CITIES & SOCIAL CHANGE

'This textbook of essays by leading critical urbanists is a compelling introduction to an important field of study; it interrogates contemporary conflicts and contradictions inherent in the social experience of living in cities that are undergoing neoliberal restructuring, and grapples with profound questions and challenging policy considerations about diversity, equity and justice. A stimulant to debate in any undergraduate urban studies classroom, this book will inspire a new generation of urban social scholars.'

Alison Bain, Associate Professor, Department of Geography, York University

'An indispensable survey of the main themes and challenges facing humanity in the urban age. Compulsory reading.'

Brendan Gleeson, Professor of Urban Policy Studies, University of Melbourne

'This book is an invaluable resource for urban social geographers. It stages a lively encounter with different understandings of urban production and experience, and does so by bringing together an exciting group of scholars working across a diversity of theoretical and geographical contexts. The book focuses on some of the central conceptual and political challenges of contemporary cities, including inequality and poverty, justice and democracy, and everyday life and urban imaginaries, providing a critical platform through which to ask how we might work towards alternative forms of urban living.'

Colin McFarlane, Durham University

CITIES & SOCIAL CHANGE

ENCOUNTERS WITH CONTEMPORARY URBANISM

Edited by
Ronan Paddison & Eugene McCann

Los Angeles | London | New Delhi
Singapore | Washington DC

Los Angeles | London | New Delhi
Singapore | Washington DC

SAGE Publications Ltd
1 Oliver's Yard
55 City Road
London EC1Y 1SP

SAGE Publications Inc.
2455 Teller Road
Thousand Oaks, California 91320

SAGE Publications India Pvt Ltd
B 1/I 1 Mohan Cooperative Industrial Area
Mathura Road
New Delhi 110 044

SAGE Publications Asia-Pacific Pte Ltd
3 Church Street
#10-04 Samsung Hub
Singapore 049483

Editor: Robert Rojek
Editorial assistant: Keri Dickens
Production editor: Katherine Haw
Copyeditor: Kate Harrison
Proofreader: Neil Dowden
Marketing manager: Michael Ainsley
Cover design: Francis Kenney
Typeset by: C&M Digitals (P) Ltd, Chennai, India
Printed and bound by CPI Group (UK) Ltd,
    Croydon, CR0 4YY

Library of Congress Control Number: 2013954632

British Library Cataloguing in Publication data

A catalogue record for this book is available from
the British Library

MIX
Paper from
responsible sources
FSC
www.fsc.org   FSC® C013604

ISBN 978-1-84860-109-3
ISBN 978-1-84860-110-9 (pbk)

At SAGE we take sustainability seriously. We print most of our
products in the UK. These are produced using FSC papers and
boards. We undertake an annual audit on materials used to ensure
that we monitor out sustainability in what we are doing. When we
print overseas, we ensure that sustainable papers are used, as
measured by the Egmont grading system.

Contents

List of Illustrations

About the Contributors

Ian R. Cook is a Lecturer in Social Sciences in the Department of Social Sciences and Languages, Northumbria University. His research focuses on the ways in which cities are governed and the circulation of policy models and expertise between cities. He has had work published in journals such as *International Journal of Urban and Regional Research*, *Urban Geography* and *Urban Studies*.

James DeFilippis is an Associate Professor in the Bloustein School of Planning and Policy, Rutgers University. His research focuses on the politics and economics of cities and communities. He is particularly interested in the processes of social change, and questions of power and justice in cities. He is the author or editor of three books. He has also written more than 30 articles and book chapters, and several white papers and policy reports.

Mónica Degen teaches cultural sociology at Brunel University. She has published in a variety of journals such as *Society and Space*, *International Journal of Urban and Regional Research*, *Senses and Society*, *Urban Studies* and *Transactions* on the sociology of the senses, urban cultures, the politics of the everyday and the experience of design and architecture. She is the author of *Sensing Cities* (Routledge, 2008) and *The Meta-City Barcelona: Transformation of a Metropolis* (Anthropos, 2008).

Geoff DeVerteuil is a Senior Lecturer at Cardiff University, Planning and Human Geography. His research interests include vulnerable populations, violence, gentrification and the social geography of health. Recent publications include *Antipode*, *Transactions of the Institute of British Geographers* and *Area*.

Tiffany Grobelski is a doctoral candidate in the Department of Geography at the University of Washington, Seattle. Her research interests lie in environmental governance, activism and how law is used to create social/environmental change. She has been conducting research on environmental advocacy groups' mobilisation of law to enhance environmental protection efforts in Poland and the European Union.

Steve Herbert is Director of the Law, Societies, and Justice Program and Professor of Geography at the University of Washington. He has done extensive fieldwork with the police, and is the author of *Policing Space: Territoriality and the Los Angeles Police Department* (University of Minnesota Press), *Citizens, Cops, and Power: Recognizing the Limits of Community* (University of Chicago Press) and (with Katherine Beckett) *Banished: The New Social Control in Urban America* (Oxford University Press).

Robin Kearns is Professor of Geography in the School of Environment at the University of Auckland. His interests span social, cultural and health geography with involvement in projects funded by the New Zealand Health Research Council ('Kids in the City') and the Ministry of Business, Innovation and Industry ('Resilient Urban Futures'). He is an associate editor of the journals *Health and Place, Health and Social Care in the Community* and *Journal of Transport and Health*.

Regan Koch completed his PhD in the Department of Geography at University College London, where he now works as a teaching fellow in Urban Studies. His most recent research was an ESRC fellowship entitled *Eating in Public: Re-imagining Collective Urban Life* which examined food-related trends in a number of US cities. More generally, his work is concerned with matters of public space, changing social practices and interventions that aim to make cities better. Regan has published articles in the *Transactions of the Institute of British Geographers* and *Urban Studies*. He also has chapters in a number of forthcoming edited collections.

Alan Latham teaches at the Department of Geography, University College London. His research focuses on issues around sociality, mobility, materiality and public space, and has focussed on cities as diverse as Auckland, New York, London, Eugene (OR), Berlin, and Champaign-Urbana. He has published in a wide range of international journals and edited collections. He is the co-author of *Key Concepts in Urban Geography*.

Loretta Lees is Professor of Human Geography at the University of Leicester. She is an international expert on gentrification and urban regeneration. Recent co-authored and co-edited books include: *Mixed Communities: Gentrification by Stealth?* (Policy Press, 2011/University of Chicago Press, 2012); *Regenerating London: Governance, Sustainability and Community in a Global City* (Routledge, 2009); *Gentrification and The Gentrification Reader* (Routledge, 2008, 2010). She has three new books coming out in 2014–15.

Gordon MacLeod is Reader in Urban and Regional Studies in the Department of Geography, Durham University. His research examines the tensions that surface between urban development, governance and politics; regional development and regionalism; and the relationships between state spaces and cities and regions, especially with regard to spatial justice. He has published extensively on these themes in a range of international journals, and is co-editor of *State/Space: A Reader* (2003) and of recent special issues of *Environment and Planning C, Urban Studies* and *Antipode*. He also edits the 'Urban and Regional Horizons' section of *Regional Studies*.

Eugene McCann is Professor in the Department of Geography, Simon Fraser University. His research focuses on the ways in which policies, especially urban policies, are circulated among communities of practitioners across the globe and how these 'policy mobilities' are related to urban politics. He is co-editor, with Kevin Ward, of *Mobile Urbanism* (Minnesota, 2011) and co-author, with Andy Jonas and Mary Thomas, of *Urban Geography: A Critical Introduction* (Wiley-Blackwell, forthcoming).

Graham Moon is Professor of Human Geography, and Co-Chair of the Population Health Strategic Research Group at the University of Southampton. He is Editor-in-Chief of the journal *Health and Place*. Professor Moon collaborated in the development and evolution of the new geography of health and in the introduction of multi-level modelling to geography. More recently his work has had an international impact on smoking cessation policy. His current research interests focus on small area synthetic estimation of health needs, area effects on smoking behaviour and post-asylum geographies. Recent publications have appeared in *Annals, AAG, Epidemiology and Community Health, Public Health* and *Housing Studies*. He co-edited the recent Wiley-Blackwell *Companion to Health and Medical Geography*.

Ronan Paddison is Emeritus Professor of Geography at the University of Glasgow. His research interests focus on the political processes driving urban change and, in particular, under what conditions local participation can contribute to the making of more inclusive and democratic cities. Recent projects have included the role of community participation in the installation of public art, and the limitations to public participation in the post-political city. He is Managing Editor of *Urban Studies* and of *Space and Polity*.

Juan Rivero is a doctoral student at Rutgers University focusing on the cultural politics of urban redevelopment. His current research looks at the relation between the planning process and the identity of iconic neighbourhoods. Since 2008, Juan has also served as the spokesman for Save Coney Island, a grassroots organisation devoted to the preservation and promotion of that neighbourhood's amusement district. Prior to coming to Rutgers, Juan was a Housing Fellow for the NYC Department of Housing Preservation and Development. Juan earned an MS in urban planning at Columbia University and a JD at the University of Chicago Law School.

Ananya Roy is Professor of City and Regional Planning and Distinguished Chair in Global Poverty and Practice at the University of California, Berkeley. Roy's research is concerned with the management and regulation of poverty, with an emphasis on the relationship between bureaucracies of poverty and poor people's movements. Her most recent book, co-edited with Emma Shaw Crane, is titled *Territories of Poverty* (University of Georgia Press, forthcoming).

Erik Swyngedouw is Professor of Geography at Manchester University. His research interests include political ecology, urban governance, democracy and political power, and the politics of globalisation. His was previously Professor of Geography at Oxford University and holds the Vincent Wright Visiting Professorship at Science Po, Paris, 2014. His forthcoming book with MIT Press focuses on water and social power in twentieth-century Spain.

Gill Valentine is Professor in Human Geography at the University of Sheffield where she is also Pro-Vice Chancellor for the Faculty of Social Science. Gill's research interests include: social identities and belonging; childhood, parenting and family life; and urban cultures of consumption. She is currently leading a European Research Council programme of research titled *Living with Difference*. She has (co)authored/edited 15 books and over 100 journal articles.

Acknowledgements

It might be only somewhat fanciful to say that this book's origins can be traced to the late 1980s at the University of Glasgow. We first met then, as undergraduate student and professor, in a political geography course. We reconnected many years later around the idea for the book. We were keen to bring together a group of top scholars to address the cutting edge(s) of urban social geography in a way that would be stimulating to advanced students. Many conversations over the phone and email and, occasionally, over food and drinks have brought it to fruition.

Clearly, the value of *Cities & Social Change* is defined by the insightful contributions of the authors who accepted our invitation to be part of it. We would like to thank them sincerely for their contributions, their enthusiasm, and their patience and fortitude as the book has moved through the publication process.

Ronan would like to add how much he has enjoyed working on the volume with the contributory authors as well as with his co-editor. He is also indebted to Tom Hutton, co-editor of the sister volume, *Cities and Economic Change* for helping to guide the structure of this text.

Thanks from Eugene go to Christiana and Sophie. He would also like to thank his colleagues and students, both undergraduate and graduate, at SFU and elsewhere, for conversations that have greatly deepened his understanding of the social geographies of cities. Special appreciation goes to Kevin Ward for ongoing chats about ideas, family, and football, and to Cristina Temenos, both for intellectual engagement and her skills as an artistic consultant.

We would also like to thank the staff at SAGE, particularly Robert Rojek who encouraged us to embark on the project, as well as to Keri Dickens and Katherine Haw who both provided expert help with the production of the volume. Their vision, enthusiasm, helpfulness, and positivity are greatly appreciated.

Ronan Paddison, Glasgow, Scotland, UK
Eugene McCann, Vancouver, BC, Canada

Acknowledgements

SECTION 1

THEORISING THE CITY

1

Introduction: Encountering the City – Multiple Perspectives on Urban Social Change

Ronan Paddison and Eugene McCann

The great buildings of civilization; the meeting places, the libraries and theatres, the towers and the domes; and often more than these the houses, the streets, the press and excitement of so many people with so many purposes. I have stood in many cities and felt this pulse; in the physical differences of Stockholm and Florence, Paris and Milan; this identifiable and moving quality; the centre, the activity and light. Like everyone else I have also felt the chaos of the metro and the traffic jam; the monotony of the ranks of houses, the aching press of strange crowds, this sense of possibility, of meeting and movement, is a permanent element of my own sense of cities ...

Raymond Williams (1973) *The Country and the City*

On being asked what it is that defines the city, and more specifically what defines the meaning of living within cities, most of us would reply in experiential terms, as the cultural critic, Raymond Williams, does in the epigraph. While our reflections of the city may embrace our imaginations of them, it is through our experience of them that our material needs are met. Cities are the spaces in which most of us live out or daily lives. But our relationships with the city involve much more than can be encapsulated in saying that it is in them that the quotidian is transacted. Cities are the arenas in which we conduct our private and public lives, in which we establish networks of social interaction, and in which we are able to secure work and provide for material needs. The sensibilities we have towards the city emphasise the diversity of attributes they encapsulate which become reflected in the ambivalent emotive appreciation we have of them. As Williams shows, cities are variously places of exhilaration and excitement, of wonder, and sometimes of fear and apprehension.

Any understanding of how cities become viewed needs to accept the role agency plays. How we relate to the city reflects the self, our positioning within the city's social make-up, the 'baggage' of the self that is brought to the daily process of living within it (Bounds, 2004). Our experiences of the city, and therefore our appreciation of it, vary. For the excluded – the poor, in particular – the celebration that surrounds the making of the postmodern city and the multiple ways in which it caters for consumption is a far cry from their experience of everyday life in the city, in which survival and 'thwarted consumption' (Bauman, 1998) are the enduring markers of everyday urban life. For those able to participate in the consumption opportunities which cities offer, the experience of living in the city will be radically different, albeit one likely to be qualified by the anxieties of everyday urban life.

These differences are graphically captured in contemporary novels of the city. In (for example) *Capital,* John Lanchester's 2012 novel of present-day London narrates a rich story centring on the experience of those living in an 'ordinary street' of terraced housing in south London, Pepys Road. Built as an unremarkable street of terraced properties at the end of the nineteenth century, Pepys Road was targeted at the lower-middle-class family 'willing to live in an unfashionable part of town in return for the chance to own a terraced house' (p. 2). For much of its history, the road and those living on it remained unremarkable. Lanchester takes up the biography of the street in more heady times, in the 2000s, by which point it had already experienced early gentrification since when, following the boom in London's financial sector, the street had become the home of the rich. But if it had become a street in which being a new arrival was confined to those enjoying a hedge fund manager's income, it was home too to some 'original' residents who had stayed on and whose lifestyle remained modest. Added to this was the story of the multiple workers who serviced the street and its new occupants, many of them immigrant, Poles as well as those from Africa and the West Indies. Much of the perceptiveness of the novel is in the ways in which it draws out what the experiences of everyday life were for the diversity of characters involved in it, their social lives and the intersections between the street's occupants and those servicing it.

Pepys Road is an imagined (but nevertheless real) space used to draw out the stories of different urban lives, stories which are not peculiar to London. In its essentials, the different experience of the wealthy and the recent immigrant, the elderly and the young *au pair,* are stories that no doubt would be repeated elsewhere in other northern cities, and increasingly in some southern cities. Defining himself around Shanghai, Tash Aw, in *Five Star Billionaire* (2013), follows the experiences of the city's diverse population in a city which encapsulates the urban explosion in China, the dazzling opportunities it creates for some, and the much more constrained lives it means for the majority.

The stories told in these literary representations of the city help explore the excitement, contradictions, conflicts and tensions arising from the social experiences of living in cities. It is these characteristics of city life that this volume intends to explore in a theoretically and empirically informed way. While the novelist has the luxury of being able to employ literary licence in developing a narrative, social scientists need to ground their arguments theoretically and, through robust methodologies, explore the social life of the city. In the rest of this introductory chapter we sketch out an understanding of the theoretical legacy and how it might inform the multiplicity of encounters in the contemporary city, before turning, subsequently, to explain the structure of the volume.

INTRODUCING URBAN SOCIAL THEORY – ALTERNATIVE PERSPECTIVES

Any understanding of urban social life is dependent on theory – reasoned arguments which define the ideas we have of the city and which seek to make them comprehensible. Fundamentally, urban theory aims to explain how and why cities develop, how they are structured and how and why they change (Hubbard, 2006). Translated into social terms this is expressed through an understanding of sociality in the city, how cities are imagined and represented, how difference is part of city life and is negotiated, and how social order is maintained – issues that are both diverse and often fraught with epistemological problems as to how they should be explored. Small wonder, then, that just as theories adopt different forms – some open to quantitative assessment and others more discursive – so too is urban theory a diverse medley of ideas.

As diverse a field as urban social theory is, what is equally true is that what defines the nature of urban encounter is itself diverse. Here, encounter can bring in classic tropes linked to city life and its complexities: 'the stranger', social distancing as a strategy aimed at the avoidance of encounter; the overarching and uneven impress of structural processes on different social groups; the experience of city life and urban materiality; the role of immaterial cultures in fashioning city life; and what living in cities means for our health. What we need to emphasise through such examples is that encounter is a multifaceted expression into the nature of city living, complex in its own right, but made patently more complex by the multiplicity of ways it becomes translated through and by different social groups within the city, and that it is mediated through the self. This hints at the potential benefits of theoretical diversity, its responsiveness to different types of research questions which urbanists exploring the social geographies of the city are likely to pose. This said, we can begin to sketch out the legacy of urban social theory, mindful of the reality that much of it is 'western' in it origins, the implications of which are returned to later.

Urban theory is a rich as well as diverse field. There is a considerable legacy of ideas on the nature of city life and its spatial dimensions on which to draw. While some have been superseded by later theoretical developments, others have not only withstood subsequent scrutiny of time but, as in the case of Simmel (1903, 1997), have been revisited in contemporary urban thinking (Frisby, 1986). What the historiography of urban social theory tends to suggest is that rather than theory developing in a strictly progressive fashion – ideas of each 'phase' being effectively supplanted by later ideas – its development has been more cumulative. Much of the Chicago School – its deterministic thinking, for example – may have been abandoned, but its models of urban social mor-phology, the iconic representation of the city encapsulated in Burgess' concentric zones, for instance, continues to be the focus of research (see, for instance, Beveridge, 2011). Perhaps it is because many of the social problems of living in cities are enduring – issues of social distance and segregation, the mixing of diverse ethnicities, problems of social disorder and crime and others – that the return to earlier urban research is tempting for its ability to throw light on contemporary configurations. Earlier theories do not neces-sarily become negated but exist to be revisited, albeit critically.

How, then, can we begin to appreciate the legacy of urban theory? Frequently its appreciation is explored historically, beginning with those early writers who sought to understand the link between cities and modernity through to contemporary accounts drawing on poststructural and postmodern ideas of the city. The approach is certainly able to demonstrate the richness of urban theory and how it has come to terms with the changing character of cities.

In reality, urban theory responds to different empirical questions. Further, it is by exploring the ambitions urban theories have that we can begin to appreciate their con-tribution to understanding the social life of cities. We argue that these ambitions can be identified by two dimensions that help to loosely position different urban social theo-ries: their *scale* and *scope*.[1] By scale we mean the perspective from which theory approaches the understanding of the city. At one extreme are theories which treat the city holistically, effectively viewing it from above, with the aim of understanding the city, or an aspect of it, as a generalised statement. In contrast, other theories commence their dissection of the city with an individual or small part of it – a neighbourhood – or a particular process or aspect of it, a view which is effectively drawn from below. Scope refers to the comprehensiveness of theory, the extent to which it seeks to embrace some overarching explanation or is more restricted in its ambitions. Expressed as a binary, what needs to be said is that in reality much urban research is conducted so that while being rooted closer to one end of the continuum linking the two poles, it remains aware of the other. Understanding the city, as the Chicago School was to readily acknowledge, meant that research needed to be conducted from both perspectives. The claim is not, then, that these two dimensions effectively classify urban theories but that they begin to shed light on the different questions urban theory has sought to address and the dif-ferent perspectives from which it has begun to explore the city in social terms.

Viewing cities from above has been a continuing tradition within urban social theory. Given their unprecedented scale, the rapidity often of their development, the contribution immigration made to their growth and diversity, and the potential threat the scale of cities constituted to social and political order, understanding how cities were emergent, how and why they developed morphologically, and what its linkages were with modernity, were questions that were bound to attract the early

---

1 The division encapsulated by these terms is not new. The difference between viewing the city 'from above' and 'below' resonates with the distinction made between extensive and intensive methods of analysing the city. For a recent usage of the division, see Stringer (2013).

attention of urban theorists. For some theorists – beginning with Engels' (1844 [1971]) depiction of the rise of Manchester and adopted later by some of the classic work of the Chicago School – unravelling the city was expressed in morphological terms. Engels' description of the city in concentric terms in which the bourgeoisie were able to distance themselves from the grime and the poverty – and indeed were able to visually cocoon themselves from it – led to a more holistic interpretation of city life rooted in capitalism. Through the use of dialectical thinking, Engels (and Marx, though he was less concerned explicitly with the city) was able to draw out the tensions and contradictions that were already apparent in the early industrial city, particularly the recurrent attempts by elite groups to maintain their privileged position and the conflicts to which this gave rise. Yet, as fertile a research territory as there was in drawing out the connections between city life with capitalism, it was not to be for more than a century that they were to become more rigorously explored by urban analysts, a rich vein of which was to be explored in the writings of Lefebvre (1991, 1996), Harvey (1985, 1989b, 1989c) and others.

Other perspectives – some of the writing of the Chicago School, in particular – were to be more immediately influential in steering how cities should be understood and studied and became key paradigms within much of the twentieth century. They were also, given the breadth of research undertaken by the School, not restricted to viewing the city from above – as a complement to this, pioneering ethnographic research unfolded the dynamics of the neighbourhoood from below (Zorbaugh, 1929). Yet, it is through the work of Burgess and his iconic concentric zone model, together with the use of biological reasoning to help explain the social patterning of the city and its dynamics, that the Chicago School was to offer a perspective that was to become so widely cited. The appeal of being able to transcend the complexities of the city and represent it in a simple geometrical model was to encourage alternative geometries, the work of Hoyt and of Ullman. It was an appeal that continued to influence urban social research over 50 years later through the factorial ecologies of the city that became fashionable following the 'quantitative turn'. In its use of biological arguments – that the dynamics of the city's social geography were somehow the result of natural processes – the School was to confront more stringent critique. Rather than being a given through 'natural' forces, the social geographies of the city and their dynamics were the result of political and managerial interventions. Here, it was to be Marxist-led – and, for some, Marxian – ideas that were to offer a more convincing explanation of the processes operating at the macro-level in the city.

A different version of the top-down perspective, while still treating the city holistically, focuses more on the individual and their interaction in everyday city life. As a response to modernity and the radically different environments in which burgeoning city populations were forced to adapt, some urban social theorists turned their attention to the ways in which the individual sought to come to terms with living in cities. In his classic essay 'The metropolis and mental life', Simmel (1903 [1997]) argued that cities created much more challenging environments than rural areas by virtue of the size and complexity of the city, so that the individual in being forced to adapt to the multiplicity of stimuli did so by becoming blasé. Such a technique was a coping strategy, but it was also one, as Hubbard (2006) has pointed out, which continues to resonate with behaviour in contemporary public spaces – the ability of the individual to be indifferent to anti-social forms of behaviour or other incivilities, providing they do not directly challenge the self. Simmel was to root the indifference of the urban citizen in the money economy of the city and the growing dependence on social interaction being transacted in terms of exchange value. The money economy of the city, then, was to erode the 'old' ties considered characteristic to rural society. Robinson (2006) has pointed out that we should be careful not to generalise this conceptualisation of the comportment of the individual in the modern city, arguing that it is the product of research and observation in only a few cities of the global north (see our discussion in the concluding chapter). Nevertheless, Simmel's argument was to lead other theorists to draw out the implications of the money economy, cities and modernity; for Kracauer (1927), for instance, they were to lead to novel forms of urban visual culture linked to consumption, an argument which, if anything, has even greater resonance in the contemporary city.

The argument that sociality in the city was materially different from that associated with the rural or, put in other terms, that the nature of city life was in some senses distinctive, already alluded to by Simmel, became explicitly associated with Tonnies (1887), Durkheim (1893) and, later, Wirth (1938). Each, like Simmel, sought to explore the nature of urban social life looking at the city holistically but looking at it from the role of the individual within the city. Tonnies' distinction between *gemeinschaft* and *gesellschaft* became translated into the distinction between rural and urban societies (though it was not a connection drawn directly by Tonnies himself). In *gemeinschaft* societies there was a strong sense of community brought about in part by their relative immobility – kinship connections were strong, as was a sense of tradition and loyalty. In contrast, *gesellschaft* societies were defined by the ascendancy of individualism, the instrumental relations between citizens centring on exchange value and by the relative loss of community. Both types of society were drawn as the extremes of a continuum so that Tonnies avoided the pitfall of binarism. Durkheim was to draw out a not dissimilar set of distinctions between the rural and the urban through his constructs of mechanical and organic solidarity respectively. Later, Wirth was to define urbanism as a distinctive way of life linked in the first instance to what he characterised as the three defining features of cities: their size, density and heterogeneity.

The frequency with which the ideas of these early writers are rehearsed reveals their continuing influence. This is not to deny of course that they have been subject to considerable criticism. Wirth has been criticized for his failure to distinguish what was distinctive about living in cities as opposed to an urban-*industrial(ising)* society. The idea, too, that cities lacked a sense of community, or were not able to show a continuing sense of community in different areas of the city and amongst different social groups living within it, was clearly not to be supported by a lot of empirical evidence. Yet, there are ways in which the influence of these early theorists remains, notably in the claim that city life is characterised by a lack of social cohesion and in which urban life is becoming, if anything, more individualistic. Though too easily over-stated, the 'loss of community thesis' continues to reappear in contemporary urban research, particularly in debates over social capital and social cohesion.

An alternative tradition in urban social theory (and research) is rooted in viewing urban processes from below. The 'cultural turn' has been a major fillip to its development – in the burgeoning use of ethnographic methods of analysis, for example – though its origins lay in the Chicago School which, while developing more holistic appreciations of the city as we have seen, were aware of the need for complementary studies which explored the city from a different perspective. Some such as Robert Park were explicit for the need for both types of study; the more micro-level analyses of particular neighbourhoods being able to unravel the complex processes linked to the city's social functioning. Park's influence here was considerable – the Chicago School generated a series of micro-level studies of the city's neighbourhoods in which new methodologies were employed to tease out the social processes at work. Subsequent work in different types of cities were to emphasise the power of ethnographic techniques of analysis: in the East End of London following Young and Willmott's (1962) path-breaking work; in Kinshasa (Macgaffey, 1991); and in more recent studies fleshing out the sociality of the street, as in Hall's (2012) dissection of a multicultural road on the southern edges of inner-city London.

Other studies, equally rooted in the perspective of the city from below, have sought to explore social processes within wider structural processes. Frequently they are concerned with 'issues' arising within the city – poverty, exclusion, difference, mobilities – that are able to use theoretical arguments to unravel urban social process, but to do so in ways which are able to show how the experience of urban living varies. Studies such as Sibley's work on exclusion (1995) has shown how social practice may exclude the participation of some citizens from particular spaces, the explanation of which drew on the writings of the anthropologist Mary Douglas and her work on pollution (1966). In his work on urban marginalisation Wacquant (2008) explores the processes linked to the causes, forms and implications of urban 'polarisation from below' in the United States and France at the end of the Fordist–Keynesian era, rooting the analysis in Bourdieu's sociology. In *Urban Outcasts* Wacquant develops a detailed empirical understanding of the 'post-industrial precariat' – based on field data and archival material – positioned within a theoretical framework developed by Bourdieu to explore the processes underpinning urban inequality.

TAKING STOCK

These examples of the range of urban social theory make no pretence at being exhaustive. Nor is their space to develop a critique of the field. Rather, the intention has been to emphasise that in dissecting urban encounters, researchers are able to express themselves in fundamentally different ways, through the perspective that is adopted and the extent to which, and how, empirical analysis can be positioned theoretically. Both traditions – the more top-down vision and the perspective from below – remain as widely used vantage points from which to understand socio-spatial processes in the city. Neither should be inferred as being better than the other where they respond to different research questions and involve different methodologies.

The diversity of contemporary urban social research reflects the wider health of urban studies as a burgeoning endeavour, in turn a reflection of the increasingly sophisticated understanding we have of cities. The need for such sophistication may have been thrust upon us by the multiple disjunctures of late capitalism – who, half a century ago, would have predicted the urban revanchism of gentrification in the late capitalist city and that the model would become globalised? Who would have foreseen the rise of super-diversity arising from deep globalisation so that (for example) a North American city's Ecuadorian population would vie in size with the largest cities in Ecuador itself? Understanding the city in an increasingly globalised world, one in which capitalism has been able to reinvent itself and the contradictions to which it gives rise, with profound consequences for the city, has been responded to by urban (social) theory in its attempts to come to terms with its complexities. Very broadly, the response reflects the basic dualism that we have sought to identify running thread-like through the history of urban social research, holistic meta-theoretical analyses co-existing alongside 'small theory' which aims to unravel the social particularities of the city. Tellingly, though, as much as our understandings of the city may have become more sophisticated and theoretically eclectic, there is a growing awareness of the deficiencies of contemporary theory in explaining urban social life.

What is clear is that urban (social) theory is firmly rooted in the development of the 'west', the implications of which have been teased out by Robinson (2006) and others (see our concluding chapter). With the global south accounting for a growing proportion of the world's urban population, the problem of so much theory being rooted in western experience has become increasingly recognised. In reality, as contemporary social scientists now accept, the production of (urban) knowledge is not only situated but it is partial. Somewhat contradictorily, an awareness of the issue has not spelt out the 'end' of the Chicago School or indeed halted the emergence of new schools of urban thought such as the LA School. Nor has an awareness of the case for studying 'ordinary cities' prevented the continued appeal to, and indeed the foregrounding of, certain cities as paradigmatic exemplars and policy role models for other cities. To complicate the picture further, some of the paradigmatic cities have emerged from recent urban research in the global south. We know a lot more about cities such as Shanghai and Rio de Janeiro than we do about Dalian or, in Brazil's case, Pernambuco. If anything, such developments lend further weight to the argument that cities are unique as well as connected and that theory may need to be more modest in its aspirations, aspiring to explain processes of structure, growth and change in particular cities, rather than in wider urban systems. What these contradictory tendencies also illustrate is that our understanding of the role theory should play in explaining urban processes – what should be its reach across the diversity of cities making up the urban world – is itself in flux.

This is not to suggest that the diversity of approaches within urban social geography, nor the debates, uncertainties and ambivalences that seem to characterise the field, are necessarily weaknesses or death knells. Indeed this volume proves that there is strength in diversity and debate. The various conceptual frameworks on display in the chapters speak to the wide range of questions that need to be addressed in cities and how they can only be addressed from multiple perspectives. Our heuristic division of the field into top-down and bottom-up approaches is, of course, just that: a heuristic. In reality, as the chapters suggest, most quality urban studies literature employs elements of both approaches. In order to understand the structural conditions that condition persistent poverty in cities, for example, it is necessary to understand how those conditions are manifest and negotiated on the ground (see Chapter 4 by DeVerteuil, and Rob Fairbanks' excellent book, *How it Works* (2009)). Approaches that combine the top-down and bottom-up approaches have produced some of the most vibrant and profound insights into cities and social change, from the Chicago School to the work of David Harvey and Neil Smith on the unevenness of capitalist development and its social and cultural consequences in cities around the world. Or from Doreen Massey's approach to place as global/ local, to contemporary post-colonial critiques of the western-centric, sweeping theorisations of urbanism and related attempts to trace alternative forms of urbanisation and globalisation, or worlding from the perspective of the global south (the work of Jane Jacobs, Jennifer Robinson, Ananya Roy and AbdouMaliq Simone spring immediately to mind).

THIS VOLUME

Our purpose in this volume is to interrogate the social experience of urban living. The subtitle of the text refers to 'encounters with contemporary urbanism'. This begs the question as to what is meant by encounter, what is included within the term, what are its limits? Answers to these questions may begin to help explain how the book has been written; what it includes as well as, through the exigencies imposed by the restrictions on space, what the volume has not been able to include.

To say 'urban encounter' hints at a variety of meanings, some of them in opposition to one another: clearly, urban encounters will involve a medley of different activities and processes linked to city living, a diversity which lends itself to the problem of ambiguity. In essence, encounter here is expressed through the multiple experiences we have through living in cities. The simplicity of the argument belies the complexities it embraces, that the experience of the city reflects who we are, what is our position in the life-cycle, what is our social positioning, what social group(s) we think we belong to, what neighbourhood we live in, how long we have lived in it and a host of other traits that define our individuality. Further, where a conventional understanding of encounter hints at conflict and tension, the choice of the term is deliberate; city life is shot through with both.

Strong continuities map out the range of issues entailed in analysing social life in the city. In their understanding of what nineteenth-century urban sociologists considered to be among the key questions city life posed, Savage et al. (2003) list issues which continue to resonate: the role of space in fashioning cities in socio-spatial terms and how this in turn influenced social interaction; how urban life influenced social relations; the impress of urban problems including vagrancy, poverty and crime; the diversity of the city; the challenge to social order; and the development of new forms of governance and control. Some of this agenda has been eclipsed by the continuing development of urbanisation particularly in the global north in which societies have become effectively urbanised, blurring the distinction important to early urban social theory of the rural and the urban. In the global south the distinction continues to have greater currency so that the interaction between the rural and the urban, the impress of the former on social life in the city, remains stronger. Yet, the agenda of what city life entailed for the early theorists is far from being replaced – rather, it has been added to, theoretically and empirically, and expressed in some cases through different language reflecting, hopefully, the changing nature of the city in late industrial society.

The volume is structured into three major sections: the imagining of city life; the experience of it; and the making of liveable cities. The rationale for the division is rooted in our experience of the city being situated against our imagination of cities, this in turn reflecting the multiple, and increasing diversity of, representations through which the city is expressed. In tracing the experience of the urban, successive chapters dissect key themes linked to social life in the contemporary city, social stratification and the emergence of lifestyle linked to consumption, the realities of what it means to be poor in the city, difference and the routes through which responding to diversity can be mapped, and the inter-relationships between urban materiality and how, through our senses, we read and appreciate the city.

The final section turns to the question of the liveability of the city and how, through its governance and through policy-making, it is possible to address issues many of which have been enduring to city life but whose form has become reconfigured under late capitalism and its pervasive and multifaceted handmaiden, neoliberalism. A consistent theme to the chapters are those questions that are recurrent in city life – liveability for whom? What is the role of elites in framing the city? What is the role of policy in contributing to social distancing and the spatial institutionalisation of privilege? What would be the contours of the just city and how is equity to be achieved? How are the discourses of neoliberalism restructuring the city? Successive chapters focus on dis/order and regulation, the walling of the city, city living and health – the 'penalty' for living in cities and health-related behaviours in the city – and the emergent discourses surrounding cities, nature and sustainability expressed through the search for environmental justice. Finally, attention turns to a question that has preoccupied much recent attention all the more so because of the growing social inequalities associated with the contemporary city, the just city.

Inevitably, the structuring of the volume has to be selective. Furthermore, in an edited volume it is important to identify themes which run through the essays. The aim here has been to frame the contributions against contemporary understandings of space and the city; often these themes are implicit in what contributors have to say though of no less importance. Key to the essays are the ways in which, far from being passive, urban space is active in the construction of urban sociality – not just as so explicitly as in the spread of urban privatism in cities in both the global north and south, but through the ways in which cities and their neighbourhoods become imagined and often stereotyped. The ways in which city spaces become labelled, stigmatised or at least categorised resurfaces in the discussions of poverty, difference and dis/order. The role class relations play within the city and of the social interactions among and between classes and other social groupings dominate other chapters, as does the role difference plays in urban social life. Finally, we draw attention to the fundamental, if sometimes disguised, ways in which power and power relations become played out with direct consequences for the experience of city life for its citizens. In our concluding chapter, we use the case of Grant Park in Chicago as a way to pursue what we see as a common, if differently stated, methodological approach that ties all the chapters together. We use the park as an entryway into discussions of a number of urban-social situations, processes, and perspectives that have shaped it over the years. Like the other chapters in the book, our conclusion suggests that the city – even mundane or small parts of the city – offers a wealth of opportunities and insights for urban social geographers. The city is there to be encountered.

2

Representing and Imagining the City

Regan Koch and Alan Latham

INTRODUCTION

Imagine you are approaching a city. What's your mental image? A skyline seems quite likely. Approach a city by plane, train or automobile and when you see the skyline you know you're getting close, right? Countless films open with an aerial scan of towering buildings, steel and glass skyscrapers, apartment blocks or clusters of shanty houses to set the scene. Search the word 'city' using Google Images and you'll find millions of these images – page after page of skylines.

All cities have a skyline, and at first glance they are merely a repetition of buildings and other big things that form an outline against the horizon. Yet many are remarkably distinct. They serve as powerful representations of particular places. New York City is probably the most widely known, but others are immediately recognisable too: Shanghai, Dubai, Hong Kong, London, Rio, San Francisco, Prague and so on. But if we consider skylines a little more deeply, we realise they are much more than just silhouettes; an awful lot goes into producing them. They are a tremendous amalgamation of raw materials: bricks, mortar, wood, stone, steel, glass and cement – literally tons and tons of this stuff. Running beneath and through them are vast infrastructural systems of wires, cables, tubes and pipes that allow them to function. These are only rendered possible by the much larger networks that bring these materials in to, and other materials out of, the city. Of course, underpinning all of this is the labour, technological know-how and human ingenuity that makes possible the construction of all the individual buildings, towers and monuments that collectively form the outline we see when looking at the city from a distance. Skylines, then, can be thought of as an *assemblage* of many things.

STARTING TO THINK WITH REPRESENTATIONS

It is the philosopher Manuel DeLanda who sparked our interest in skylines. He notes that they are more than just brute materials: they are also expressive. As assemblages of all sorts of materials, skylines become representations, and as such, they do things.

In some cases, the physical skyline of a town is simply a sum of its parts but the rhythmic repetition of architectural motifs – minarets, domes and spires, belfries and steeples – and the counterpoint these motifs create with the surrounding landscape, may produce emergent expressive effects. In the twentieth century skyscrapers and other signature buildings were added to the skyline as a means to make it unique and instantly recognisable, a clear sign that the expressivity of skylines had become the object of deliberate planning. (DeLanda: 2006a: 261)

Thinking of skylines as a form of representation, then, can help to imagine a city's past and future. Where once the largest buildings in the skyline were of religious significance, now these have been surpassed in height and stature by structures with civic, cultural and (most often) commercial functions. Their predominance at the city centre speaks to the concentration of wealth and power in cities. The transference of expressive skyline features between cities – and the ongoing drive to produce new ones – further suggests the endurance of skyline configuration as a powerful strategy to project an image of wealth, dynamism and innovation in cities. Many contemporary skylines are dotted with construction cranes that reflect the reshaping and reproduction of these qualities and imaginaries, while others are notable for their lack of building projects or those that sit uncompleted.

But skylines are not merely windows into the past or imagined future, their expressive properties continuously involve them in the unfolding present. Through myriad forms of representation, skylines become, in Lefebvre's (1991) terms, part of how the city is conceived, perceived and lived. They find their way into corporate logos, city branding material, postcards, T-shirts, movie posters, video games, advertisements and commercials. The Manhattan skyline, portrayed in a Woody Allen film, a Marvel comic book, the rap lyrics of Jay-Z or any episode of *Sex in the City* or *Friends* is in its own way as real as the physical buildings themselves. Through these practices of representation, the skyline itself becomes something much greater than 'just' a collection of buildings.

REPRESENTATIONS AND URBAN IMAGINATIONS: AN OVERVIEW OF THE CHAPTER

We have prefaced this chapter with a consideration of skylines to exemplify the three themes we want to develop in the following pages. Firstly, we want to highlight the ubiquity of representation and imagination to urban space. Cities teem with representations of all different kinds. Bound up with these representations are multiple types of imaginations and imaginings. Secondly, we want to illustrate the activities that representations enable, the many things they are involved in, the work that they do. Representation and imagination are not simply some kind of by-product of urban life. Rather they are central to the very ways in which cities are ordered, managed and made sense of. Thirdly, we want stress how the various practices and processes of representation and imagination ensure that cities are

always more than just the raw materials that comprise them. They help to give the
city its expressive materiality and processual capacity. As we will see, representation is not an easy concept to work with. It includes all manner of writing, theory,
artistic practice, imaging, calculation and cartography. It is used in every social
field from art, culture, politics, business and law. Further, new technologies in
media, communication, digitisation and software have further muddled up any
clear distinction between 'reality' and 'representation' (Amin and Thrift, 2002;
Dodge and Kitchin, 2007; Thrift and French 2002) just as they have blurred
(although not dissolved) the distinction between the real and the imagined. In this
chapter, we want to cultivate an urban imagination that can critique the powers of
representation where need be, but which can also (and we would argue more crucially) work productively with representation – and the associated imaginaries they
may entrain – in attending to the multiplicity of urban life.

The chapter is divided into four parts. In Part One we draw on a key figure in the
history of western urban planning, Daniel Burnham, to examine the 'view from
above' and the way in which devices such as maps, plans, tables and diagrams have
been used to imagine and address particular urban problems. Part Two draws upon
the work of radical French urbanist Henri Lefebvre to move to a series of critiques
highlighting the limitations and dangers of these dominant ways of representing the
city. In Part Three we attempt to move beyond (but not discard) the well-established
critiques of representation to exploring some ways in which popular representations
and imaginations are implicated in the production of urban life. Part Four outlines
a range of possible ways in which urban studies might go about engaging more
expansively with representations and the work that they do.

PART ONE: VIEWS FROM ABOVE: IMAGINING THE MODERN CITY

> From these office windows will come to us the feeling of look-outs [visages]
> dominating a world in order. (Le Corbusier, cited in Vidler, 2000: 31)

In 1906, architect Daniel Burnham moved his practice to the 18th-floor studio
of the Railway Exchange Building in Chicago. His firm had completed the
building – one of the world's tallest at the time – two years prior and the spe-
cially conceived space at the top was meant to provide his staff with a good
vantage over the city and the shores of Lake Michigan. Surrounding the building
was a city undergoing incredible change, from being a backwater village of some
200 residents to a bustling metropolis of 1.7 million people in the span of 70 years.
But Burnham was interested in more than just a skyline view. He was in the business of making Big Plans. He had been a pioneer in the development of the modern
skyscraper. He had also been commissioned to draft comprehensive city plans for
Cleveland, Washington, DC, San Francisco, and Manila and Baguio in the Philippines.
Before any of this he had masterminded the 1893 World's Columbian
Exposition. The Exposition presented a model version of Burnham's ideal city,

employing a wide range of innovative representational technologies to conjure up his vision – panoramas, dioramas, models, re-enactments, the first commercial cinema – and it introduced the Ferris wheel, lifting exhibition visitors out of the crowd and offering them a bird's eye view from above (Larson, 2003). In all of these projects, Burnham demonstrated a strong awareness of the power of representation as both a practical tool and as a key component in stimulating urban imaginations. So in 1906, when it came to devising a plan for the actual city of Chicago, the city in which he grew up and made his name, Burnham was to make his biggest plan yet. He wanted to bring about a modern City Beautiful (see Wilson, 1989) that could rival any of the world's great cities. Moving his firm to the 18th floor offered new potential to help realise such a vision. It offered the possibility of distance from the chaos and congestion below, literally embodying a new way of making the city legible and manageable.

Of course, Burnham was not the first to apply such techniques to city planning. Yet the *Plan of Chicago* ([1909] 1993) that Burnham co-produced with architect Edward Bennett was in all sorts of ways an important precursor and a catalyst for a powerful set of planning techniques that coalesced into a coherent body of practice in the first half of the twentieth century (Ross, 2013). Through an extensive series of representations: perspective drawings, bird's-eye-view sketches, watercolour prints, photographs, plans and blueprints, the *Plan* laid out a tremendous reworking of Chicago's urban fabric. It addressed the need for new streets, railroads, parks, waterworks, recreation areas and more. As the *Plan* was distributed well beyond Chicago, it became influential in developing the idea that large-scale plans were needed for the effective and orderly growth of cities, and that representations were powerful tools that could help make them happen. In reading the *Plan* as a general set of theoretical–practical tendencies, we can draw parallels with ways of knowing manifest in a vast range of contemporary urban academic disciplines, policy initiatives and political rhetoric. These have not been universally shared nor gone uncontested by all urban actors, but running through these sorts of imaginations are some particular ways of understanding cities that are tightly bound up with certain techniques of representation. We will briefly outline four of these.

The city as a problem to be solved: Four habits of imagination

Rational detachment: Burnham's offices being moved high above the city presents a quite literal enactment of the idea that detachment enables objective decisions to be made. This thinking has its origins in Cartesian understandings of the mind as separate from the body and of 'the logical' as superseding 'the sensory'. It also extends a way of solving problems though the act of distancing, which allows for a functional look at how interconnected parts work in serving instrumental purposes. Furthermore, the *Plan of Chicago* speaks to a wider way of imagining cities that emerged through rational planning. Knowledges based on abstraction – plans, maps, tables, models – are valorised over personal and emotional attachments to places. Representations can facilitate this by both creating information (giving a problem a certain definition or shape) and neutralising it (through making this information technical). Distancing oneself from the city enables a view in which rational decisions can be made.

A will to order: The moral failures, biological threats and barriers to economic success perceived in industrial cities implied a need to bring order to chaos. The City Beautiful movement, of which Burnham was a key proponent, was premised on faith in the utility of unifying and efficiently arranging interconnected parts of the city. It was believed, for example, that linking together distinct functional zones with landscaped streets and punctuating them with neoclassical architecture would inspire a sense of community among urban residents and increase economic productivity. There is a paradox here. Cities are imagined as possessing a natural order. Burnham, like many generations of urban thinkers, was fond of organic metaphors: the city centre was said to be its 'heart', parks were the vital 'lungs', transport networks a 'circulatory system' and great highways 'the legs' upon which the city could further expand. And yet, conversely, cities are often described as 'unruly' and in need of taming. The production of architectural renderings, planned forms and interventions to the existing fabric are justified for their contribution to correcting the urban ills and restoring vitality. Urban imaginations that seek to order are both derived from and operate through such practices of representation. They become embedded in discourses that portray parts of the city as objectionable yet repairable. The urban fabric becomes connected with the larger project of modernity – ordering the unknown and the invisible, making them known and visible, making them available for use (Mitchell, 1991).

A universal notion of the public interest: The *Plan of Chicago* was made possible by an elite network of successful businessmen who saw no real difference between their best interests and those of the wider city. Along with Burnham, their commitment to decisive action was based on a universal notion of the public realm in which 'the city' is a representation of 'the people'. Such imaginaries propel the idea that powerful interests and technocratic experts are best placed to make decisions about how urban neighbourhoods should develop. The history of urban planning is marked by grand schemes positing universal good for an abstract public and by urban actors with high intentions and an unquestioning trust in their own motives and ideas. A number of civic leaders, planners and architects became highly influential in acting on this notion. Perhaps most notably Ebenezer Howard, Frank Lloyd Wright and Le Corbusier each designed and promoted their own utopian 'ideal city' under the premise that their plans for radical reconstruction could not only solve urban crises but also elevate humanity to a new level of social harmony (see Fishman 1982; Hall 1988; Pinder 2005). What has become clear in hindsight is how impractically rigid their notions were given the dynamic and heterogeneous nature of urban life. Universal appeals to a singularly imagined 'public good' however, are remarkably enduring.

A reduction of complexity: This habit of thinking runs through each of the previous three: detachment inherently involves setting some details aside, attempts at ordering can easily flatten out heterogeneity and a universal notion of the public provides little room for difference or change. Burnham was attuned to this dilemma. He developed the *Plan* based on his understanding of what was best for the city but intentionally left things somewhat vague. His intention was to be more impressionistic than prescriptive. As C. Smith (2006) suggests, Burnham's aim was to enlist readers to a cause, not the details of the plan. The very task of planning requires an isolation of some features of a city in order to rework them towards particular ends. Representations enable planners to anticipate possible outcomes, make comparisons, visualise alternatives and ultimately select and make interventions.

Distance and Abstraction

Plan of Chicago was never realised in its entirety but it left an undeniable mark on the city. The industrial city that Smith described as 'choking on its own success' (2006: 37) was gradually transformed through the construction of long, straight roads, grand monuments and buildings, forest preserves and waterfront parks that endure today. As a set of representational practices, the *Plan* enabled a vision that could be articulated, distributed, debated, modified and enacted. These developments are illustrative of just some of the work that representations do and enable more generally for cities. They present a set of resources for dealing with the challenges that arise through urbanisation. Throughout the middle of the twentieth century these techniques became increasingly institutionalised. This paralleled developments in the social sciences more broadly where a range of urban subdisciplines were coming to be defined by their ability to address socio-economic problems through the application of scientific methods. The so-called 'quantitative revolution' in the 1950s and 1960s brought in the widespread adoption of inferential statistics, computation and abstract modelling, promising new ways of representing the city in even more objective, rational and calculative terms (see Barnes 1996, 1998; Livingstone, 1992). As a result, knowledge production in urban geography, urban planning, sociology, economics and other urban-oriented social sciences came to be based on representational practices such as cartography, diagramming and statistical analyses. The 'view from above' had become – for those professionals charged with planning, managing and understanding cities at least – the dominant form of imagining the urban.

PART TWO: CRITICAL VIEWS: CITIES A NEXUS OF POWER

> If today one wants a representation of the 'ideal' city and of its relations to the universe, one will not find this image with the philosophers and even less in an analytical vision which divides urban reality into fractions, sectors, relations and correlations. (Lefebvre [1968] 1996: 160)

If Daniel Burnham represents the rise of a certain kind of mainstream, rationally oriented, modernist imagination, we can trace through the figure of the radical urbanist critic Henri Lefebvre the emergence of an explicitly alternative way of thinking about cities. More than any other twentieth-century social theorist, Lefebvre drew attention to the ways in which 'the lines between the material and the ideal, the objective and the subjective, the physical and the perceptual, tend to blur when you look at how they work out in the spaces of the city' (Tonkiss, 2005: 2–3). Lefebvre's writings span much of the twentieth century and have spawned an academic cottage industry of secondary analyses and translations. In his native France he is remembered mostly for his critique of everyday life, his engagements with the Situationist movement and as a broker in the 1968 student uprising. He is more revered in Anglo-American academic circles, however, where his later work on urbanisation and space have made him an iconic figure in urban studies and critical geography (Goonewardena et al., 2008; see also Elden, 2004; Merrifield, 2006; Sheilds, 1998). Two of his texts in particular remain profoundly influential in contemporary urban scholarship.

The first, 1968's *Le Droit à la Ville* (*The Right to the City*), was a collection of provocative essays Lefebvre had written throughout that decade. Visits to French New Towns, the architecture of Le Corbusier's 'machines for living' and the worldwide growth of suburban sprawl horrified Lefebvre, confirming his fears of the modern impulse to separate spaces, simplify complexities and flatten out social experience. In his texts, Lefebvre suggests the city to can be understood as a kind of ouvre – a work in which all citizens participate. The 'social centrality' of the city thus demands that all citizens have a 'right to the city' (Lefebvre, 1996; Mitchell, 2003). In doing so, he laid down an imperative for social justice in and through urban space. This demand was both taken up and challenged by sociologist Manuel Castells who argued that traditional urban sociology was incapable of identifying answers to urban problems such as poverty, criminality and race riots (see Castells, [1972] 1979). Soon after, the geographer David Harvey (1973) began arguing the need for a radical analysis of capitalist urbanisation. What opened up in both fields was a Marxian political economic analysis of cities that drew attention to the ways in which ideology and power structures work to alienate, marginalise and control urban inhabitants.

Lefebvre's second key text, *The Production of Space*, was his 57th book and the capstone of his illustrious career. Although written in 1974, it was not widely read in the Anglophone world until its 1991 English translation. Central to the book's thesis is the idea that space should be interpreted not as some dead, inert object or passive surface but as organic and alive; composed of 'great movements, vast rhythms, immense waves' (Lefebvre, 1991: 87). His conceptual triad of 'representations of space', 'spaces of representation' and 'spatial practices' has been profoundly important in shaping critical understandings of the spatialities of urban life (see Soja, 1989, 1996). Importantly it is the 'lived' realm of spatial practice that not only transcends the others but also provides opportunities for humanity to resist the dominating forces of abstraction and ordering. Through Lefebvre's valororisation of spaces of embodiment, desire and expression, critical theorists began to understand these aspects of urban life as equally important to the building of cities as physical raw materials.

Re-presenting the city in critical urban studies

Although there have been debates over issues of methodology, epistemology and sub-stance, the broad field of critical urban studies (including geography, sociology, plan-ning and architecture) is united by the imperative to attend to the social injustices constitutive of contemporary urbanisation (see Brenner, 2009). Further, the notion of space as 'socially produced' has become axiomatic within the urban canon. These understandings owe a great deal to Lefebvre, but are situated within a wide range of urban scholarship that has challenged conventional planning and inspired a range of alternative urban imaginations. What is important to our discussion here is that repre-sentation is folded into this tradition of critical urban studies in at least three key ways.

Firstly, representations are seen to obscure the workings of power and domination that structure everyday urban life. Following the lead of approaches in social and cultural studies, deconstructing representations has become a major domain of urban scholarship. In particular, representational practices such as cartography and mapping (Cosgrove, 1999; Harley, 2001; Pickles, 2004), advertising and consumer 'brandscapes' (Klingmann, 2007; Zukin, 1991), city branding (Greenberg, 2008; Kearns and Philo, 1993; Patterson, 1993) and planning/regeneration discourses (Hall and Hubbard, 1998; Mele, 2000a, 2000b; Wilson, 2007) have been dissected to reveal power relations in action. Further, urban locations such as shopping malls (Goss, 1999), parks (Mitchell, 2003), plazas (Low, 2002; van Deusen Jr., 2002), restaurants (Zukin, 1995) and entire city centres (Macleod, 2002) have been repeat-edly 'read' for the ways in which representations work to exclude particular citizens.

Secondly, through the development of 'cultural' and 'symbolic' economies represen-tation is said to have replaced material production as the key engine of capitalist urban development. There is no shortage of analysis and case studies to support the increas-ing entanglement of economy and culture (Harvey, 1989a, 1989b; Lloyd, 2006; Molotch, 1996; Power and Scott, 2004; Scott, 2000; Zukin, 1995, 2009) with analyses shifting between positing whether such developments are best described as a 'cultura-tion of the economy' (Warde, 2002) or an 'economisation of culture' (Miles, 2007).

Thirdly, alternative voices and forms of representation in cities are understood as being continuously suppressed. Projects aiming to expose the ideological character of dominant representations through critique have been amplified by incorporating insights from feminist, post-colonial and queer studies. Questions of representation have centred on the politics of asking 'who has the power to produce authorised representations of the world?' and 'what/who are the legitimate objects of represen-tation?' (Söderström, 2005: 13; see also Rose, 1993). Urban imaginations and prac-tices of city planning have been challenged by these developments. Emphasis has been drawn to ways in which the built environment (and the processes of construct-ing it) fail to embrace the diversity of contemporary cities (see Sandercock, 1998) Likewise, urban theory-building has been critiqued for drawing almost exclusively on the experience of a handful of wealthy, western cities. Scholars such as Robinson (2006), Simone (2004a) and Gandy (2005a) have shown how African cities tend to be ignored, exoticised or pathologised by urban scholarship that views them as either exceptional or in need of developmentalist intervention.

To summarise, one of the key legacies of critical urban scholarship has been the ongoing questioning of power and its work though representations. However, there is an enduring sense that this realm is one of artificiality, a realm that is somehow not 'real' – or less real – to the material business of cities (see Lees, 2002). As we will see in the next section, however, everyday urban life is deeply bound up in myriad practices of representation. These practices may be laden with power, but this power is not always of the repressive sort. Further, that these practices cannot be seen from above does not mean that they are invisible.

PART THREE: VIEWS FROM THE EVERYDAY: REPRESENTATIONS AND COLLECTIVE LIFE

The kind of critical urban theory sketched out by Lefebvre and developed with such vigour by writers like Castells, Harvey and others, rightfully places questions of representation and imagination at the core of urban scholarship. However, for these writers representation often exists as either a kind of alienation – a way for the powerful to realise their domination – or an escape – a way in which the powerless find some small way of maintaining their autonomy. But perhaps we can talk about representation and imagination in more prosaic terms, as simply part of the day-to-day, ordinary reality of urban life? Perhaps we can think about the way that all sorts of representational techniques and practices provide ways for people to navigate and orient themselves within cities? That is to say, as part of the normal going-on of city life, urban dwellers are involved in a whole range of representational technologies and practices that are neither invisible nor part of some grand scheme of domination by the powerful.

Take, for example, how mass communication technologies such as the newspaper helped the inhabitants of rapidly expanding industrial cities in the nineteenth century make sense of the new environments and circumstances within which they found themselves. It is difficult to imagine just how strange and alien the new European and North American metropolises of the nineteenth century must have felt. The emerging industrial city was remarkable not simply for its size. It was also remarkable for the novelty of its social organisation. Innovations such as factory work, hourly pay, tenement housing, public transit, mass literacy, commercial entertainments, department stores and their associated retail districts, to name just a small number of examples, all created a world that was both radically novel and often disturbingly fluid. In such a world the newspaper came to be an essential agent in providing urban dwellers with guidance in how to get on. They also provided a sense of how the city as a whole hung together. As the Chicago School sociologist Robert Park – who had worked as a newspaper reporter before entering academic life (Lindner, 1996) – wrote in early study of the relationship between the newspaper and urban life:

> The newspaper is the great medium of communication within the city, and it is on the basis of information which it supplies that public opinion rests.

The first function which a newspaper supplies is that which was formally performed by the village gossip. (1925: 39)

In Park's account, the newspaper came to stand in for more traditional forms of authority that previously were provided through face-to-face relationships. However, newspapers did rather more than this. Through the narratives they delivered, newspapers offered a series of ongoing, evolving, representations of urban life. As a technology of representation the newspaper offered a kind of mimesis of the urban experience itself. Schwartz describes how in late nineteenth-century Paris the popular press 'featured a written scenario of life on the boulevards – a sort of literary voyeurism' (1999: 26). One can see parallels with the figure of the flâneur whose goal was to keep abreast of everything abroad within the city. But while the whole point of flâneurie is to observe but not be directly involved, the role of the newspaper reporter – and the newspaper – is to tell what has been seen back to the city itself. Schwartz highlights how this constant re-telling brought the newspaper directly into the 'sensationalization of the everyday' and through this sensationalism 'the press ... promoted the shared pleasures and identification of individual city dwellers that transformed them into city dwellers' (1999: 26). Of course much of this reportage focused on the exceptional and was not necessarily representative of daily urban life in the strict sense of the term. However, as historians like Schwartz (1999) and Fritzsche (1996) have shown, the reporting of events within cities did generate a very real democratisation of urban life in a number of ways.

Firstly, the way in which events were made available to a mass reading public created a collective sense of involvement in the daily ebb and flow of urban life. City newspapers, Fritzsche (1996: 125) writes in *Reading Berlin, 1900*, 'brought to light the public places and amusements that city people had fashioned, charted the manifold rhythms and tentative arrangements of the metropolis, and thereby extended the geographic, social, and imaginative bounds of Berlin'. Secondly, the newspaper acted as a kind of guide and commentary on the social mores of the big city. As Fritzsche (1996: 60) writes to explain the explosion in newspaper publication and readership that occurred in late nineteenth- and early twentieth-century Berlin: 'thousands of confused newcomers arrived in Berlin's train stations every year, the great majority from small villages, many of them Poles and Jews who spoke German poorly, and all hungering for information to orient themselves in the big city'. The newspaper offered a cheap and generally reliable source of information on topics ranging from employment openings, housing opportunities, how one should comport themselves, 'whether to throw away cherry pits or orange peels, how to behave on the streetcar, the proper conduct of pedestrians' (Groth in Fritzsche, 1996: 61). In short, newspapers co-constructed a sense of how to go about making oneself an *Echter Berliner*, a real New Yorker, a savvy urbanite. Indeed, a central characteristic of urban newspapers was their willingness to trade in the argot of the boulevards and the streets. Thus, New York's newspapers were full of references to a whole new constellation of characters, places and phenomena of often less than aristocratic etymology: straphangers, rubberneckers, panhandlers, muggers, hookers, subways, movies, rush hours, skid rows, tenderloins, automarts, nickelodeons, candy stores, luncheonettes.

As Allen (1995: 17) writes of nineteenth-century New York: 'Mass communication traded in the lingua franca of slang when they wanted to speak as one with the city. Millions were reading, listening, laughing, and learning – and all the while talking.'

Thirdly, the fact the city newspaper gave so much space to reporting mundane, everyday events and encounters created a sense of the city dweller as a participant in a wider public drama. In describing the popularity of the *fait divers* – a literary genre which focused on dramatising human interest stories such as crimes or other extraordinary events in Parisian newspapers of the late nineteenth century – Schwartz stresses that the importance and, indeed, transformative power of this genre of reportage lay in its ordinariness:

> [*Fait divers*] constructed a new kind of public life by thrusting ordinary people, even innocent victims and murderous transients, onto a vast stage for inspection by the 'universalizing' eye of the newspaper reader. The fait divers indicated that all life, no matter how banal, could be rendered spectacular through sensational narrative. In addition fait divers' precise location in contemporary and ordinary Paris meant that readers could identify with the narrative. At any moment they might find themselves the subject of a notorious fait divers. (1999: 39)

Throughout the twentieth century there was an explosion in related and new forms of representation. Innovations in printing technologies made literary genres such as paperbacks, magazines, comic books and catalogues affordable to a mass audience. Simultaneously, advertising came to fill not just the printed spaces of the city. It also filled up posters, handbills, shop signs, billboards, bus stands and light displays, in effect making these an inherent marker of urbanity (see Fritzsche, 1996; Leach, 1994; Rappaport, 2001; Schivelbusch, 1995). Other new media technologies, particularly those of radio, film and television, that were at first extraordinary, became an everyday aspect of how cities were made sense of, portrayed and inhabited (Charney and Schwartz, 1995; Sklar, 1994). As new modes of distribution made these media less expensive and more widely accessible, representations came to shape not only how urban life was imagined, but also how it was lived. We can think of the ways that the spread of cinema at the start of the twentieth century created not only new spaces for socialising, but also helped generate new rhythms of leisure (see Bowser, 1990; Field, 1974). Further still, these representational practices were involved in the continuous stretching of the urban beyond what might conventionally be recognised as the city to people and places far from the great metropolises of the nineteenth century.

PART FOUR: MACHINIC CITIES: REPRESENTATIONS AT WORK

Thus far we have considered representation from three different angles, so to speak. One might find similarities with de Certeau's (1984) well-known chapter 'Walking in the City in *The Practice of Everyday Life*. Standing atop the World Trade Center he contemplated how being high above the city enabled an imagining of the urban fabric as a static text that could be read. Recognising the limits of this view, he suggested that 'it is below – "down" – on the threshold where visibility ends that the city's common practitioners dwell' (1984: 93). We want to suggest a different stance. We want to highlight the usefulness of refusing to valorise a particular vantage point. Our understanding of the varying modes of representation that swirl through urban life is that they fold promiscuously into one another in ways that continuously constitute what cities are. This leads to three key points:

1. *Cities are ordered, managed and held together through representations.* Take, as an example, the emergence of urban electricity networks that began to be established in the late nineteenth century and are still being rolled out in places throughout the world. Electrification brought a whole new set of capacities to cities and much has and can be made of the new patterns of inhabitation and experience this afforded (Graham and Marvin, 2001; Hughes, 1993; Schivelbusch, 1995). As cities started to become thickets of wires and cables, electricity companies were dependent on a range of representational technologies to make these emerging power grids (themselves representations) function: blueprints, service plans, postcodes, training manuals, qualification certificates, electricity meters, energy bills. Electricity networks are now so embedded into how cities operate that monitoring and regulating and maintaining them across urban space is vital to the very capacity of cities to function. In a similar manner, we can understand how cities are ordered, managed and held together by tracing the historical development of a whole range of representational infrastructures that support urban systems: water and sanitation utilities, land registries, local authority and zoning jurisdictions, natural hazard and emergency response plans, transportation infrastructures and wirelesses networks to name just a few examples (see Melosi, 1999; Mitchell, 1996; Schwieterman and Caspall, 2006).

Rethinking Maps

Traditionally the domain of geographers, cartographic practices are currently fostering new urban imaginations in all sorts of exciting ways. Whereas critical discussion has traditionally framed maps as a tool of power and authority, urban artists, designers, architects, activists and community groups have been putting them to use for a host of 'exploratory, experimental, playful, popular and even subversive activities' (Pinder 2007: 454). Rather than being seen as having a purely mimetic function, mapping is being more broadly conceived as a means of navigational interpretation (November et al., 2010). Freed from the demand to represent territories with objective accuracy, a new generation of map-makers and 'user cartographers' are critiquing hegemonic power structures while creating alternatives and most generally using maps as 'a way of making sense of things' (Abrams and Hall, 2006: 12; Wood, 2010).

Much of this creativity has been driven by an awareness of the need to respond to changing political, social and economic realities in cities. For example, in India the

(Continued)

(Continued)

'Maps for Making Change' project has brought together grassroots activists and NGO workers to train them in digital cartography and to explore how such skills might be used in struggles for social justice. Outcomes have included mobilising slum dwellers to engage with Mumbai's Development Plan, mapping social services for sex workers in Delhi and tracing the lives of migrant workers building Bangalore's Metro. In New York, the Center for Urban Pedagogy brings expertise in the arts and graphic design together with urban practitioners to create educational projects to empower people in acting on a range of issues to facilitate change. They have developed toolkits to help urban residents locate and analyse proposed developments in their neighbourhoods. Their resources also help residents navigate the concepts and procedures required to participate meaningfully in consultation processes. The centre's 'making policy public' projects seek to map and make legible what are often complicated administrative and regulatory regimes in areas such as street vending, social benefits programmes, the juvenile justice system and immigrants rights. These practices illustrate how the field of cartography and related forms of representation can create 'new potentialities for social action and new configurations of social life' (Pickles, 2004: 171).

2. *Cities are enormous spaces for the creation, processing and distribution of representations.* Film production is a case that illustrates this point. Films are not just moving images of cities; they are largely made in cities. Los Angeles has long been the undisputed centre of the global film industry. Yet in the past few decades, places as diverse as Mumbai, Hong Kong, Cairo, Lagos and Wellington have gained prominence as hubs in the production of film and television. This wider distribution of the industry is in no small part due to work that extends beyond actual filming and includes representational processing as part of a much larger media-related supply chain. What makes each of these cities a hub is the clustering of studios, screenwriters, production companies, distribution networks and the variously skilled individuals required for putting a film together (take note of how long the credits are after the next film you watch). However, we also want to emphasise forms of representation that work in a slightly different register. New technologies in media, communication, digitisation and software are very much about taking elements from the lived world and re-presenting them back into new ways of sensing, knowing and acting (Kitchin and Dodge, 2007; 2011; Thrift and French, 2002). Take Garmin – the world's leading producer of GPS devices. Garmin devices include GPS systems for aviation, marine and automotive navigation, laptops and PDA receivers, personal fitness training devices and handheld GPS devices. From pretty much anywhere on or near Earth, Garmin's products are capable of providing real time and location in a range of representational formats that can be embedded into maps, navigation systems, databases and software programs. The process that makes these systems possible involves communication between these ubiquitous devices and orbiting satellites. Yet the production of these representations is rooted in very particular places. In the case of Garmin, the headquarters

and the main research and design facilities are located in Olathe (suburban Kansas City) while the devices themselves are primarily made in Sijhih City (suburban Taipei). Crucial to the point we are making is that the world we inhabit is in all sorts of ways tied to these representational capacities which are located in, and a product of, particular cities. That is to say, the multifarious creation, processing and distribution of representations, and indeed the ability to process and generate further representations, are a fundamental part of how urban economies function. Think beyond film and GPS devices to the wider worlds of publishing, fashion, advertising, news production, software design, video games, art and architecture (see Grabher, 2001, 2002; Lash and Lury, 2007; Lash and Urry, 1993). Each of these industries will have key sites of production yet the ubiquity of their end products makes it easy to overlook the specific geographies that produce them.

3. *Cities are key sights for the consumption of representations.* Population density alone renders cities as pivotal sites of consumption. But the nature of contemporary urban life means that this is more than just a matter of scale. Cities are both 'consuming spaces' and host to a range of spectacularly mediated 'consumer spaces' (Jayne 2006; see also Clarke, 2003; Berman, 2006; Mort, 1996; Rothman, 2003). The consumption of goods has long structured city life. However, the past 30 or so years show a marked orientation of the urban towards consumption – and not just of goods, but services, images, architectures and experiences (see Zukin, 1991; 1995). Consider for example that today, on average, 120,000 tourists will visit Paris; 45 million people annually. Visitor experiences will in all likelihood be informed by a range of representations consumed prior to arrival: novels, films, paintings, travel shows, hotel brochures, websites and travel literature. The act of touring the city will further be mediated though things such as guide books filled with maps, suggested itineraries and strategies for 'doing Paris'. Many first-time visitors will rush to the Louvre, where as many as 20,000 people per day crowd around the *Mona Lisa*. Others will make the Eiffel Tower an immediate priority. The reason for doing either is not simply because these are nice things to look at; they are also powerful representations of the city's historical and cultural status. The experience of 'doing Paris' might be seen as incomplete without experiencing them first-hand and perhaps getting a photo to prove it. The point here is that consumption is often tied up in a whole range of representational processes and practices. Cities are not only involved in the production of these but are the testing grounds and sites for their consumption. Much scholarship has been concerned with theorising and tracing how, in a neoliberal era, cities are said to compete in an urban hierarchy. Thus, facilitating consumption becomes a key concern of investor-developer-city governance groups in the competition to secure investment, jobs and tourists (Cronin and Hetherington, 2008; Florida, 2007; Hall and Hubbard, 1998; Harvey, 1987, 1989b). Yet these kinds of strategies are just one dimension in the diversity of sites and practices of representation that are folded into urban inhabitants' everyday lives. Long before and after the tourist's trip to Paris, for example, the same kinds of material objects that helped to (re)present Paris – literature, films, websites,

maps – are involved in the navigation of life within their own city. Even more prominently, and in a multitude of ways, urban life gains its texture and meaning through signs, symbols and images that are continuously reshaped through processes of urbanisation.

Urban imagining through representations: What are streets for?

As cities grow in complexity the components that constitute them open up new possibilities and challenges. Cities have been theorised as 'machinic' in this way – as a set of constantly evolving systems or networks that intermix categories like the social, technical, biological, economic, cognitive and corporal in emergent ways that are often systematic without being structural (Amin and Thrift, 2002; DeLanda, 2006a; Latham and McCormack, 2004). What we have been arguing is that representations are part of this machinic assemblage. This makes them always *more*-than-representational: they are active performers in processes of abstracting, transferring, rendering, holding together, processing, distributing and projecting. As Cronin (2006) suggests in regard to urban advertising, representations are so ubiquitous that they give a certain sense of 'alreadyness' to everyday urban life as a conceptual and lived realm. To work with them productively requires following the actions and imaginations they enable across the lines of management, production and consumption suggested above.

Take, for example, a question that has been on our minds lately in our own research on urban public life: 'What are a city's streets for?' The answer of course varies from place to place, but in the last 100 years or so it has come to be that in most cities the street is understood first and foremost as the domain of the automobile. It is not just that this is the natural order of things, or that legislation has made things this way. Rather, a great number of material cultural developments fixed this idea into popular imagination and practice. Things such as curbs, guardrails, signage, designated pedestrian crossings, signals, media coverage of accidents, even education campaigns urging people to 'look both ways' and teaching children that streets are not safe all work together to create a certain sense of what streets are about (see Norton, 2008; Urry, 2004; Vanderbilt, 2008). Each of these developments works as a type of representation that helps to reinforce the primacy given to automobiles. Historically however, urban streets were a mix of uses jostling together. Over time, however, the multiple uses of streets were gradually stripped out or at least confined to the sidewalk. Eventually even sidewalks came to be understood as primarily about movement. What we have been asking ourselves is: Could we develop more socially and economically vibrant – not to mention more fair and socially just – ways of provisioning city streets and sidewalks? Absolutely. But doing so will require a tremendous range of practical interventions, policy experiments and material reconfigurations to make transformation happen (see Dennis and Urry, 2009; Urry, 2004).

Figure 2.1   Representations organise streets – changing representations may radically change how a street works. 1. Signs such as this quite clearly make streets the domain of cars. 2. Zebra crossings require drivers to attend to pedestrians. 3. Bike lines give a portion of the street to cyclists. 4. White bike memorials testify to the unequal relationship between bikes and vehicular traffic. 5. Shared space designs force cars to attend to pedestrians and cyclists through the absence of clear instructions. 6. Adding chairs and tables may further complicate the uses of a street

Representations can and will play a role in re-imagining streets in at least four general ways. Firstly, technical modes of representation such as harm data, accident mappings, health statistics and actuarial tables can demonstrate the dangers and harms that come with letting cars dominate cities. Second, representations can also work at an affective and emotional level in conveying some of these same messages. Think, for example, of the American organisation Mothers Against Drunk Driving campaigns and their commercials; the solemn power of roadside memorials; or the placement of white bicycles to indicate where cyclists have been killed. Third, various techniques are needed to visualise, plan and mobilise support for initiatives such as pedestrianised zones, bike lanes, congestion charges, road-pricing schemes and expansions of public transportation. Representations supporting these initiatives compete with more established imaginations and forms of representation that suggest these sorts of changes are unfeasible, dangerous, economically damaging and so on. Fourthly, and perhaps most ubiquitously, a number of quite mundane forms of representation – demarcations, lines, crosswalks, bike lanes and road signage – are put to use in the provisioning of the public realm to facility safety, efficiency, fairness and the sharing of space. Changing the way streets are used may well depend on the invention of new representational devices that effectively alter the grammar of the street. The wide blue lanes that mark bicycle crossings at major traffic intersections in Copenhagen – an idea that has in various forms been transported to cities such as Portland, Oregon and Brisbane, California – is a good example.

Urban Utopia and Dystopia

To lift oneself out from the urban fabric, to view the city from above as Burnham did, shrinks the city, abstracts it, makes it appear eminently knowable, and as a result eminently perfectible. And, indeed, there is a strong current of urban thinking that is driven by the impulse to create the ideal city: a city that is not defined by its contradictions, disjunctions, by its opaqueness, but rather by its orderliness, by its rationality, by its completeness. This utopian impulse – utopian because it foregrounds an imagining of another ideal city in place of the actual existing city – has driven a great deal of progressive thinking. Urban theorists as diverse as Patrick Geddes, Ebenezer Howard, Raymond Unwin, Leonid Sabsovich, Le Corbusier, Bruno Taut, Frank Lloyd Wright and Kenzo Tange, to name just a few examples, have put forward proposals aimed at thoroughly transforming urban life through the construction of new, idealised, urban forms (see Eaton, 2001; Pinder, 2005).

But it is not just academic urban thinking that is energised by utopianism. There are many commercially driven renderings of ideal future cities. Perhaps the most famous is Walt Disney's EPCOT (Experimental Prototype Community of Tomorrow) Centre in Orlando, Florida, which was transformed from a vision of an ideal city into a theme park. But the utopian impulse can be found in all sorts of surprising places: in world exhibitions such as the General Motors sponsored Futurama exhibit at the 1938 New York World's Fair; in advertisements for planned communities in places as diverse as São Paulo, Manila, Guayaquil, Cairo, Lima and Los Angeles; in the rhetoric of business consultants and journalists, who see the outline of a fully realised global urban future in the rapid development of ultra-connected, ultra-modern aerotropoli in places such as Chongqing and Chengdu in in-land China, to say nothing of Hong Kong or Dubai (see Davis and Monk, 2007; Harvey, 2000a; Kasarda and Lindsay, 2011).

The power of such utopic thinking arises from the ways it conjures up the possibility of imagining cities wildly different to those we might know. Nonetheless, the actual cities, or parts of cities, that have been produced as a result of these utopian flights rarely match the radiance of the ideals with which they are fuelled. Take, for example, the anthropologist James Holsten's (1989: 3) analysis of the construction of Brazil's new capital Brasilia in the 1950s and early 1960s. 'Brasilia', Holsten writes, 'was built to be more than merely the symbol of [The New Age of Brazil]. Rather its design and construction were intended to create [The New Age] by transforming Brazilian society.' And yet, for all its modernity and architectural brilliance (the city was named a UNESCO world heritage site in 1987), Brasilia has been swamped by informal settlements, and riven by inequality. Like Rio de Janeiro and São Paulo before, Brasilia has failed to transcend the profound social divisions that define so much of Brazilian society (see Caldeira, 2000). In a similar way, many of the modernist social housing projects built throughout North Europe and North America with such idealism in the 1950s and 1960s have over time atrophied into dystopian landscapes, populated only by the unwanted 'outcasts' (Wacquant, 2008) of urban society. They have created – at least so it seems – the very kind of city they were meant to banish. And, lastly, as Mike Davis and Daniel Bertrand Monk show in their anthology *Evil Paradise: Dreamworlds of Neoliberalism* (2007), many of the supposed utopian spaces of the current global economy are built on profound (if often hidden) exclusions and power asymmetries. This is not say that utopian – and indeed dystopian – imaginings of the city cannot be productive. Imagining any good city requires perhaps at least some degree of utopian thought. But as Matthew Gandy (2005a) has shown in his discussion on the future of Lagos, focusing too much on either the utopia or dystopia can distract urban scholars from considering the more practical, tried-and-tested ways of improving urban life.

These strategies for ordering and managing traffic in cities feed into a broader set of projects that envision new ways of creating cities and neighbourhoods less dominated by automobiles, trying to *domesticate* them in more broadly inclusive and democratic ways (Koch and Latham, 2013) This is being done through a range of innovations and experiments. For example:

- In Bogotá, 120 km of streets are closed to automobile traffic on Sundays and public holidays. This is to encourage walking and cycling by making their experience both more enjoyable and less dangerous.

- Activists in San Francisco have transformed parking spaces into temporary parks, mini-golf courses, sun lounges, libraries and other creative uses. 'Urban Park(ing)' projects have now spread to cities in Europe, Asia, South America and Africa.

- City councils and cyclist groups across the UK and US organise 'Bike to Work Breakfasts', encouraging people to cycle by offering them breakfast at publicised locations.

- In over 300 cities around the world, on the last Friday of the month, hundreds even thousands of cycling enthusiasts join en masse to travel as a group through their cities in an assertion of their presence (and to have a good time).

- Food vendors in New York and LA not only use sidewalks and streets to trade, but have increasingly taken to hiring parking spots for the day, organising festivals that close streets temporarily, and using Facebook and Twitter to create impromptu gatherings.

- In Paris, since 2002, stretches of road along the river Seine are converted into urban beaches in summer months. Sand, palm trees and deck chairs are used to cover the spaces normally given over to traffic.

These interventions work through representational techniques that aim to provoke a consideration of how streets might be otherwise configured. In other cases, existing representational devices can be worked with or reproduced. For example, in Jakarta, zebra crossings exist all over the city but are largely ignored by drivers. Recent projects have used dancers and choreographed routines as a way of attempting to (re)establish their symbolic power as a way of making Jakarta safer for pedestrians. This strategy stands in direct contrast to cities in Holland where street signage, pedestrian crossings, demarcating lines and other traffic-regulating representations are being *removed* from streets as part of a 'shared space' concept that makes drivers actively negotiate with pedestrians and cyclists. In some cases, successful experiments come to represent how less automobile-dominated forms of urbanity can be achieved. Think, for example, of Curitiba or Copenhagen. For roughly a century, car ownership has been understood as representing freedom, mobility and personal choice. Counter-representations of pollution, danger and harm might gradually come to serve as a mobilising force for alternative sorts of urban imaginations. Of course, these changes will depend on much more than representations – they are just one part of the machinery that makes cities what they are and what they will become.

CONCLUSION

If we return to our discussion of skylines at the start of this chapter, we are reminded of the material and expressive properties immanent to the vast array of assemblages that comprise the city. Cities are swarming with images, maps, texts, plans, diagrams and on and on. This does not create some kind of reified world of illusion in the manner of Debord's *Society of the Spectacle* ([1967] 1983). Rather, representation is simply part of how the world is. Or, put another way, representation is part of how the world gets done. As Shields writes, 'Representations are ... complex formations of material, techniques and ideologies in which social practice is indissolubly linked to social thought and imagination' (1996: 228). This linkage means that representations are clearly bound up with power in all sorts of ways. Cities as they exist simply could not have been built without the tools and capacities of simplification, elaboration, abstraction and action that representations enable. Architects, planners and policy-makers derive much of their capacity to shape cities through these 'views from above'. At the same time, such ways of knowing are also complicit in many forms of oppression. The dominant representations can – and indeed often do – obscure a wider diversity of perspectives, exclude the less powerful and marginalise alternative viewpoints. But representations can also be a more or less benign way of sense-making, evaluation, getting things done or imagining alternative possibilities. Highlighting the more ordinary forms of representation used in everyday life makes this clear. There is productive potential in all of these understandings of the power of representation. The challenge – as we see it – comes in understanding how this power is put together, put to use, enacted.

Following Lefebvre and many others, it has become commonplace in urban scholarship to emphasise space as constructed. What concerns us, however, is precisely how spaces get constructed and to ask how all sorts of representational techniques and practices are deployed in these constructions. In pressing for a more expansive engagement with representations – understanding them as material and expressive, as part of the machinic assemblages of cities – our hope is that we might stimulate urban imaginations and foster more productive forms of urban scholarship. We think this means four things. First, urban studies need to move beyond straightforward critiques of representation and attend more to the generative capacities of the representational. Second, urban scholars need to consider their own embeddedness within a range of representational practices. This implies thinking about the limitations and potentials of established ways of working. Third, we might become more proficient at making sense of cities if we cultivate a more syncretic ethos towards various forms of representation. This would of course demand an expansion in our repertoire of representational techniques and strategies. Fourth and following, we might then embrace a more experimental ethos that puts representations to work in communicating concerns, expressing alternative voices and imagining possible futures.

SECTION 2

EXPERIENCING THE CITY

3

The 'New' Middle Class, Lifestyle and the 'New' Gentrified City

Loretta Lees

INTRODUCTION

This chapter will explore the rise of the 'new' middle class, also known as the 'cultural new class', and how their lifestyles, culture and consumption have impacted on cities. The focus will be on the 'new' city. In the global north this is the postmodern, post-industrial city that is undergoing an urban renaissance. And in the global south it is associated with the late modernisation and in some cases industrialisation of certain cities that are more connected with global flows. Before turning to the rise of the 'new' middle class in these 'new' cities I want to make four points.

Firstly, the 'new' middle class is not the only new class to be associated with the 'new' city. Two other groups are also significant – a new class of super-rich transnationals and an underclass of working or workless poor. Their lifestyles too are having an impact on the contemporary city, but it is the lifestyles of the 'new' middle classes that governments and policy-makers world-wide are drawing on in the creation of the 'new' city. Indeed, as we will see, governments are actively displacing and fragmenting the underclass of working and workless poor from, and in, our cities. As Slater (2006: 744) points out with reference to the leading edge of global urbanism – gentrification:

> It is as if the middle classes are the only characters occupying the stage of gentrification, with the working-class backstage, both perennial understudies and perennially understudied. This is particularly disappointing, for middle-class gentrifiers are, of course, only one part of a much larger story.

We need detailed class-based research on the remnant urban working classes (if indeed they still exist in the 'new' city), the urban working and workless poor (especially in-migrants to the rapidly urbanising cities of the global south); and importantly their lifestyles and relations with the supposedly urbane middle classes. Governments are also seeking to attract the super rich through tax breaks and other means, but that is another story. But, regardless of this, we need much more research on the *non*-middle classes in the contemporary city. Indeed, many authors now argue that it is not possible to study the experiences and identifications of any particular class in isolation from other classes (e.g. Slater et al., 2004). People are categorised by other people, and these categorisations influence how people identify themselves individually and collectively. Structural inequalities are reproduced through these categorisations making class something that remains hard to manoeuvre. Future work on class and lifestyle transformations in the 'new' city must be sensitive to *all* classes and their lifestyles.

Secondly, although the bulk of the literature drawn on here is from the Anglo-American experience, the emergence of a 'new' middle class is not limited to Anglo-American cities. As a result of the economic and political changes related to globalisation, the 'new 'middle class has risen in cities as far apart as Moscow, Mumbai and Shanghai. Yet literature on the 'new' middle class in these cities is, as yet, limited. We should not assume that the emergence of the 'new' middle class in these very different city and national contexts is the same, for the politics, practices and lifestyles will all be contextually and culturally inflected, although to some degree the experiences of class inequality in the 'new' city may have become globalised. Much more work needs to be done in the vein of comparative urbanism on class, lifestyle and the new city in the global north *and* the global south (see Lees, 2012a, 2012b; Robinson, 2006).

Thirdly, as this chapter will show it is now evident that there is not a singular 'new middle class' living in the city, if ever there was, but a fragmented 'new middle class'. As such the term 'new middle *classes*' should really be used instead (see also Butler and Watt, 2007). I am also conscious that the 'new' middle classes in developed world cities are no longer 'new', they are half a century old! Yet even if highlighting the word 'new' has less purchase today, it is still useful to differentiate this post-industrial middle-class population from the previous industrial middle-class population. As Butler (1997: 1) states:

> The middle class used to have a very clear image; they got married and Dad went to work, Mum stayed at home and they had a couple of kids and lived in a nice house with a garden in suburbia and they stayed married. Times have changed and so have the middle class.

And in developing world cities it is also useful to differentiate this 'new' class from both current social groups and previous social categorisations in their very different social, economic and political contexts.

Fourthly, renewed attention on the central city by academics, policy-makers, the media and governments has meant much less attention to the changing world of the inner and outer suburbs in cities. Now that gentrification has gone mainstream, what has the impact of this been on lifestyles in the inner and outer suburbs, indeed the exurbs and rural areas? We need much more comparative research into the differences and similarities between these different spaces in cities around the world. We can no longer compare the gentrified inner city with the modern suburb, for suburbia itself has changed!

In what follows I look at class and lifestyle in the contemporary Anglo-American city, connecting a discussion of class and related lifestyle transformations to the transition from the industrial or modern city to the post-industrial or postmodern city. I then move on to outline the features of the so-called 'new' city and the impact of the 'new' middle class on it, before turning to the notion of the 'creative city', which in part criticises the 'new' city, yet produces many of the same effects. Within these sections I also outline the somewhat different story of the emergence of the 'new' city and 'new' middle classes in newly modernising cities like Moscow, Mumbai and Shanghai. By way of conclusion I discuss the key role that the 'new' middle classes could play in the 'sustainable city', but this brings me back to the point that they are not (and should not be seen as) the only class in town!

CLASS AND LIFESTYLE TRANSFORMATIONS

In the West, in the transition to a post-industrial, postmodern city, long-standing ways of thinking about class have become as unsettled as has class itself. In the modern, industrial city the Marxian concept of class was defined in relation to the mode of production. Social classes emerged out of the social division of labour which occurred as the means of production became privately owned. In its pure and most rigid form, Marxist class analysis is based on a two-class model, the proletariat being dependent on the bourgeoisie, the owners and controllers of capital. This two-class model, however, did not allow for the emergence of the 'new' middle class that was to be born in the economic, social and cultural transition to post-industrialism and postmodernity. As Neil Smith (1987: 161) explains:

> The two-class model of classical Marxism does give us considerable insight into capitalism as a whole, but as a tool for comprehending specific experiences of social and political change, it must be refined considerably ... For examining the gentrification of a neighbourhood the two-class model would have the effectiveness of a chain saw for wood carving. Not that the two-class model is intrinsically blunt; it is necessary for cutting and shaping the block out of which our more intricate carve of gentrification can be fashioned ... Just as the two-class model cannot cut the sharp outlines of gentrification, the intricate, more refined, and more contingent tools of class analysis appropriate for portraying gentrification in a given locality are ineffective for explaining the larger historical and theoretical patterns of capitalist society. They would be as nail files to a forest.

Smith was forced to confront the inadequacies of Marxist class analysis because class was no longer what it used to be. In the economic, social and cultural transition to postmodernity, to the post-industrial city, social class fragmented along different lines. The working class declined, more people became middle class and the middle class itself became fragmented along identity lines (hence the 'new' middle class), and an underclass grew as the welfare state went into decline. Class was no longer the source of identity, politics or social behaviour (lifestyle) in the ways it used to be. The changes to class structures cannot be disaggregated from the related changes in the economic structure of advanced capitalist cities and to changes in the nature of households. Post-industrialism was both an economic, social and cultural process that had a significant impact on the city.

The 'new' middle class emerged out of the structural changes that were to affect Anglo-American cities after the Second World War. Economic changes that led to a focus on the service sector rather than the manufacturing sector. Changes in the social structure that afforded greater status and power to professional and techno-logical workers – 'unlike the old middle class ... the professional managerial class was not independent of the capital-labor relation but was employed by capital for the purpose of controlling, managing, and administering to the working class' (Ehrenreich and Ehrenreich, 1979, cited in Neil Smith 1987: 153). Changes in the knowledge base of the economy and society caused R&D (research and design) to become more important and there was increased concern with technological change and the associated advent of advanced information systems and intellectual technol-ogy. Jameson (1984) shows how there was a 'constitutive' relationship between cultural postmodernism, the new technologies and multinational capitalism. Structural changes like the expansion and contraction of the Keynesian welfare state, and from the mid-1970s onwards the neoliberal de-regulation of the labour market and the concomitant re-regulation of workplace relations, the globalisation of the economy, and the demise of trade unions caused profound changes in the experi-ences of class, gender relations and cultural expectations; they also caused significant changes in lives and lifestyle (see Harvey, 1989b). From the 1970s onwards in Anglo-American cities, households had less children (in part due to the birth control pill), marriage was increasingly delayed or in some cases not undertaken at all, non-traditional gay and straight partnerships were undertaken in public view, and women entered the workforce in increasing numbers. Significantly the number of professional dual-career households increased and the central city provided them and other non-traditional households with the structures that would enable them to undertake the everyday tasks of social reproduction. Social classes became what Neil Smith (1987) called fuzzy categories defined by economic, social, political and ideological conditions.

In order to understand this new class transformation and differentiation in west-ern cities it is useful to draw on Albertsen's (1988) conceptualisation of postmod-ern culture. Albertsen (1988) argued that high-modernism was high-Fordism's culture and that 'explosive' postmodernism emerged as an oppositional culture when high-Fordism was flowering in the 1960s. High-Fordism refers to the high point of Fordism: the system of mass production and mass consumption charac-teristic of highly developed economies in the 1950s and 1960s. High-modernism (a culture of standardisation and the establishment) declined and 'implosive' post-modernism (the dissolution of the Fordist model of standardised consumption into diversified and aesthetisised consumption, the rise of an experimenting culture industry after the youth revolts of the 1960s, the growth of the service class, and the advent of 'disposability' in ways and styles of living) arrived in the late-Fordist

1970s, emerging as the 'new' culture of the establishment in the first half of the post-Fordist 1980s. In social philosophy a general delegitimation of the grand narratives of progress and emancipation occurred as 'high-Fordism' gave way to stagnating 'late-Fordism' and fragmented 'post-Fordism'. Such a conceptualisation tallies well with gentrification research that has shown distinct differences between first-wave and second-wave gentrifiers and their gentrification practices (see Butler and Lees, 2006; Lees et al., 2008). As David Ley (1996, 2003) has said of gentrification, initial entrants into gentrifying districts in Canadian cities in the 1970s commonly had left-liberal sympathies and endorsed the sentiment of social difference, but as the process of gentrification unfolded and prices inflated a more conservative ethos took hold. Jon Caulfield (1989) similarly distinguished between early and later gentrifiers, the former or pioneer gentrifiers he names 'marginal gentrifiers' (see also Rose, 1984), for whom gentrification was an emancipatory social practice (see Lees, 2000). Marginal gentrifiers (Ley's 'cultural new class') were socially marginal figures like lesbians, gays, single parents and activists, and economically marginal figures like public sector workers and those in the artistic professions such as artists and architects. The inner city offered them cheap housing, child care and other support networks that were missing in the suburbs. Their non-traditional anti-suburban (anti-establishment) and pro-urban values defined their 'new' middle-class identity, lifestyle and cultural values.

The birth of a 'new' middle class in cities of the global south is a different story, here a new global middle class is emerging and growing in particular cities in emerging economies, the result of globalisation. But whereas

> ... urban thinking in much of Europe and North America is obsessed with the contours of postindustrial society, urbanization in the Global South is driven by the simultaneous expansion of 'old' and 'new' spatial economic shifts; cities are being reshaped by the expansion of manufacturing and heavy industrial activities, as well as the growth of high-tech off-shoring and outsourcing activities and smaller pockets of service sector innovation. (Lees et al., 2008: 166)

This middle class is not 'new' to define it from a previous 'old' middle class, rather it is 'new' because in some cases a middle class as such did not exist before. Importantly, this emerging 'new' middle class is now in competition with the 'new' middle classes in cities of the global north for jobs and resources. They are a new and emerging market and companies are tailoring products and services to their needs/desires. Yet behind this hegemonic image of 'modernity', Fernandes (2006) shows that the new middle class in India is a more complex and less self-evident social group than we are led to believe. She argues that India's 'new' middle class has its roots in the colonial character of English educational policies replicated in India and that English now, as then, remains the predominant form of mobile social capital. For her, the middle class in India today are part of a larger historical continuity. There are, then, important histories to the 'new' middle class in the global south that we need to attend to.

Globally there are important geographies to these changes in social class. There are emerging 'new' middle-class groups in some cities (which must be studied in place/context), whilst in other cities the middle classes are stagnant or even in decline. Social class is very dynamic, it is not stable on a global basis, and it is variable on a country-by-country, region-by-region and indeed city-by-city basis.

GENTRIFICATION AND THE 'NEW' MIDDLE CLASS

In the United States after the Second World War, fuelled with federally financed loans, those that could fled the inner city and moved to the suburbs. This became known as 'white flight' and American inner cities became synonymous with those left behind – urban blacks and the underclass. The American inner city was labelled 'a concrete jungle' – a violent wilderness full of crime, disease, pollution, social/economic malaise and racial unrest. The American inner city, abandoned by the de facto federal urban policy of suburbanisation, became removed from the mainstream with a concentration of the working class and the workless poor (Wilson, 1987). For many commentators (both in the media and policy-makers) this signified 'the death of the city'. In his *Voices of Decline*, Beauregard (1993) investigated these narratives of decline that emerged in the US post-war and shaped policy responses to the perceived 'urban crisis'. He shows well how these narratives of decline ignored or sidelined the important issues of race and poverty. Although less extreme and less visceral, there was a similar exodus from British and other European inner cities to the suburbs, but this tended to be a class flight, it did not have the racial dimension particular to the United States. As Jonathan Raban commented in his book on London, *Soft City*:

> A combination of class fear and railway engineering turned a vast stretch of residential London into a no-mans land ... Camden Town, Holloway, Islington, were abandoned to the hopelessly entrenched working class. It is only in the last decade or so that a new middle class, trendy and pioneer, have replaced these buffer areas, between the nobs and mob of N1 and NW1. (1974: 80)

At the same time as the death of the city was being proclaimed, the city in certain developed economies was being reborn through processes of gentrification (see Lees et al., 2008, 2010) or what some termed 'an urban renaissance' (Lees, 2003a). The 'urban wilderness' of the inner city became the 'new urban frontier' (Smith, 1986, 1996) and 'the new city' (Sorkin, 1991). And central to this process, some would argue, were 'the *new* middle class' that Raban (1974) mentions above.

Once they had abandoned the inner city, the middle classes in the UK and the US found it difficult to buy properties back in the inner city as mortgage companies red-lined (refused to lend on) the older housing stock located there. However, by the mid-1970s in the United States, the United Kingdom, and elsewhere in developed world cities, the confluence of i) an emerging anti-suburban sentiment, ii) the blossoming of white-collar financial and service industries in the ruins of post-industrial cities, and iii) a swath of university-educated men and women – middle-class baby-boomers – who were seeking jobs, money, culture and adventure – led to the emergence of a 'new lifestyle' in the inner city. This new lifestyle was seen to be much more exciting, dynamic and adventurous than the life that the baby-boomers' parents were seen to experience in the suburbs. The American media dubbed these young people 'pioneers' as they began to settle in the decayed inner city. They were seen as 'urban homesteaders' and 'urban settlers', terms which as Smith (1986) rightly points out legitimised their processes of conquest, as they took over poor and working-class areas of the central city, displacing the indigenous populations and remaking (gentrifying) the central city as a middle-class space (see Figure 3.1).

David Ley (1994, 1996) was one of the first to offer a more detailed and sophisticated theoretical and empirical analysis of who this 'new' middle class, these pioneer gentrifiers, were. His book, *The New Middle Class and the Remaking of the Central City*, examines the creation and self-creation of a 'new' middle class

Figure 3.1   The 'new' middle class in the central city: a gentrifier in the Lower East Side, New York City (photo: Loretta Lees)

of professional and managerial workers associated with the process of gentrification. He looks at their impact on central housing markets, on retail and leisure spaces in the inner city, as well as their effects on urban planning and urban policies. Investigating the social history and cultural politics of pioneer gentrifiers, Ley identifies a 'new cultural class' that emerges during the transformation to a postmodern, post-industrial society; a class inspired by counter-cultural youth movements; a class that sees the inner city as an oppositional space to the con- formism of the suburbs. Ley links their counter-cultural attraction to the inner city as part of the simultaneous rise of a generational protest (post-war baby- boomers) against the perceived tyrannies of 'corporate society'. He reveals how in a critique of both modernity and mass culture, pioneer gentrifiers sought the oppositional space of the central city, thus distancing themselves from the con- formity, standardisation and under-stimulation of the suburbs. He quotes a pioneer gentrifier who was an artist:

> Artists need authentic locations. *You know artists hate the suburbs.* They're too confining. Every artist is an anthropologist unveiling culture. It helps to get some distance on that culture in an environment which does not share all of its presuppositions, an old area, socially diverse, including poverty groups. (Ley, 1996: 195, emphasis added)

Ley argues that this new middle class were behind the rehabilitation of central cities across the world. They are, he is clear, a privileged class who desired to build a new convivial city – a city to live in and enjoy, a city which promoted social equity and quality of life. Yet for Ley (1996), the new middle class become liberated in the central city to consume, whether that is cappuccinos, art, litera- ture or cinema; their (anti-capitalist, left-liberal) cultural politics are thus cut from beneath them.

As the 'cultural turn' began to take hold in geography, there was, for a short while, a turn away from focusing on the economics and politics of class in the city towards looking at representations of class and especially how class was inter- cleaved with other forms of difference, such as ethnicity, gender and sexuality, in the city (see Fincher and Jacobs, 1998). The gentrification literature became increasingly interested in the lifestyle differences between fractions of the middle class living in the city. Sociologist Tim Butler has been at the forefront of attempts to conceptualise the differences between the gentrifying middle classes (see Butler with Robson, 2003). His research in central London has shown that 'geography matters', and that the new middle classes are fractured along identity lines, usually associated with lifestyle, value systems and income; and that they seek out places (neighbourhoods) that contain 'people like themselves'. He finds significant differ- ences between more left-liberal gentrifiers in the London neighbourhoods of Brixton and Stoke Newington, and the more corporate, conservative gentrifiers in Barnsbury and Battersea. Butler's research makes important points about the rela- tionship between social and spatial structures, and argues for an incorporation of 'sense of place' into studies of how 'class works'.

More recently, authors in/on the global south have also begun to explore the relationship between the 'new' middle class and gentrification. Wang and Lau (2009) identify a specific gentrifier fraction within the 'new' middle classes in Shanghai who possess cultural competence to decode and appreciate an urbane lifestyle. They find that these members of the 'new' middle class are attracted to an image of elite life and are willing to pay for the symbolic value of elite residential enclaves. Yet, interestingly, this thesis about the agency of the 'new' middle class in gentrification in Shanghai contrasts with He's (2007) account of large-scale state-sponsored gentrification under market transition, motivated by the Chinese government's pursuit of economic and urban growth at any cost (in this case the cost is large-scale residential displacement). In He's (2007) account the state is the instigator of gentrification as they consider low-rise traditional houses built pre-communism and declining workers' villages, factories and warehouses built in the socialist period to be inappropriate for a global city image (see Figure 3.2). And the 'new' middle classes are the willing consumers of the global and metropolitan styles of building that are seen by China's elite to represent modernity and change (see Figure 3.3). The result is that the aspirant world city Shanghai is undergoing a fundamental class remake in a much more rapid and drastic way than its western counterparts (Lees, 2012a). Low-income people have been pushed to the outskirts of Shanghai – nearly a million households have been relocated over the last 12 years – removed to new housing away from their employment and their social networks. Their lives and livelihoods have often been destroyed (He, 2010).

Figure 3.2 The pre-gentrified neighbourhood of Shenjiazhai in Shanghai (photo: Shenjing He)

Figure 3.3   Gentrified Liangwancheng in Shanghai (photo: Shenjing He)

Figure 3.4   The architecture of gentrification in Ostoshenka, Moscow (photo: Oleg Golubchikov)

Badyina and Golubchikov (2005: 124) have looked at gentrifiers in Moscow and argue that 'in many respects this cohort shares its identity with the new upper classes colonizing the "elite" districts in the major world cities'. In a similar vein to Shanghai, gentrifiers in Moscow are symbolic of change, in this case from the Soviet Union to the New Russia. The 'Europeanisation' of neighbourhoods is a way of creating social distinction from the rest of Russian society and, like in Shanghai, the new architecture of gentrification is used to represent this value change (see Figure 3.4). The following box summarises the general characteristics of the 'new' gentrified city world-wide.

Characteristics of the 'New' (Gentrified) City (Source: Lees, under review)

1   The erasure of the proletariat in central cities (class change).

2   In some cities the whitening of the central city (racial/ethnic change).

3   The creation of a culturally homogeneous inner-city population that, ironically, will damage creativity and the economy (the suburbanisation of the central city).

4   The creation of a global inner-city aesthetic that will make cities around the world all look and feel the same (placelessness – the 'ageographia').

THE 'NEW' CITY

As first-wave gentrification in western cities mutated into second-wave gentrification, as a pioneering counter-cultural gentrification mutated into a more corporate form of gentrification, a 'new' city emerged (see Butler and Lees, 2006; Hackworth and Smith, 2001; Lees et al., 2008). Michael Sorkin (1991) was at the forefront of characterising this 'new' city in the US. For Sorkin the 'new' American city was a deindustrialised and deterritorialised city; he points to three characteristics:

1   The loosening of ties to any specific place – the new city is placeless. These new cities are all the same, offering uniform historic gentrifications and festival markets. He labelled it an 'ageographia' – an ageographic city – referring to the creation of placelessness.

2   There is an obsession with security, control and surveillance.

3   The new city has a distinctive landscape both material and ideological. It is a city of simulations – a television city – in which new buildings must rely for their authority on images drawn from history.

For Sorkin the 'new' American city was unreal, a dystopic Disneyland trying to relive positive memories from the past, repackaging them as the future of cities. The 'new' city was a nostalgic city yearning for the features and values of the past through new urbanisms such as pseudo-historical market places, gentrified zones and corporate enclaves. This was a city that was being (re)created by an image-driven postmodern culture in which the real nature of social order was being effectively concealed by elaborate simulations. The displaced and disadvantaged had no access to this constructed vision of pleasure. Spaces that served the working class were decreasing whilst those that served the 'new' middle classes were increasing. It was a revanchist city using postmodern architecture and styles to overwrite and delete the cities 'others' with new middle-class commercial and leisure spaces. Taken from the French word *revanche* (meaning revenge) the revanchist city refers to the political shift from a liberal welfare state characterised by redistributive policy, affirmative action and anti-poverty legislation, to an era of neoliberal revanchism characterised by a discourse of revenge (see Smith, 1996).

Mike Davis' (1990) *City of Quartz* gives us a useful description of the 'new' city that emerged in Los Angeles and presents a similar picture. A Marxist, Davis looks inside of the 'new' city of Los Angeles, searching for the hidden truth of it, and finds a class-based dystopia. He discusses how downtown LA had become a carceral city, a fortress built out of fear, where the middle-class corporate workers worked and ate in hermetically sealed enclaves never to meet the 'other LA'. In his discussion of 'Fortress LA' he illustrates the revanchism in the 'new' city well – the middle class fears of the working and underclass – evidenced by the walled enclaves, security guards, the privatisation of public space and surveillance in downtown LA. Mike Davis' thesis tallies well with Neil Smith's (1996) revanchist city thesis, for the 'new' city is a revanchist city, in which the middle class seek revenge on those that they feel have stolen the central city from them – the poor, ethnic minorities, the homeless, and so on. This revenge can be seen in LA's official policy of containment towards the poor. Homeless people are restricted to small areas, enforced by security, surveillance and police violence; public parks have little seating, and furnitures like 'bum proof' benches are constructed, what Davis calls – 'the architecture of the evicted'. Davis' analysis makes it clear that capitalism's power lies primarily in land ownership, and that any real challenge to the existing social order must have land ownership as a central concern.

Neil Smith's (1996) *The New Urban Frontier: Gentrification and the Revanchist City* was explicit in challenging the idea that gentrification was the simple outcome of new middle-class tastes and a new demand for urban living. He locates gentrification, as a process, in the larger shifts in political economy and culture in the late twentieth century that led to the emergence of a 'new' city. In particular Smith begins to document the relationship between public policy and the private market and how they came together to conspire against the underclass, working and workless poor. As Smith (1996: 88) states:

> Gentrification is part of a larger redevelopment process dedicated to the revitalization of the profit rate. In the process, many downtowns are being converted into bourgeois playgrounds replete with quaint markets, restored townhouses, boutique rows, yachting marinas and Hyatt Regencies. These very visual alterations to the urban landscape are not at all an accidental side-effect of temporary economic disequilibrium but are rooted in the structure of capitalist society every bit as deeply as suburbanization.

By way of contrast with Smith (1996), Sharon Zukin's (2009) most recent book *Naked City* offers a thesis of the 'new' city of New York that is much less critical of pioneer gentrifiers like artists, while being very critical of second- and third-wave gentrification. This is important because it is this distinction between first-wave and subsequent waves of gentrification, temporality and context, that has been missed (or underplayed) in recent critiques (e.g. Slater, 2006, 2008, 2009). Zukin (2009) argues that as cities have gentrified, educated urbanites have come to prize what they regard to be 'authentic' urban life: old buildings, art galleries, boutique shops, upscale food markets, ethnic restaurants, and so on. For the new urbanite these signify a place's authenticity, in contrast to the bland standardisation of the suburbs and now also the exurbs. Zukin explains how the desire of the 'new' middle class to consume authentic experience has become a central force in making cities more expensive and more exclusive. She shows how the escalating demand for authenticity has driven out the very people who first gave the neighbourhood its authentic aura, e.g. immigrant groups, the urban working class and artists.

The creation of the 'new' city is well under way now in cities around the world – the outcome of a new global urbanism and new processes of state-led gentrification (see Lees and Ley, 2008; Lees et al., 2008; Smith, 2002). Zukin (2009) shows how over time neighbourhood distinctiveness became a tool used by economic elites to drive up real estate prices and effectively force out pioneer gentrifiers and indigenous groups in New York City; Badyina and Golubchikov (2005) show how a similar process has played out in Moscow. They show how the neoliberal state followed the lead of market forces (led in turn by the new global urbanism that Smith (2002) discusses) and assigned residential buildings in the neighbourhood of Ostozhenka, in central Moscow, for demolition, due to their 'state of disrepair', and thus the households in them for resettlement (that is, immediate displacement).

Figure 3.5 The 'new' city of Moscow (photo: Oleg Golubchikov)

Like Zukin (2009), Badyina and Golubchikov (2005) are sceptical of this 'new' city of Moscow (see Figure 3.5), concerned by 'the loss of historic value, and architectural integrity, privatization of public space, growing social polarization, and undermining of the social mix and equality achieved under Soviet socialism' (2005: 126). In Cape Town, South Africa, Visser and Kotze (2008) show how state policies and interventions focused on inner-city regeneration are underpinning new forms of gentrification. They too are critical about attempts by the city to launch the city into the global arena, promoting Cape Town's central city as a destination for global business, investment, retail, entertainment and leisure. They assert: 'Consequently, the CBD narrative is not about *who is there*, but rather *who is not*' (2008: 2589).

A discussion of consumption-led urbanisation would not be complete without some reference to China – where consumerism has become a recent and very powerful ideology (see the images in Figures 3.6 and 3.7). Shengjian (2004: 131) discusses the development of Shanghai's city-maps (from *The Shanghai Times*, *Shanghai Wednesday* and *Shanghai Weekly*), new guides to city life that stand at the forefront of fashion and consumerism, and try to invent new fashions. These guides take great pains to seek out fancy shops and entertainment, and perhaps most interestingly new places in the unromantic and unattractive parts of the city that might lead to a new fashion (a process called 'Sou Dian'). The guides can be seen to be acting like Anglo-American pioneer gentrifiers seeking out exciting and stimulating city places. But gentrification, as a process, has not simply projected out of Anglo-American cities to the rest of the world. The politics of gentrification and of the 'new' city needs to be understood across different global contexts, indeed gentrification in newly emerging world cities like Mumbai and Shanghai has a new even sharper-edged form (Lees, 2012a, 2012b). As Andrew Harris (2008: 2423) says:

> The 'social tectonics' invoked by Butler with Robson (2003) in their study of gentrifiers in London become, in the phrase of Mike Davis (2004: 23), the 'brutal tectonics of neo-liberal globalisation' in Mumbai. The 'spectre of displacement' that Freeman (2007) raises in relation to gentrification pressures in New York is reconfigured through the spectral narratives that dominate the nervous system of Mumbai's housing, where more people live in shacks or on pavements than the entire population of London. (Appadurai, 2000)

As I stated in the introduction to ths chapter, we need much more comparative work on new urbanisms in the 'new' city, work on class, lifestyle, and the 'new' city in the global north *and* the global south (Robinson, 2006).

THE CREATIVE CITY

Richard Florida's (2002) *The Rise of the Creative Class: And How It's Transforming Work, Leisure, Community and Everyday Life* has become an international bestseller

Figure 3.6   A shared kitchen in a lilong house in Shanghai (photo: Shenjing He)

Figure 3.7   A trendy restaurant in a gentrified lilong house in Shanghai (photo: Shenjing He)

and Florida is paid substantial sums of money to talk to policy-makers and governments around the world. Florida's creative city thesis argues that cities and regions
can no longer compete economically by attracting companies or by developing
mega projects like sports stadiums and downtown development districts, rather, to

capitalise on the new economy, policy-makers must attract the 'creative class', that is gays, youth, bohemians, professors, scientists, artists, entrepreneurs, and so on. The creative class are seen to be the key to economic growth in the contemporary city/region (see http://www.creativeclass.com). Florida's 'creative class' has a lot in common with David Ley's (1980, 1994, 1996) gentrifying 'new middle class' (Lees et al., 2008: xx). Indeed, Ley conceptualised this 'cultural new class' well before Florida published his creative class thesis! The interests and lifestyles of Florida's creative class and Ley's new middle class are the same: they value diversity in the city, historic architecture, quality of life; their values are about social and environmental sustainability. They are urbane, interested in the progressive aestheticisation of central cities. They are very different to the conservative middle classes whom cities traditionally tried to attract but who preferred to live in the suburbs, indeed they are anti-suburban, preferring bike and hiking trails to roads and highways. The creative class (or Bobos – bourgeois bohemians) manages to combine a bourgeois work ethic with bohemian culture. The creative class desires tolerance – Florida asserts that those cities most tolerant of, for example, the gay population will be more successful in attracting and keeping the creative class. Florida's 'creative city' is 'the emancipatory city' found in the gentrification literature (see Lees, 2000; Lees et al., 2008: 209–12). It is a liberal, tolerant, liberating city of possibility, the main difference being that Florida is explicit in making it a vehicle for new economic growth.

Florida's thesis, however, is an ambivalent one, as he himself recognises that his model of urban and economic renaissance both invites the creative class and stifles the diversity and creativity that it seeks, as gentrification progresses. In his 2005 book *Cities and the Creative Class*, he laments: 'With gentrification comes an out-migration of bohemians ...' (2005: 25). Nevertheless, Florida's (gentrification) thesis has become big business. This ambivalence is echoed in the politically ambivalent arguments that are contained in his 2002 book, which, as Peck (2005: 741) states, 'mixes cosmopolitan elitism and pop universalism, hedonism and responsibility, cultural radicalism and economic conservatism, casual and causal inference, and social libertarianism and business realism'. Florida's text expresses the confusion and unease that has occurred as pioneer gentrification's left-liberal cultural politics are destroyed by the very same process of gentrification. Florida, like Ley, realises that the creative class ultimately destroys the creative city and in its place creates the gentrified city, which has many of the revanchist and inauthentic features of the 'new' city. So although Florida's creative city thesis is quite critical of a number of the features of the 'new' city, especially those that are more corporate in nature, it leads to the gentrified, 'naked city' that Zukin (2009) discusses. For successfully attracting the creative class inflates house prices (limiting more creative types from moving in), erodes the social diversity that creative types desire, destroys authenticity, and in so doing erodes the creativity of the creative class itself.

Peck's aptly titled essay 'Struggling with the creative class' talks about the way that Florida's creative-city thesis works 'quietly with the grain of extant "neoliberal" development agendas, framed around interurban competition, gentrification, middle class consumption and place marketing ...' (2005: 740–1). He is interested in why this text has struck a chord with urban elites – why they have been persuaded that their cities must make efforts to establish the right kind of climate and environment to attract and keep the creative class. Peck argues that it is the seeming success of those creative cities, like San Francisco, that it have risen to prominence on the back of Florida's work that has spurred other cities near the bottom of Florida's 'creativity index' into action. Disinvested cities and areas of cities are seen to be bereft of 'creativity', and Florida's 'creative city' is increasingly seen to be the way forward for a healthy economic present and future in cities world-wide. Peck (2005: 749) discusses Portland, Oregon, which has been promoted as a case study of compelling creativity for other cities; its lessons include:

> identifying creative leaders; building new systems of communication within the local community; enabling artists and other creatives to build sweat equity in emerging creative neighbourhoods; promoting the adaptive reuse of buildings; supporting festivals and other street level events; and above all, being 'authentic'.

But in addition the creative-city thesis melds well with the discursive strategies of the neoliberal project, which deploys carefully selected language to fend off criticism and resistance, and is organised around a narrative of competitive progress (Bourdieu and Wacquant, 2001; Tickell and Peck, 2003) and morally persuasive attempts to elevate the social and economic capital of the lower classes (Lees, 2003a, 2008). The creative class are a compelling class, whose aspirations are hard to argue against.

Singapore's government recently purchased the services of Richard Florida to tell them how to create the creative bohemian environment (missing in this otherwise successful city-state led by 'authoritarian developmentalism') that he prescribes as a key attraction for the creative class. The result was that the Singaporean government has worked to develop certain creative industries and has even gone so far as to liberalise restrictions on a variety of activities ranging from public displays of homosexuality to bungee jumping to busking, drinking and gambling – all in the name of creativity (Ooi, 2008).

One of the main messages of Florida's creative class thesis is that we need a new analytical, conceptual and political mindset that accepts the fact of this new class and that they need space to actualise their identities. I began this chapter with Neil Smith's (1987) discussion of the inadequacies of a two-class Marxist model – Florida too argues that the old categories of class analysis are inadequate for these new times and for this new class. Florida (2002: 68), like Ley (2003), discusses the intangible creative capacity of the creative class, and in addition he argues that this creative capacity is a form of property for this class that marks them as different and moves them away from the capitalist class formations that traditionally revolved around ownership and control of property. Like Ley's (1996) pioneer gentrifiers, Peck (2005) comments:

> Creatives want edgy cities, not edge cities. They contemptuously reject suburbia, the 'generic' of chain stores and malls, and places that are orientated to children or churches. Indeed, any of the mundane and time-consuming

tasks of social reproduction are also spurned by creatives, amongst whom 'marriage is often deferred and divorce more common'; they prefer more spontaneous associations in localized 'mating markets' (Florida, 2002: 177) ... *Homo creativus* is an atomized subject , apparently, with a preference for intense but shallow and non-commital relationships, mostly played out in the sphere of consumption and on the street. (Peck, 2005: 745–6)

Importantly, Florida (2002) reminds us that the creative class rely on an army of service workers to service their needs; workers in low-end jobs that do not pay properly 'because they are not creative jobs' (2002: 322)! The creative city is an emancipatory city for the creative class, but not for the inner city's 'others', where by way of contrast it can be revanchist (see Smith, 1996). And this revanchism has and will play out differently in different cities and contexts around the world. In the UK revanchism has been directed at the mostly white population living in residualised inner-city council housing, a population that the BBC TV series *Little Britain* has represented as 'white trash' and 'chavs'. This population has been more than ridiculed and stigmatised by the media, and government policy is trying to dilute or socially engineer it out of existence by demolishing public housing and building mixed communities in its place (see Lees, 2008). Below market value, low-income, private housing lived in by the working and workless poor has also become the focus of mixed communities initiatives (see Allen, 2008). In the US, HUD's HOPE IV Program of poverty deconcentration, which demolishes monolithic concentrations of (mainly African-American) public housing, displacing large numbers of (black) residents from the central city and rebuilding neighbourhoods as mixed-income communities, has enacted an even more revanchist fourth-wave of gentrification (see Lees et al., 2008: 185–7).

CONCLUSION: TOWARDS A SUSTAINABLE 'NEW' CITY?

Brenner et al. (2010), amongst others, are adamant that despite its disruptive, destructive consequences, the global economic crisis that emerged in 2008 will not significantly undermine the neoliberalising tendencies of the last three decades. The neoliberal regime that was consolidated during the 1990s and early 2000s (leading to third- and fourth-wave gentrification – see Lees et al., 2008) may, they suggest, be recalibrated or reconstituted but it will not die ('zombie neoliberalism'). If anything, the recession will act to religitimate neoliberalism. Indeed, the political machinery of the neoliberal state remains intact and its policy agendas for cities are unlikely to change substantially: agendas like privatisation, increased regulation by the market, securitisation and gentrification. Erasing the 'cultural mindset' of gentrification is unlikely to happen because policy-makers around the world have come to believe that the 'new' middle or creative classes are the saviours of our inner cities (Lees, 2009). Previous crises have seen the deepening and strengthening of the current system of power. The stimulus packages designed to return the economy to 'normal' and the rehearsal of urban policy initiatives show Anglo-American governments to be attempting to strengthen neoliberalism and the neoliberal city. The Obama administration is making moves on urban policy, an urban czar has been appointed (former Bronx borough president Adolfo Carrion Jr.) and $20 billion in stimulus money is being directed to urban programmes. The impact of these urban programmes is yet to be seen.

Different authors have different takes on the 'opportunities' that the current recession will lend our cities. For David Harvey (2009b) the current crisis offers an opportunity, as do all crises, for the reconfiguration of society within a different ideological framework. However, a more equitable society is not necessarily the outcome of this process. Richard Florida (2009) argues that we need to use the economic crisis as an opportunity, a strategic moment, to throw overboard the demand for the key products and lifestyles of the old order, and begin building a new economy, based on a new geography (the geography of the creative class), new lifestyles (those of the creative class) and new products. Florida argues that some cities should be allowed to decline naturally and that a new geography of US cities will emerge, a new spatial fix. This new geography will be related to the new economy and the spatial movements of the new middle class.

Whatever we believe, or hope for, the world-wide recession is bound to alter the 'new' city to some degree and the ways in which we, as urban geographers, conceptualise contemporary cities. Political economy and the rent gap (see Lees et al., 2008: Chapter 2) are re-emerging as important explanatory vehicles. In a recent editorial I discuss the reversal of Neil Smith's rent gap – with actual rent being high and potential rent being low in the current recession (see Lees, 2009). What might the implications of this be for processes of gentrification? Only time will tell.

Peck (2005: 760) has called the creative-city thesis 'cappuccino urban politics, with plenty of froth', and he is right to dismiss it in this way. Yet the world-wide recession has blown off (discredited) some of the froth. With the froth suspended in mid-air, perhaps now it is time to ask if there is anything we can salvage from the creative-city thesis that might lead us in the direction of a just city (see Marcuse et al., 2009). Some authors would assert that there are no positive features in the creative-city thesis, but I would argue that there are some possibilities (alongside the contradictions) (see Lees, 2004 on the paradoxes and possibilities of the emancipatory city). In my mind the possibilities emerge out of the three 'S's: environmental sustainability, economic sustainability and social sustainability. Ley's cultural new class, like Florida's creative class value the three 'S's: they prefer walking to driving, they prefer the small independent shop over big chains and shopping malls, they prefer socio-cultural diversity to social homogeneity. In a recession the consumer is more thrifty; more conscious of class differences, and of the instability of economic life. Now is the time to blow away the cappuccino froth for good, and to push a move towards a more sustainable future for cities world-wide. And that sustainable future must not be a 'new' middle-class vision of the future of cities, but one that seeks to reshape that 'new' middle-class vision, re-creating it into something more inclusive of all classes and groups, something truly socially sustainable. A reassessment of the key terms – quality of life, livability and lifestyle – is essential. Currently these terms enact a 'new' middle-class rhetoric that needs to be 'socially mixed' to include the lifestyles and voices of other social classes and groups, especially those that have been most marginalised, stigmatised, displaced and dispossessed in the 'new' city. Rather than making policy assumptions about the 'new' middle class as 'good/ economic/property-owning' and the working/workless poor as 'bad/uneconomic/ non-property-owning', policy-makers need to figure out the pros and cons of the lifestyles of all these social groups and to think how 'together' they can take our cities into a more socially sustainable future.

Gentrifying slums in Santiago, Chile, in the name of modernisation (see Lopez-Morales, 2010) is not socially sustainable, neither is the redevelopment of cities for the sake of keeping up with a globalised economy that causes the marginalisation of the poor (as is happening in Karachi, Pakistan). As Clark (2005: 252) states: 'In places characterized by a high degree of social polarization, short on legally prac-tised recognition of the rights of users of place and long on legally practised recogni-tion of the rights of owners of space, the conflict inherent in gentrification becomes inflammatory'. In cities desperate to enter the world stage quickly and with little welfare provision, or interest in welfare provision, the creation of a 'new' (gentrified) city has particularly visceral results (Lees et al. (in press) (see box below)).

A Comparative Urbanism of the 'New' City

Western cities	Emerging world cities
(remnant) welfare state	No/limited welfare state
Democratic urbanism/planning	Authoritarian urbanism/planning
(positive?) gentrification	(visceral) gentrification
In/direct displacement low income groups	Large scale evictions/direct displacement low income groups

---

Now is the time to exploit the contradictions that have arisen in the construction of the 'new' city moving us towards the just city. Marcuse (2009) argues that if the needs of the *in*cluded can be linked to the needs of the *ex*cluded, 'a powerful force for change can be brought into existence' (p. 252). Marcuse makes the important point that:

> Intellectuals and idealists, arriving at critical positions by virtue of pursuit of their own thought processes or examination of the moral values of their society, are technically included, but support opposition to that in which they are included. (2009: 253)

Perhaps, then, the creative class or the cultural new class, which as we have seen includes intellectuals and idealists, can be even more creative and help move society towards a more equitable, just and sustainable urban future. This is something that the Urban Resource Centre in Karachi is trying to do. Aware that it cannot fight international capital and the forces that are determining the shape and form of Asian cities, it has developed a four-point city planning agenda through which it hopes to promote more just urban development (see Hasan, 2007). Activist researchers in the global north and the global south need now to get together urgently to discuss how we might promote and indeed enact a social justice agenda in 'new' cities around the world (see http://www.inura.org/ – the international network for urban research and action).

Useful web sources

- www.creativeclass.org (the creative class)
- www.urckarachi.org (the Urban Resource Centre)
- www.inura.org (on resistance)
- www.members.multimania.co.uk/gentrification (on gentrification)
- www.economist.com/node/13063298?story_id=13063298 (on the new middle class in emerging markets)
- www.globalresearch.ca/index.php?context=va&aid=19280 (Latin America's new middle class)
- www.newurbanism.org/ (New Urbanism)
- www.lboro.ac.uk/gawc/ (globalisation and cities)

4

Being Poor in the City

Geoff DeVerteuil

INTRODUCTION

There has been a long-standing academic fascination with urban deprivation, spanning nineteenth-century social reformer investigations into the impoverished inner city (Ames, 1897; Booth, 1902), to the Chicago School of Urban Sociology obsession with the 'zone of transition' (Park and Burgess, 1925), to more recent forays into subaltern studies (Gregory, 1994; Spivak, 1988) and revanchism and the post-justice city (Mitchell, 2001; Smith, 1996). A 2009 conference in Toronto entitled 'Lumpen-city' asserted that 'research on marginalized urban residents has been an academic cottage industry throughout the history of the social sciences'.

The focus of this chapter is on how the lower class experiences poverty, not only socially and economically but especially spatially. Geographical interest in poverty has been uneven, waxing in the 1970s with the emergence of a distinct Marxist and radical geographical project, and waning by 1995 when Andrew Leyshon bemoaned the omission of 'poverty' from the *Dictionary of Human Geography* (Johnston et al., 1994). Geographical work has been dominated by those who adhere to a more statistical approach, and those radical geographers who tend to use the poor more as ciphers to illustrate and critique the deleterious impacts of broader political and economic restructuring in a neoliberal age. As a way to respond to these omissions, I focus on how poverty is actually experienced in the city, which moves beyond external categorisations of poverty that deny poor people's own understandings of their experiences, and towards an approach that actually grasps the spatially embedded experiences of poverty. More specifically, I examine how space both constrains *and* enables the everyday experience of poverty.

I organise the chapter into the following sub-sections. Firstly, I provide further material on conceptualising poverty as marginalisation. Secondly, I trace the (uneven) evolution of geographical thought on poverty. The discussion is necessarily wide-ranging, spanning social geography, welfare geography, political geography and urban geography, as well as beyond the discipline itself, given the sometimes sporadic attention paid to poverty in geographic circles. Thirdly, and comprising the bulk of the chapter, I concentrate on the experiences of poverty through a series of case studies.

These case studies highlight the constraining and enabling role of urban space in experiencing poverty, and also raise interesting points about how poor people are labelled and stigmatised, as well as state-led responses to poverty – areas of concern that are treated in detail in the final two sections.

CONCEPTUALISING POVERTY

Before considering the relationship between poverty and urban space, it is worthwhile beginning with some background material on how poverty is defined, measured and conceptualised, both in isolation and in relation to other axes of marginality. Poverty is usually defined in *absolute*, *relative* and *subjective* terms. The first involves a fixed benchmark, recognising the fact that there are people who make insufficient money to afford minimum necessities for survival. While useful in the global south where many go hungry, have insufficient shelter and live without sewage and running water, the absolute measure is less effective in the global north (Philo et al., 1995). A disadvantage of using an absolute measure is that most in the global north now have access to the basic necessities of life; another (conflicting) disadvantage is that it is extremely difficult to choose an objectively defined minimum set of necessities, and that this minimum standard will necessarily change over time. For instance, indoor plumbing and electricity would now be regarded as necessities in the global north, but this is not necessarily true in other countries, nor was it true in the global north 100 years ago. A relative conception of poverty defines individuals as poor if they have significantly less income than others around them. Typically, relative measures of poverty define poor individuals as having less than some percentage of median equivalent income (usually 40 or 50 per cent). A major advantage of this approach is its simplicity and transparency; it requires no a priori decisions about what constitutes a minimum necessary basket. For instance, in Canada, those 'worse off' are defined by low-income cut-offs determined by the federal government, which involves income levels at which families or unattached individuals spend 20 per cent more than average on food, shelter and clothing (i.e. 70 per cent of their income on food, shelter and clothing), based on the consumer index, and for different family size and size of the city (Statistics Canada, 2007).

Finally, there is a subjective approach to defining poverty, more popular in Europe than in North America. This approach argues that individuals are poor when they feel they do not have enough to get along. Proponents argue that the best way to assess how much income people need to make ends meet is to ask them. Thus, subjective poverty lines are constructed from surveys that ask questions such as: 'Living where you do now and meeting the expenses you consider necessary, what would be the very smallest income you and your family would need to make ends meet?' Of course, answers to this question increase with the respondent's income, and estimates of subjective poverty lines take this phenomenon into account (van Praag and Ferrer-Carbonell, 2006). Nonetheless, a clear consensus among scholars in the field of poverty research is that the relative approach is the most straightforward to use in the context of measuring poverty in the global north. Nonetheless, Gilbert (1998: 617) notes that while there is little doubt about the (absolute) material deprivations associated with poverty, (relative) poverty measurement are themselves a social construction 'based on the norms of a particular society; therefore poverty definitions ... [are] open to political contestation', particularly the variable indexes across different nations.

Poverty is most obviously connected to class position, and this has drawn the attention of many great thinkers, writers and reformers – including Friedrich Engels, Karl Marx, Mohandas Gandhi, Martin Luther King Jr., George Orwell – who have dedicated considerable energy in defining poverty (and attendant class exploitation), its pernicious consequences, and approaches to eradicating it. Nonetheless, poverty also interacts with a variety of other key social denominators that relate to power, opportunity and life chances, such as (but not limited to) race, gender, sexual orientation, (dis)ability, religion and age. Interest in these key social denominators has expanded with the so-called 'cultural turn' in human geography, moving beyond radical geography's focus on class-based exploitation to incorporate the concept of 'oppression' based on race, gender, sexual orientation and so forth (Leyshon, 1995; Young, 1990). For instance, in racially divided countries like the United States, Brazil and South Africa, the relationship between racialised others and poverty is strong. Even in the most generous welfare states of the global north, single mothers with children encounter everyday difficulties around survival, child care and housing (Davies, 2001). While some have worried that the importance of class-based exploitation (and poverty more specifically) is being diluted by an equivalent focus on identity, the ability to incorporate multiple oppressions is essential in a world that no longer (if it ever did) revolves solely around class relations (Castree, 2006; Katz, 2006; Ruddick, 1996b).

GEOGRAPHY, POVERTY AND URBAN MARGINALITY

Up to this point in my discussion, the contribution of geography to poverty as marginality has been itself marginal; this is also to say that other social sciences, especially anthropology and sociology, have made important contributions to first-hand accounts of poverty, particularly through ethnographic and grounded methodologies that geographers have begun to adapt (DeVerteuil, 2009). Here I begin the discussion with Janet Kodras' (1997) insights into the interactions of geography, poverty and marginality. To her, poverty was necessarily place-bound and geographical, resulting from a specific interplay between the market that distributes economic resources, and the state, whose role is less central, serving to counter or reinforce economic disadvantage. She viewed this process as necessarily scale-dependent, with broader global and national market and state processes that create poverty sieved through particular local contexts, creating place-specific variations in patterns of poverty. She provided five case studies to show the very different place-specific outcomes of poverty, ranging from deindustrialised Detroit to the working immigrant poor of Silicon Valley to the under-developed and isolated Eastern Kentucky (see also Milbourne, 2004 on the place–poverty relationship).

Geographical interest in poverty has waxed and waned over the past four decades (DeVerteuil, 2009; Milbourne, 2004). It was only in the 1970s, with the critique of spatial science and the advent of radical geography and welfare geography, that poverty became a central concern to (some) geographers. Geographers began focusing on social issues such as poverty (but also crime, racial discrimination, inequality) to better society, using geographically sensitive research. The Marxist approach to space and poverty was eloquently set out in David Harvey's *Social Justice and the City* (1973). Harvey explained how the capitalist city regressively redistributes from the poor to the wealthy, resulting in the unfairly structured 'location of jobs and housing, the value of property rights, and the price of resources to the consumer' (p. 86). In order to alleviate the worst excesses of the capitalist city, Harvey advanced the concept of 'a just distribution justly arrived at', with the aim of achieving 'territorial distributive justice'. In the more radical section of the book, however, Harvey departed from the more normative concepts to focus on accumulation, class struggle and the inherently unequal outcomes of capitalism that could not necessarily be alleviated by the capitalist state. Heavily influenced by the book, Marxist geographers would seek to unveil the causes and consequences of poverty (Peet, 1975; see also Badcock, 1984; Coates et al., 1977). Subsequently, welfare geography would adopt Harvey's more normative concepts but retained the quantitative bent of spatial science, as well as borrowing liberally from welfare economics, shedding light on 'who gets what, where and how' (e.g. DeVerteuil, 2000; D.M. Smith, 1987; P.J. Smith, 1994).

During the 1980s and early 1990s, there was a pronounced shift away from the entire idea of modelling and mapping poverty (and issues of distribution, access and the rectifying state found in more radical geography). These concerns were being superseded by more identity-based, post-structuralist frameworks whereby race and gender (and other key social demarcators) were now central in understanding oppression, rather than solely exploitation. Upon seeing no entry for 'poverty' in the *Dictionary of Human Geography* (Johnston et al., 1994), Leyshon (1995: 1023) worried that 'a broad, socially orientated political orientation is being replaced by a more inward-looking "identity politics", which is practiced in the main by and for middle-class academics, a development which augers badly for emancipatory political projects'. By the late 1990s, however, there was renewed interest in the geographies of poverty, spurred by conceptual innovations and empirical pressures. Conceptually, work by Sibley (1995) provided a psychoanalytical framework for understanding exclusion, while Wolch and Dear (1993) were advancing multi-scalar understandings of homeless production and survival. A body of quantitative work, armed with more extensive databases and innovative spatial-analytic tools, proved insightful into the broader patterns of poverty, inequality and place-marginalisation (e.g. Chakravorty, 2006; Dorling et al, 2007; Gregory et al., 2001).

Empirically, renewed interested came from a surge in poverty in the 1990s, the result of intensified globalised competition that produced a more flexible, lean and down-sized post-industrial production, bifurcation of labour markets and falling wages, welfare-state contraction and the collapse of socialist economies. Sassen's polarisation thesis (1991) conceptualised the social order of global cities, where she hypothesised that the influx of low-skilled immigrants to service the global elite had, with the demise of Fordist production and wages, widened the gap between the rich and the (working) poor. In her words (2001: 339):

> new conditions of growth have contributed to elements of a new class alignment in global cities. The occupational structure of major growth industries, characterised by the locational concentration of major growth sectors in global cities, in combination with the polarised occupational structure of these sectors, has created and contributed to growth of a high-income stratum and a low-income stratum of workers. It has done so directly through the organisation of work and occupational structure of major growth sectors and indirectly through the jobs needed to service the new high-income workers, both at work and at home as well as the needs of the expanded low-wage workforce.

Another reason for renewed interest was the increasing sense that space mattered fundamentally to the intensification and perpetuation of poverty, rather than (or in addition to) the 'culture of poverty' explanations put forth by Oscar Lewis (1966). Lewis argued that poor people are partly to blame for their predicament because their own maladaptive behaviour to poverty reproduces and sustains itself across future generations. Perhaps the most prominent of these spatial constructs was Julius Wilson's concept of concentrated poverty and the jobless ghetto (1987, 1996). Concentrated poverty (usually measured as 40 per cent poverty rates per census tract, representing a 'critical mass') is different from incidence of poverty, in that the former has important *spatial* implications, a place effect if you will:

> the concentration of poor families and children in high-poverty ghettos, barrios, and slums magnifies the problems faced by the poor. Concentrations of poor people lead to a concentration of the social ills that cause and are caused by poverty. Poor children in these neighborhoods not only lack basic necessities in their own homes, but also they must contend with a hostile environment that holds many temptations and few positive role models. Equally important, school districts and attendance zones are generally organized geographically, so that the residential concentration of the poor frequently results in low-performing schools. The concentration of poverty in central cities also may exacerbate the flight of middle-income and higher-income families to the suburbs, driving a wedge between social needs and the fiscal base required to address them. (Jargowsky, 2003: 2)

Wilson's concepts, however, were criticised in that they lump together unlike populations; that poor people may derive some benefits from living in high-poverty neighbourhoods (services, support networks, ability to organise); that they obscure the racial dimensions of slum formation; and that they further stigmatise inner-city populations and their behaviour. Nonetheless, Wilson was among the first social scientists to claim that the spatial concentration of poverty magnified the plight of the poor, effectively isolating them from mainstream opportunities and culture. As Crump (2002: 583) argued, '[Wilson's] analysis takes an important spatial turn when he advances the hypothesis that the geographic concentration of low-income people in urban ghettos leads to a magnification of the problems associated with poverty'. Figure 4.1 shows the isolation and abandonment typical of Chicago's South Side ghetto.

Figure 4.1   Chicago South Side, 2008 (photo: Geoff DeVerteuil)

Wacquant (1999) builds on these insights by identifying the symptoms of a new regime of urban marginality in the late twentieth century in North American (and to a lesser extent European) cities, the outcome of four structural logics: deepened inequality, the disappearance of full-time employment, the retrenchment of the welfare state, and the spatial clustering and stigmatisation of poverty. One outcome has been the mass incarceration of young men, to the point where some speak of a 'carceral continuum' designed to entrap redundant populations (see also Peck and Theodore, 2008).

A final reason for the surge in interest in the geographies of poverty stems from the urbanisation of poverty in the global south (Davis, 2006; Nijman, 2008; Pacione, 2005). Indeed, the living conditions and spatial patterning of the poor in the mega-cities of the global south is among the most critical issues of the twenty-first century (UN-HABITAT, 2003). Almost all of humanity's population growth over the next 40 years will be in these mega-cities – places like Cairo, Jakarta, Lagos, Mexico City, Mumbai, São Paulo – and almost all of this growth will be in peripheral, slum-like developments (Davis, 2006). These developments contain low-quality, poorly serviced, temporary dwellings, and represent the inability of cities in the less developed world to provide enough housing for all of the people. Mumbai alone has between 10 million and 12 million slum-dwellers; Figure 4.2 shows the edge of the notorious Dharavi neighbourhood, one of the largest slums in Asia and under pressure to be redeveloped, given its highly accessible location (Mehta, 2008; Nijman, 2008; Pacione, 2005).

Despite the utility of the statistical as well as radical treatments of poverty within human geography, little insight is garnered on the actual experiences of being poor in the city. While the statistical perspective is useful to gain a 'big picture' of poverty patterns, and the radical perspective useful in explaining poverty with regards to macrostructural forces, both give the appearance of imposing their own agendas upon the poor without really understanding their everyday lived experiences (see also DeVerteuil et al., 2009). Both perspectives paint a picture of a vulnerable, passive and powerless group largely constrained (rather than enabled) by space, but is this necessarily the case? By focusing on experience, I can humanise the poor without romanticising them or denying their agency. So while sympathetic to both the state and radical approaches, neither privileges the actual experiences of poverty – a subject that has been largely studied through more grounded, ethnographic techniques. These techniques have a long-standing legacy within urban anthropology and urban sociology, and have spawned a vast array of 'ethnographic poverty studies', in the words of Fairbanks (2009: 19). These studies range widely in terms of their populations, from the homeless (Duneier, 1999) to drug dealers (Bourgois, 2003), familes with children (Kozol, 1988), the working poor (Anderson, 1992) and recovering addicts (Fairbanks, 2009). In what follows, I elaborate three case studies that speak to experiencing and surviving poverty across a variety of contexts in the global north and global south.

Figure 4.2   Mumbai Dharavi, 2008 (photo: Geoff DeVerteuil)

EXPERIENCING POVERTY IN THE CITY

This section emphasises that city space is both constraining to poor people's experiences and survival (as we have already seen from the radical and statistical approach respectively) but also life-sustaining (Gilbert, 1998; Ruwanpura, 2006). In her study of survival techniques of impoverished single-parent women in Worcester Massachusetts, Gilbert (1998) found that space is both constraining and enabling. Space is constraining in terms of limiting, through class (and sometimes racial) segregation, the personal networks of the women. This insularity necessarily limits the ability to find suitable employment, child care and housing. Conversely, this very place-rootedness can act as a potential resource to connect to employment, housing and child care, and develop personal networks. As Gilbert argued (1998: 608): 'while the spatial boundedness of women's lives help to determine where and with whom women develop networks, it also affects women's survival strategies indirectly because their use of place-based networks can be enabling as well as constraining'. Following on from Gilbert, I use studies that primarily employed qualitative methods rather than statistical or macro-structural, as they miss the fine-grained, intimate and everyday experiences that occasionally transcend the constraints of space.

Homeless survival in global north

IS MOBILITY A PART OF SAFETY

The first case study focuses on the survival techniques and experiences of poverty for homeless individuals in large cities of the global north. Like people the world over, those experiencing homelessness routinely seek the social and material resources requisite for their subsistence. Since they are resource-poor by definition, the characteristics of the immediate locale greatly affects their ability to adapt to life on the street or in shelters, especially since different locales or places have different 'carrying capacities' and thus structure subsistence patterns differently. For over 20 years, geographers have sought to understand how homeless survival is itself place-dependent and place-bound (e.g. DeVerteuil, 2003, 2006; Rollinson, 1990; Rowe and Wolch, 1990; Ruddick, 1996a; Takahashi, 1996; Wolch and Dear, 1993).

Of key interest here is the relationship between space and homeless survival techniques, particularly through the lens of mobility. As May (2000: 737) states, 'it is clear that the experience of homelessness cannot be considered apart from the experience of movement of varying kinds and at a variety of scales'. A persistent theme within the geographical literature has been whether mobility is positive/enabling or negative/constraining to the experiences and survival techniques of homeless people. To some researchers, mobility can be understood as advantageous for subsistence patterns.

For instance, Rahimian (1990) suggests that mobility should be seen as an adaptive coping mechanism, while Dear et al. (1994: 207) contend that 'geographic mobility is essential to material well-being'. DeVerteuil (2003) found that voluntary mobility across institutional settings, especially emergency shelters, enabled certain homeless women to avoid literal homelessness in Los Angeles. Along similar lines, Wiseman (1970: 18) explains how the Skid Row alcoholic, despite his supposed weakness and impoverishment, will redefine multiple settings to survive:

> He is in an environment that any outsider would label as bleak and comfortless, offering nothing but destitution, shame and despair. Yet his strategies for survival indicate a remarkably indomitable and creative spirit ... The essence of creativity is redefinition, that is, the ability to mentally free an object from one meaning or mental framework and then convert it into raw material to serve another purpose in another context. Such strategies are essentially what the Skid Row resident uses in order to survive both physically and psychologically. He begins to locate things that can become resources to supply food and shelter if they are used in a way other than generally intended. Even the institutions and organizations created specifically to provide necessities as a charity can be redefined and 'worked' so as to offer more than bare comfort.

For example, Skid Row alcoholics depend on the County Jail, missions, out-patient clinics and social welfare organisations for everyday subsistence, rather than as means to salvage their lives in the long term. As such, mobility can represent 'the ability of the homeless to exercise some measure of autonomy within a highly constrained residential environment' (DeVerteuil, 2003: 363).

On the other hand, excessive mobility – especially the involuntary kind – can produce negative experiences and survival techniques, essentially isolating and alienating the person from a normal, stable existence (Kozol, 1988; Snow and Anderson, 1993). Moreover, there is the risk of becoming institutionally dependent (Rowe and Wolch, 1990). This is particularly a problem among the mentally disabled, who frequently and involuntarily cycle across an array of unrelated, inappropriate and inadvertent institutional settings, such as jail, prison, shelters and the street (DeVerteuil, 2003). Starkly, in 1998 the Los Angeles County Jail was the largest 'mental hospital' in the United States (Butterfield, 1998).

A retrospective housing history of Ann, who in 1999 was staying at an emergency shelter in Los Angeles, may be instructive to illustrate the positive and negative aspects of mobility (DeVerteuil, 2001). A 31-year-old Caucasian woman, Ann was originally from Melbourne, Florida, and in 1997 she was living in her own apartment. Despite her university education, her job history was characterised by tedious, dead-end employment in tele-marketing and telephone assistance. She worked for a Directory Assistant company until she lost the job in February 1999. However, she did not tell her parents for four months, at which point her money had run out. Her parents supported her for several months while she looked for a job. However, on 3 May 1997, her parents threatened to financially cut her off unless she enrolled in an eating disorder counseling programme. Through his connections, her father knew of a treatment program in Abilene Texas. Ann arrived there a day later, losing her apartment in the process. The programme embodied a highly structured routine of counseling, dieting and isolation.

Ann found her time at the treatment center unbearable. She was uncomfortable with the discipline and the counselor's techniques. After ten days, Ann left this suffocating environment with no specific destination. Her departure initiated a series of disconnected and haphazard residential movements that would eventually lead her to Los Angeles. As a first step, she decided to spend her meagre funds to take a cab to the Salvation Army (Abilene) – an emergency shelter that she found more amenable and certainly less structured. After a week, however, the Salvation Army began charging $7 a night, so Ann sought new residential options. The in-house social worker recommended the nearby 'Hope Haven', which combined emergency shelter with transitional housing. Although more accommodating, Ann was not interested in staying in Texas; her new tele-marketing job was a dead-end, and she still wanted to see California.

Ann's arrival in Los Angeles only prolonged and deepened her residential instability and institutional dependency. Out of money, her father arranged to pay for a series of suburban motels over a one-week period. These solutions were short term, however, and Ann was looking for a more long-term residence to bide her time. While frequenting the Pacoima referral center, the Palms Mission emergency shelter had an opening. Ann arrived at the shelter in July 1999. She applied for the unattached individual welfare program, which paid $221 a month (known as General Relief) soon thereafter, although it took several months before the first cheque arrived. Her initial experience with the welfare bureaucracy was discouraging: 'I had to wait all day just to fill out an application. It's like we're just ... fill this form, then fill this one, you know "hurry up and wait". It's high security, they check your purse or bag, and there's a metal detector for when you go in.' Between the shelter, GR/Food Stamps, and an erratic flow of loans from her parents, Ann was finally able to stabilise her residential patterns. Nonetheless, at the time of the interview (October 1999), she was running out of time at Palms Mission, and had not yet secured a job (although she had attended several GROW meetings). After having spent almost three months there, she had this to say about the Palms Mission: 'It's not structure that I'm after but they don't manage their residents, they don't interfere when people start complaining, they say "fight among yourselves and if you complain a little too much, we'll kick you out".'

It is clear from the retrospective narrative that her initial (and particularly negative) institutional stay set off an extended bout of residential instability. While avoiding literal homelessness, Ann was forced to string together an inadvertent array of residential settings, including three shelters and three motels across two states. This cycling was a product of limited income and low welfare payments.

Hollywood, Survival and Marginal Space

Susan Ruddick's (1996a) study of punk youth in 1970s' and 1980s' Hollywood makes a very direct link between space, marginality, identity and survival. Their ability to squat in abandoned buildings and cemeteries in the 1970s enabled them to define and sustain a distinct sub-culture that resisted larger pressures to conform: 'The sustenance

(Continued)

(Continued)

of a distinct identity by punks, and their self-identification as *punks*, rather than as runaways or homeless youths, was intimately bound up in the perpetuation of their squatting subculture, itself dependent on access to and control over particular material and symbolic spaces within the Hollywood area' (1996a: 99). The symbolic importance of space was itself intertwined with the ability of punks to live independently of social services, family and police harassment. Once those free, controllable spaces were lost – for instance, the Hollywood Cemetery was closed off in 1980, followed by the demolition of many squatted apartment buildings – the teen population was increasingly caught between street-based survival (e.g. drugs, prostitution) and the spaces of social services. As Ruddick (1996a: 122) suggested, by the 1980s, 'more youth [were] passing into casual prostitution and drug dealing because of a lack of alternative countercultural networks and supports'.

Figure 4.3   Recycler and Hollywood sign, 2005 (photo: Geoff DeVerteuil)

Working poor communities in global cities

The second case study highlights the experience of poverty for working poor communities in the global north. Wilson and Keil (2008) consider the (working) poor to be the real 'creative class' of the city (as opposed to Florida's gentrifying class), contributing immensely to the current urban economy and deploying remarkable ingenuity in their everyday survival. Day labour sites – where men sell their casual labour to employers at designated (and sometimes non-designated) locations – are but one manifestation of this extreme flexibility among the working poor (Peck and Theodore,

2008; Wilson and Keil, 2008). Recent research on the working poor in London (Datta et al., 2007; May et al., 2007) has identified important labour-market shifts. As a global city, London has experienced significant income polarisation as a result of its increasing reliance on migrant labour, what Datta et al. (2007) calls the new 'migrant division of labour'. In-migrants from high-income countries have been crucial in helping meet a still growing demand for high-skilled workers, while in-migrants from the global south and Eastern Europe have emerged as a critical source of labour for London's expanding low-wage economy. Through July 2005, a team of 11 researchers completed a structured questionnaire with 341 workers in four sectors of the London economy known to employ high numbers of low-paid workers. The authors found that fully 90 per cent of those interviewed in contract cleaning, hospitality and catering, home care and the food-processing industries were born outside of the UK, with as many as half arriving in Britain in the last five years, demonstrating ethnic segregation at the bottom end of the labour market. The vast majority (90 per cent) of workers earned less than the London Living Wage, which was £6.70 in 2005; on average, they earned £5.40 an hour and would make around £10,200 a year before taxes, which is just a third of the London average annual salary of almost £30,000. This influx has had the effect of squeezing London's more established ethnic groups, including Afro-Caribbeans, Bangladeshis and Pakistanis, who continue to suffer disproportionately high levels of unemployment. Massey (2007: 55) sees this polarisation as working together, not despite each other, because greed and need are part of government policies in London and sustaining global city status under conditions of neoliberalisation.

While Datta et al. (2007) have examined the means by which low-paid migrant workers survive in a rapidly changing and increasingly unequal, post-Fordist labour market, using an array of short-term, day-to-day 'tactics' that enable them to 'get by', we know relatively little on why these same impoverished immigrant groups in global cities – Sassen's floating pool of cheap, unskilled labour (2001) – do not seemingly suffer from the sharpest edge of polarisation: the condition of being homeless. This paradox has been acknowledged only in passing by the homeless literature. For instance, in Los Angeles the typical poor person is a working-class Latino, but the homeless are disproportionately White and African-American; in London, the homeless are disproportionately White, despite the massive increase in immigrant poverty over the last ten years. A current explanation is that poverty and homelessness for impoverished immigrant groups in global cities are mediated by a tendency to accept overcrowded conditions (Baker, 1994; Molina, 2000) and the presence of strong social and family networks (Baker, 1994), as well as the crucial role of an ethnic/immigrant shadow state, in which third-sector, ethnically based institutions have emerged to deal with the glaring gaps in the global city and the receding welfare state.

Preliminary research into these issues using interviews of Central American (Los Angeles) and Bangladeshi (London) social service organisations reveals a broadly similar pattern of survival techniques (DeVerteuil, 2011). While very different culturally, both groups suffer from inner-city segregation, high rates of poverty and relatively slow rates of assimilation. It was also found that across the sample of social service agencies interviewed (nine Central American and six Bangladeshi), all confirmed that their respective communities featured strong social networks, the willingness to overcrowd and a well-developed ethnic shadow state (supported by higher government) that worked to keep their co-ethnics off the street. Spatially, the concentration of services within the original destination neighbourhood of the immigrant group – Pico-Union for Central Americans and Tower Hamlets for Bangladeshis – created a dense network of helping institutions that actually strengthened the safety net for those at risk of homelessness. This Do-It-Yourself (DIY) welfare system enabled vulnerable individuals to avoid the more mainstream social service system, an important consideration given persistent linguistic, cultural and religious barriers.

Survival strategies in the global south

The third case study relates the even more precarious situations facing the poor in the global south. As previously mentioned, levels of absolute poverty and inequality are much higher in the global south, particularly in the ever-growing mega-cities. Here I focus on the experiences of two marginal groups – recyclers and recovering alcoholics – whose survival patterns point to the tension between living in marginal space yet needing access to prime space for their everyday income. In her study of street children in Kampala (Uganda), Young (2003: 609) illustrates how space both enables and constrains survival patterns: 'particular places provide different opportunities for survival, as street children are often drawn to those parts of the city where income can be earned'. Constrained by dominant society and excluded from prime spaces, street children are forced into marginal space such as garbage dumps. However unpleasant, these spaces also provide important safe havens, niches for survival and basing points for engaging in street activities such as begging and stealing. Relying upon extensive fieldwork in Delhi, Kaveri Gill (2009) traces the everyday experiences of scavengers and recyclers, as well as how they fit into the chain of the informal economy. The waste pickers must navigate a complex array of caste, state and private-market constraints to earn a living, as well as geographical limits on their mobility and place of residence. Hayami et al. (2006) focus on the chronic nature of poverty of the waste pickers; of how they remain marginalised and spatially segregated from the mainstream population yet perform an inherently useful task in the urban economy. In Mexico City, Brandes (2002) used fine-grained ethnographic methods to outline the survival techniques of recovering alcoholics, and of how they rely on the marginal locations and spaces of Alcoholics Anonymous (AA) while also attempting to gain access to prime spaces in order to avoid old drinking buddies and haunts, and thereby maintain sobriety. Needless to say, the vast majority of the men were unemployed or under-employed:

> Scarcity not only produces personal hardship on a daily basis for recovering alcoholics, but also produces feelings of envy, inadequacy, and resentment whenever members find themselves unable to contribute on a regular basis to the common good. As a self-help group, dedicated to enhancing the health and well-being of its members, Moral Support (Mexican AA) experiences as precarious an existence as that of its individual members. Moral Support ... is indelibly affected by poverty. (Brandes, 2002: xvii)

The men saw the AA group as a way to (re)create a village atmosphere within the metropolis while also regaining social acceptability. Unfortunately, the location of AA was invariably in the cheapest, poorest parts of the city that were also ridden with bars, liquour stores and street drinkers, representing distinct threats to everyday sobriety. The ability to access the prime spaces of Mexico City were understandably difficult for such an impoverished group.

The Material Environment of Poverty in São Paulo

While unique in terms of sheer size, São Paulo also typifies many of challenging trends in the global south. As Brazil's most obviously global city, São Paulo's economic centrality has nonetheless not guaranteed a life of dignity and everyday subsistence for a majority of its citizens. The poor are far worse off, in relative and absolute terms, than those in the global north, given that they must endure higher levels of segregation, informality (especially with housing; 20 per cent of Paulistanos live in self-constructed dwellings) and violence (Budds and Teixeira, 2005; Caldeira, 2000; Fix, 2007; Fix et al., 2003). To the outsider looking in, the most prominent feature of São Paulo is the blatant contrast between rich and poor, to the point where one recognises a dual built environment – one formal and legal, the other self-produced and illegal. Everyday survival in the *favelas* is marked by a large informal economy, including recycling, most of which is done by single men. These collectors create living environments made out of the refuse of urban culture, thereby transforming its meaning and performing an important environmental service (dos Santos, 2009). Nevertheless, the collectors face enormous opposition to their activities in rich neighbourhoods, and surprisingly strong opposition to their semi-permanent residences in poor communities. The image below shows an organised protest in central São Paulo to another challenge facing collectors: a fair price for their material.

Figure 4.4 Collector collective protest, São Paulo, 2004 (photo: Geoff DeVerteuil)

The case studies from across the three sub-sections above raise interesting points about how poor people are labelled and stigmatised, as well as state-led responses to poverty – areas of concern that I focus on in the final two sub-sections of this chapter.

PROCESSES OF LABELLING AND STIGMATISATION

The experiences of the poor in the global north and south cannot be divorced from their marginalisation due to labelling and stigmatisation. Takahashi (1997: 903–4) defined stigma as the 'processes of social relations that lead to and reproduce definitions of "outsider" and "other"; such processes serve to define and label specific groups as being undesirable and dangerous'. She identified three dimensions of stigma that results in individuals and groups becoming devalued because of some marked difference or 'socially disqualifying attributes': (1) non-productivity relates to functionality (i.e. the more functional individuals being more acceptable than less functional individuals) and participation in the labour market, consumption and stable membership in social and spatial communities; (2) dangerousness relates to unpredictability, criminality, contagion – risky behaviour that lie outside of social norms; and (3) personal culpability relates to the degree to which the individual can be held responsible (and thus blamed) for their circumstances. She then focuses on the spatial expression of these social stigmatisations, whereby the landscape inherits stigma from the presence of stigmatised groups, and stigmatised places can transfer stigma onto people who live there, even if they are not themselves of low status. Wacquant (1999) essentially makes the same point about territorial stigma and relegation in an age of advanced marginality. He senses that 'the new marginality displays a distinct tendency to conglomerate in and coalesce around "hard core", "no-go" areas that are clearly identified – by their own residents, no less than by outsiders – as urban hellholes rife with deprivation, immorality and violence where only the outcasts of society would consider living' (1999: 1644).

The processes of labeling and stigmatisation are intimately linked to power. In this respect, Sibley (1995) identifies the routine practices whereby the 'included' exclude, reject and control the weak, the 'other', ambiguity, and so forth. Persons who are part of the non-stigmatised, 'included' group wish to homogenise, purify and protect their own status by erecting boundaries that exclude those that do not belong or who are defiling. This process occurs both in the global north and global south; it is not uncommon for homeless people in the global south to suffer from stigmatisation and exclusion, even though their conditions are only marginally worse than most of the impoverished population (Speak and Tipple, 2006). However, and building on the previous sub-section's emphasis on survival despite marginalisation, the power to exclude is never complete, allowing for some measure of agency and initiative. In the next sub-section, I emphasise the incomplete power to marginalise from a state-centered perspective.

RESPONSES TO POVERTY

Up until the 1970s, the role of the capitalist state in the global north was to ostensibly buffer those most vulnerable to the (inequitable) workings of the labour market (DeVerteuil, 2009). At the urban scale, this led some geographers to note the emergence of a distinctly 'public city' (Dear, 1980), in which the most vulnerable groups and places were supported – if grudgingly, and sometimes more for containment purposes – by the state. And at least until the mid-1990s, one could still detect in the United States the presence of 'welfare neighbourhoods', where welfare had intricately insinuated itself into the everyday practices of welfare recipients and local merchants (e.g. many local grocers rely on Food Stamps, up to 80 per cent, while also giving credit to customers on welfare), the local welfare office (e.g. recipients know and trust the case managers) and landlords (e.g. many tenants depend on welfare subsidies to pay rent) (DeVerteuil, 2005).

However, this idealised 'welfare/public city' concept has been undermined by various restructuring trends, including the reduced role of the public sector in service provision, the growing tendency for the state to magnify and contain, rather than alleviate inequality, combined with the increasingly unequal gap between the rich and the poor, and the worsening conditions of the most disadvantaged populations – the homeless, the severely mentally ill, welfare recipients (Fairbanks, 2009). To a certain extent across all developed nations – and especially in the United States – the welfare state has reduced its support through devolution, privatisation and dismantlement, deteriorating the living conditions of the welfare-dependent (Peck, 2001). Of course, this process has been very uneven, with certain jurisdictions enthusiastically embracing the post-welfare trend while others retaining some measure of support for the worst-off (DeVerteuil et al., 2009).

Within this context, the responses to visible poverty in cities are conditioned not only by the process of labelling and stigmatisation, but also by economic pressures to bolster city images in a post-welfare period of intense inter-urban competition: what Mitchell (1997) called the aligning of local conditions (urban landscapes congruent with liveability) with the demands of global capital. In particular, Smith (1996) deemed the increasing array of punitive measures used against homeless people (and poor people more generally), especially the proliferation of anti-homeless ordinances that clear visibly poor people from prime urban spaces, as part of a 'revanchist' urban policy at the behest of the upper classes and city managers. These vengeful policies have apparently been exported to other contexts, including the United Kingdom (Anti Social Behaviour Orders, Public Drinking Exclusion Zones and Town Centre Partnerships, for example) (Coleman, 2004; Johnsen and Fitzpatrick, 2007) and beyond. The marginal spaces occupied by the poor are seemingly under siege, not only from these anti-homeless policies but also a more systematic gentrification and upgrading of central-city districts. The image in Figure 4.5, taken in recently gentrified Downtown Miami in February 2009, exemplifies the increasingly prominent constraints on the uses of space by poor people.

Figure 4.5 Image of anti-homeless ordinance in Downtown Miami, 2009

The situation in the global south is perhaps even gloomier, as the middle and upper classes continue to impose their mastery over city space. While slum densities continue to skyrocket, the established middle and upper classes are expanding their living space. From Lima to Cairo to Manila, these more powerful groups are pushing to create insulated living spaces that further displace and segregate the very poor (squatters, itinerant street hawkers and entrepreneurs) from prime urban spaces (Fernandes, 2004; Roberts, 2005). The state frequently abets these restructurings of urban space by bulldozing squatter settlements and explicitly supporting middle-class housing. Exacerbating these trends has been the dramatic retrofitting of the built environment at the behest of more globalised actors, particularly 'as developers create new types of office, residential and commercial space to meet the demands of [global] business and the new elite' (Shatkin 2007: 3). As Robinson (2002: 547) notes, these 'calculated attempts at world or global city formation can have devastating consequences for most people in the city, especially the poorest, in terms of service provision, equality of access and redistribution'. Despite the well-argued fact that mega-cities in the global south follow different trajectories from first-world global cities (as well as among themselves) for reasons of history, culture and economy (Robinson, 2002), there can be no doubt that many are emulating global north built environments, particularly the production of expressly global and privatised CBDs (Central Business Districts) (Grant and Nijman, 2002).

But if the experiences of poverty have demonstrated anything, it is that poor people are remarkably ingenious and resourceful, to the point that they even manage to resist some of their imposed exclusions. As DeVerteuil, May and von

Mahs (2009) contend, too often the current revanchist and post-justice literature on anti-homeless measures in the global north frame the poor as passive. When resistance is identified in this literature, it is most likely to be spectacular (riots, occupations, legal challenges) rather than the everyday resistance through survival tactics that were described earlier in the chapter. Rather than hapless victims, the poorest are remarkably tenacious, even in the face of overwhelming state forces, as Duneier (1999: 312) observes:

> Many politicians incorrectly think that, if only they were to pass more laws to make life difficult for disreputable people working the sidewalks, these people would go away ... [But] surely, the people working and/or living on the sidewalks cannot be done away with so easily, even if it were desirable. Those determined to make 'an honest living' will keep deploying their creativity, competence ... as the men and women on Sixth Avenue do, to survive.

This does not mean that we should romanticise resistance among the poor; rather, we should recognise that their persistence *is* resistance, not in terms of radically overthrowing the social order, but of transgressing it on an everyday basis (DeVerteuil, Marr and Snow, 2009).

Finally, these current trends speak to the need for more, not less, direct research *with* the poor, and perhaps even *for* the poor. Participatory action research is an emerging methodological approach to understanding the experience of poverty in human geography. For instance, Heynen's research on the geographies of food distribution for the very poor (Heynen, 2010) focuses on the work of local Food Not Bombs. This organisation is a feeding programme that operates in defiance of anti-homeless ordinances that outlaw free public food distribution, with the stated aim of making the problem of urban hunger more visible to the general public. Johnsen et al. (2008: 194) allowed homeless people to use auto-photography to illustrate '"hidden" spaces that do not typically feature in public (or academic) imaginations of homelessness, and provided more nuanced understandings of the use, meanings and dynamics associated with other, apparently already "known" spaces'. This extension of standard research practice necessarily empowers the research subjects and suggests a way forward in understanding the intricacies of poverty survival and perhaps even alleviation.

Pedagogic guide

The Poverty Site

http://www.poverty.org.uk/
This site is entirely statistical and provides 100 poverty indicators, thus helping to monitor social exclusion in the UK.

Inequality

http://www.inequality.org/
This site chronicles America's growing economic divide, with resources for journalists, teachers, policy-makers and citizens.

World Bank

http://web.worldbank.org/
Data and research on poverty, inequality and social safety nets from around the world.

Understanding slums

http://www.ucl.ac.uk/dpu-projects/Global_Report/home.htm
This set of studies of slum conditions, policies and strategies was commissioned and compiled in preparation for the United Nations Global Report on Human Settlements 2003 – The Challenge of Slums.

5

Living with Difference: Reflections on Geographies of Encounter

Gill Valentine

DIFFERENCE: THE HALLMARK OF THE CITY

Difference is a hallmark of cities. The size and density of urban populations means they are sites of proximity where all different sorts of people are brought together. The issue of diversity and juxtaposition has been at the heart of geographical attempts to understand urban life. At the beginning of the twentieth century a group of scholars – most famously Robert Park, Ernest Burgess and Roderick McKenzie – carried out detailed studies of where different kinds of people lived in the city. They became known as the Chicago School of Human Ecology because they used an analogy with plant communities to interpret the residential patterns of Chicago and to develop a theory of how 'natural communities' emerge in cities. This work was very influential in Geography in the 1960s and led to the development of techniques to map segregation within cities on the basis of ethnicity and class (e.g. Peach, 1975). However, this work was heavily criticised by radical geographers and black political activists (see P. Jackson, 1987) for its narrow empiricism and the assumptions made about 'race' (that it was an essential category), which is now out of kilter with contemporary understandings of identity and 'difference'.

In the 1970s and 1980s, influenced by understandings of 'race' as a social construction rather than a 'natural' difference, geographers sought to explain and challenge such patterns of inequality in cities as products of structural processes – in particular focusing on the role of the housing market in shaping urban space and producing racial segregation (e.g. Anderson, 1991; S.J. Smith, 1987). In the USA and to a lesser extent the UK, attention also focused on the spatial concentration of the underclass (those on the bottom rung of the social ladder whose experiences are characterised by inter-generational poverty, welfare dependency and unemployment/unstable employment) in inner-city 'ghettos'. Here, debates about the origin and definition of the underclass focused on both individual and structural explanations for social polarisation in major cities (Robinson and Gregson, 1992). During this period, cities in the affluent West were generally in decline being characterised by deindustrialisation and structural unemployment. The juxtaposition of difference in this context of social polarisation led to tension and conflict. Trapped in poverty with little access to employment or wider opportunities, some marginalised groups, with little stake in society, turned to crime, drug dealing and violence as a way of earning a living as well as self- and social respect. For some young unemployed white men who had lost their relatively privileged status as working-class men, their anger at their structural circumstances was displaced by blaming scapegoats such as minority ethnic groups, lesbians or gay men or women (Fine et al., 1997). As such, during this period, 'difference' was synonymous with fear of otherness (Davis, 1990; Valentine, 1989) with particular groups, at different times and in different spaces, becoming demonised as 'dangerous others' including young people, minority ethnic groups, homeless people and those with mental ill-health, etc.

However, in the late twentieth century, globalisation placed major European and North American cities at the centre of the world economy. The rapid growth of the service sector and creative industries produced a well-paid group of middle-class professionals who wanted to live in the centres of cities because of the proximity of work and entertainment opportunities. As a result, post-industrial gentrification changed the social and physical make-up of many city neighbourhoods. This process was theorised by Marxists such as Neil Smith (1982) as a movement of capital back into the city in what became known as the 'rent gap' thesis.

In the 1990s, as a product of the 'cultural turn' in human geography, explanations for patterns of difference in the city shifted towards symbolic as well as material processes of inclusion and exclusion. Whiteness became understood not only as a structural advantage, but also as a standpoint and cultural practice (Frankenberg, 1993). Likewise, explanations for gentrification which had focused on production took a cultural turn, understanding it as a product of consumption in which individuals were perceived to be buying into particular lifestyles and identities. Here, too, feminist analyses began to recognise links between gentrification and women's changing position in the labour market as well as to draw attention to the increased visibility and development of gay enclaves in major North American, European and Australasian cities facilitated by the growing confidence of lesbians and gay men to claim sexual citizenship and the commodification of gay lifestyles as chic cosmopolitanism (Knopp, 1998). Here, the historical shift from industrial society to new modernity, in which individuals are assumed to be released from traditional constraints and to have more freedom to create their own individualised biographies, choosing between a range of lifestyles and social ties, has resulted in the more open public expression of a diverse range of social identities and ways of living (including greater visibility of people with disabilities, transgender and transsexual people, different religions and spiritual beliefs and the 'grey' lifestyles of older people, facilitated in part by equality legislation).

At the same time, the twin forces of the global economy and global conflicts have accelerated patterns of transnational migration at the beginning of the twenty-first century dramatically intensifying the connections between different peoples, cultures and spaces. This supermobility has created what Vertovec (2007) has termed 'super diversity' in contemporary cities across the globe (e.g. Law, 2002; Yeoh, 2004).

Thus after a decade or more in which the city was characterised as site of crime, conflict and withdrawal (e.g. Davis, 1990; Mitchell, 2003; Smith, 1996; Valentine, 1989) the city of the twenty-first century is being re-imagined as a site of connection. Iris Marion Young was one of the first commentators to celebrate the city as a site of difference. She described city life as 'a being together of strangers' (Young, 1990: 240). More recently Doreen Massey (2005: 181) has referred to our 'throwntogeth-erness' with others in the city; Laurier and Philo (2006: 193) describe the city as 'the place, above all, of living with others'; while Sennett (2001) argues that: '[a] city is a place where people can ... enter into the experiences and interests of unfamiliar lives ... to develop a richer, more complex sense of themselves'.

Much of the writing that is associated with what might be regarded as a 'cosmo-politan turn' (a stance that implies openness towards diversity) in thinking about the city celebrates the potential for the forging of new hybrid cultures and ways of living together with difference (evident in place marketing strategies) but without actually spelling out how this is being, or might be, achieved in practice (Bridge and Watson, 2002; Sennett, 1999). Rather, it is implied that cultural difference will somehow be dissolved by a process of mixing or hybridisation of culture in public space (e.g. Young, 2002). For example, Mica Nava (2006: 50) describes the everyday domestic cultures in many of London's neighbourhoods as signalling 'increasingly undifferen-tiated, hybrid, post-multicultural, lived transformations which are the outcomes of diasporic cultural mixing and indeterminacy'. She further argues that, what she terms the 'domestic cosmopolitanism' of London, represents a 'generous hospitable engagement with people from elsewhere, a commitment to an imagined inclusive transnational community of disparate Londoners' (Nava, 2006: 50).

Focusing on the micro-scale of everyday public encounters and interactions Eric Laurier and Chris Philo (2006), claim that low levels of sociability, for example in terms of holding doors, sharing seats and so on, represent one 'doing' of togetherness – one facet of mutual acknowledgement. Laurier et al. (2002: 353) write: 'The massively apparent fact is that people in cities do talk to one another as customers and shopkeep-ers, passengers and cab-drivers, members of a bus queue, regulars at cafes and bars, tourists and locals, beggars and by-passers, Celtic fans, smokers looking for a light, and of course ... as neighbours.' Ash Amin (2006: 1012) refers to such civil exchanges (after Lefebvre) as 'small achievements in the good city'. Likewise, Nigel Thrift (2005) has argued that the mundane friendliness that characterises many everyday urban public encounters represents a base-line democracy that might be fostered. He talks about overlooked geographies of kindness and compassion and about the potential for leaching these practices into the wider world (Thrift, 2005). Richard Boyd (2006) goes one step further to suggest that civility has a vital place in contemporary urban life and should be understood as form of pluralism predicated on moral equality. However, I want to argue that the extent to which these everyday spatial practices and civilities truly represent, or can be scaled up to build, the intercultural dialogue and exchange necessary for the kind of new urban citizenship that commentators (Isin, 2000; Staeheli, 2003) are calling for, needs much closer consideration.

Some of the writing about cosmopolitanism and new urban citizenship appears to be laced with a worrying romanticisation of urban encounter and to implicitly reproduce a potentially naïve assumption that contact with 'others' necessarily translates into respect for difference. In this chapter I therefore draw on original material from a research project about white majority prejudice, to think more closely about what Sennett (2000) refers to as the importance of the 'collectivity of space'. I begin by critiquing some of the work celebrating urban encounters through using empirical examples of where contact with difference leaves attitudes and values unmoved, and even hardened, before going on to consider debates about what kind of encounters produce what might be termed 'meaningful contact'. By this I mean contact that actually changes values and translates beyond the specifics of the individual moment into a more general positive respect for – rather than merely tolerance of – others. In doing so, I identify a paradoxical gap that emerges in geographies of encounter between values and practices.

The empirical material employed in this chapter comes from a qualitative research project funded by Citizenship 21 as part of a two-stage investigation into the nature of prejudice (Valentine, 2010). This study addressed negative social attitudes towards a range of minority groups, including lesbians and gay men, transsexuals, disabled people and so on, not just minority ethnic and migrant communities. In the first stage MORI (a social research company, now known as MORI IPSOS) conducted a nation-wide questionnaire survey about prejudice for Citizenship 21. The survey asked respondents which groups, if any, they felt less positive towards. It was completed by 1,693 adults who were interviewed across 167 constituency-based sampling points. The data was weighted to reflect the national population profile. The results of the poll were published in a report titled *Profiles of Prejudice* (Citizenship 21, 2003).

The subsequent qualitative study upon which this chapter draws was funded by Citizenship 21 to understand some of the patterns identified in the national survey. It involved nine focus group discussions and 30 in-depth autobiographical interviews with white majority participants. The research design included both group and individual methods because previous research has shown that some individuals feel more comfortable expressing particular attitudes in a social context with others, whereas others may only talk freely in a private, one-to-one situation. The focus groups were used to look at shared values and general issues, whereas the individual interviews were designed to examine the particular processes that shaped individuals' biographies and the development of their social attitudes. Like the survey, this qualitative research focused on the white majority informants' attitudes towards a range of minority and marginalised social groups (including, for example, disabled people, lesbians and gay men, transsexual people, gypsy and travellers, women, children and young people, asylum seekers, minority ethnic and faith-based communities). In this sense this research extends much of the writing about geographies of encounter because it focuses on a complex range of intersecting differences rather than adopting the more common bipolar approach of considering only relations between white majority and minority ethnic groups.

The qualitative research was based in three contrasting UK locations: London, the West Midlands and the South West. Details of the specific locations are withheld to protect the anonymity of those who participated in the study. The quotations presented in this chapter are verbatim.[1]

PARALLEL LIVES?

There is increasing evidence that contact between different social groups alone is not sufficient to produce respect. Indeed, many everyday moments of contact between different individuals or groups in the city do not count as encounters at all. In a study of social interactions in urban public places in Aylesbury, UK, Caroline Holland and colleagues (Holland et al., 2007) found that although their research sites were frequented by a range of different groups, this did not necessarily mean that there was any contact between the diverse inhabitants. Rather, their observations suggested that while different groups co-existed and even observed each other, nonetheless there was little actual mixing between different users who self-segregated within particular spaces, carving out their own territory. A similar study, by Dines and Cattell (2006) in East London, UK, found that good relations tended to emerge in spaces such as a park attached to a school where the parents' interests and attachments to place were able to converge and evolve. Likewise, Amin (2002) has observed that city streets are spaces of transit that produce little actual connection or exchange between strangers. A process exacerbated by the emergence of a mobile phone culture, which, Cameron (2000) has observed, contributes to incivility in public space as individuals move in and through locations while locked in the private worlds of their conversations with remote others. While other studies have also provided evidence that low-level incivilities still persist, with so-called 'respectable people', including the middle-aged and elderly, being most likely to be rude to strangers in interpersonal encounters (Phillips and Smith, 2006).

Beck (2002, 2006; also Beck and Sznaider, 2006) argues that although an internalised globalisation of society has occurred, not everyone sees themselves as part of this cosmopolitanism or will chose to participate in interactions with people different from themselves. Spatial proximity can actually breed defensiveness and the bounding of identities and communities (Young, 1990). Both the Home Office (2001a) and the former Chair of the UK Commission for Racial Equality, Trevor Phillips (2005) (now head of the new Commission for Equality and Human Rights), have raised concerns about self-segregation within some UK communities and similar fears are evident in a Council of Europe report to investigate the resurgence of intolerance and discrimination in Europe (Report of the Group of Eminent Persons of the Council of Europe, 2011).

---

1 Three ellipsis dots are used to indicate minor edits of a few words. Where [edit] is used this is to indicate a more significant chunk of text has been edited out.

Intolerance and Prejudice in Europe

Europe is witnessing unprecedented levels of mobility (within and beyond the European Union) and population change as well as rising levels of insecurity generated by post 9/11 terrorism and the current global financial crisis. As such, the Council of Europe is concerned about the rising levels of intolerance towards minority groups and support for xenophobic and populist parties in some parts of Europe. There are 85 cities in the world with somewhere between 100,000 and 1 million foreign-born residents, and 30 of these cities are in Europe (Zick et al., 2011: 28).

A study by Zick et al. (2011) found that negative attitudes towards minority groups are widespread in Europe. They conducted a survey of 8,000 people aged 16+ from France, Germany, Great Britain, Hungary, Italy, the Netherlands, Poland and Portugal (a representative sample of 1,000 people from each country). These countries were chosen to reflect the diverse geography of the European Union. Over half of all the European respondents stated that there are too many immigrants in their country, and a similar percentage described Islam as a 'religion of intolerance'. A majority of the respondents also supported sexist statements. Prejudices were most evident in Poland and Hungary and least prevalent in the Netherlands. For example, over 70 per cent of survey respondents from Poland expressed anti-Semitic views compared with only 17 per cent from the Netherlands, and 88 percent of the Polish respondents opposed same-sex marriage for lesbians and gay men compared with 17 percent of Dutch respondents (Zick et al., 2011).

Such attitudes matter because they can be translated into actual discrimination and hate crime. The *Intolerance, Prejudice and Discrimination* study (Zick et al., 2011: 14) found that respondents who expressed most prejudices are also more likely 'to oppose the integration of immigrants, to refuse them equal political participation and to use violence against them'. The European Council is concerned that rising intolerance might also cause the creation of parallel or segregated societies within European cities, the loss of democratic freedoms and possible clashes between the perceived rights and freedoms of different minority groups (especially between freedom of expression and religious freedom).

The European research from the *Intolerance, Prejudice and Discrimination* study (Zick et al., 2011) suggests that prejudice towards minority groups increases with age and is also associated with feeling politically powerless, being disadvantaged and holding authoritarian political views (e.g. wanting a strong leader, or supporting the death penalty), and is reduced by education and income. In contrast, positive attitudes towards difference can be fostered by contact – particularly firm friendships with, or trust in, others.

A report by the UK Home Office community cohesion independent review team described a picture in which: '[S]eparate: educational arrangements, community and voluntary bodies, employment, places of worship, language, social and cultural networks, means that many communities operate on the basis of a series of parallel lives. Their lives often do not seem to touch at any point, let alone overlap and promote any meaningful interchange' (Home Office, 2001: para 2.1). Indeed, Debbie Phillips (2006) has recently demonstrated that contrary to popular stereotypes of British Muslims as self-segregating and culturally inward-looking, her research participants had a range of housing aspirations and neighbourhood preferences, and some had sought to live in mixed neighbourhoods. However, these preferences for greater interaction with people from other backgrounds were frustrated by white self-segregation in the suburbs, institutional racism in housing markets and racial harassment.

Indeed, it is close proximity which often generates or aggravates comparisons between different social groups in terms of perceived or actual access to resources and special treatment. The West Midlands site where this research was conducted is an area of relative social and economic deprivation. Many of the informants were in comparatively low-income or unstable forms of employment and had either housing or health concerns relating to themselves, their children or older parents. They told community-based narratives of injustice and victimhood, for example that migrants are stealing jobs, that minority groups such as Muslims, lesbian and gay men and disabled people are receiving unfair cultural support or legal protection and so on. In both forms of account – of economic and cultural injustice – minority groups were represented as dependent on the State. This position of parasitism was contrasted in these narratives with the perceived unacknowledged rights and contribution to society of the white majority community. The research in London was conducted in one of the most culturally diverse boroughs, having an indigenous white working-class population as well as significant Afro-Caribbean, South Asian and Turkish communities and a growing number of refugee and asylum seekers. This area has also undergone a process of gentrification in the past ten years and so is also socio-economically diverse. Here, the white majority interviewees' accounts were also laced with examples of perceived economic and social injustices. These included claims that minority groups were taking advantage of the welfare system and receiving preferential treatment in terms of benefits, housing and health care as well as receiving financial and political support for their own faiths, languages and wider cultural practices. In each research location such narratives provided the basis for the interviewees' justifications of their openly held prejudices towards minority groups in the local neighbourhood (Valentine, 2010), as these quotations demonstrate:

> *They forget that they've been born and bred here* [referring to British minority ethnic groups] *but they're not putting anything into the country … you know they're taking … you know people who haven't worked for over 20 years and they're getting this, that and the other, to me they're not putting anything in … Because most people round here they're workers, they've always worked and everything and everybody works.* (woman, 60s, West Midlands)

R1:　　　　*To be truthful, it's like they had a mosque put on Station Road and on a quiet day, like a Sunday morning you will hear it, yeah.*

R2:　　　　*Wailing*

R1:　　　　*To be truthful when I hear it I do, I will say I feel like I'm in some other country, do you know what I mean?*

Interviewer:　Its cultural strangeness?

R3:   *Yeah it is strange.*

R4:   *It doesn't mix.*

R1:   *No, it don't feel right to have that on your doorstep anyway. But they've built that when they should I think have other important things to build ....*

R2:   *There's schools and hospitals that are needed and they build a mosque. They closed the children's hospital ... that children's hospital had been there for years and years.*

Interviewer: *so the mosque you're saying?*

R2:   *It was taken from taxpayers' money*

R1:   *It came from the council it shouldn't have ... it's a grievance.* (London, focus group)

In the context of such personal and community insecurity it is possible to see why some people find it hard to have mutual regard for groups they perceive as an economic or cultural threat. Indeed, being prejudiced can actually serve positive ends for some people, for example by providing them with a scapegoat for their own personal, social or economic failures (Valentine, 2010). This means that prejudiced individuals can have a vested interest in remaining intolerant despite positive individual social encounters with communities/individuals different from themselves. Perhaps not surprisingly, then, everything from hate crimes and violence, to discrimination and incivility, motivated by intolerance between communities in close proximity to each other, are commonplace. The geography literature documents many examples of socially mixed neighbourhoods that are territorialised by particular groups and rife with tensions over different ways of 'doing' and 'being' in shared space (Watt, 1998; Watt and Stenson, 1998; Webster, 1996). These include not only power struggles and conflicts over the ownership and control of public space between different ethnic groups but also between people of different ages – particularly between teenagers, who often feel unjustly marginalised in public space by adults, and the elderly who are commonly fearful of groups of young people in what in effect are often age-segregated neighbourhoods (Valentine, 2004, Vanderbeck, 2007). Indeed, contact with any manifestation of difference – in the neighbourhood or elsewhere – can breed frustration and indeed generate different scales of resentment from rudeness in one-to-one situations to the threat of vigilante action. The following quotations illustrate some of the everyday tensions in neighbourhoods and workplaces:

You know they have come from a country where they chuck their rubbish in the street and that's it, that's the end of it. Dogs come and eat it whatever, and the cats, and it rots away and it stinks and everything. And they seem to think that they can still do [it] here ... they don't abide by our rules. (West Midlands focus group)

I can remember at least on one occasion, working with a colleague who's got a physical disability and I guess getting pissed off with his immobility in the classroom. Cos I was kind of like ... well I was kind of running what was going on and he would be, kind being slow or immobile or whatever.
(male, 30s, London)

Even where contact is instigated between different social groups, for example in the institutional space of the school, rather than generating intercultural exchange it can actually be socially divisive. Here the social studies of childhood and youth literatures includes evidence of the repetition of gender, sexual, class and race practices amongst young people which cement, rather than challenge, animosities (Valentine, 2004).

Nonetheless, despite the often parallel lives of different groups within the city, it is true that people do – as Laurier, Philo, Thrift and others have observed – generally behave in courteous ways towards strangers in public space including the performance of everyday acts of kindness. Thrift (2005: 147) characterises these everyday moments as providing 'resevoirs of hope'. However, the evidence of my research on white majority prejudice is that we should be careful about mistaking such taken-for-granted civilities as respect for difference. As Cresswell's (1996) seminal book – *In Place/Out of Place* – demonstrated, the production of space is shaped by normative codes of behaviour. Encounters in public space therefore always carry with them a set of contextual expectations about appropriate ways of behaving which regulate our co-existence. These serve as an implicit regulatory framework for our performances and practices. As Smith and Davidson (2008) argue – echoing in some respects the classic work of Elias (1978) – urban etiquette matters because 'publicly reiterated performances of social mores define an individual's persona' (p. 233). Since the enlightenment, dominant western discourses have associated civility and etiquette with notions of moral and aesthetic development. Individuals therefore regularly act out mundane and ritualised codes of etiquette such as holding open doors for, or exchanging banalities in queues with, 'others' because these conventions are sedimented into public modes of being and are constitutive of our self-identities as citizens. Indeed, for some of my informants, behaving in a civil or decent way in public, regardless of your privately held views and values, is what Britishness is all about. As such, this urban etiquette does not equate with an ethics of care and mutual respect for difference. For example, Jim, who admits to holding openly, in some cases quite extreme, prejudices, nonetheless describes the civilities he exchanges with new migrants in his neighbourhood.

All these ... have come over, you don't know if there's a terrorist amongst them ... There's one, there's a college up here, and he comes home and comes [past] here, and ... he talks pretty good English. At first he didn't want to talk English, you know what I mean? I don't know why, I'm talking. Then all of a sudden he got to know me like. Cos I used to clean the car outside there sometimes, outside their house, clean my car, you know what I mean. He'd stand on his step and he used to watch me, like and talking and I used to go 'alright'. And I go out now, since I started saying hello to him, and they come out to chat ... like we've all, been neighbours for years [laughs]. (male, 60s, West Midlands)

Such civil encounters represent a tolerance of others in shared space. However, tolerance is a dangerous concept. It is often defined as a positive attitude yet it is not the same thing as mutual respect. Rather, tolerance conceals an implicit set of power relations. It is a courtesy that a dominant or privileged group has the power to extend to, or withhold from, others. Waltzer (1997: 52), for example, writes: 'toleration is always a relationship of inequality where the tolerated groups or individuals are cast in an inferior position. To tolerate someone else is an act of power; to be tolerated is an acceptance of weakness.' The danger of everyday civil encounters therefore is that they obscure or leave untouched this question of who has the power to tolerate, and therefore wider issues of equality and mutuality (Weymss, 2006).

Moreover, some of my informants argued that encounters in contemporary public space are regulated by codes of so-called 'political correctness' to such an extent that they feel obliged to curb the public expression of their personal prejudices and negative feelings. Their actual attitudes are only allowed to leak out in 'privatised' spaces, such as at home or when part of a 'closed' group of friends. These are spaces where they know their opinions will be shared and validated, and that even if challenged, will have no wider public or personal consequences for them. In this way, anti-discrimination legislation regulates public civilities but not private moralities; while prejudice-reduction initiatives rarely address spaces like the home. This quotation captures the privatised nature of many prejudices.

I don't think we'll change people's attitudes. I mean I know just from like doing my job in working for the Council, they've got a policy of you know fair discrimination ... I think it makes people in fear of it ... it makes people think more before they speak, be more careful about what they say about minority groups, so you know you can't sort of like, voice your opinions, so I think it makes people tread on egg shells. (male, 20s, West Midlands)

Moreover, some informants who identified themselves as holding liberal values and of having a conscious desire to be non-prejudiced, nonetheless described themselves as being fearful of contact with minority groups because of what Sennett (2003: 22) might term the 'anxiety of privilege'. They talked about being aware of, and uneasy about, their own economic and cultural positions of power, yet did not know how to show respect across the boundaries of inequality. Fearful of being condescending or 'getting it wrong' and causing offence, they eschew encounters with difference (an option in part facilitated by their privilege) and in doing so produce the very effects of which they are fearful, as this woman describes:

If you see someone in a wheelchair I do think oh there's someone in a wheelchair and you know how people say you know all the bad things that happen to disabled people, like people talking to the person pushing them or shouting or whatever... All this flashes through my mind and I think act normal, act normal, ... My brain automatically goes onto things you shouldn't do and the things you are told are bad ... and I get paranoid that I'm going to do one of these things ... I can't act natural. (woman, 20s London)

In both situations – where a person holds prejudiced values and yet behaves in a polite way in public encounters with minority groups; and where a person holds liberal values and yet behaves in an implicitly disrespectful way towards others by avoiding encounters with difference – a clear gap is evident between individuals' values and practices in public space. If we are to produce meaningful contact between majority and minority groups which has the power to produce social change, this gap needs to be addressed. We need to find ways in which everyday practices of civility might transform prejudiced values and might facilitate liberal values to be put into practice.

SPACE OF INTERDEPENDENCES AND CULTURAL DESTABILISATION

Writing in the aftermath of race disturbances which took place in three British cities (Oldham, Burnley and Bradford) in 2001, Amin (2002) recognised that proximity on its own is not enough to bring about social transformation. Rather, he argued that we need to create spaces of interdependence in order to develop intercultural understanding. If, as Ahmed (2000: 279–80) argues, 'collectives are formed through the very work that we need to do in order to get closer to others', then the question for geographers is what work needs to be done – and in which kinds of spaces – to generate this interdependence?

Creating Dialogues Across Difference

In 2008 the Council of Europe published a white paper on intercultural dialogue – *Living Together as Equals in Dignity*. This argued that the skills or competences to enable people to live with difference are not necessarily automatically acquired but rather need to be taught and practised from childhood. It identified the need for such training at school but also through life-long educational programmes and informal education. A number of initiatives have been developed by groups within specific countries to find practical responses to how we might live with difference. For example, the Bielany Cultural Centre in Warsaw hosts a series of events including lectures, films, performances, photography and art exhibitions to bring people together from different communities to challenges stereotypes and to encourage participants to improve their knowledge of each other (www.yepp-community.org/yepp/cms/index.php). There are also pan-European initiatives as well; for example the Council of Europe holds annual youth peace camps to bring together young people from regions of Europe where there are conflicts. They take

(Continued)

(Continued)

part in education and training sessions about human rights, conflict resolution and inter-cultural dialogue (see the Report of the Group of Eminent Persons of the Council of Europe, 2011 – www.coe.int).

There are many non-western consensus based ways of developing dialogues across difference too. Indaba is one such concept. This is a Zulu or Xhosa term from south-ern Africa, for an important meeting held by izinDuna (principal men), in which the participants gather together in a space to address and resolve a problem or conflict. Everyone has an equal voice and the group stays in communion with each other until they can find a common position or story upon which they can all agree (although there are similar consensus models in other parts of Africa too). This southern African model of addressing conflict was recently adopted by the Archbishop of Canterbury, Rowan Williams, at the decennial Lambeth Conference of Anglican bishops, to create a dia-logue across difference between those members of this global faith network who are opposed to the ordination of gay bishops, and blessings for same-sex partnerships and those who want equality for lesbians and gay men.

For Amin (2002: 959) interdependence is best achieved in what he terms the 'micro-publics of everyday social contact and encounter' rather than engineered through larger-scale events like public festivals or policies framed in terms of rights and obli-gations at the national scale. These 'micro-publics' include: sports or music clubs, drama/theatre groups, communal gardens, youth participation schemes and so on. They represent sites of purposeful organised group activity where people from dif-ferent backgrounds are brought together in ways that provide them with the oppor-tunity to break out of fixed patterns of interaction and learn new ways of being and relating (Amin, 2002). Sandercock (2003) shares Amin's characterisation of micro-publics as sites of not only cultural exchange, but also cultural destabilisation and transformation. This analysis is extended further by Nava (2006) who uses the term 'domestic cosmopolitanism' to signal that she understands cosmopolitanism to emerge from engagements with otherness, not just in the micro-publics of the city (which she defines somewhat differently from Amin to include more abstract sites such as the street and the shopping centre, as well as spaces organised around pur-poseful activity like the baby clinic, the gym and the dance floor), but also in the space of the home. Here, she argues: 'the intimate albeit mediated form of TV must also be included here insofar as, cumulatively it generates in the familiar domestics-cape of the living room an increasing deterritorialisation of the globe by normalising difference in the spheres of music, fashion even politics although often against the message of individual programmes' (Nava, 2006: 49–50).

Rather than leaving to chance the emergence of openness to otherness, some writ-ers have argued that the commercial hospitality industry (Bell et al., 2007) and also design (Fincher, 2003; Fincher and Iveson, 2008; Rishbeth, 2001) can play impor-tant potential parts in fostering integration and interaction between different groups. Bell (2007), for example, argues that hospitality should not merely be seen as an instrumental or economic exchange but might also offer broader possibilities for transforming urban public culture; while Fincher and Iveson (2008) suggest that the creation of conviviality as a state of encounter should be an intent of planning. Here, they identify the characteristics of particular spaces where they believe this productive activity can be produced or facilitated. Libraries, they argue, are spaces of encounter that have a *redistributive function*. They offer free and – facilitated by design – equal access and a safe space for individuals and groups. The information resources and provision of areas to sit and read or drink coffee can enable users to mutually negotiate their common status as library users and to build social capital. Community centres in contrast are spaces which emphasise *recognition*. Social encounters in these spaces are relatively informal and can quickly become familiar or home-like through repeated visits. As such, these encounters are not completely incidental like meetings on the street, but neither are they as organised and purposeful as 'micro-publics' such as sports clubs and drama groups. They can also operate as therapeutic spaces because they provide the chance for individuals to show an interest in or support for the well-being of others (Conradson, 2003).

These diverse accounts of how we might begin to build – what Ash Amin (2004: 43) has called a 'politics of connectivity' through specific spaces – however, need to be treated with a degree of caution for two reasons. First, inter-group contact – while potentially beneficial in reducing majority prejudice – can be very stressful for minority groups. They may be unsure of how they will be received (Crocker et al., 1998); may not welcome the burden of representation (Bassi, 2003); and may even dread such encounters because their experiences of marginalisation and discrimination taint their willingness to engage in relations with majority groups. For example, deaf people's everyday experiences of discrimination in public space – as a cultural and linguistic minority – are so negative that they have developed separatist spaces of withdrawal from hearing society and are often reluctant to engage with hearing people unless it is on their own terms (Valentine and Skelton, 2003, 2007). Whereas, other studies have identified *gendered* and *generational* divisions in terms of opportunities for, and types of encounter between respondents from minority ethnic communities and the white majority population (Uitermark et al., 2005; Valentine et al., 2009). For example, different generations have their own normative values and practices because of the particular socio-economic and political contexts within which they are born (Vanderbeck, 2007); while the voices of women are often underrepresented in formal 'community' consultation processes and organisations. We need to think more carefully therefore about which types of encounters are sought, and by whom, and which are avoided, and by whom. The same contact may be read and experienced very differently both between, and within, majority and minority groups (cf. Bell et al., 1994) and may have unrecognised negative outcomes for particular individuals. As such we need to pay more attention to the *intersectionality* of multiple identities (not just to ethnicity), and particularly to consider which particular identifications these purposeful encounters with difference are approached through, and how these encounters are systematically embedded within intersecting grids of power (Valentine, 2007).

Second, if a common ethics of care and mutual respect emerges from these particular kinds of purposeful, organised micro-public encounters – which I am not necessarily sure it always does – then how can this connectivity be sustained and scaled up in both space and time beyond these moments?

SCALING UP A POLITICS OF CONNECTIVITY

Ash Amin (2002) argues that 'micro-publics' are spaces that can transmit wider intercultural understanding and social transformation because they are sites of cultural destabilisation. Taken at face value this expectation appears plausible. Research on the causes and transmission of prejudice (Allport, 1954) suggests that when an individual has a negative experience with a member of a minority group as part of routine everyday encounters, this moment is often mobilised to produce and justify powerful negative generalisations about the whole population that the minority individual is seen to represent. We might expect therefore that positive encounters with individuals from different social groups in micro-publics, such as the sports club, drama group or communal garden, might also produce correspondingly powerful positive changes in attitudes towards minority populations in general.

However, the evidence of my research is that this is not the case. Positive encounters with individuals from minority groups do not necessarily change people's opinions about groups as a whole for the better, at least not with the same speed and permanence as negative encounters. In other words, in the context of negative encounters minority individuals are perceived to represent members of a wider social group, but in positive encounters minority individuals tend to be read only as individuals. In the following quotations, informants describe friendships and family relationships with individuals who are lesbian and gay, and who are of dual heritage yet they then go on to articulate homophobic and racist comments respectively, demonstrating the limits of encounter with difference:

> I'm an open guy, I've had some gay friends and lesbians. I got on very well with them, and I find them funny. I find them, in the most part to be quite well educated as well, you know. They know how to party, I'm all for that. I just think there could be people out there that well, it's [social change] going ... just a wee bit too fast ... I mean when you see the [lesbian, gay and bisexual pride] rallies at Parliament Square and places like that. I mean I've been working in my van and I've been sitting parked up, and you see two guys ... and then they're really camp and they're trying to get their message across. They're going about it in completely the wrong way, because all they're doing is disgusting people. When you have families and mothers and kiddies walking along the pavements, and they're camping it up and two guys kissing and ... they're going over the top, they're not going to get much of a sympathy vote there. (male, 50s, London)

> R1:   I've got blacks in my family, my grandson's half baked. I'm not racist
>   but they've let them all in, they're taking over the country.

R3:   *I think she's got a very good point*

R2:   *My son can't even get a flat* [edit]

R1:   *There's nothing worse than when you're standing, especially in the street, and walk to the bottom and you walk from the bottom to the top and you haven't heard an English word spoken.* (focus group, London)

These examples of the failure of individual contact to produce generalised respect for difference explain why there was no contradiction between Jim's story – quoted earlier – of exchanging everyday civilities with his neighbours who are asylum seekers while cleaning his car, and his support for a right-wing, anti-immigration political party.

The reason that such individual everyday encounters do not necessarily change people's general prejudices is because they do not destabilise white majority community-based narratives of economic and/or cultural victimhood. It is these narratives – that have a geographical dimension, differing in their focus in different places according to specific local socio-economic contexts – which enable people to justify their prejudice, and not to recognise their own attitudes as constituting prejudice, because they believe their views to be predicated on well-founded rationales (Valentine, 2010). This informant explains when prejudice is not prejudice but fair comment:

Obviously there's prejudice in the world that we live in. [It's a] prejudice society. But obviously prejudice is a logical response to sort of phenomenon and so therefore if it can be explained, if you have a certain doubt or a certain feeling about something then if, if it can be explained you know logically then therefore then it isn't prejudice. (male, 40s, London)

The certainty in respondents' justifications of their prejudices makes them hard to challenge, especially where groups feel they have little ability to control events and that they are being treated unfairly. I would suggest therefore that more emphasis needs to be placed, not just on immediate contact experiences, but on how people's accrued histories of social experiences and material circumstances may also contribute to their feelings about urban encounters from both sides (i.e. from the perspective of participants from both majority and minority groups). In particular, how do 'real' and 'imagined' feelings of injustice (here, I refer to imagined injustices in the sense that some identified threats are symbolic or future-oriented) – inhibit an emotional bridge being made between people's attitudes to particular individuals and their attitudes to wider social groups.

Encounters never take place in a space free from history, material conditions and power. The danger is that contemporary discourses about cosmopolitanism and new urban citizenship, by celebrating the potential of everyday encounters to produce social transformations, potentially allow the knotty issue of inequalities to slip out of the debate. Yet, the informants who participated in my research that had the most cosmopolitan and non-prejudiced attitudes were those who considered their own lives to be full of opportunity and who were most optimistic about their own futures. I argue therefore that we need to scale back up from recent preoccupations with contemporary manifestations of the 'contact hypothesis' to acknowledge the relationships between individuals' prejudices and the processes through which communities become antagonised and defensive in, firstly, the competition for scarce resources and, secondly, in the debate about conflicting rights. Here, I use resources not just to refer to work, housing, benefits and so on, but also to the provision of financial and legal support for cultural practices and different ways of living. I use rights to refer not only to the rights of groups to social and political equality and to live free of discrimination; but also to the rights of individuals, for example, to freedom of speech. Such an approach also requires the need for researchers to reflect on the research tools that might provide the most effective ways of exploring and understanding the transmission of values and practices. This might include, for example, employing methodological techniques that are not commonly used in researching geographies of encounter, such as life histories, biographical interviews or intergenerational studies.

CONCLUSION: DIFFERENCE MATTERS

This chapter has reflected on the question of how we might live with difference. On the one hand, the positive focus on social transformation that characterises much of the writing about cosmopolitanism provides a welcome antidote to a previous emphasis on cities as sites of social exclusion and conflict. On the other hand, however, I remain wary about being too quick to celebrate everyday encounters and their power to achieve cultural destabilisation and social transformation.

Specifically, the evidence of my research is that proximity in the city does not equate with meaningful contact. While taken-for-granted normative codes of behaviour in public space mean that people do commonly behave in courteous, and sometimes kind ways towards others, this is not the same as having respect for difference. Indeed, there is often an uncomfortable gap between some people's professed liberal values and their actual practices, and vice-versa those who hold prejudiced views can nonetheless willingly exchange public civilities with individuals from the minority groups despite their politics. Rather, everyday convivial urban encounters often mark instead a culture of tolerance which leaves the issue of our multiple and intersecting identities (including generational differences), specifically, the identifications through which these encounters are approached and the differential capacity of particular voices to participate unaddressed; as well as the question of who has the power to tolerate.

Even if a respect for difference can be produced from particular kinds of purposeful, organised micro-public encounters (i.e. if the contact is meaningful), it still leaves the question of how this can be scaled up beyond the moment, given that white majority prejudices appear to be rooted in narratives of economic and/or cultural victimhood, which themselves are a response to a risk society, in which old securities and certainties are continually being eroded by unprecedented socio-economic change (Beck, 1997).[2]

As such we need an urban politics that addresses inequalities (real and perceived) as well as diversity; that recognises the need to fuse what are often seen as separate debates about prejudice and respect with questions of social-economic inequalities and power (cf. Fraser 1997). Here, the respondents' resentment towards what they dubbed 'political correctness' suggests that there is a general lack of understanding of diversity, difference and rights, as well as misunderstandings about resource allocations which have important implications for the work of equality bodies. In particular, there is a need to address issues about the perceived fairness of resource distribution between majority and minority populations. Urban policies to develop meaningful contact also need to build the capacity to participate of those who are commonly marginalised within purposeful organised groups. In sum, this chapter reiterates calls by Philo (2000) and others for a re-materialisation and re-socialisation of human geography: a return to focusing on socio-spatial inequalities and the insecurities they breed, and to trying to understand the complex and intersecting ways in which power operates.

ACKNOWLEDGEMENTS

I wish to thank Ben Anderson and Ian MacDonald who conducted some of the interviews and focus groups as part of this study. The paper on which this chapter is based was previously published in *Progress in Human Geography*. I am grateful to Sage for giving the editors of this volume permission to reproduce this edited version of it and to the European Research Council for its support to develop these ideas through an Advanced Investigator Award (grant agreement no. 249658): *Living with Difference in Europe*.

---

2 It also leaves the issue of whether the home – as a space where values are contested and reworked between intra-familial generations – might also be a potentially important site of social transformation.

6

The Everyday City of the Senses

Mónica Degen

INTRODUCTION

City living is in vogue in the twenty-first century. Formerly decaying inner-city neigh-bourhoods have been dramatically spruced up and made into attractive spaces to live in or visit. Whether it is New York's Harlem, Berlin's Kreuzberg or the historic centre of Mexico City, their desirability is advertised by estate agents and tourist guides alike. Indeed, the radical restructuring of the urban material landscape is a crucial feature of what has been described in British circles as an 'urban renaissance' (DETR, 1999; Lees, 2003a). This is reflected in the redesign of street-layouts, the building of new squares and public spaces and the commissioning of flagship architecture in redeveloping city centres. Yet, 'looking good' alone is not enough in an ever more competitive global market. One crucial feature has been the conscious animation of public places through events, retail, bars and restaurants to create a certain atmosphere or ambience of place. Hence, we are witnessing the gradual move from the 'post-industrial' or 'entrepre-neurial city' (Cronin and Hetherington, 2008; Hall and Hubbard, 1998) that does not just look different but, more importantly, needs to elicit a variety of exciting sensations to remain competitive in an expanding 'experience economy' (Lonsway, 2009; Lor-entzen, 2009). The management of this new experiential landscape has become a key tool in controlling and organising public life in the city in late modernity.

We encounter the city foremost as a corporeal space. We assimilate our immediate surroundings through the senses, perceiving before we understand what happens around us and are guided through spaces with assistance from our whole sensory body. A nauseating stench alerts us to rubbish bins in a corner; the warm sunshine on our skin relaxes us; a shrill ringing of a bicycle bell makes us aware that we are in somebody's way. The interplay of different sensory perceptions contributes to our spatial orientation, frames our awareness of spatial relationships and facilitates the appreciation of the qualities of particular places. Indeed, as I will argue in this chapter, the management and organisation of urban atmospheres is of crucial importance in contemporary urban policy. A focus on the senses in the city allows us to analyse the experience of the city as a political domain that links the personal lives of its diverse users with broader structural changes in the city's politics and economy. Of course, this landscape is not set in stone but is constantly fluctuating and transforming through the myriad bodies, spatial practices and uses of those living in the city. The senses thus link the physical constitution of the city, its streets and buildings, with a living social landscape.

In this chapter I examine the importance of the senses in structuring and mediating the everyday life and experience of the city. The chapter begins with a brief summary of the historical evolution of sensory approaches that emphasise the social and spatial character of the senses rather than reducing human perception merely to a psychobiological system. This is followed by a discussion of the ways in which sensory dynamics are underpinned by and frame power relations in the city. The last section evaluates how within contemporary urban living the senses have been consciously adapted, manipulated and framed to market and brand urban places.

THE SENSES AND THE CITY

A focus on sensory experience in the city started to emerge at the beginning of the twentieth century as urban centres throughout the West were morphing into modern metropolises and undergoing unprecedented changes and developments. Two writers in particular, Georg Simmel and Walter Benjamin, outlined the value of a sensory approach for understanding the novel experiences shaping life in the modern city. In particular, they analysed how urban individuals negotiated new sensations elicited by technical innovations, such as the car and electricity, which were transforming urban perception. Benjamin, for example, writes about how pedestrians are forced to constantly check traffic lights and concludes that 'technology has subjected the human sensorium to a complex kind of training' (1997: 31). Likewise, Simmel (1971) famously examines how modern city experience is unique in its sensory over-stimulation and how individuals protect themselves from this sensory accost by adopting a blasé attitude or aloofness to the environment. In his essay 'The Sociology of the Senses' (1997 [1907]), Simmel further examines how the senses are involved in mediating and ordering human interaction: 'That we get involved in interactions at all depends on the fact that we have a sensory effect upon one another' (1997 [1907]: 110). In this short piece, Simmel already foreshadows some of the themes that have since become central to sensory geographies, namely that sensory perceptions are shaped by social values and underpin social hierarchies and distinctions; that each sense establishes a particular relationship with our surroundings; that senses supplement each other, in other words we sense holistically; and finally, that sensory paradigms transform over time. Simmel's and Benjamin's legacy has been not only to show how the senses are crucial in understanding the distinctiveness of urban culture but also that an explicit focus on the sensory relations in public spaces helps us to assess broader social changes in society. In other words, changes in economic and cultural practices transform the sensory perceptions surrounding us. Hence, the move from an agrarian society to an industrialised society means that certain sensations disappear or are replaced. For example, the smell and sound of cattle in cities was overtaken by the noise of cars and the stench of industrial fumes. In more recent times, the ring of mobile phones and people talking loudly into their handheld devices indicates the introduction of a new technology in everyday life. Both writers show through their studies the importance of microanalysis in understanding the everyday dynamics of metropolitan life.

Tokyo's contrasting sensescapes

Figure 6.1   The neon landscape of Tokyo (photo: Eugene McCann)

Tokyo is the world's largest urban agglomeration (35 million inhabitants) and though part of a global city network it is at the same time a notably different sort of world city from New York or London. While Tokyo has undergone rapid and uncontrolled development, global investment has not been a major factor in its urban restructuring, as 'the dominant presence in Tokyo is that of transnational Japanese corporations' (Waley, 2007: 1466). In addition, Tokyo has a much less ethnically mixed population than Paris or Seoul and many more factories than any other post-industrial city (Waley, 2007). Tokyo provides an intriguing blend of western and Asian culture producing its own localised form of modern globalisation. The city's unique urban features (shaped by history, culture, economy and politics) can be ascertained through the mapping and experiencing of the sensory landscape of the city. This is a city of contrasts which becomes most perceptible at night when its radiant sea of neon and video screens bring the buildings themselves to life. When walking through city-centre areas such as Shinjuku, one is quickly enveloped by the crowds. Within seconds one can move from the shrill, flickering landscape of giant neon adverts hanging off skyscrapers and promoting largely Japanese products to narrow side streets of one-storey houses where electricity cables tangle loosely overhead. Leaving behind a sea of colours and cacophony of the whirrs and plinks of pachinko parlours mixed with the garish calls of sellers for electrical goods on the busy main streets, one can drift into a more serene space hearing the murmuring sound of a Shinto priest involved in daily prayers on a street corner while commuters rush by. A traditional Buddhist temple stands next to a spaceship-looking high-rise, the smell of incense lapping the street, the glow of a metal vending machine irradiating the dark. The contrast between new and old, the unruly development of its urban landscape is similarly palpable in contrasting tastescapes. Within the newly built areas of the city, vertical tastescapes predominate. Restaurants are squeezed onto every floor of a high-rise and each opening of the lift door exposes the visitor to a distinct and disarming environment: green bamboo and a bridge over running water in one; the lulling sounds of a Hawaiian bar in the next. Yet step outside, walk into a narrow alleyway and soon you are surrounded by wooden latticework, white noren (shop curtains) and the dimly lid red lanterns of small ramen bars. The smells of miso soup and grilled fish mix with beer and the sound of laughter and shouts of 'Kampai!' (Cheers) echo from inside.

Figure 6.2 Sensing the street in Tokyo (photo: Eugene McCann)

However, much of this work/the work on the sensory-experiential dimensions of urban life fell into oblivion and, until the 1970s, space was very much viewed by many social scientists as something that was in the background of society, an abstract space, determined by geometrical measures and coordinates. The emergence of so-called 'humanistic geographers' (Buttimer and Seamon, 1980; Ley, 1974; Relph, 1976) started to challenge this view by recovering the importance of experience in the making of space, the most prominent being Yi Fu Tuan. Tired of the positivistic spatial science models, he wondered what qualities make a place unique and interrogated the ways in which places obtain emotional and cultural meanings for humans. In his book *Space and Place* (1977), Tuan argues that spaces become places through our routine activities in them and the emotional attachments and investments that people develop over time. Space is transformed into place as it acquires definition and meaning: 'What begins as undifferentiated space becomes place as we get to know it better and endow it with value' (1977: 6). As we use places on a daily basis, we attach particular experiences and memories to them – they become meaningful. Think about the first time you came to university, the buildings and spaces you encountered were 'things', something abstract, with no personal meanings for you. Over the time of your degree, the different spaces on campus, the lecture halls and common rooms start being associated with specific activities or happenings that have occurred in these spaces. Tuan emphasises precisely the importance of our embodied experience, of sensory engagements in creating places. It is through smelling, touching, seeing, hearing and tasting that we get to know places and they become familiar. The senses, for Tuan, 'constantly reinforce each other to provide the intricately ordered and emotion charged world in which we live' (1977: 11). Place starts with where we are situated bodily.

In the early 1990s, anthropologists such as Howes (1991), Classen (1993) and Stoller (1989) started to research in depth the largely neglected world of sensations. Focusing on non-western cultures and exploring the changing role and meaning attributed to the senses throughout history, their work emphasises the crucial relation between cultural frameworks and sensory perception. As Classen's (1993) study of the Ongee people in the South Pacific shows, their world order is based on the sense of smell. Hence, space for the Ongee is not a fixed and static area that can be captured by the eye but a fluid entity constantly evolving. This anthropological work has highlighted that sensory orders are organised by culture and express cultural values and, as cultures change over time, so too do their sensory orders (Classen, 1993). Sensations are socially constructed: 'perception is a shared social phenomenon ... it has a history and a politics which can only be comprehended within its cultural setting' (Howes, 2005: 4–5). For example, in our contemporary media-saturated western society, the visual sense has become the most dominant with regards to 'transparency' and truth. However, as Classen illustrates, this was not always the case and '[i]n the pre-modern West ... smell was associated with essence and spiritual truth, while sight was often deemed a "superficial" sense, revealing only exteriors' (Classen, 1993: 7).

One can also identify strong variations between individuals' sensory thresholds shaped by the cultural backgrounds they have become accustomed to. For example, a western body is likely to feel dazzled and overwhelmed by the haptic environment, smellscapes and soundscapes of an Indian bazaar, where he or she needs to 'weave a path by negotiating obstacles, and remain alert to hazardous traffic and animals (such as monkeys, cows and dogs)' (Edensor, 2000: 135). In such a sensory context, western sensibilities feel assaulted: 'The jumbled mix of pungent aromas (sweet, sour, acrid and savoury) produces intense "olfactory geographies", and the combination of noises generated by numerous human activities, animals, forms of transport and performed and recorded music, produces a changing symphony of diverse pitches, volumes and tones' (ibid.: 135). Yet, it is precisely such divergent sensescapes that distinguish one place – one city – from another, and such sensory differences, such as the aromas of an Arab souk, become either exoticised or shunned by many westerners.

What these writings reveal is that perception is not subjective but socially shaped. Indeed, Howes notes how one can identify different 'communal sensory orders' across various societies. Sensations cannot be reduced to purely 'natural' or biological ways of capturing our environment as the way we sense and the meanings we attribute to particular smells, sights or tastes are culturally learned. It is precisely the researchers' role to analyse 'the social ideologies conveyed through sensory values and practices' (Howes, 2005: 4). As we will see in the remainder of this chapter, social judgements such as rejection or acceptance of particular social groups or places are often wrapped up in sensory qualifications. Low explains how the senses '[function] as a social medium employed by social actors towards formulating constructions/judgements of race-d, class-ed and gendered others' (2005: 405). Consequently, each society produces its own sensory hierarchies linked to an established social order and in which the dominant group will be linked to the valued senses and positive sensory formations, and the subordinate groups will be associated with what are regarded as inferior and polluting senses (Howes, 2006: 164). Smith (2007), for example, examines in his historical analysis of slavery, segregation and racism in North America how the irrational structure of racism was justified through sensory paradigms which facilitated 'the rule of feeling' to bypass reason. In particular, he highlights the importance of analysing how racist and discriminatory ideologies are not just visually mediated and articulated, but invoked and supported through an array of sensory paradigms to create racial stereotypes.

At the same time as the emergence of anthropological research on the senses, geographical approaches started to explore the relationship between sensing, embodiment and place-making. Pivotal was the work of Porteous (1985, 1990) who challenged the occularcentric bias of geographical research and suggested that landscapes, as much as being visually ordered, are perceptually mapped as 'smellscapes' and 'soundscapes'. Each sense contributes to our geographical knowledge and experience in distinctive ways. Conceiving our geographical encounters in terms of interacting 'sensescapes' has framed a range of recent explorations on the experiential dimensions of the city such as 'sensory landscapes' (Degen, 2008; Law, 2001; Rodaway, 1994), the 'emotional qualities' of cities (Parr, 2001; Pile, 2005) and the politics of materiality and decay in urban environments (Edensor, 2005; Till, 2005). A common theme within these different approaches is that they establish clear connections between the making of space and the intangible qualities that produce the lived geographies of the city. Most significantly, Rodaway's (1994) notion of 'sensuous geography' has shown that the senses are intrinsically geographical in that they order space and structure our 'sense of place'. As a result, urban geographers and sociologists have started to 'foreground spatialities that are normally occluded in understandings of city life' (Pile, 2005: 3). These points have also been picked up in architectural studies where a new multisensory research agenda has started to challenge the dominance of the eye in this discipline (Adams and Guy, 2007). At the forefront is the work by the Finnish architect Pallasmaa (2005), who argues that architecture – the building of physical spaces – has been reduced for too long to a visual, aesthetic enterprise which focuses too much on maps and the drawing board. Instead, Pallasmaa proposes an architecture steeped in the specific embodied perception of buildings and places: '[e]very touching experience of architecture is multisensory; qualities of space, matter and scale are measured equally by the eye, ear, nose, skin, tongue, skeleton and muscle' (2005: 41).

Arguably the hardest challenge has been to find a language to write about these more visceral, corporeal and emotional qualities that comprise urban life. The difficulty lies not so much in how to communicate sensory, visceral experiences verbally but, more importantly, in how to 'translate' these non-linear and non-narrative moments of experiencing and being-in-the world.[1] To date academics have appropriated a range of different media from non-linear writing styles (Stewart, 2007), the use of photographs (Edensor, 2005), maps (Lynch, 1979) or more recently websites (for an overview see Rose et al., 2009) and film (Kosinets and Belk, 2007). Work linked to 'non-representational theory', led by Nigel Thrift has noted that we might have to experiment and find different, less linear forms of research and expression to capture or convey adequately some of these 'non-discursive' experiences in the city (Amin and Thrift, 2002; Thrift, 2004). This school of thought suggests viewing the city as a pulsating force-field of encounters between all kinds of entities such as bodies, materials, passions or technologies (Amin and Thrift, 2002: 84) and to focus on moments, things, actions and events in order to capture these evasive experiences that move beyond the remits of representation (see also Buckingham and Degen, 2012).

As we have seen, a range of scholars from different disciplines have developed a variety of theories about how sensory perception frames and is framed by the social world. Possibly the most prevalent argument is that while the visual might be regarded as the dominant sense, it is embedded and folded through the other senses. A less challenged argument has been that much of the existing literature on the senses tends to be theorised from the position of 'a singular body'. Yet, bodies are highly differentiated. Bodies are male, female, single, parent, white, black, young, old, able or disabled, and so on, and they engage in a variety of ways with the world. The point I am making here is that our particular embodiment shapes our perceptual awareness of the world. Studies on disability (Butler and Parr, 1999; Gleeson, 2002; Imrie, 1996), for example, have called attention to the way the physical environment impairs people's movement and experiences in the city. A study on visually impaired people[2] (Anvik, 2009) shows how the body actively adapts to perceive and manage the environment through the senses, not as a 'compensation strategy' for the lack of

---

1 I have to thank Iliana Ortega-Alcazar for highlighting this point to me.

2 Thanks to Donna Reeve for making me aware of this article.

sight, but by constructing alternative scopes of action and relations to space, as one research participant states:

> I think sighted people under-estimate the 'feeling' of space. As a blind person you are able, at least when you are on own ground, to feel you are placed in the right position in relation to where you are heading. In the pedestrian area of my town centre for instance, I know and experience space through the way I feel the ground, how the sounds and the echoes of the street are, what kinds of smells there are and lots of other sensations. [...] (Quoted in Anvik, 2009: 155)

Anvik's (2009) work highlights the importance of bodily practice and sensing in the construction of space. As she explains, space cannot be reduced to a location but places are created in the engagement and relationship between the body and its physical surrounding. From an epistemological point of view this means 'to bring the body, with all its emotions, cognition, knowledge and experiences into both the methodological and analytical field' (Anvik, 2009: 147). In our recent research on urban experience in designed environments (Degen and Rose, 2012; Degen, Rose and Basdas, 2010; Rose, Degen and Basdas 2010; and see www.urban-experience.net) we applied such an embodied method, which we describe as 'walk-alongs' (see also Kusenbach, 2003). It consisted in accompanying individuals (sometimes with their families and friends) in their routine uses of the town centre, from walking with them to get a sandwich in their 30-minute lunch break, to spending three to four hours with them on a Saturday shopping spree. Our aim was to gain access to their immediate sensing and embodiment in spaces. We recorded the spatial use and feeling of the space through our own embodied experience while simultaneously observing participants' actions, movements and uses of bodies. As Lee and Ingold (2006) argue, walking with people, living and moving as others do, can bring us closer to understanding how different individuals perceive their multisensory environments and constitute place through everyday practices. While both in Anvik's research and our own one could argue that the researchers' presence affect individual's experiences, such participatory methods allow to engage, if only temporarily, in other people's experiential world and to consider this experience reflexively (see also Pink, 2008). In our research we found that different bodily practices in city centres such as shopping, caring, socialising or maintaining (i.e. the work done by cleaners, police or private security) can frame an individual's bodily sensing. The particular activities that our body (and mind) are involved in, inform our perceptual sensibilities and shape both the perceived environment and our bodily dispositions. So, for example, when socialising or caring for others such as children the surrounding urban space fades into the background and becomes a minimal perception, related to not walking into things while one is watching the child. What this points towards is that levels of perception are far from uniform, but are instead fluctuating. While our senses work together in offering information on the environment, our ears, nose and eyes might notice or engage more intensely with certain sensations while others are blanked out or get ignored. Sensing in the city is therefore not consistent but configured by changing intensities.

PLANNING CITIES AND SENSORY IDEOLOGIES

Every incursion into urban space – such as the introduction of new pavements, the addition or removal of trees, the sand-blasting of a building façade or the building or demolition of a building – transforms the sensescapes of this particular place and with it our urban experience. In our daily uses of the city we tend to forget that cities are human-made products and that, consequently, the morphology of the public spaces of the city structures and expresses the values of a society (Dovey, 1999; Lefebvre, 1991). Urban landscapes can be understood as ideological constructs whose physical structure reflects and maintains relations of power and the senses are crucial in mediating, structuring and contesting social power relations in space.

By analysing the historical development of cities such as Athens, Rome or Venice, Richard Sennett (1994) illustrates how the physical spatial order, social relations and public imaginary of places are intricately linked by underlying sensory regimes. These sensory regimes order, divide and structure spaces to serve particular interests and influence social relationships in the city: 'The spatial relations of human bodies obviously make a great deal of difference in how people react to each other, how they see and hear one another, whether they touch or are distant' (Sennett, 1994: 17). A good example of this sensory ordering of social relations is the Jewish quarter of Venice built during the sixteenth century. Jewish inhabitants were regarded as a threat to trading relations and associated with destabilising the existing Christian order of the city and polluting properties. Hence they were segregated into a marginal area of the city, the ghetto (literally meaning the place were the foundry was located), so that other people would 'no longer [have] to touch and see them' (Sennett, 1994: 216). As this example shows, the senses play a determining role in establishing socio-geographical meanings and social hierarchies in the social production of space. We can explore this point further by examining how smells in particular have guided the development of the western urban form.

In his study of the changing role of smell in French society, Corbin (1986) illustrates how in the eighteenth and nineteenth centuries the olfactory sense featured predominantly in medical and public health theories and thus played a vital role in shaping their view of the world. Indeed, it was believed that illness and death could travel through bad air, as putrid odours were regarded to be the materialisation of infection. The control of currents and ventilation became crucial in urban planning as well as the conscious implementation of spatial distance and the uncrowding of private and public places was regarded as ways of preventing illness. Paris was radically restructured according to the rules of Baron Haussmann who became Napoleon III's chief urban planner in 1853 and purified the city by demolishing great parts of working-class housing, and building grand boulevards and parks in Paris that would brush out the darkness of the city and its foul smells. As Corbin points out, the most obvious threats 'which aroused the vigilance of sanitary reformers were the odors of excrement, corpses and decaying carcasses' (1986: 27) – a stench that was covering Paris. Famously the new urban structure was also designed to control the potential revolutionary, unruly behaviour of the poor: 'The width of these streets was finely calculated moreover in terms of Hausmann's fears of the movement of crowds in revolt. The street width permitted two army wagons to travel abreast, enabling the militia, if necessary to fire into communities lying beyond the sides of the street wall' (Sennett, 1994: 330).

In the nineteenth century a major shift occurred in the social imagination of smell which started to equate foul smells not only with death and illness but also with filth, dirt, poverty and misery. Strong odours became associated with the lower social classes, adding a sense of disgust and fear of illness. Soon the working classes were associated with fetidity and dirt, 'the secretions of poverty' regarded as precisely stemming from their social disorder and undisciplined behaviour. Across Europe cities started to follow Paris' lead and overthrew their medieval city walls, relocating businesses with unpleasant smells outside the city, and widening roads. Businesses such as abattoirs or skin yards where the smells of rotting meat and putrefying skin lingered day and night were relocated in more peripheral locations, often close to working-class housing, which throws up questions about environmental justice that are still pertinent today as we witness the relocation of toxic factories in developing countries next to densely lived areas. City reformers supported the idea that sunshine and the circulation of air purified and the ruling classes were eager to separate themselves from the unruly lower classes that were perceived to live amongst, and emanate, strong odours, and moved out of the 'old city' into new spacious bourgeois residences. Gradually smell started to define the social and moral order in the city and increasingly played a determining role in urban spatialisation:

> Haussman's policies could be interpreted – and not unreasonably – as a 'social dichotomy of purification' … a social division of stench … now in force in the city […]. [I]t was thought that purification requirements must be selective, quite apart from the fact that disinfecting the space reserved for bourgeois activities could only enhance property values. Wealth increased when the volume of refuse and the strength of its stench decreased. On the other hand, purifying rented premises crowded with apathetic workers would do nothing for the time being but add inordinately to landlord's expenses. The quest for profit strengthened this social distribution of odours. (Corbin 1986: 134–5)

As this quote highlights, the smellscape of places and their associated social imagery determined the economic value of places. To put it simply, the salubriousness of places was determined by economic interests, which, as we will see, is still a dominant feature in contemporary urban regeneration projects.

From the above discussion we can conclude that sensory frameworks are an important element in the planning of the city, needed to maintain a particular social order in place. Yet, what determines the right order in cities? The work of Mary Douglas (1966) is helpful here – she explains that what makes spaces *ordered* is that they are regarded as pure:

> [D]irt is essentially disorder. There is no such thing as absolute dirt: it exists in the eye of the beholder. If we shun dirt, it is not because of craven fear,

still less dread or holy terror. [...] Dirt offends against order. Eliminating is
not a negative movement, but a positive effort to organize the environment.
(1966: 68)

Again, we can see here how sensory dimensions, mainly visual and tactile, underpin
the ordering of the environment. By eliminating or avoiding unwanted sensuous experience we construct pure, structured environments. Sensory ideological dimensions
are implicit in urban renewal schemes which order place, as they delineate what is the
right order, what is pure – what is considered as dirt. However, such classification
schemes are not just limited to places but also apply to people. The work on 'geographies of exclusion' by Sibley (1995) clearly illustrates how associations, images of
places and the perception of their inhabitants are informed by cultural discourses of
purity which lead to subtle exclusionary practices, and are shaped by those in power.
For Sibley, exclusionary practices are based on particular notions of purity that regard
anything outside this artificially constructed realm as imperfect and inferior:

> Exclusionary discourse draws particularly on colour, disease, animals, sexu-
> ality and nature, but they all come back to the idea of dirt as a signifier of
> imperfection and inferiority, the reference point being the white, often male,
> physically and mentally able person. (1995: 14)

Drawing on Douglas, he argues that those that do not fit into a group's classification scheme are those that are considered 'impure', as polluting the environment
through their mere presence, secreting sensory pollution. As Cresswell (1996) further illustrates, through his discussion of travellers or graffiti artists, people themselves are regarded as carriers of threatening disorder. Unsurprisingly, much city
planning is precisely concerned with the control of spatial movement and spatial
segregation. Social hierarchies are played out in space through sensory descriptions,
or associations help to define who and what is pure or impure, who is allowed in a
place, who is considered 'out of place'. Perceptions and feelings attached to sensory
experiences are filled with ideological values. Hence, we can talk of sensory ideologies which are socially constructed and therefore raced, classed and gendered. These
sensory ideologies influence how people perceive themselves and others in space
and what sensory perceptions are considered to be legitimate in public space. The
construction of urban place is not only a geographical, political or economic matter
but intersects with socio-cultural expectations, in particular with social perceptions
of the senses (Dawkins and Loftus, 2013). Urban planning's concerns with maintaining (social) order, purifying the city from social groups that are identified
as polluting and dangerous and thereby controlling fear in the city, have actively
informed modernist and contemporary planning. The modernist city, with its aim
to counter the excess and chaotic development of the industrial city, famously
focused on rationality and functional organisation. The visual sense was given priority
alongside the facilitation of movement. Rationalisation had inevitable effects on the
character of public space, which became more functional as streets transformed
from being places for encounters, to become places of flow and consumption.

Similarly, the use of new materials such as concrete, glass and steel facilitated the building of individualised mass-produced housing, such as the tower block. Sennett (1990) describes this as the 'compulsive neutralization' of modern city planning. The aim of this 'transparent city', symbolised by the increased use of glass, can be understood as wanting to achieve complete visibility, without exposure to other senses. This emphasis on spatial (and sensory) distance and visibility in the modern city can be read as aiding the neutralisation of strangehood and the controlled exposure to the unknown.

The need to manage, control and manipulate sensory experience is still very much at the forefront of contemporary urban development and policy. Much research on contemporary urban change has focused on the visual attempts by local authorities, planners and developers to redesign and beautify city centres, creating a new optical order and emphasising the 'aesthetisation' or stylisation of the urban space (Boyer, 1988; Hubbard, 1996; Zukin, 1995), yet neglects to attend to how the other senses play an active role in the transformation of the environment. Similarly, studies on the experience of these new urban environments tend to emphasise visual reactions by city users. Yet, as I will show in the rest of this chapter, urban regeneration is put into effect through a conscious re-organisation of all the sensescapes and transgressed, accepted or resisted through the whole human sensorium.

CONTEMPORARY URBAN LIVING AND THE SENSES

Most western cities suffered major disinvestment and decline in the late 1960s and 1970s due to a combination of factors such as economic downturn, de-industrialisation and suburbanisation. During the 1980s a range of political and economic changes took place that would deeply alter the development of cities. Spearheaded by the US and UK governments, a new culture of deregulation, privatisation and liberalisation grew across the globe which would dramatically affect urban politics and planning (Hall and Hubbard, 1998; Harvey, 1989a). In fact, a new spatial logic emerged, reflected in major urban restructuring, as modernist industrialism was replaced by post-industrial flexible accumulation (Harvey, 1989a, 1989b). Simultaneously cities across the globe began to acquire more power as the hold of the nation state was regarded as diminishing in providing the main regulatory force for a new global economy. Hence, cities actively started to compete with each other to attract an ever more footloose global investment in the form of financial and legal services, the leisure and retail industry, international corporations or tourism.

As the 'urban question' moved towards an emphasis of economic rejuvenation through global markets, city policies moved from a concern for welfare issues and social politics to economic politics, hence from managerial forms of governance to an entrepreneurial approach (see Harvey, 1989a, 1989b). The effect on the urban landscape, from cities in the global south such as São Paolo, Kuala Lumpur or Johannesburg to those in the global north such as Chicago, Manchester or Moscow, has been an astonishing degree of investment and development that has 'seen cities across the world take on a new character and a new dynamic that has forced issues of culture and consumption more predominantly to the fore' (Hetherington and Cronin, 2008: 1).

Let us examine in more detail the social and public life that these regenerated landscapes produce. While urban renewal is nothing new, each urban restructuring period has had distinct aesthetic values and spatial ideologies ingrained in them. What has been distinctive to urban change since the 1990s is an explicit focus on stylisation and use of urban design, often understood as a concern with visual coherence, to frame spatial identity. This attentiveness to the visual and wider experiential impact of place needs to be understood as part of cities' trend to market themselves as attractive investment locations so that 'city space and architectural forms become consumer items or packaged environments that support and promote the circulation of goods' (Boyer, 1988: 54). Consequently, environmental improvement schemes feature strongly in regeneration projects, aiming to erase the 'aura' of marginality and decline of places, which is perceived to be ingrained in their public spaces through obsolete sensescapes:

> Physical renewal is usually a necessary if not sufficient condition for successful regeneration. In some instances it may be the main engine of regeneration. In almost all cases it is an important visible sign of commitment to change and improvement. (Jeffrey and Pounder, 2000: 86)

Hence, the first step of a regeneration scheme is to rearrange the spatial and sensory order of space within particular aesthetic parameters. As Miles and Miles (2004) point out, while city centres have historically tended to reflect an eclectic mix of historical styles without a unifying theme, contemporary developments increasingly use an overarching aesthetic code reflected in matching textures, colours, use of materials, an emphasis on spatio-visual landscaping and consistent theming of an area. Indeed, one can identify the emergence of a similar global urban aesthetic as the physical, spatial and sensory landscape is redesigned and stylised according to a common script that successfully sells on an international market (Degen, 2008). Yet, what does this global urban aesthetic consist of and how is it implemented?

A run-down working-class neighbourhood, red-light district or dilapidated industrial zone within the city centre is earmarked for redevelopment. It is often defined as a 'no-go' area for residents of the city, shunned either because it is associated with poverty, urban decline and desolation due to years of disinvestment by local authorities. Its sensescapes reflect different stages of decay and marginality. In some cities this sensory geography might reflect a waning working-class life: a bustling street-life; the sound of people eating and watching television slipping out of open windows; the smell of food being prepared; or street-vendors loudly selling their goods. In other cities one might encounter the carcases of once thriving industrial neighbourhoods: empty, grey, ruinous buildings; a musty smell mixed with urine; closed shop shutters and overgrown pathways. Crucially, these places are sensuously opposed to the modern, forward-looking and efficient business-oriented picture that the city wants to portray to a global audience – and that the area is profitable real estate. Hence, the regeneration scheme aims to achieve what Miles (2000) has termed a 'cultural-recoding' of place – a physical re-organisation of the sensory-spatial landscape that brushes away any controversial or negative associations with the past. This strategy is complemented by a careful regulation of the activities, uses and, thus, sensory experiences available in the neighbourhood. Through a conscious management of the sensory modalities in the neighbourhood, social groups, place identities and spatial practices get shifted around, controlled, supported or erased. An excellent account of the contradictory effects that global capital has on the everyday lived experience of urban space is offered by Huang (2004) in her analysis of East Asian cities. By focusing on the private, sensory experience of walking in Shanghai, Hong Kong and Tokyo as represented in film, and juxtaposing the contradictory impact that the global landscape of skyscrapers produces next to traditional dwellings, she shows how 'the lived space of everyday life is shrinking to make room for rezoning, construction of infrastructures, space modification – all in the name of urban development' (2004: 11).

To illustrate these rather abstract claims, let us take as an example the regeneration of Castlefield in Manchester, UK. Once part of the industrial centre of Manchester's cotton industry after the Second World War it became a forgotten space in the city; an industrial wasteland. Manchester City Council soon realised the potential of an area of industrial warehouses, canals and large open spaces close to the city centre for tourism and real-estate development and nominated Castlefield Britain's first Urban Heritage Park in 1979. To invite people into this once shunned area, a new landscape was produced which involved emptying the basin area of unsightly businesses that permeated Castlefield with the uncontrollable smells and sounds of car-repair workshops or scrap-yards. Sights or buildings

Figure 6.3   Castlefield after the regeneration (photo: Mónica Degen)

that might reflect social inequalities or echo uncomfortable memories such as broth-els, poor working-class housing or abattoirs were demolished. Canals were cleaned, hollowed out and expanded further into the area, so that their glittering surfaces would be easily visible from the main access road. To attract visitors, new paths and benches were built in to offer vantage points as part of a tourist trail to visually consume the superimposed layers of Castlefield's hygienised history.

It is common in these types of developments that formerly cluttered and sensuously oppressive spaces are given a makeover and transformed into spacious, ordered, light-coloured environments. New design is mixed with sandblasted heritage features – hence providing through the sanitised past an element of place distinction and also connoting with the use of contemporary design the city's forward-looking, entrepre-neurial spirit. Places are reinvented to conform to twenty-first-century sensibilities and economies. What stands out in contemporary regeneration schemes is the expres-sive concern about the quality of public space. Hence, they tend to include flagship public spaces, in the case of Castlefield the Outdoor Event Arena, which is a vast, 3,500m^2 stage for events and performances inaugurated in 1993. The surrounding history is transformed into heritage, re-coded as a cultural asset, and buildings' mean-ings are altered by new cultural uses: a Sunday school becomes a furniture design business; warehouses transform into exclusive lofts; a hospital becomes a hotel. Increasingly, cities rely on analogous spatial techniques, using a common design lan-guage despite local differences, homogenising the look of place and thereby making regenerated spaces experientially interchangeable. The sensory values embedded in this global 'designer heritage aesthetic' are those of order, purity and cleanliness.

Alongside restructuring the built environment, the key purpose of regeneration is to attract new users and spatial practices, thus to create a particular form of public life, often defined in the regeneration plans as 'vibrant', 'cosmopolitan' or 'mixed-use' – suggesting that what was there before did not fulfil these criteria (for a critique, see Degen, 2008; Lees, 2003a). Depending on the overall organising concept of the regeneration – whether it is retail, culture, leisure or housing-led – particular types of businesses, activities and policies are put into place to stimulate specific uses and practices. In Castlefield, an up-market 'Mediterranean leisure lifestyle' became the organising concept behind its redevelopment. Castlefield was marketed as an exclusive place, offering expensive residential living and using its water features as an attraction. Furthermore, in accordance with Manchester's aim to support '24 hour city living', café culture was promoted in the area by opening a string of designer bars alongside the canals, all with extended licensing times. Convivial sensescapes such as the mellow sound of laughter and chatter coming from bars, music from buskers, and the odours and tastes of European-style food were expected to settle in the area. A range of Mediterranean-themed open-air events were organised in the open spaces, purposefully designed to cater for a middle-class taste, playing jazz or world music.

Social groups that lacked the disposable income or middle-class cultural capital were not targeted and felt excluded by the events. Indeed, the working-class uses and sensescapes promoted by the staging of a regular bank-holiday market on Castlefield's main through-road – where vendors and customers would haggle loudly over cheap clothing and bric-à-brac; where the whiffs of juicy burgers would mix with the sweet smell of sugary doughnuts and the jolly-go-round tunes of a children's fun-fair – were regarded as unsuitable for Castlefield's quality regeneration scheme by its mainly middle-class residents and city officials and therefore closed in 2000. We can see here, how the spatial practices and sensory landscapes implemented by regeneration bodies aim to submit areas to a new public life by manipulating the sensory geography and thereby attracting or deflecting the uses and engagements by particular social groups. However, this is not a straightforward process, and spatial contestations emerge as different groups make their claims to the city. So, as the bars and cafés of Castlefield became more popular in the mid-1990s they started to attract a greater number of customers, in the summer easily reaching 10,000. Simultaneously more residential developments were built. Soon conflicts emerged between the sensescapes produced by the bar crowd – pumping music, loud screaming and singing, the stench of beer, empty bottles on the ground – and the residents' expectations of an exclusive and quiet lifestyle. Indeed, residents perceived these sociable sensescapes as overpowering Castlefield's more sedate European atmosphere. Most bars in Castlefield have now closed as other areas of the city have become more fashionable. We can conclude from this that while city officials aim to adopt strategies to fix sensory perceptions and control the lived experience of places, sensory experiences are fluid, evasive and slippery and thus get constantly reworked, embedded and lived through local practices (see also Law, 2001 for an excellent account on how Filipino domestic workers subvert both the dominant cultural sensescapes of Hong Kong).

While my discussion of sensory planning ideologies shows that the trend to control urban experience is nothing new, the increased pressure on cities to brand themselves and promote their unique place-differentiating qualities to investors, residents and visitors has led to a more conscious engineering of urban atmospheres (Ashworth and Kavaratzis, 2007; Degen et al., forthcoming; Julier, 2007; Klingman, 2007). This emphasis on branding means that cities have moved from the external promotion of particular venues, sights or activities to constructing coherent place identities that will appeal to particular social groups, similar to commercial product. Branding consists of constructing particular sets of associations, establishing particular meanings and lifestyles that are linked to the consumption of a product, so that 'everything a city consists of, everything that takes place in the city and is done by the city, communicates messages about the city's brand, in the same way that this is true for corporations' (Karavatzis, 2009: 34). While there is as yet no agreement on a single successful branding formula, urban branding relies on the combination of both the hard and soft attributes of the city; from the attractiveness of the urban landscape or transport and communication networks to the existence of a vibrant lifestyle or the assurance of safety (see Kavaratzis, 2009 for an overview). These softer qualities that relate to the atmosphere – the 'feel' of a place – are those mediated through bodily sensations. The rising importance of culture as an economic motor, has led city governments to increasingly pay attention to these 'soft' qualities of urban perception and consciously manage and produce unique 'place-distinguishing' urban cultures and lifestyles (Degen, 2010). Howes notes how the senses have become central in contemporary product branding: 'Just as product design (functionality) has been subsumed within sensory design (aesthetics), so the idea of brand image has been superseded by brand sense. Whereas brands used to be distinguished by their name and visual logo, now the idea is that they should ideally register as many senses as possible' (Howes, 2007: 1). Howes further argues that the five senses are progressively enrolled to establish a distinctive and memorable brand experience. Contemporary urban regeneration and the branding strategies that go hand-in-hand with the promotion of neighbourhoods can be seen as an extension of this trend into the urban realm. The currency that contemporary cities trade in is not just their image but the lived experience that they promise. The sensuously perceived 'ambience' is as important as the physical location itself. Ironically, because of the standardisation in the architectural appearance of cities due to globalisation processes such as regeneration, intangible features such as local public life or the local 'feel' provide the necessary differentiating aspects (and images) for city developers and marketers. Concurrently, as the cleansing powers of regeneration schemes brush through the city, new bohemians and trendy tourists actively search for the next 'cool neighbourhood' that provides richer, less controlled and more complex sensory experiences. As Zukin critically suggests, it becomes the hunt for an 'idea' of authenticity, a search for aesthetic codes, sensory experiences and forms of consumption outside the mainstream, so that 'the cutting edge becomes "the next new thing" and soon enough, "the next neighbourhood" of gentrification' (2008: 745).

BARCELONA: SENSING URBAN CHANGE

Figure 6.4   Plaça dels Angels, El Raval, Barcelona (photo: Mónica Degen)

During the 1980s Barcelona's city council started to redevelop El Raval, once the city's infamous red-light district. With the nomination of Barcelona to host the Olympic Games in 1992 it became imperative to transform the city centre and exploit the occasion as an image-building exercise to market Barcelona as a truly avant-garde and cultural city. Not surprisingly, the regeneration of El Raval consisted of designating this working-class neighbourhood as a new 'cultural quarter' and thereby attracting a range of new cultural infrastructures such as universities, research centres and cultural institutions. Its flagship development became starchitect Richard Meier's Museum of Contemporary Art. Walking across El Raval's narrow streets, with balconies almost touching each other above, one is quickly sensuously immersed in the local life, having to negotiate the sidewalk with people and beeping mopeds; being assaulted by a cacophony of TV blaring, voices and hammering tools coming from shops and balconies; and being subjected to the musty smell of the sea nearby mixed with sewage and urine sometimes, and clean laundry or food at other times. And then, suddenly one stands in a vast minimalist square, the Plaça dels Angels, lacking any seating or decoration, yet serving as a visual stage to Meier's imposing modernist white building. Due to its scale, smells do not linger as readily, sounds are muffled, tactility is minimised by the smooth surfaces, no street furniture disrupts their uniformity. A hierarchical relation of the senses is afforded by the spatial design of the environment in which the sensuous rhythms of the place heighten the visual sense, whereas odours, sounds and tactile experiences are transformed into a supporting feature.

At first these new regenerated spaces stood in stark contrast to the rest of the neighbourhood; however, over time locals have appropriated these spaces, especially the square in front of the Museum of Contemporary Art, and gradually they have become immersed into the sensory rhythms of El Raval. In the morning dog-walkers let their pets defecate on this square, and groups of skate-boarders take over the ramps of the museum – their rattling rhythms mixing with the chattering voices from young tourists and locals that gather with beers in the early evening, while the homeless people assemble their cardboard shelters in the cavities of the museum. The order and purity imposed by the 'designer heritage aesthetic' becomes sullied by the manifold sounds, smells and textures as it is digested within the neighbourhood's daily life.

Figure 6.5   Contrasting sensescapes, new and old in El Raval, Barcelona (photo: Mónica Degen)

CONCLUSION

Focusing on the senses in urban life connects the lived, imagined and physical city. Cities are not just material, economic or political landscapes but actively experienced and therefore lived entities. The senses reveal city living as an ongoing, embodied and active process, a constant negotiation between an imposed order and individual agency. While dominant groups try to shape and direct sensory, and thereby social, relations in the city, individuals personalise, appropriate or adapt to these sensescapes in a variety of ways. As I have shown, contemporary urban redevelopment does not only restructure the city physically and economically but radically transforms its somatic landscape. The re-framing of the sensory landscape through physical urban development is supported and enhanced though a broader array of urban policies (e.g. event policies, zoning policies, policies that regulate opening times and environmental sound pollution) that aim to control the bodily sensations and experiences available, which I have described as a *management of atmospheres*. These processes may also be understood as the creation of new moral and civic landscapes organised around particular aesthetic and cultural values to attract a middle-class public. As Pine and Gilmore highlight, in the contemporary 'experience economy', 'experiences represent an existing but previously inarticulate genre of economic output' (1999: ix). So, on the one hand, one could argue that we are witnessing a standardisation and, even in some cases, a commercialisation of urban sensations as public life and spaces become branding tools to sell the reinvented city on a global circuit. Yet, simultaneously, urban life evades being captured as diverse social groups appropriate these new spaces in unexpected ways, imposing their own sensory meanings and uses. Ultimately, researching the senses not only offers a new lens to understand urban conditions but provides a practical sensuous framework to assess the subtler politics in everyday spaces where tensions are palpable.

Paedagogic Guide Listing

Websites

www.urban-experience.net
www.bbc.co.uk/worldservice/specialreports/saveoursounds.shtml
www.emotionmap.net

Films

Lost in Translation (for thinking through urban life and the senses, sensory overload, cultural differences and senses).
Be Kind Rewind (a good analysis of gentrification, sensory attachments, the link between sense of place and attachments).
Slumdog Millionaire (for offering an insight on the sensescapes of slum living).

Books and Journals

Degen, M. (2008) *Sensing Cities: Regenerating Public Life in Barcelona and Manchester*. London: Routledge.
Rodaway, P. (1994) *Sensuous Geographies: Body, Sense and Place*. London: Routledge.
The Senses & Society – a journal which presents cutting-edge research around the senses.

SECTION 3

THE LIVEABLE CITY

7

Dis/Order and the Regulation of Urban Space

Steve Herbert and Tiffany Grobelski

INTRODUCTION

If you visit Seattle as a tourist, there is a good chance you will make your way to Pioneer Square. The area is on the National Register of Historical Places, a testament to both its centrality to Seattle history and its well-preserved architecture, much of which dates to the late 1800s. The Pioneer Square area was important to the American Indians who lived there prior to Anglo-European settlement (Thrush, 2008) and served as the economic hub of the city in its early industrial development. Today, it lies just to the south of the financial district with its towering skyscrapers, and just to the north of two large sports stadiums.

One of the main tourist attractions in the neighbourhood is the Underground Tour. The Tour takes its guests underneath the streets of contemporary Seattle to visit an even older version of the city. The underground buildings predate the great Seattle fire of 1889, which destroyed much of the downtown. When Seattle rebuilt after the fire, it raised downtown's elevation because the previous urban grid was at sea level. For a city whose sewage system drained directly to the adjacent Puget Sound, this lack of elevation was problematic; at high tide, materials were more likely to flow in rather than out. What remained after the fire was preserved, and provides tourists an opportunity to imagine life in 1880s Seattle.

Unsurprisingly, the Tour emphasises the rough-hewn nature of that era. As a port city whose economic engine was the timber industry, Seattle attracted hundreds of itinerant men, whose thirst for vice was not easily slaked. Single-room occupancy hotels became common, as did saloons and houses of prostitution. In the hands of the Tour's operators, the disorderly nature of early Seattle is transformed into a tourist commodity.

When tourists exit the Underground Tour, they are very likely to encounter another manifestation of what many call disorder – a significant number of homeless people. Pioneer Square's history includes a long-standing role for missions and other forms of social support for the disadvantaged. Today, several emergency shelters and day service centres continue to draw the downtrodden to Pioneer Square. Many of those individuals cluster in one of three city parks, one of which abuts the Underground Tour's offices.

This is a version of disorder that is unwelcome to many in Seattle. Indeed, Seattle is an American city with an unusually robust effort to monitor and potentially arrest those without homes and others who spend considerable time in public space (Gibson, 2003). A leader in the development of so-called 'civility codes' – which penalised a range of behaviours in which the homeless regularly engage (see Mitchell, 1997) – Seattle now employs an even more stringent effort at social control. This regime of control essentially relies on various forms of trespass law to exclude people from large swathes of the city. Once excluded from a place, individuals are subject to arrest if they reappear (see Beckett and Herbert, 2009).

This brief story from Seattle illustrates one of the central tensions in urban life. On the one hand, cities are regularly celebrated as places where heterogeneity is welcomed, where a range of experiences is possible, where licentious behaviour is allowed and even encouraged. In a city, one can encounter a variety of ways of life, and can expand one's horizons in unexpected ways. The hustle and bustle of urban life is exciting because its turbulence generates uncertainty. Banal predictability gives way to the thrill of the new and unexpected. In this way, some lack of order is considered a public good, and a reason to be an urbanite. Sennett (1992), for example, touts the 'uses of disorder' as opportunities for personal growth, just as Young (1990) celebrates cities as places where we can daily encounter social difference and thereby learn to practise more capacious forms of citizenship.

On the other hand, some forms of disorder are regularly shunned. Vagrants, street alcoholics, prostitutes and homeless people rarely find a welcome place in urban space. Their ostracism is historically commonplace (Chambliss, 1964; Dubber, 2005; Sibley, 1995). In many cities in the United States, and increasingly the rest of the world, this repulsion is exercised through strong policing tactics that make the disadvantaged a constant target for surveillance and potential arrest. Their presence is linked to crime (Wilson and Kelling, 1982) and seen as a threat to business (Ellickson, 1996). The urban downtrodden are marginalised in multiple ways.

At the same time, the flow of urban life must be subjected to some constraints to make daily time–space patterns manageable. All manner of mechanisms exist to order the flow of goods, people and services, from the formal rules of traffic to the informal manoeuvres that prevent sidewalk collisions. Despite their confusing swirls of heterogeneity, cities remain surprisingly ordered places.

We use this chapter to explore the importance of both order and disorder in urban life. Cities are impossible to imagine without each of these linked concepts, because each is central to the urban experience. Order provides multiple public goods – it enables the efficient flow of people and products; it helps ensure public health; it provides psychic comfort to urbanites. Yet disorder is just as central to cities. Confusion, movement and difference are inherent to the urban experience. Indeed, this vibrancy and sense of adventure is what attracts many people to cities. Litter, congestion and outlandishness cannot be avoided in vibrant cities.

However, it is no easy matter to define just what constitutes order and disorder, and to decide how they are to be balanced against one another. For this reason, the politics of order are consistently robust. Further, the regulation of order requires a strong role for the police, whose visible presence in everyday life makes them a perpetual focal point for a range of symbolic politics (Herbert, 1996; Manning, 1977). Indeed, one can learn much about the political climate within a given city through an investigation of how order is defined and maintained.

We move through four sections in this investigation of urban order and disorder. In the first, we review the various mechanisms by which cities are rendered orderly, and explain the various functions that order helps to accomplish. In the second, we explain how and why disorder is also an unavoidable component of urban life, and explore its significance. In the third, we illustrate how the tension between these two concepts can generate a volatile politics, and we provide an in-depth exploration of these politics through an analysis of recent controversies over so-called 'broken windows' policing. In the fourth section, we review the analysis and offer some observations about the continuing symbolic significance of order and disorder in cities.

ORDER IN THE CITY

If you are an urbanite, you are likely to be highly mobile. You must move from home to work or school, you need to visit friends and family, you wish to get to a restaurant or a movie or a concert. To accomplish all of these time–space manoeuvres, you plan accordingly and you profit from past experiences. You learn bus and train routes, you master traffic patterns well enough to know which streets to favour at what times, you generate a well-developed sense of the time required to get to particular destinations. As you move through urban space, you encounter hundreds, perhaps thousands of other city dwellers. You pass them on the sidewalk, you sit next to them on the bus, you cruise past their cars on city streets. Although you might bump shoulders or otherwise engage in slight contact with another person, a typical city sojourn involves no physical interactions at all. And, quite often, you arrive at your destination right on time.

This navigation of urban space is so commonplace it is unremarkable; it occurs millions of times a day in a typical city. But it is no small accomplishment, on both an individual and collective level. In fact, this production of urban order relies on a wide array of formal and informal mechanisms.

The government does much to generate this order. It provides regularity to the landscape through zoning laws. It builds and maintains the infrastructure to enable the flow of traffic – of people, of machines, of various forms of waste. It creates and arms police forces who insinuate themselves in daily life to attempt to instill order.

Order is also generated through cooperation between the government and the private sector. Local urban authorities increasingly work in partnerships with businesses to 'revitalise' downtown areas – make them attractive places to visit, live and work. City regeneration efforts often focus on crime control, where certain spaces, especially those reserved for higher-end consumption, are closely monitored for appropriate behaviour (see the 'CCTV' box below). Private companies are being given greater discretion in the control of such spaces and in defining who should be the target of such control (Coleman and Sim, 2000; Coleman et al., 2005).

But order is not just an effect of government or public–private action. It arises just as much from millions of unscripted actions, most of them engaged in unconsciously by urbanites. Consider a busy city sidewalk. Though crowded, such sidewalks rarely witness much physical contact. That is because of the infinite and infinitesimal manoeuvrings that occur – the anticipations of others' movements, the slight anglings of shoulders, the sudden accelerations and decelerations. This collective ballet represents one of many informal practices that make cities surprisingly orderly.

Cities would not function without both these formal and informal ordering mechanisms. Order provides multiple benefits. For starters, the economic underpin-nings of cities require it. Cities are centres for the production and circulation of goods and services. These activities require the efficient movement of people and materials. Cars, trucks, trains, ships and planes must move in and out according to somewhat predictable timetables. Workers and shoppers must be able to arrive at their destinations within certain parameters. And the experience of movement should be as smooth and uninterrupted as possible (Phillips and Smith, 2006).

Waste must also flow efficiently. Economic production often generates copious amounts of pollution which need to be channelled to minimise threats to health and well-being. Trash and sewage must be disposed of appropriately. A significant amount of city planning thus is devoted to creating infrastructure to accomplish the orderly disposal of health-threatening substances.

Order also works to regulate social interactions. Despite their social heterogeneity, cities remain remarkably segregated places (Massey and Denton, 1991). Through a set of formal and informal practices, urbanites are sorted in urban space according to both class and race. Social divisions are reinforced through spatial divisions. And even in those milieu where different social groups are in close proximity, lines of separation persist. In his classic examination of a city beach, for example, Edgerton (1979) noted how urbanites maintained bubbles of privacy in a way that minimised interaction with others (see also Morrill et al., 2005). In a more drastic example of minimising interac-tion with different social groups, Caldeira (2000) characterises São Paulo, Brazil, as a city of walls. There, a proliferation of enclosed and monitored residential spaces ensures that, even though the physical distances between different social groups have decreased, they interact less. The private order thus created allows residents to avoid what they perceive to be the problems of the city. Yet these patterns of urban residen-tial segregation make it difficult to maintain what might be considered organising principles of life in modern cities: openness and free circulation (Caldeira, 1996).

In short, multiple collective manoeuvres – some deliberate, some unconscious – enable urbanites to share public space in a way that maximises access. This is another consequence of order. Public areas like parks and plazas are ostensibly open to all. Practices that generate order can work to ensure that people can enter, occupy and exit places with relative ease. In this way, people can share public space with minimal disruption. Think of the unspoken rules of forming lines and of taking turns that occur spontaneously at public gatherings. Without these, public order would regularly be threatened when urbanites gather in shared space.

As the above discussion suggests, the production of order in cities is enabled through both formal social control and informal social control. The former relies largely on the efforts of state authority; it is created through law and other forms of regulation, and is enforced by the police and other agents of coercive power. It is largely 'top-down' in its orientation. Informal social control is more 'bottom-up'; it arises from the workings of mundane interactions among city dwellers. It references the less coercive, but no less potent, forms of control that are enforced through gossip, baleful stares, ostracism and other forms of collective punishment. Each is critical to the processes of making cities orderly, and each is discussed in greater detail below.

The formal production of urban order

The complexity and heterogeneity of the city generate challenges that require a formal role for the state. The ability of urbanites to inhabit, modify, move through and share space requires that presumptively impartial state authorities regulate how space can be accessed and used. An impressive welter of laws exists to regulate land use and to define the parameters of allowable action. These laws are created and enforced by a large number of bureaucratic actors and organisations. Urban order could likely not exist without the formal pursuit of social control.

Zoning law is an obvious example of the formal imposition of order onto city space. Zoning works by apportioning urban space by land use and density. The categories for land uses typically include residential, commercial and industrial, although some zones allow some mix of these. Zoning can thus work to keep incompatible land uses segregated. For example, an industrial zone can be kept apart from housing developments. Zoning can also work to make some parts of the city denser than others. Some residential zones, for example, will include clusters of apartment buildings and other forms of multi-family dwellings. Many suburban neighbourhoods, by contrast, will be limited to single-family homes. Zoning and other restrictions, such as building codes, can regulate land use at a fairly minute scale. Rules can determine the look, height and width of buildings, their distance from the street and how much parking must be included. Such rules are often even more minute in private housing developments that possess their own codes and covenants. In these 'privatopias' (McKenzie, 1996), residents may be restricted on the colours they can use to paint their houses or whether they can possess an outdoor basketball hoop.

There is an obvious utility to zoning (Popper, 1988; Reps, 1965; Toll, 1969). Some land uses are less safe and more polluting than others. When these are separated from residential zones, public health is better protected. Further, if landowners seek to protect property values, then zoning can be beneficial. Someone who purchases a single-family home, for instance, appreciates any guarantees that zoning law can provide that only compatible land uses will remain adjacent to their properties. Through helping ease the movement of goods and services, and by providing some stability to real-estate markets, zoning aids in the preservation of daily capitalist activity (Underwood-Bultmann, 2010).

Yet there is little question that zoning can be a defensive gesture, an opportunity to ensure that people do not mingle with others who are less desirable. Suburban zoning practices, for example, have long been criticised as key mechanisms in maintaining class segregation (Dreier et al., 2005; K. Jackson, 1987; Teaford, 1979). When suburban land uses are restricted to large homes on large lots, then only the affluent can find a home there. In this way, homogeneity along lines of race, class and political allegiances can be maintained (McGirr, 2002). Zoning thus works to maintain capitalist relations and to perpetuate cultural distinctions.

The criminal law represents another major manifestation of formal social control. Urbanites are prohibited from all manner of behaviour and threatened with punishment when they offend. Laws regulate whether and when we can cross the street, where we can drive and park our cars, whether and where we can smoke cigarettes or drink alcohol, what drugs we can consume and the extent to which we can use violence to resolve disputes. Although most of us can go years without our behaviour generating any suspicion that would lead to interactions with formal agents of authority, the spectre of the criminal law hovers above all aspects of urban life. And the police, highly visible as they are in their uniforms and patrol cars, provide a potent symbol of the coercive authority that can be exercised in law's name.

Further, when the police act, their principal goal is to maintain order (Wilson, 1968). In most instances, the police do not actually enforce any law when they respond to an incident. Yet they invariably take action, typically with the intent of restoring some measure of peace (Bittner, 1967). The police's ability to successfully assert their authority to restore peace is deeply connected to their capacity to control territory (Herbert, 1997). Most exercises of police power involve convincing or forcing one or more individuals to relocate. This can occur quietly when an officer steps between disputants or more dramatically when an officer forcibly restrains a reluctant citizen.

The collective expectation that police will maintain socio-spatial order is made most obvious when public order fails, such as during instances of civil unrest. When order breaks down, and the police are unable to restore it – such as during the 'Rodney King' riots in Los Angeles in 1992 or the 'Battle of Seattle' during the World Trade Organization meetings in 1999 – the legitimacy of the police can suffer immensely (Herbert, 1997, 2007).

There are other mechanisms besides zoning and criminal law enforcement that manifest formal social control in action, but these examples hopefully suffice to illustrate how cities are importantly ordered through government action. Just as important to urban order, however, are informal means of ensuring social control.

CCTV

In 1993, in a town near Liverpool, a two-year-old boy was brutally murdered after being abducted from a shopping centre. Evidence from closed circuit television (CCTV) surveillance cameras was used to capture the offenders. This high-profile incident, along with changing national politics of law and order, led to a massive expansion of video surveillance in Britain, with little public debate or resistance

(Norris and Armstrong, 1999). Since then, CCTV has been an integral aspect of policing public space in Britain.

The development of CCTV in public spaces has largely been driven by efforts at city regeneration: creating a safe, consumer-oriented environment in the city centre. Behind such efforts are images of a modern tourist city that will attract investment and consumers. CCTV proponents argue that cameras can help create such an environment by detecting and deterring crime, and making people feel safer, thus increasing consumption-oriented visits to city centres. As such, construction of a CCTV scheme depends crucially on an alliance between the local government and private capital, giving business interests much discretion in deciding who poses a danger to city regeneration (Coleman and Sim, 2000; Coleman et al., 2005).

A much-debated aspect of public CCTV is the extent to which such systems provide security from criminal threat. Evidence suggests that CCTV is most effective not at controlling serious crimes, but low-level activities which are not illegal, such as loitering (Williams and Johnstone, 2000). Many who use crime data to bolster CCTV's effectiveness do not consider that CCTV may simply displace crime to areas not in view of the cameras, as well as divert police attention from those less protected spaces (Williams and Johnstone, 2000).

The presence of surveillance cameras may have various effects on safety – or perceptions of safety. Their presence may make people less likely to report incidents to the police (Fyfe and Bannister, 1996), hampering community policing efforts. In some cases, as with certain members of the homeless population in Vancouver and Toronto, vulnerable groups may feel safer in spaces under surveillance; what is captured on camera might validate claims of harassment or other abuse, providing some access to justice (Huey, 2010). Yet a well-established criticism of public CCTV is that it makes social judgements possible, protecting the affluent consumer class at the expense of marginalised groups (Graham and Wood, 2003).

CCTV systems, and other forms of increased surveillance, are being adopted in cities all over the world, sometimes with disconcerting results. In Mexico City, CCTV cameras on public transit and other types of digital surveillance were proposed in 2002 in an attempt to import New York's crime control policies. Yet a disregard of local circumstances, in particular Mexico City's lack of technological infrastructure, did not allow for meaningful implementation of such systems (Mountz and Curran, 2009). In Quito and Guayaquil – Ecuador's two largest cities – urban regeneration policies are being enacted in particularly repressive forms. Indigenous people, already historically excluded from Ecuadorian society, are being removed from a public space that is increasingly monitored and reserved for tourists (Swanson, 2010). Such urban policies, diffused from northern cities, can compound already deep inequality in the global south.

The informal production of urban order

The threat of formal punishment can serve as an inducement to behave in a particular fashion. Most of us prefer to avoid jail or to otherwise run afoul of the authorities. Yet we equally fear the disapproval of peers. We seek to avoid becoming the object of unflattering gossip. We want to be included, not excluded, by groups with whom we wish to associate. We seek not to attract disapproving looks. This fear of informal sanctions compels us to abide by often implicit norms. The daily patterns of cities are importantly enabled through the means by which informal social control can, in the words of Ellickson (1994), generate 'order without law'.

Think of typical behaviour in a public urban setting, such as at a bus stop or in a public park. Most of us engage in subtle behaviours to minimise our physical and verbal contact with others. At the same time, we are often quietly alert to what is occurring around us, so that we can react appropriately. If we are with friends, we generally observe norms about how loudly to interact with each other.

One way to appreciate the power of these informal rules is to consider how we feel and react when those rules are broken. When individuals are loud, when their physical appearance is unkempt or when their body odour is strong, most urbanites experience discomfort. Disruptions to the patterned existence of urban neighbour-hoods are a source of anxiety for city dwellers; their sense of daily security is max-imised when predictability is high (Herbert, 2006). As we live in and move through urban space, we expect others to abide by customs that regulate appearance, behaviour and interactions.

One custom that we expect people to observe is avoidance (Lofland, 1998). City dwellers presume that others will do all they can to uphold standards of privacy and civil inattention (Goffman, 1963). At a city beach, for instance, towels are used to mark space for oneself; they form an informal boundary that others are expected to respect (Edgerton, 1979). At other public areas, like bus stops, urbanites studi-ously avoid much contact, and only engage each other politely and quickly. This degree of avoidance is especially pronounced in suburban settings with large land lots (Baumgartner, 1991), but is present in city interactions, as well. Some of this avoidance is aimed at minimising the threat of danger. In crime-prone neighbour-hoods especially, residents become adept at reading places and people to make sure they lessen their vulnerability (Anderson, 1992; Ley, 1974; Merry, 1981).

Sometimes, however, city dwellers are active agents of informal social control. Elijah Anderson (1992), for example, stresses the important role of the 'old heads' in black-dominated urban areas. These are respected male elders who attempt to use their stature to influence young people. Jane Jacobs (1961), in her classic study of the life of cities, emphasises the importance of what she terms 'public characters' who help build a pattern of trust in urban neighbourhoods. Even those who are sometimes seen as impediments to informal social control, like street-level vendors, are actually strong agents of it. In his intensive ethnography of magazine vendors who operated on New York's streets, Mitchell Duneier (1999) found that they did much to infor-mally police each other, and to assist those with drug problems and other afflictions.

Of course, not all agents of informal social control are beneficial. Real-estate agents and bank officers, for example, continue to often use race in making deci-sions about what homes to show or whether to issue a home loan (Holloway and Wyly, 2001; Massey and Denton, 1991; Orfield and Ashkinaze, 1991). The implicit assumption appears to be that home-buyers wish to live near like-raced people. In this way, real-estate agents and loan officers work to reinforce urban segregation patterns. Similarly, employers are guilty of making similar assessments when mak-ing hiring decisions. As a consequence, black males, especially those with criminal records, find it very difficult to secure employment (Pager, 2007).

Regardless of its form and intent, informal social control is a powerful shaper of urban order. Our ability to negotiate the sharing of urban space is predicated on countless actions and reactions, all of which rest upon unspoken norms and values. That said, this collective valuation of order is not all that characterises city life. A degree of disorder is inevitable in cities, and sometimes is even welcomed. It is to a consideration of the role of disorder in urban life that we now turn.

DISORDER IN THE CITY

Cities require order to function economically, to ensure public health, to enable mobility, and to make daily life manageable. Yet cities also offer opportunities to step outside drab predictability. A mix of cultural groups inhabits most cities. Indeed, cities are often ports of entry for new immigrants. Most cities also witness a steady influx of rural people, most of them looking for new opportunities. Further, the sheer number of people in cities generates a degree of congestion, pollution and moment-to-moment uncertainty. To stroll down an urban sidewalk usually means encountering difference and some measure of physical vulnerability. Rates of crime are often higher in urban areas versus rural ones, and thus urban dwellers live with some degree of daily risk.

The prospect of intermingling with difference is an attraction for many city dwellers. Cities can offer a wide range of cultural experiences and other opportunities for personal discovery. Cities also offer multiple chances to participate in festive and sometimes raucous events, from carnivals to concerts to casinos. The possibility of encountering the new, the different, the avant-garde is ever-present in vibrant cities.

Looked at this way, disorder is just as much a desirable fundament of city life as is order. Yet in some respects, disorder is less obviously good. Pollution, noise and congestion are often social liabilities. Few of us thrill to see dilapidated housing or littered sidewalks. Neighbourhoods characterised by visible poverty are generally avoided. Indeed, such neighbourhoods have historically been understood sociologically to be characterised by their lack of organisation. The concept of social disorganisation was a central one to the 'Chicago School' of sociology that developed in the first half of the twentieth century. According to some of the key Chicago sociologists, such as Clifford Shaw, Henry McKay and Edwin Sutherland, many urban neighbourhoods witnessed perpetual change, as new residents moved in to displace the old. This constant process of turnover led social norms to lose their power, and to thereby enable higher levels of social deviance. This dynamic beset poor neighbourhoods most critically, and was seen as an explanation for higher comparative levels of crime in impoverished communities (see Shaw and McKay, 1942; Sutherland, 1955).

Yet the argument that poor communities are disorganised appears harder to sustain if one looks closer. Ethnographies of disadvantaged communities often reveal a high level of social organisation (see Gans, 1963; Liebow, 1967; Stack, 1987). In other words, it is not so much that these neighbourhoods lack an internal structure, but they are organised along lines that differ from middle-class communities. One can gain appreciation for this point from in-depth examinations of groups oriented towards

crime, such as street gangs. These were the quintessential example of social disorganisation, according to Chicago School theorists. Yet these groups are often extremely
tightly structured, which is unsurprising when one recognises that they are businesses
(see Bourgois, 1995; Jankowski, 1991; Padilla, 1992; Williams, 1989). The notion of
social disorganisation may represent a class-based judgement of seemingly different
groups rather than an accurate depiction of sociological reality. This point was brought
home clearly in an interview that Katherine Beckett conducted with a social worker.
The interviewee works with poor people who are targeted by new forms of trespass
law in Seattle's Pioneer Square. He was convinced that these laws were squarely aimed
at those who are poor, and are enforced in a way that reflects a strong class bias:

> It's definitely a class thing, there's no doubt about it. Now, how do you con-
> trol the masses, huh? Most of the, time, I work with Indians an awful lot here
> and many of them are indigent. Many of them have alcohol problems so they
> hang out in the parks, which is the only place on the streets you can go. They
> sit there and have a drink, because that's the cheapest high they can get, to
> endure their meager existences and of course here comes the police, we want
> to clear them out because we're having those big ships come in from Alaska.
> You don't want those drunk Indians sitting on that park bench—that's just
> terrible. It's alright for the drunk Alaskans to sit down there and puke, but
> it's not alright for the Indian guy. (Beckett and Herbert, 2009)

Just as these trespass laws may be enforced based on a strong class bias, other policies
against street activities, when imposed in other world cities, might similarly reflect a
cultural bias. Policies used in North American cities, and dominant notions of childhood, are shaping perceptions of street begging in Ecuador. Based on her ethnography
of indigenous women and children who beg on city streets, Swanson (2010) understands urban begging as a way women and children move forward within the constraints of Ecuador's racist social structure and capitalist economy. Moralistic rhetoric
accuses these people of being lazy, manipulative, and of exploiting their children for
emotional appeal. Such rhetoric is used to justify exclusionary policies against these
groups. Among indigenous families, however, children are considered active producers,
and child circulation is a long-standing practice in an economy of organised caring.
This discussion of social disorganisation makes clear that the concept of disorder is
not simply a naïve description of reality but a value-laden term. It can perform significant cultural and political work. This is especially evident in contemporary discussions about urban policing, much of which are oriented towards the reduction of what
many describe as visible disorder. There is no better place to understand the important
and volatile politics of order and disorder in urban areas.

ORDER, DISORDER AND THE POLICING OF BROKEN WINDOWS

Disorder became a much more prominent issue in urban areas in the early 1980s,
largely as a consequence of two related developments. The first was the rise of visible

homelessness. This reality resulted from multiple dynamics, but economic shifts and a reduction in government spending for housing were the most important. The decline of the industrial base meant fewer well-paying jobs. When these job losses occurred just as public housing declined, a surge in homelessness resulted (Burt, 1992; Wolch and Dear, 1987).

This rise in homelessness was accompanied by another key development – the increased popularity of the so-called 'broken windows' theory. This theory, first formulated in a magazine article by James Q. Wilson and George Kelling (1982), sought to draw a connection between visible disorder and more serious crime. According to the theory, an unrepaired broken window in an urban neighbourhood can serve as a precursor to crime. Wilson and Kelling asserted that the broken window would symbolise a lack of informal social control. This would embolden criminals, who would perceive the neighbourhood as poorly defended. As criminal activity increased, neighbourhood residents would become even more fearful, and would withdraw from public life. This would further erode informal social control, and a negative feedback loop would be set in motion that would cause significant neighbourhood deterioration.

A close reading of Wilson and Kelling's essay makes plain that they are not really referring to broken pieces of glass as the key symbols of disorder. Instead, they are focused on people. In particular, they isolate individuals who spend a considerable amount of time in public space, many of them regularly engaged in deviant acts, like prostitution, public intoxication or drug use. They also include panhandlers and homeless people. In other words, the key indicators of a neighbourhood in decline, for Wilson and Kelling, are particular people whom they consider disorderly.

One of the most significant implications of the theory involved the police. Most urban police departments are fairly reactive. Officers wait for citizens to phone in complaints, and then proceed to the incidents to which they are dispatched. Officers also seek primarily to arrest more serious criminals, those guilty of felony offences. Wilson and Kelling found this problematic. Police departments, they argued, should be more proactive, and they should focus more on minor offences. In that way, the police could do their part in fixing broken windows. If the police placed pressure on the low-level crimes perpetrated by those they considered disorderly, Wilson and Kelling argued, they could prevent more serious crimes, and avert the cycle of decline that would otherwise beset disadvantaged communities. Thus was born so-called 'broken windows' policing. This meant that the police would place increased pressure on the homeless and others who spend considerable time in public space. One of the more well-publicised of such efforts was deployed in New York City, where it came to be known as 'zero tolerance' policing.

New York's Zero Tolerance Policing

The most heralded instance of broken windows policing occurred in New York City in the 1990s. There, the broken windows philosophy morphed into a particularly vibrant form – 'zero tolerance' policing. This evocative language was used to convey just how stringent the New York police would be towards the disorderly. Particularly prominent

(Continued)

(Continued)

symbolically were 'squeegee men' – individuals who would clean windshields of cars idling in traffic and then demand payment. Key actors – like Mayor Rudolph Guiliani and Police Commissioner William Bratton – vilified the squeegee men and emphasised how the police's strong tactics would restore order to an unruly city (Bratton, 1998; Silverman, 1999).

Fortunately for the political fortunes of Guiliani and Bratton, these tactics coincided with significant reductions in more serious crimes. Because of this, each of these public officials loudly trumpeted the alleged effectiveness of using the broken windows philosophy to great effect. (During his unsuccessful run for president in 2008, Guiliani used his record in New York City to suggest that he could similarly protect the United States from the threat of terrorist attack.) The New York example was justified in efforts to implement broken windows policing throughout the United States (Kelling and Coles, 1998) and throughout much of the world, including the global south (Mountz and Curran, 2009; Newburn and Jones, 2007; Swanson, 2007).

Yet the actual story is more complicated than the simplistic tale told by Guiliani and Bratton. In the specific instance of New York City, the link between zero tolerance and crime reduction was likely purely coincidental. The decline in New York's crime rates began before Guiliani became mayor (Bowling, 1999). Further, crime rates dropped across American cities, almost none of which adopted policing tactics similar to New York's (Greene, 1999). It is therefore likely that crime reductions occurred because of factors other than policing, most notably the decline of the crack cocaine epidemic and improvements to the economy (Karmen, 2006).

Indeed, rigorous tests of the alleged linkage between disorder and crime that forms the crux of the broken windows argument fail to find a strong connection (Harcourt, 2001; Sampson and Raudenbush, 1999; Taylor, 2001). Because of this, there is strong reason to question the underlying justification of intensive and sometimes strong-armed policing done in the name of either broken windows or zero tolerance.

The police were aided considerably in their effort to implement broken windows policing by new laws. Many of these were termed 'civility codes' because they ostensibly sought to promote orderly behaviour in public space. These codes made illegal a range of behaviours that the homeless (and others considered disorderly) regularly engage in, like sleeping in parks, sitting or lying on sidewalks, engaging in 'aggressive' panhandling, or public elimination (see Foscarinis, 1996; Mitchell, 1997). In the United Kingdom, Anti-Social Behaviour Orders (ASBOs) performed much the same function, through providing the police with the ability to define the limits of acceptable behaviour and to arrest people who stepped outside those limits (Flint and Nixon, 2006). Similar efforts are also under way in Germany (Belina, 2007) and France (Dikeç, 2002).

In Seattle, these civility codes are now enhanced by even stronger measures. In essence, Seattle has expanded the use of trespass law to make it easier for the police to monitor and arrest those frequently derided as disorderly. For example, people can be excluded from public parks for violating park rules. These exclusions can be for up to a year. A violation of an exclusion order makes an individual subject to arrest. Those individuals who are charged with drug-related offences are very likely to be given a Stay Out of Drug Area (SODA) Order. SODA zones are predetermined areas that are reputed to possess long histories of hosting drug-related activity, such as on-street sales. Any one in Seattle charged with a drug-related offence will almost always be served with a restriction that prohibits them from entering one or more SODA zones. These new mechanisms significantly increase the power of the police to place pressure on the 'disorderly' population, as evidenced by notably higher rates of arrest for misdemeanour offences (Beckett and Herbert, 2009).

There are a wide range of concerns generated by these formal efforts to reduce what many consider disorder. One issue is the focus on individual behaviour that lies at the core of broken windows. The theory is very much preoccupied with those individuals who congregate frequently in public space, and seeks to deter them from doing so through the threat of arrest. This emphasis on individual behaviour occludes from analysis the social forces that generate disadvantage in the first place, and make affordable housing too scarce (Herbert and Brown, 2006). It also can detract attention from the wider forces of gentrification that often accompany efforts to deploy broken windows policing (Mitchell, 1997; Raco, 2003).

This is connected to a second issue – the symbolic and political significance of the term disorder. If individuals are characterised as disorderly, then they become politically less significant (Harcourt, 2001). It thus becomes easy to enforce stringent laws against them. It also enables the police to use their authority with some vigour, and at some risk to constitutional protections meant to extend even to disadvantaged populations (Beckett and Herbert, 2009).

As less than complete citizens, those considered disorderly lose their full place, in both literal and symbolic space. This is an additional concern. It is especially a concern for the disadvantaged themselves, whose contributions to social life become occluded (Duneier, 1999) and whose ingenuity in ensuring their survival is typically ignored (Snow and Anderson, 1993). It is also a concern for the wider body politic, whose sense of the need for an inclusionary public space becomes weaker (Bannister et al., 2006; Caldeira, 2000). In the process, some of the importance of vibrant, diverse public spaces becomes lost (Cooper, 2007: Dixon et al., 2006).

As this discussion reveals, there is a deeply political dimension to the order–disorder couplet. As much as order possesses a functional utility in urban life, as much as its production is a necessary formal and informal accomplishment, its too ardent pursuit can have significant consequences. Some citizens lose status and see their freedoms curtailed. Larger social issues are ignored in the quest to reduce what some see as disorder. And some of the larger challenges of urban life – the abilities to confront and reckon with social difference, and to recognise a

sense of collective responsibility for the downtrodden – are largely avoided, in ways
that diminish us all.

CONCLUSION

On a sunny Seattle morning, a police sergeant is accompanied on his rounds by
two social workers from a downtown emergency shelter. The sergeant leads them
on a tour of three Pioneer Square parks, all of which typically attract a significant
number of homeless people. His hope is that the social workers could assist individuals in finding shelter. This, he hoped, would reduce their presence in public
space. At one point, the group is walking towards a set of public benches, all of
which were occupied by homeless people at rest. The sergeant stops, points at the
benches, turns to the group accompanying him and asks, 'Now, whose responsibility is this?'

It was impressive that the sergeant asked the question. In so doing, he implicitly
recognised the futility of his efforts in the face of widespread social disadvantage.
The 'disorder' he sought to address springs from a range of social, economic and
political dynamics over which he possesses absolutely no control. That the police
are asked to 'clean up' after the consequences of urban capitalism is one of the more
problematic aspects of the broken windows discourse and the attendant politics of
urban disorder.

Those who seek to continue to help us understand these politics are best advised
to recognise that order and disorder are sewn deeply into the fabric of urban life.
Cities necessarily host each. The flow of people and goods, the shared presence of
many in finite spaces, the persistent need for physical and psychic comfort – all of
these ensure that formal and informal practices will persist to generate some degree
of order. At the same time, cities are waste-producing, heterogeneous and somewhat
unpredictable. Disorder therefore is equally unavoidable, and equally central to the
urban experience.

Yet it is clear that the politics of order and disorder can be problematic, particularly if one seeks to improve the life circumstances of the disadvantaged. It is difficult
to find very much justice in practices that enable the downtrodden to be dismissed
as broken windows and policed in draconian fashion. Future research focused on
urban disorder should thus remain attentive to the key practices through which that
disorder is framed, and the policies that are generated as a consequence. Disorder is
in the eye of the beholder.

Further, even if visible homelessness can be characterised in such terms, it is
critical to remember that it is the result of wider social and economic dynamics
that beg for consideration. Students of disorder, then, must continue to interrogate the range of policies that generate social disadvantage, the manifestations of
which are frequently visible in the urban street. Disorder, in other words, is a term
that requires careful unpacking, both because of the political work that it can
perform and because of the unseen processes that make it an issue in the first

place. This is what makes the sergeant's question so poignant and appropriate. As much as members of urban society might wish to simply call the police to use their territorial power to rid places like Pioneer Square of unwanted individuals, social disadvantage is not really a police matter. It is the result of processes that are an inherent part of urban capitalism.

For those of us who enjoy and study cities, disorder is an unavoidable reality. We must accept it and understand it to fully appreciate what it means to be a member of urban society.

Web Resources

The Project for Public Spaces. http://www.pps.org/
Right to the City. http://www.righttothecity.org/

8

Walling the City

Gordon MacLeod

At some point walls were used as protection against threats from the outside, whether from beasts or hostile human marauders. No one can object, on moral or social grounds, to walls built for such purposes ... But, since these early days, walls have come to play a more ambiguous and increasingly divisive role. They have become boundary walls ... com[ing] to reflect, and to reinforce, hierarchies of wealth and power; divisions among people, races, ethnic groups, and religions; and hostilities, tensions, and fears. (Marcuse, 1997: 103–4)

INTRODUCTION: URBAN WALLS AND ENCLOSURES

Urban scholars have long been concerned to examine how inequalities of wealth and differences in class, ethnicity and culture are expressed in the social geography of cities (see Chapter 3). Notable examples include Stedman Jones's (1971) analysis of London's Victorian slums, Burgess's (1925) concentric zoning of neighbourhoods in 1920s' Chicago and prognoses of a growing 'culture of poverty' in the 'black ghettos' of US cities in the 1960s (Banfield, 1970). Over the last two decades, however, critical urban scholars have offered compelling testimonies to indicate that escalating social divisions are being expressed in ever more dramatic inscriptions in the metropolitan landscape. In a widely acclaimed contribution, Mike Davis (1990) excavates beneath Los Angeles's glitzy cosmetic facade to reveal a discordant terrain where the feverish protection of luxury lifestyles has fuelled a rapid rise in ultra-secure suburban gated communities often displaying an 'armed response' welcome to outsiders. At the same time, LA's corporate citadel, Bunker Hill, redeveloped in the 1980s to feature a galaxy of hermetically sealed hotel complexes and enclosed malls de-linked from the traditional pedestrian routes to the old centre, 'is programmed to ensure a seamless continuum of middle-class work, consumption and recreation, without unwonted exposure to Downtown's working-class street environments' (Davis, 1990: 230).

Davis's ground-breaking investigation into Los Angeles as a 'fortress city' unlocked new ways of seeing physical and social segregation in cities in the global north and south: a notable example being Teresa Caldeira's (1996, 2000) stunning portrayal of São Paulo as an intensely partitioned 'city of walls'. In response to escalating fear of street crime and violence, a series of fortified enclaves defended by walls, surveillance technologies and armed guards act to shape ever-widening gulfs in economic opportunity, social status and substantive citizenship. Martin Murray (2004, 2008) uncovers a similarly 'precarious urbanization' in Johannesburg. Here the formally instituted racial segregation that had prevailed under South Africa's Apartheid political regime has been succeeded by a social apartheid, where wealthier middle classes, panicked by sensationalised media reports and impelled by avaricious insurance companies, have retreated to neighbourhood enclosures, often protected by private security and cordoned-off roads and with privatised services and amenities. Meanwhile Manila is a fast-globalising metropolis increasingly punctuated by suburban cellular office blocks, upscale malls and secluded gated compounds all linked by freeways and flyovers around which the poor are excluded, ignored, displaced and marginalised (Connell, 1999).

In another pioneering essay, 'The Rise of the New Walled Cities' (1995), Dennis Judd contends that this upward trend in the enclosure of commercial and residential space has become a defining feature of US cities, while others have signposted how the authority inscribed through such walls is intensified by extensive surveillance and muscular policing (McLaughlin and Muncie, 1999). Some commentators also infer that recourse to walling is part and parcel of an increasingly fragmenting urban-regional landscape, variously defined as a postmodern urbanism, post-metropolis, patchwork urbanism and splintering urbanism (cf. Borsdorf and Hidalgo, 2009; Dear, 2000; Graham and Marvin, 2001; Low, 2001; MacLeod and Ward, 2002; Soja, 2000). Murray further contends that:

> The spatial dynamics of postmodern urbanism promotes the steady expansion of social polarisation and spatial fragmentation ... By cordoning off urban glamour zones ... from the rest of the city, postmodern urbanism not only condenses the intended and unintended spatial consequences of 'siege architecture', but also transforms dwindling public spaces into battlegrounds where the urban poor struggle for dignity and survival. (Murray, 2004: 146)

Trends like these are leading many scholars to analyse *and* critique these widening social divisions, spatial partitions and erosions of public space: not least in that they are widely perceived as anathema to conceptions of the 'good city' premised upon a civic acceptance of others as neighbours and citizens (Amin, 2006; Caldiera, 2000; Jacobs, 1961; Kohn, 2004; Low, 2003). Of course, as discussed in the next section, there is nothing new in urban settlements experiencing the segregation of different classes and ethnic groups into strictly demarcated districts. But the contemporary urban condition appears to be mapped by internal demarcation lines drawn with such intensity, they surely demand analysis. In offering one modest step, this chapter poses the following questions: What types of 'walls' and barriers are punctuating the city? Where are they concentrated? In what ways are walls 'fragmenting' contemporary cities? How might these differ from the walls and fortifications associated with earlier eras? How generalised are processes of walling? How might we explain the contemporary walling and enclosure of urban space? In responding to this last question, it is contended that 'walling' is intricately intertwined with ever-more diverging lines of social, economic, cultural and political lines of privilege, power, mobility and immobility; and that these diverging lines find their imprint in the landscape and territorial shape of metropolitan regions: what Agamben (2006) terms a new metropolitan spatialisation, one increasingly characterised by a precarious governance amid the cacophony of (a de-amplified) urban politics (MacLeod, 2012).

ANCIENT FORTIFIED CITY TO MODERN INTEGRATED URBANISM

the medieval city reminds us of the paradoxes, exclusions and segmentations that have always been associated with city form and urban organisation. (AlSayyad and Roy, 2006: 2)

Before investigating the present-day enclosure of cities, we should be mindful that walled cities are as old as the act of city-building itself. Stretching back to 7000 BC, Jericho is distinguished as an early example, enclosed within a defensive wall, fortified towers and a ditch to deter outside aggressors. Around 3000 BC, the Mesopotamian city of Uruk, thought to be the largest in the world at the time, housed between 50,000 and 80,000 residents all within a walled area of 6 km (Atkins et al., 1998). As urbanisation advanced and defensive schemes formed in response to the strategies of intruders, Lanciani (1967; in Coaffee and Murakami Wood, 2009) documents how, between the fifth century BC and the third century AD, Ancient Rome was fortified around seven different contours. And in due course the walls of medieval cities came to reflect society's distribution of power and patterns of social stratification. Typically the citadel on the hill was the pivotal fortress that enabled the temporal and spiritual lords to dominate. This was surrounded by residents, workers, merchants and crafts people, all encircled by a city-wide wall separating *citizens* from the agricultural serfs outside[1] (Marcuse, 1997). Durham and Newcastle in north-east England, and Venice, Florence and Rome in Italy were examples where walls embodied spatial enclosure and protection while simultaneously offering urban citizens a mode of commerce, governance and culture long before the rise of nation-states (Atkins et al., 1998; Coaffee and Murakami Wood, 2009; McLaughlin and Muncie, 1999).

As the epigraph at the beginning at the chapter emphasises, walls have become increasingly ambivalent over time. The onset of modernity and the industrial revolution heralded three foundational consequences for urban settlements. Firstly, technological

---

1 The regular positioning of the Jewish ghettos outside this wall but immediately adjacent to it served to symbolise both the rejection of Jewish communities by, and their necessity to, the dominant society (Marcuse, 1997).

advances in military weaponry eroded the physical and symbolic potency of stone walls as an adequate defence. Secondly, radical transformations in the mode of production and the constitution of class relations revolutionised the urban socio-economic order so that intimidation and insurrection were more likely to ferment *inside* a city's perimeter walls or partitions. And thirdly, the bourgeois era saw embryonic nation-states increasingly assume an intricate assemblage of power around which to map territory and to orchestrate the means of military protection and violence across nations, enabling a regulatory control of cities and distributing a bio-political governmentality *through* urban populations (Joyce, 2005; Marcuse, 1997). Nowhere did these processes combine with such dramatic effect as in mid-nineteenth-century Paris; a city that had become synonymous with street insurrection (Benjamin, 1968; Harvey, 2003). Instructed in 1853 by France's Emperor, Napoleon III, Paris's Prefect, Georges-Eugène Haussmann, began radically transforming it into the first modern European metropolis. By the 1870s, infrastructures like sewage, water, public monuments, parks, lighting, bridges, and railway stations had all been formed around a network of wide and open boulevards that literally blasted through the old medieval city.

Described as 'the most spectacular urban innovation of the nineteenth century and the decisive breakthrough in the modernization of the traditional city' (Berman, 1983: 150), Paris's boulevards formed a spatially integrated urban landscape permitting a hitherto unimaginable circulation of people and traffic within and through the city. In effect, it 'opened up the whole of the city, for the first time in its history, to all its inhabitants' (ibid.: 151). Haussmann's sidewalks were also extravagantly wide. Lined with furniture and lush with trees, they brimmed with bustling terraced cafés, restaurants and boutiques, all helping to make 'the new Paris a uniquely enticing spectacle [and] a visual and sensual feast' (ibid.). But building the new Paris also entailed demolishing working-class *quartiers*, thereby displacing tens of thousands. As Berman (1983: 153) outlines, 'in tearing down the old medieval slums, [Haussmann] inadvertently broke down the self-enclosed and hermetically sealed world of traditional urban poverty'. Moreover, 'as [the poor] see, they are seen: the vision, the epiphany, flows both ways ... The glitter lights up the rubble, and illuminates the dark lives of the people at whose expense the bright lights shine.'[2] Haussmann also pioneered a series of semi-enclosed 'interior streets' vis-à-vis glass-covered gallerias, arcades and, not least, the department store (McLaughlin and Muncie, 1999).

By the 1880s, Haussmann's Paris was acclaimed to be the standard bearer for modern urbanism across the world. Berlin, Barcelona, London, Chicago, Santiago and Saigon (now Ho Chi Minh City) were among numerous cities where unitary street systems were orchestrated to integrate districts while infrastructure networks like

---

2 In his pamphlet *The Housing Question*, Engels (1872) rails against the 'method ... called "Haussmann" which has now become general, of making breaches in the working-class quarters of our big cities'. And he continues: 'No matter how different the reasons may be, the result is everywhere the same: the most scandalous alleys and lanes disappear to the accompaniment of lavish self-glorification by the bourgeoisie on account of this tremendous success, but they appear again at once somewhere else, and often in the immediate neighbourhood.'

sewage and water served to '"cleanse" city spaces thereby emancipating "good" working-class people from the risks of immorality' (Graham and Marvin, 2001: 44).[3] Across Europe and North America in particular, city governments and planners committed to civic improvement and urban beautification transformed conveniently located spaces into signature urban parks, none more quintessential than New York's Central Park. And as the 'progressive era' of the early twentieth century unfolded, and spirited by blueprints ranging from Ebenezer Howard's Garden City to Jacob Riis's reforms for New York's slums, open public spaces were seen to be beneficial for health, hygiene and recreation as indeed for instilling 'civilising' virtues, especially for the working classes living in the still congested inner cities (Banerjee, 2001).

Throughout the mid-twentieth century, many state-centred projects deployed modernist architecture and 'progressive' city planning in an endeavour to mould a 'rational' urban model – an 'integrated urban ideal' so to speak (Graham and Marvin, 2001) – with an aspiration, at least in principle, to erode the inequality and squalor that had bedevilled medieval and industrial cities. Caldeira (1996) identifies Brasilia to be the embodiment of this political commitment to a public city. In due course, though, Brasilia came to symbolise modernism's failure: as contrary to the planners' aspirations for an egalitarian landscape it became Brazil's most segregated city, featuring 'streets only for vehicular traffic, the absence of sidewalks, enclosure and internalization of shopping areas, and spatial voids isolating sculptural buildings and rich residential areas' (Caldeira, 1996: 317). With Brasilia's experience replicated across much of the world during the 1960s and 1970s, confidence in modernist urban planning waned, not least its 'progressive' credentials and its capacity to work in 'the public interest' (Sandercock, 1998). This paradigmatic crisis, and what was to become a related recourse to the re-liberalisation of certain infrastructure networks from the orbit of public sector planning, has become crucial in facilitating more splintered urban landscapes (Graham and Marvin, 2001). Increasingly planners have been forced to acknowledge that their cities are 'collages of fragmented spaces', 'defined by multiple identities, aspirations, life worlds and socioeconomic and time-space circuits' (Graham and Marvin, 2001: 112). Nowhere is this more evident than in the dramatic upsurge of walled and gated communities.

TWENTY-FIRST-CENTURY WALLED AND GATED COMMUNITIES: RECALLING ANCIENT ROME'S *POMERIUM*

Gated enclaves give materiality to what Rose (1999), deploying Foucault, has termed the 'powers of freedom', the forms of governing that presuppose

---

3 An essential aspect of the drive for cohesion was the construction of the 'underground city' through the 'knitting together of necessary underground utilities' as well as aboveground street networks and transport and communication grids (Mumford, 1961, in Graham and Marvin, 2001: 52).

> the freedom of the governed. In other words, the enclave is an important tech-
> nology of rule, a form of rule that operates through the double helix of liberty
> and sovereignty, of freedom and protection. (AlSayyad and Roy, 2006: 8)

Some mention could have been made above about how, in the mid- to late-nineteenth
century, gates and barriers helped maintain the privileged character of elite residential
districts in West London[4] and Manhattan, and likewise throughout the twentieth
century in places like Hollywood, Los Angeles[5] (Atkins, 1993; Davis, 1990). But as
Blakely and Snyder (1999: 4) reveal, these gated sanctuaries represented 'uncommon
places for uncommon people'. In contrast, early twenty-first century expressions are
mushrooming in most major metropolitan regions and increasingly epitomise part of
mainstream housing development. A typical 'gated community' is a housing formation that is *walled or fenced physically* thereby precluding 'general public access to
streets, sidewalks, parks, beaches, rivers, trails, playgrounds: all resources that without gates or walls would be open and shared by all the citizens of a locality' (Atkinson
and Blandy, 2005: 178). They are also often *walled in an institutional sense* through
legal agreements – covenants, controls and restrictions (CC&Rs) – which tie residents
to a common code of conduct and can enforce all sorts of limitations, from the age
range of residents, the hours and frequency of visitors, house décor and fixtures (the
basketball hoop being a serial offender), visibility of 'industrial' automobiles, to the
number and size of family pets (Judd, 1995; Knox, 2008).

In *Fortress America: Gated Communities in the United States*, Blakely and Snyder
distinguish three notable forms. Firstly, *Lifestyle Communities*; lush-green outer
suburban reserves designed exclusively for groups like retirees or premised upon
specific leisure pursuits like golf, as well as custom-built master-planned communities extending to towns like Disney's Celebration in Florida (McGuirk and Dowling,
2009; Ross, 2000). Secondly, *Prestige Communities* manifesting as exclusive preserves for the rich and famous, not least sports and movie stars, alongside premier
executives,[6] all of whose purported desire for 'urban buzz' has seen a recent trend

---

4 Peter Atkins (1993) offers a fascinating analysis of how, akin to the spirited aspiration
to foster a more 'open' city, public reaction from pressure groups and local authorities
lobbying Parliament led to a removal of many street barriers in Victorian London and
thereby altered the balance between public and private space.

5 Beckett (1994) outlines how the fact that so many of Los Angeles's white residents
arrived to escape the growing integration of eastern cities has always made it economically
and racially segregated. Egalitarian nineteenth-century ideals about socially 'promiscuous'
cities, developed by academics and planners in Chicago and New York, never really
rooted in LA, and after the Watts riots of 1965 and the 'Rodney King' riots of 1992, a
growing demand was created for 'gated' communities.

6 Some of the gated apartment blocks sell the idea of being able to enjoy their space as
if in other places and times (past and future). Indeed, the residents of enclaves in London,
Los Angeles, São Paulo, Cape Town, Istanbul and Lebanon – because they are networked
into global economic flows and corresponding lifestyles – are in certain respects culturally
closer to each other than to their own cities.

for prestige compounds to be parachuted into downtown glamour zones alongside newly gentrified neighbourhoods (Minton, 2009). And thirdly, Blakeley and Snyder identify *Security Zone Communities*. Built primarily in response to a growing fear of crime, these can take the form of the 'perch' (so-called because it is not developers but long-term residents who have retro-fitted gates) and the 'barricade' concentrated mainly in poorer areas. Blakeley and Snyder's diverse case studies thereby disavow a popular conception that 'gatedness' is a preserve of the rich:

> Poor inner city neighborhoods and public housing projects use security guards, gates, and fences to keep out drug dealing, prostitution, and drive-by shootings and regain control of their shared territory. Other neighborhoods, frightened by spillover crime from nearby areas or irritated by traffic, have obtained city permission to take their streets out of public use, limiting access to residents only … Whether crime is rampant or infrequent, the threat actual or perceived, the fear itself is very real. (Blakely and Snyder, 1999: 100)[7]

Recent estimates suggest that eight out of ten new urban housing projects in the US are gated, and the trend is growing rapidly in Latin America, Asia, Africa, Russia and other Eastern European countries (Glasze et al. 2006; Hirt and Petrovic, 2011; Knox, 2008; Lemanski, 2006; Murray, 2008). Caldeira (2000) reveals how homes in São Paulo's gated condominiums are often advertised in glossy magazines as an opportunity to live out 'First World' lifestyles in 'Third World' cities (see box). In Manila, walls and gates are the portents of virtually all new suburban developments, built-by-design to deny the heterogeneity of a contemporary Asian metropolis (Connell, 1999). Thus, amid the spectre of early twenty-first-century precarious capitalism, all classes are engaged in *voluntary ghettoisation*. And here 'security' appears to have become more than just a positional good, as signalled in the quote from AlSayyad and Roy, afforded the status of 'freedom': 'freedom, not just from crime but also from such annoyances as solicitors and canvassers, mischievous teenagers, and strangers of any kind, malicious or not' (Blakely and Snyder, 1999: 18).

São Paulo: 'Defensive Urbanism' as a Way of Life

During the last two decades, Brazil's major cities have been routinely portrayed as enduring political mismanagement, widespread corruption, runaway crime and street violence. Whether such narratives exaggerate or reflect reality, a deepening sense of fear and disorder has led many to choose a way of life perhaps best described as

---

7 Drawing on results from the 2001 American Housing Survey, Sanchez et al. (2005) found a prevalence of low-income, racialised minority renters living in gated communities (GCs), and the extent to which US public housing projects are walled and gated is illustrated by results showing that tenants are nearly two and a half times more likely than owners to live in GCs (Atkinson and Blandy, 2005).

'defensive urbanism'. For the number of Brazilian residents who have sought refuge in gated communities, called condominiums *exclusivos* or *condominios fechados*, has sky-rocketed. In São Paulo, the first such secured development was *Alphaville*. Located in north-western São Paulo, eight miles from the city centre, Alphaville has 32,000 perma-nent residents and is surrounded by a four-metre-high cement wall topped with barbed wire (see Figure 8.1). It has 1,100 armed security officers who screen visitors, patrol streets and maintain constant vigilance over suspicious characters. Like the estimated 300 other such residential estates that have proliferated on São Paulo's urban fringe, Alphaville is divided into distinct specialty zones. Alongside residential areas, the com-pound includes its own private shopping mall, supermarkets and recreational facilities, while also extending to 'open' retail trade, office and service locations. Consequently, the daytime population rises to around 130,000 people. Alphaville offers a seques-tered refuge, perhaps a self-sufficient mini-universe. And significantly (see Section 4 of this volume), the enclosure also has three helipads. For such composites, the adver-tisements present:

the image of islands to which one can return every day, in order to escape from the city and its deteriorated environment and to encounter an exclusive world of pleasure among peers. The image of the enclaves, therefore, is opposed to the image of the city as a deteriorated world pervaded by not only pollution and noise but more importantly confusion and mixture, that is, social heterogeneity. (Caldeira, 1996: 309)

At the same time, São Paulo's poor fend for themselves in rows of dilapidated high-rise apartment complexes, 'auto-constructed' peripheries and slums. And yet, throughout the city, *all* residents are assaulted by a barrage of neon signs, massive television screens and garish billboards presenting glorifying images of material abundance, opu-lence and luxury chic.
Adapted from Caldeira 1996, 2000; Murray, 2004.

And yet the process has deeper implications for analyses of cities and social change: as many of these gated landscapes also feature new modes of micro-urban governance and political expression[8] (MacLeod, 2011; Webster et al., 2002). Indeed Davis (1990: 153) contends that the 'most powerful "social movement" in contemporary Southern California is that of affluent homeowners, organized by notional community designations or tract names, [and] engaged in the defense of home values and neighborhood exclusivity'. Across the USA, the Homeowner Association or Common Interest Development is increasingly significant as a non-profit organisation elected by home-owners in gated suburban estates and enclosed inner urban condominium blocks. As well as drawing on the afore-mentioned

---

8 While the presence of gated communities is clearly becoming global, the political ramifications are more closely reported in US academic and legal literature. An English-language understanding of the politics of non-US developments represents an urgent research agenda.

CC&Rs, Common Interest Developments (CIDs) and Home-Owner Associations (HOAs) impose statutory levies to maintain 'community'-owned amenities like roads, sidewalks and parks and to deliver services like refuse collection, security, recreation and leisure (Knox, 2008; Low, 2003; McKenzie, 1994). Four out of five homes in the USA built since 2000 are located within HOA sub-divisions, prompting McKenzie (2006) to reason that this housing revolution represents the 'forced obsolescence' of traditional neighbourhoods featuring individually owned homes on public streets with public services in favour of privately governed common-interest communities with private streets, services and governments. The following example is most revealing:

> East of Seattle, across beautiful Lake Washington, lies the gated community of Bear Creek. An exclusive community … [whose] … residents … enjoy their environmental amenities (paid for with steep fees) without sharing them with the public because they own everything, even the streets and the sewers. Bear Creek's citizens like their private government and are not inclined to tax themselves to help solve Seattle's problems. As one resident put it: '[T]he citizens have moved ahead of government. The government has not kept up with what people want'. (Dreier et al., 2001: 30)

McKenzie (1994) interprets examples like Bear Creek to be about the upper-middle-class pursuit of a 'privatopia' – a putatively utopian lifestyle via a privatised life in an exclusive neighbourhood – thereby enabling a 'civic secession' or societal exodus. The privatopia may be intensified by entry gates and even private dedicated highways, customised water, energy provision and other privatised infrastructures (Graham and Marvin, 2001); thereby eschewing obligations to a city-scale mode of 'collective consumption' (Castells, 1977) and perhaps, in turn, signalling the erosion of an urban or metropolitan public sphere (Dreier et al., 2001; Section 4 of this volume). Just as the proliferation of CIDs and HOAs has elicited a private provision of 'community' facilities in favour of those governed through municipal oversight, so democracy itself is increasingly determined by property ownership, with renters denied any voting rights (Low, 2003). Blakely and Snyder (1999: 140) reveal the post-democratic disposition of residents in one gated community in Plano, Texas:

> 'I took care of my responsibility, I'm safe in here, I've got my guard gate; I've paid by [home-owner association] dues, and I'm responsible for my streets. Therefore, I have no responsibility for the commonweal, because you take care of your own.'

In considering such trends, McKenzie usefully invokes comparison with an earlier historical urban form:

> Taken together, these things – home-owner associations, privatisation and gated communities – resemble the construction of a pomerium. The pomerium

is an ancient concept dating to pre-Roman times and used in the demarcation of Rome itself ... It was a symbolic, sanctified boundary that separated civilisation from barbarism, order from chaos and civil peace from anarchy. The pomerium was, in essence, an imaginary line drawn around the spiritual city. Instead of surrounding an entire city, today's emerging pomerium demarcates the protected islands of walled and gated private communities. (McKenzie, 2005: 190)

On parallel lines, AlSayyad and Roy (2006) interpret gated CIDs and HOAs as exhibiting a territorialisation of citizenship more akin to medieval fiefdoms: inscribing citizenship rights within quasi-urban enclaves often directly antithetical to modern 'big city' government while imposing 'freedoms' that are at times actually contrary to national law. They go on to argue that:

Today, property matters in the way occupation mattered in the middle ages. In both cases, urban citizenship is premised on the management of a secessionary space of internal regulations and codes. (AlSayyad and Roy, 2006: 7)

It is, moreover, a secessionary citizenship actively encouraged by powerful developers, whose sophisticated marketing techniques shape the demography of new 'master-planned communities' (Low, 2003; McGuirk and Dowling, 2009). For Knox (2008: 1–2) this is indicative of how 'people's sense of "community" and "neighbourhood" have become commodified: ready-made accessories furnished by the real estate industry'. And while some urban authorities find the new 'pomerium' troubling in terms of compromising the urban polity and democracy (Dear and Dahmann, 2008), others actively foster the local privatism of HOAs, given how in practice they deliver costly neighbourhood services while municipalities can still secure property taxes from residents (Lang and Nelson, 2007; McKenzie, 2006). In north Las Vegas, for example, government mandates that new housing be in CIDs: one neighbourhood, Bonanza Village, was literally refashioned into a 'walled community' by city authorities – in the face of dissenting protests from residents – to make it resemble newer fashionable gated enclaves and integrate it more in accordance with glitzy downtown redevelopment (McKenzie, 2005).

SPLINTERING CITIES? CORPORATISATION, ENCLOSURE, SECESSIONARY COMMONS, SPATIAL GOVERNMENTALITY

The domiciliary 'walling' outlined above can be understood more fully by examining analogous transformations in the metropolitan landscape. Perhaps the most obvious expression of contemporary urban 'enclosure' beyond the gated community is the indoor shopping mall (McLaughlin and Muncie, 1999). The first enclosed mall, Southdale, opened in 1956 in the Minneapolis suburb of Edina, largely as a response to the extreme weather often endured in the American Midwest. Interestingly, and in yet another recalling of Europe's past, its designer, Victor Gruen, modelled Southdale on the late nineteenth-century gallerias and arcades of Milan and Paris while also envisaging it as 'a practical answer to suburbia's crying need for a social and cultural center' (Kowinski, 1985: 158–9). Following its success, and convinced that the environmental designs of suburban malls could be applied to revive jaded or distressed city centres, Gruen went on to design the first enclosed downtown mall, Midtown Plaza, in Rochester in the early 1960s (Goss, 1993). By the 1970s, enclosed malls were competing with open-air shopping centres across the US landscape: urban designers and developers encouraging consumers to appreciate the 'total ambience' that integrates climate control, a carefully planned retail mix, pedestrian flow, security and aesthetics while City Mayors identified signature malls as part of their 'trophy collection' alongside an atrium hotel, domed sports stadium, and redeveloped waterfront (Frieden and Sagalyn, 1989; Judd, 1995; Robertson, 1995).

Consequently, during the late twentieth century, over 200 American cities witnessed their downtown streets converted into vast pedestrian malls: many enclosed via a glazed galleria and connected via ducts and skyways to adjacent arcades, office towers, atriums, food courts and hotels (Isenberg, 2004). Again Minneapolis was at the vanguard, as during the 1960s its downtown was the first to experience *overhead* pedestrian bridges connecting discrete corporate and consumer towers into a linked assemblage whilst a labyrinthine network of *underground* tunnels manoeuvred white collars from public transit station to workplace – all without recourse to conventional streets (Boddy, 1992). Boddy interprets this to be an 'analogous city', offering spatial familiarity and ontological security to generations raised in suburbia that might otherwise fear the unpredictability of organic street life. Davis (1990: 229) also reveals how the *Los Angeles Times* critic Sam Hall Kaplan similarly denounced his city's corporate citadel, Bunker Hill, as an 'air-dropped piece of suburbia' which has 'dammed the rivers of life' downtown. And the 'downtown megastructure' – typified by John Portman's Renaissance Center in Detroit, Bonaventure in Los Angeles and Peachtree in Atlanta – offers an astonishing exhibit of this fortified cellular urban enclosure (Goss, 1993; and see box below). Boddy, unable to conceal his ambience of foreboding depression, contends how:

> seamlessly sutured into the downtown corpus, these reshaped pedestrian routes not only replace, they transform. Their status as infrastructure makes their unspoken agendas – to make the city less public in the name of public amenity – all the more frightful … [And] … Their conflation and reversal of private and public […] makes them an excellent entry to the broader anti-metropolitan forces at work in our cities. (1992: 126–7)

Fortified Downtown Enclosure: The Peachtree Center, Atlanta, Georgia

Peachtree opened in downtown Atlanta in 1967 and was an instant success with architectural critics, media and the public. But by the late 1980s, Peachtree Plaza had usurped
an entire downtown: 16 buildings clustered around the aluminium cylinder housing the
Marriott Hotel, anchoring the 'honeycomb complex' of Atlanta's ever expanding, enclosed
downtown business district. But as the enclosure swallowed more and more of downtown
Atlanta's premium activities, the 'real' city streets were being left almost deserted to
pedestrian traffic, especially by nightfall. As with many such mega-structures, entrances
are few and, given their close monitoring by bellhops, rendered unwelcoming to the
non-consuming or non-hotel-accommodated 'publics' of Atlanta. Indeed Portman's own
interpretation of Peachtree almost alludes to a rejection of the city surrounding it: 'I'm
building a city that will become the modern Venice. The streets down there are canals for
cars, while the [indoor] bridges are clean, safe, climate controlled. People can walk here
at any hour' (quoted in Oney, 1987: 184). Portman goes on to claim that 'downtowns
are dangerous … [and that] … I couldn't see abandoning the cities to the poor' (ibid.).
The result of this architectural philosophy is that Peachtree Center sits astride downtown
Atlanta like a colossus: the glassed-in skyways connecting the various atriums and lobbies
isolate the inhabitants of Peachtree from the 'dangerous' street below (see Figure 8.2).
As city streets become less trafficked the contrasts between 'public street' and 'privatised
enclosure' become ever more pronounced. Peachtree helps foster a *spatial apartheid*
separating Atlanta's white middle class from its black and poor. As the second-storey sky-
walks, atriums and shops become the preserve of office workers, tourists and suburban
commuters, the streets below are left to minorities and those who ride the bus.
  Adapted from Judd, 1995: 152–4.

Analysis of the transformative effect of such enclosures on metropolitan spatialisation
demands an appreciation of tectonic shifts under way in American society during the
1980s. The momentous loss of manufacturing jobs, a virtual collapse in federal housing programmes, a clipping of welfare provision, and 'community release' for the
mentally ill and infirm all left many city streets to be populated by escalating numbers
of homeless and walking-wounded located at the sharp end of a merciless Reaganom-
ics; simultaneously disquieting a new generation of aspirational urban professionals
as they ran the gauntlet towards those skyway and megastructure entrances (Boddy,
1992: 138; Boyer, 1993; Zukin, 1995; see also Chapter 4 in this volume). This
was *roll-back neoliberalism* unravelling at pace, with the higher echelons of political
office heralding a fundamentalist faith in 'the market' as allocator of resources
(Peck, 2010; Wilson, 2004). Perhaps certain corporate developers had become conveniently attuned to this when proclaiming that enclosed shopping malls represent
the new 'medieval marketplaces' and 'town squares' (Judd, 1995). To be sure, across
urban America, growth coalitions have enrolled cardinal market players like mall
developers, mall management companies and other private sector consortia in
downtown renewal, just as concessions negotiated through Tax Increment Financing
and the increasing proliferation of Business Improvement Districts have endowed

private interests with considerable power and control over urban space (Turner, 2002; Ward, 2007). English cities, too, are increasingly subject to corporate takeovers, as hitherto emblematic public spaces in London, Liverpool and Manchester are reconditioned to host privatised corporate and consumer palaces (MacLeod and Johnstone, 2012; Minton, 2009).

Not that the corporatisation-enclosure of urban space is a peculiarly Anglo-American phenomenon. In bestowing developers with immense power amid the endeavour to attain global status, Metro Manila's government has *de facto* licensed an 'unprecedented privatization of urban and regional planning' (Shatktin, 2008). And surfacing on the metropolitan regions of other South-East Asian cities, such as Jakarta, Kuala Lumpur and Ho Chi Minh City, are titanic privatised enclosures where elite gated communities are packaged alongside 'bundled' retail, commercial and leisure complexes often linked by tolled highways custom-built for the auto-dependent middle classes, permitting them to secede from *the city's* dilapidated transport infrastructure and its threatening exterior of streets, pollution and poor (Dick and Rimmer, 1998; Douglass and Huang, 2007). It is precisely amidst this *splintering urban* landscape that Graham and Marvin (2001) locate the crucial role of *secessionary networked spaces* – not least the private roads,[9] customised utilities and infrastructures outlined in the previous section of this chapter – which enable an emergent neo-bourgeoisie to enjoy a smartly zoned and cosseted time-geography intertwining the sports utility vehicle (SUV), gated privatopia, downtown citadel, lifestyle centre, elite school, entertainment venue, airport, hotel and distanciated-connected workspace. To some extent, this amplifies the 'civic secession' alluded to earlier, perhaps even mapping the contours of a swaggering *secessionary commons* for the well-heeled. Related to this:

> In many cases [erstwhile] 'public space' is now under the direct or indirect control of corporate, real estate or retailer groups which carefully work with private and public police and security forces to manage and design out any groups or behaviour seen as threatening to the tightly 'normalized use'. With secessionary street spaces those not seen to belong are actively pursued with the latest CCTV and surveillance technologies as attempts are made to 'sift' the quasi-public spaces in search of people transgressing the normative ecologies of the splintered metropolis. (Graham and Marvin, 2001: 232)

This struggle to censor those unsettling the normative ecologies of deluxe enclosures, grander boulevards and premier secessionary spaces, alongside those marginalised in the wake of ruthless dispossessions waged through neoliberalisation, sees urban

---

9 Direct highway connections to the gates of CIDs are not uncommon: the 10,000 'community' in Weston, Fort Lauderdale, and built by the Arvida corporation, has been furnished with dedicated expressway links straight to Miami airport (Graham and Marvin, 2001: 273).

governance becoming preoccupied with what some term *spatial governmentality.*[10] A mode of zonal crime control calculated to 'produce security' in specific sites – pacifying and purifying through architectural design, streetwatch technologies and property law – spatial governmentality is primarily concerned to reduce, relocate or redistribute crime *rather than fully eliminate it* (Merry, 2001; Murray, 2004; Robins, 2002).[11] Stern policing dispensed variously by official cops, private security and Business Improvement District 'ambassadors' further aims to prohibit 'disorderly' behaviour and remove 'incivilities' like panhandling and informal trading, as populist calls for a 'clean and safe' downtown, 'zero tolerance' of homeless, and a 'risk-and terror-free zone' resonate with a neo-bourgeois ambience of simmering fear and insecurity (Coaffee, 2009; Paddison, 2009; see also Chapter 7 of this volume). It is in this context too that political pleas to preserve genuinely democratic public places open to all citizens run against the morally hegemonic enforcement of market discipline which decrees an extension of privately managed revenue-inducing spaces for consumption (Staeheli and Mitchell, 2008; Turner, 2002). Of course, the spatial governmentalities commandeered to sustain such accumulation risk fostering 'interdictory spaces', thereby compromising the diversity so often cherished about city downtowns, while perhaps also licensing an authoritarian or *revanchist* landscape and vernacular (Flusty, 2001; MacLeod, 2002; Smith, 1996; Swanson, 2010).

Perhaps, then, a key question to consider here is the extent to which any walling of twenty-first-century cities is being sculpted by the mutually reinforcing processes of neoliberal corporatisation, architectural enclosure, social secession and spatial governmentality. Perhaps, too, the associated circulation of technologies, spaces, governmentalities and policies (e.g. policies for education and health which incite choice for privatised disaffiliation) are promoting what Atkinson (2008) terms 'mobile circuits of exclusion'. These enable a conscious or subconscious shunning of relegated people and territories, and for higher-income groups to either 'hardwire indifference' or be insulated from the negative externalities of poverty and widening disparities between rich and poor. Returning to São Paulo, we witness perhaps the most breathtaking of all 'mobile circuits of exclusion', as growing numbers of the city's neo-bourgeoisie elevate themselves above the four million residents struggling with the precarious bus system by choosing to commute from their gated compound to executive office via private helicopter (AlSayyad and Roy, 2006). With the less ostentatious upper- and middle-income groups increasingly being conveyed to their destinations by luxury automobile, to actually step on the streets of São Paulo is fast becoming a signifier of class (Caldiera, 2000). Likewise the flipside of Manila's flourishing private mega-malls is that the central city has only one remaining publicly

---

10 In this sense, it becomes evident that the political rationalities of neoliberalism are not therefore strictly limited to free-market rule (Dikeç, 2007; Peck, 2010). As with all fundamentalist doctrines, they are fraught with tensions and contradictions.

11 In Merry's (2001: 16) view, whereas 'modern penality is largely structured around the process of retraining the soul rather than corporal punishment, recent scholarship has highlighted another regime of governance: control through the management of space'.

accessible park (Connell, 1999). All of which prompts non-trivial questions about the future hope of cities like Manila and São Paulo being *public* places, and spaces of civic sociability and extended community. For, as Caldiera outlines:

> in a city of walls and enclaves such as São Paulo, public space undergoes a deep transformation. Felt as more dangerous, fractured by the new voids and enclaves, broken in its old alignments, and privatized with chains closing streets, armed guards, guard dogs, guardhouses, and walled parks, public space in São Paulo is increasingly abandoned to those who do not have a chance of living, working, and shopping in the new private, internalized, and fortified enclaves. As the spaces for the rich are enclosed and turned inside, the outside space is left for those who cannot afford to go in. (1996: 319)

LIMITS TO WALLING

> City spaces are always exposed, including the 'gated' communities that try everything possible to shut themselves off, but are still crossed by the fumes of the city, and the nightly escape of younger residents looking for entertainment in the city's more lively areas. (Amin and Thrift, 2002: 22)

> cities provide actual spaces where the workings of [official] regimes do not reach. (de Certeau, 1984)

In critically evaluating the walling of contemporary cities, it would be interesting to position Caldeira's compelling portrayal of São Paulo as a precarious dystopian landscape characterised by defensive walling, enclosure, capsular enclaves and a configuration of 'different worlds' between affluent and poor, alongside Berman's (1983) portrayal of Haussmannised Paris as a fledgling city of modernity characterised by a freshly inaugurated circulation 'throughout the whole city', of 'openness ... to all inhabitants', and of the worlds between rich and poor becoming, if not communal, at least recognised, and instituting an 'epiphany' flowing both ways. Perhaps from this a conclusion might be drawn that the social ecologies of 1870s' Paris and contemporary São Paulo are tugging in opposing trajectories. For as with many other twenty-first-century cities and their proliferation of enclosures, 'mobile circuits of exclusion' (Atkinson, 2008) and secessionary commons, the Brazilian metropolis appears built-by-design to insulate against the rich and powerful ever being directly confronted by the universe of slum-dwelling or the very *visibility* of bare life survival, thereby narrowing the scope for certain feedback loops to engender an aura of contrition and regard. And given what seems like a ceaseless erosion of genuine public spaces, at times actively authorised by elected city mayors and governments, are we to conclude that cities are regressing as spaces of openness, as sites of democracy, perhaps in a sense becoming post-democratic (MacLeod, 2011; Swyngedouw, 2011)? Might we be nearing the end of the 'public city'?

While much of the evidence presented above might indicate this to be so, several questions demand immediate attention. The first relates quite simply to the fact that the juxtaposition of Berman's Paris and Caldeira's São Paulo is based on *my selective* reading of *their particular* portrayals: and it does not constitute a systematic comparison of the two cities as they have unfolded during the last 150 years.[12] And while Paris has not been at the forefront of recent debates on walling, it is worth reminding ourselves of the thousands of poor displaced in Haussmann's Parisian renaissance (what Harvey (2008) characterises as an early instance of large-scale 'accumulation by dispossession'). And the quick introduction of glass-covered galleries, arcades and department stores (see earlier in this chapter) also permitted the bourgeoisie to avoid unwelcome interaction with lower classes and to erect new 'walls of cultural distance' – in dialect, manners, dress, eating habits, leisure and consumption – from the plebeian lower orders (McLaughlin and Muncie, 1999: 112). Here, perhaps the paradox between openness and enclosure requires to be analysed in more dialectical and relational terms (Merrifield, 2000).

Secondly, while the work of scholars like Davis and Caldiera, and geographers like Neil Smith (1996) and Don Mitchell (2003), have all been justifiably commended for their original and insightful respective investigations of urban inequality and injustice, some within the scholarly community are uneasy, viewing such contributions as illustrative of a recent genre of urban dystopianism. Lees (1998), for one, expresses misgivings about certain critical perspectives resonating akin to 'war correspondents' reporting from the urban street as if it were some incessant battlefield. Amin and Thrift (2002) similarly contend that certain 'doomsaying academics have made pessimism into a high art form', while Judd (2005: 127) avers that 'hyperbole may have become the principal methodology of today's urban scholarship'.[13] It is not so much Caldiera and others researching cities in the global south that Judd has in his sights as those analysing US cities, in particular Davis and members of a self-styled 'Los Angeles School' (Dear and Flusty, 2002) whose 'version of a dystopian urban future has swept through the community of scholars who study cities and become ... [something of]... a hegemonic interpretation' (Judd, 2005: 126).

We can, of course, recall how in his forensic dissection of the Peachtree Center, Judd was at the vanguard in alerting us about the fortification of US cities. And in this article penned a decade later, he acknowledges that, to be sure cities in America

---

12 While a recent debate has emerged in urban geography concerned to identify a pathway for comparing cities, there is no scope here for developing the discussion (Ward, 2010).

13 In defence of Davis and others, perhaps it is us as readers – students, teachers, researchers – who are drawn in by, fascinated, while equally appalled by, what we are reading in these terrific narratives and analyses of cities (see also Merrifield, 2000). And in looking to convey the messages to our respective audiences (and while just re-reading the introduction to this chapter) perhaps *we* are the dystopianists. 'Fortress LA' is just one chapter in Davis' *City of Quartz* (1990), but the preceding and subsequent chapters offer fascinating explanatory insights into the historical and political processes which have helped to initiate the fortified landscape. And the same applies in Caldeira's extended analysis of São Paulo.

and many countries have become more unequal: income and wealth gaps are increasing rapidly and urban governmentalities are shaping a displacement rather than eradication of homelessness. And relatedly cities across the world contain downtown fortifications, gated communities and enclosed malls. But for Judd (2005: 127) it then 'requires a great leap of faith to conclude that sanitized, enclosed, privatized, fortified enclaves are replacing all public spaces'. He goes on to contend that too often the exceptions – such as LA itself, and Baltimore and Detroit, which do, in the form of Harbor Place and Renaissance Center, respectively, contain 'virtual reservations' for visitors who rarely venture beyond the 'tourist bubble' – are being used to prove the rule; and that the physical renovation of central cities in the last 25 years has resulted in:

> cities all over North America ... becom[ing] safer, more pleasant environments for local residents and visitors alike. A traveler to cities in North America, Europe, and many other places can observe that cities are becoming more, not less, accessible to the tourist *flaneur* ... Local residents and visitors are not confined within barricaded spaces and enclaves in most cities of the United States or in any city in Canada or Europe. With few exceptions, such an experience greets visitors only in the most dangerous and crime-ridden cities in the world. (Judd, 2005: 128)[14]

And in their analysis of Ho Chi Minh City, Vietnam, Douglass and Huang identify that while the city's public space is diminishing, the parks are exceptionally well used and that, in turn, 'public life' is brimming:

> public streets and sidewalks are the places that have become the spaces of community and city life ... Along these streets people meet and engage in conversations, dwellers of shops put out chairs and spend their day in the public's eye. Men play board games, and children play sports and practice traditional dancing. At night motorcycles with entire families on them slowly ride through central areas in the cool air to see other people doing the same. Benches in public squares become filled with families. All of these scenes in public spaces reveal the liveliness of the city in its own forms of conviviality through the variety of social uses of these spaces ... Even Vietnam travel agencies proclaim that 'Life in HCMC resides in the city streets, markets, shops, pavement cafés and vendors selling their goods on the sidewalks'. (Douglass and Huang, 2007: 21–2)

---

14 In a characteristically judicious and droll chronicle, Judd urges those urban scholars busily berating the ersatz and unwelcoming landscape of renascent cities to just briefly reflect on their own personal experiences: 'having attended conferences in exotic settings and walked about the streets in search of exceptional restaurants, they (we) should know that the *noir* fantasies often spun over a good wine in these restaurants should be treated with a dose of irony, if nothing else' (2005: 129).

What these reflective promptings also raise is the spectre of agency. I say spectre, because sometimes it can feel that, in the imagery and prose deployed in much debate on fortification and walling, agency remains the preserve of ambitious architects, rapacious developers, manipulative politicians and revanchist cops. Fortunately, there is a fast growing body of literature, often drawing on the theoretical promptings of Foucault, Lefebvre and de Certeau (Lees, 2003b; Mitchell, 2003; Ruddick, 1996a), and more recently thinking around urban democracy and the relationship between 'publics' and 'public space' (Iveson, 2007; Staeheli and Mitchell, 2008), offering critical insights into the agency, rituals of resistance and endeavours to nurture 'spaces of escape' undertaken by those who might seek to transgress the normative ecologies of urban fortifications, such as homeless, skateboarders and protesters. And in this regard, it is surely worth reflecting on how so many of the insurgent movements for political democracy, economic egalitarianism and social justice throughout 2010 and 2011 have been pushing at the very limits of elite-led endeavours to wall and enclose contemporary cities. Indeed, incidents like the tightly policed preclusion of Occupy London to enter the now 'private' Paternoster Square near St Paul's Cathedral, alongside the revanchist military tactics being waged on civil activists in Wall Street and Zuccotti Park, New York, have in some senses translated these protests into a question about the urban commons, the limits to enclosure and the degree to which contemporary cities are democratic (MacLeod, 2012).

ACKNOWLEDGEMENTS

The author would like to thank Eugene McCann and Ronan Paddison for their guidance in framing the chapter, and also for their considerable patience in awaiting its production. Colin McFarlane also provided inspiration on certain themes discussed here.

9

Health and the City

Graham Moon and Robin Kearns

INTRODUCTION

> By 2015, half the population of the developing world will be living in cities and is expected to double in the next 30 years. By 2030 these cities can be expected to triple their land area. Urban health challenges to improve the quality of life for the urban poor are indeed daunting. (World Bank, 2009)

> Good quality urban areas can be stimulating and offer opportunities not found elsewhere. But the urban environment places stresses and strains on human health and wellbeing that contribute to tens of thousands of deaths each year and a considerable burden of ill health. Major issues include air pollution, climate, obesity and mental health. Most of these problems are not unique to urban areas, but are important because of the high numbers of people living there and the aggravating impact of factors associated with urban areas, such as high levels of vehicle emissions, poor housing and a lack of good quality green space. (UK Royal Commission on Environmental Pollution, 2006: 5)

In these two quotes we see the essence of the connections between health and the city. With urbanisation comes population concentration, the stresses of faster and more complex lifestyles, overcrowding, and pressures on natural resources and the services that promote, protect and repair our health. The consequence is that cities and the accompanying processes of urbanisation are often bad for our health. To this end, urban health is now emerging as a specialist sub-discipline specifically concerned with the links between urbanisation, urban living and health (Leon, 2008; Vlahov and Galea, 2003). While much of the recent impetus for this emergence comes from public health and epidemiology, the field has inherent interdisciplinarity. Geography and urban planning are partners in this task; it is not enough to simply catalogue health problems as 'urban', we need to identify and think through the circumstances that constitute health problems for particular people with particular consequences, in, between and across *places* that manifest their 'urbanicity' in particular ways.

This chapter provides a critical assessment of current research on urban health. We do not seek to be comprehensive though we draw attention to key themes. We tend to stress more recent work and also aim to point to emerging research directions. The first section considers the well-established notion of the 'urban penalty'. We begin with a reflection upon the equation of urban with poor health and the implicit corresponding assumption that rurality is in some way associated with better health. We then consider the historical relevance of the urban penalty to cities in the developed world and its contemporary importance in the global south before moving to wider agendas linking health to utopian city planning and a short consideration of the health advantages of living in the city. The second substantive section of the chapter examines health-related behaviour in the city. Here we consider key current research topics: the walkable city, the food desert and spaces of drinking and smoking. For our third theme, we turn to the question of how the state of urban health can be collectively managed. We examine the idea of governance at international and local levels, before considering how sites of health care in cities change in significance through both political ideology on the part of providers and place-loyalty on the part of users. We then examine a view of primary care that takes attention beyond clinical settings into the lived environments of everyday city life. Our last substantive section considers those marginalised in the relentless churning of socio-spatial processes that make up urban life. We examine the place of stigmatised groups and specifically mental health care users in the city. We consider the places they and care providers are developing to, at least potentially, maintain journeys towards independence. The chapter concludes by identifying areas where research on urban health could usefully concentrate in the next few years.

THE URBAN PENALTY

The idea of the 'urban penalty' refers to a central and well-established paradox in the links between health and cities: that urban mortality rates have been observed to be significantly higher than those in rural areas, in spite of the much better accessibility to health care generally enjoyed by urban residents. The urban penalty is a construct most clearly evidenced in the cities of the nineteenth-century industrial revolution in developed economies, and in the juxtaposition of slums and affluence in the rapidly growing cities of the global south. In these circumstances, its common basis appears to include economic instability, population growth and changing modes of socio-economic organisation.

It is important to think critically about the urban penalty. The juxtaposition in urban areas of poor health and better access to health care is perhaps not surprising. Almost 50 years ago it had become evident that improvements in health over time had stemmed more from improvements in sanitation and nutrition; health care was not unimportant but it was a relative sideshow (McKeown, 1979). The urban penalty is also an idea that posits a particular conception of the city, and indeed a countervailing and equally stereotypical perception of rurality. The city is 'other', antithetical to 'normal' human health, bringing together, in one place, various health-damaging factors. Ill-health flows from the way the city is, in a fashion, reminiscent of environmental determinism. In opposition we can observe an alternative construct – the rural idyll (Halfacree, 1995; Mingay, 1989) – which sees humans in their natural state, living healthy lives in situations removed from the artificial disturbance of (excess) concentration into urban places. This crude binary opposition (urban penalty – rural idyll) is arguably most evident in the rapidly urbanising regions and nations of the 'global south'. Yet even in such cases, the contrast between cities and villages is troubled when, for example in China, urban pollution and its ill-effects literally spill out into the countryside (Chan and Yao, 2008).

When urban developments and policies are planned or enacted with health in mind, the urban penalty can be reduced. Equally, the rural idyll can be at least as challenging to health as urban residence (Philo et al., 2003; Watkins and Jacoby, 2007). Rural poverty, isolation, the greater visibility of stigmatised conditions and limited services can all conspire to create a rural penalty that can easily overcome the rural idyll. Empirical work confirms that 'penalties' are not exclusively urban. In the UK context it appears that health inequalities are similar in urban and rural areas. Analogous socio-economic groups enjoy (or suffer) similar experiences (Phillimore and Reading, 1992). Only in remote rural areas is there a clear absolute health advantage. Data from the most recent Health Survey for England provides further evidence of the limited health differences between urban and rural areas. For self-reported health there is some evidence of a very slight gradient in favour of rural advantage but for long-standing illness the (equally slight) gradient is generally reversed. More recent research in Scotland has cast this finding in a temporal context (Levin and Leyland, 2006). Inequalities in all-cause mortality increased between 1981 and 2001 and the increase was actually greatest in remote rural areas. There was also differentiation by sex and age. Men experienced greatest inequalities in urban areas and women in remote rural areas. Elderly people in remote rural areas were most affected.

The classic manifestations of the urban penalty were in industrialising nineteenth-century cities in the now developed world and in the burgeoning cities of the present day global south. For the former, two case examples summarise matters. The much-cited work of John Snow on cholera transmission in mid-Victorian London is a classic tale of epidemiological inquiry (Brody et al., 2000; McLeod, 2000). Snow's work spanned the 1849 and 1854 cholera epidemics and highlights the recurrent presence of epidemic disease in the overcrowded and insanitary conditions prevailing at the time in London and other 'western' cities. What Snow contributed to uncovering was the interplay of sewage and (drinking) water in the aetiology of cholera. This interaction was a product of the contemporary urban condition. For most city dwellers, housing was poor quality. Occupancy levels were high and overcrowding rife. Drinking water was of poor quality and waste disposal was inadequate. These conditions were compounded by poorly regulated industry and associated pollution. Our second case example is equally highly cited. Friedrich Engels' *The Condition of the Working Class in England in 1844* is a classic account of the insanitary conditions that accompanied the industrial revolution (Engels and Kiernan, 1987). Engels focused extensively on the city of Manchester where the health consequences flowing from rapid population growth, uncontrolled industrial development, poor housing, immigration and poor sanitation were particularly marked. He indicates that mortality rates from infectious diseases were over four times higher than rural areas. With supporting examples from Leeds, Bradford and Edinburgh, Engels summarises his assessment of central Manchester thus:

> on re-reading my description, I am forced to admit that instead of being exaggerated, it is far from black enough to convey a true impression of the filth, ruin, and uninhabitableness, the defiance of all considerations of clean-liness, ventilation, and health which characterise the construction of this single district, containing at least twenty to thirty thousand inhabitants. (Engels and Kiernan, 1987: 43)

Arguably we are currently seeing history repeating, if not exacerbating, itself in the even more rapid urbanisation that is occurring in the global south, given the emergence of the mega-city phenomenon (Douglass, 2000).

Academic work in historical urban (health) geography has continued to emphasise the urban penalty. Combating the urban penalty with legislation that improved sanitation and raised housing standards was by no means a straightforward process (Kearns, 1988). Alongside the changing economic fortunes of the urban population and their political representation, factors such as climate played a part (Williams and Mooney, 1994). Nor was the impact of the urban penalty experienced equally (Mooney, 2002). The gap between male and female mortality changed as infectious disease mortality, which impacted most on women, began to decrease as sanitation improved (Mooney, 2007). Beyond the UK, historical work has considered the urban penalty in imperial Germany (Vögele, 2000) and Iberia (Reher, 2001; Reis, 2009). The latter works offer confirmation of a particular impact on male health and the importance of action by urban governments in the fields of sanitation, housing standards, public health surveillance and poverty relief. It also shows that the regular employment opportunities available in cities could, in some circumstances, counter the penalty and even set up an urban premium if rural employment conditions were particularly bad.

In turning to the present-day urban penalty in the global south it is salutary to note that the countervailing idea of the urban premium retains some currency. For example, Woods (2003) reminds us that, historically, cities in the Far East experienced better health than neighbouring rural areas. This contrast was confused by poor reporting of mortality, varying definitions of the urban and differences in cultural practices between urban and rural areas. There is little dispute, however, about the existence of an urban penalty in the present-day global south.

Case Study: The Urban Penalty in Africa

In Kenya, although the urban–rural mortality gap has narrowed as a consequence of reducing infant and maternal mortality in rural areas, urban mortality improvements have stalled and even reversed. A review of the changing patterns of and explanations for rural/urban differentials in under-5 mortality links draws attention to growing

(Continued)

(Continued)

national planning and policy problems associated with rapid urbanisation. In the history of African colonisation, urban mortality was initially observed to be low because it was controlled in Europeanised cities, and data on non-European populations was limited. This was particularly evident in situations where there were early expressions of public health measures, such as the installation of sewerage and water-supply systems. Since the 1950s, inequalities have widened. While some urban populations have become richer, and better educated and housed compared with rural counterparts, recent population growth has been associated with heightening measures of poverty, unemployment, crowding and poor nutrition. Such influences are taking a particular toll on child survival rates in Nairobi, a city once dubbed 'The Green City in the Sun'.
Adapted from Gould, 1998.

The situation observable in Nairobi is not atypical of the global south and is largely a result of hyper-growth in urban populations that has exceeded what might be termed the 'carrying capacities' of the cities, resulting in failures in governance, declining environmental conditions and socio-economic breakdown (Fotso, 2007). Generally the urban penalty in the global south is reducing when attention has been focused on urban poverty alleviation, but in cases where such programmes have not been possible, the penalty is increasing and the gap between urban and rural well-being is widening. More specific policy pointers suggest the effectiveness of community participation, intersectoral cooperation, the promotion of resilience rather than the targeting of vulnerability, and the provision of accessible primary care in disadvantaged urban environments (Few et al., 2003; Harpham, 2009).

The association that we have highlighted between insanitary conditions, socio-economic deprivation, industrialisation and the urban health penalty begs two questions. Firstly, as at least one disciple of Engels would have had it: what is to be done? Secondly, we might ask whether there exist any countervailing arguments: what are the health advantages of urban places? (That is, what is the potential for an 'urban premium'?) In terms of action against the urban penalty, it is important to recognise that even at the time of Snow and Engels, there was a clear recognition that mortality burdens were excessive in urban areas. While debate raged about the proximate and distal causes of this mortality excess, for example between sanitary and miasmic theorists, there was a general recognition that the problem required coordinated action rather than a *laissez-faire* approach and some level of state intervention was probably in order. In the UK the 1840s saw the creation of the Health of Towns Association and the Metropolitan Sanitary Association, both dedicated to encouraging sanitary reform. The Public Health Act, 1848, began a process of empowering local authorities to intervene to improve the health of urban populations. Eventually slum clearance programmes were initiated, new sewer systems such as Bazalgette's London sewer network were put in place and town-planning legislation developed (Hall, 2002: Chapter 3; Porter, 1999: Chapter 7; P.J. Smith, 1994). Similar processes took place in other western countries (Corburn, 2009; Ladd, 1990; Peterson, 1979) including the establishment of public housing in countries such as New Zealand (Ferguson, 1994).

Perhaps the ultimate expression of these processes was the 'garden city' (Hebbert, 1999; Howard, 1945). In this utopian town-planning movement the alleged evils of the city, including its health problems, were to be addressed by amalgamating the conveniences of the city with the supposed healthfulness of the country (Figure 9.1). The idea spawned planned communities, new towns and, as we shall see later, both the healthy cities movement and what in many ways is its antithesis, the sprawling, and often health-damaging, car-dependent suburbia characteristic of much of urban USA and Australia. These latter health-corroding outcomes of suburbia are arguably ironic given that suburbia was originally believed to be, and sold as, a healthy alternative to the central city – a refuge from crowded tenements with open space and better sanitation. The urban penalty thus continues to be a challenge for town planning; a discipline that has always contained an overt commitment to health improvement (Sloane, 2006). Today urban sprawl provides the common agenda (Johnson and Marko, 2008). It underpins the continuing urban penalty on a global scale and is compounded in the global south by continuing poor sanitation.

To conclude this section, we need to stress how the health advantages of living in cities are unequally experienced. As we stated earlier, it would be wrong to simply label cities as unhealthy places. Just as cities contain the extremes of deprivation that

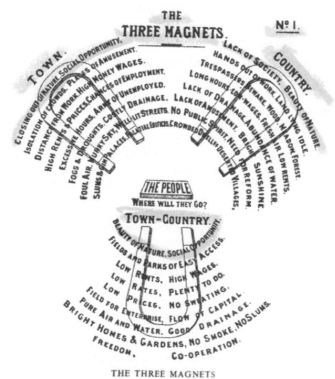

THE THREE MAGNETS

Figure 9.1 Reconciling the city and country: Howard's classic 'three magnets' diagram (Howard, 1945)

are associated with poorest health and lowest life expectancy, so too they also hold extremes of wealth and privilege. The more affluent areas of cities worldwide will tend to house those people who enjoy the best health on a national and international scale. They will also house those who are in the best position to purchase good health care in the face of adverse health events. An example of this polarisation is provided by the oft-quoted gap of six years in male life expectancy (four for women) between the electoral wards containing the London Underground Jubilee Line stations at Westminster (stereotyped as affluent central London) and at Canning Town (equally stereotyped as deprived East London) (Greater London Authority, 2007). At nearly 78 years for men and 84 for women, life expectancy in Westminster is high by any standards. Just 16 km separate the two tube stations yet the differences in life expectancy are stark (72 years for men and 80 for women in Canning Town). They are yet more marked in Glasgow where the adjoining communities of Drumchapel and Bearsden have a life expectancy gap of almost ten years. Perhaps the most obvious health advantage enjoyed by urban areas is access to health care. As we have already noted, this may matter surprisingly little for health outcomes. Moreover, the concentration of health care provision in urban areas may not always be high quality, particularly in primary care (Guagliardo et al., 2004; Hyndman and Holman, 2001; Moon and North, 2000). In quantitative terms there is almost inevitably an urban premium – even to the extent that over-provision can result and be contested on the grounds of historical privilege (Moon and Brown, 2001).

Case Study: Health and Heat Waves: A Contemporary Urban Penalty in the Global North?

Urban areas have long been known to generate heat islands – higher temperatures compared to surrounding rural areas. When this effect is compounded by a heat wave, excess mortality can result, particularly when it is accompanied by high humidity, pollution (Besancenot, 2002), and a reduced availability of services to deal with heat-related health problems. The urban penalty associated with heat waves concentrates on elderly people and other vulnerable groups who lack the personal resources to combat the effects of heat. It is likely to be exacerbated by the impact of global climate change (Kovats and Akhtar, 2008). Clearly some parts of the world are more likely to experience excess heat and indeed be better prepared for its health effects. For example, São Paulo and Delhi see less excess mortality in comparison to the ongoing health problems associated with the urban penalty (Hajat et al., 2005). Equally clearly, both as a reflection of structural discrimination and also as a consequence of less experience with heat waves, these impacts are best documented in the USA and Europe.

The 1995 Chicago heat wave (Klinenberg, 2002) is perhaps the best documented. A combination of sustained high temperatures in excess of 40°C and excess humidity led to about 600 additional deaths in mid-July 1995. Most were elderly economically disadvantaged males, with African-American people being disproportionately represented. Older women, with better social networks, were more likely to survive. The ability to afford a functioning air-conditioning system was crucial. There was little evidence to suggest that the heat wave simply brought forward deaths that would have occurred anyway in the near future; there was a real, tangible and immediate effect on health. Studies of heat waves elsewhere in the USA have suggested that heat-related mortality is less socially specific in its impact outside heat wave periods (Smoyer, 1998); deaths tend to be associated with the established peak locations of urban heat islands (Johnson and Wilson, 2009); and the level of urbanisation is an important correlate of levels of mortality (Sheridan and Dolney, 2003).

The 2003 European heat wave was concentrated in August. Its effects were felt most in France where national holidays ensured that services were less able to respond. Estimates of the mortality impact in France suggest in excess of 11,000 deaths (World Health Organization, 2003). European housing traditionally does not have (or need) air conditioning so technological responses were limited. Again, elderly people living alone with poor social networks were most vulnerable; older people living in institutions tended to fare relatively well. There is some suggestion that, unlike the USA experience, mortality tended to concentrate on older women, and again, the hypothesis that heat waves simply provided an early 'harvest' of anticipated deaths is disproved (Toulemon and Barbieri, 2008). Rey et al. (2007) provide a reminder that excess mortality in urban areas during heat waves is an established epidemiological fact: six major heat waves in France between 1971 and 2003 were each characterised by a high death rate. Nonetheless, societal learning is also possible; mortality in the heat wave of 2006 was lower than expected as the population adapted following the experience of 2003.

HEALTH-RELATED BEHAVIOUR AND CITIES

Health-related behaviours include smoking, alcohol consumption, diet and physical activity. People may choose to pursue particular behaviours or combinations of behaviours, but that choice is constrained and framed by socio-economic circumstance and opportunity. Health-related behaviours are important because they are implicated in the aetiology of a wide range of chronic health conditions; inequalities in health outcomes are usually complemented by inequalities in health-related behaviours. As concentrations of population, retail provision and consumption opportunity and built environments that reflect changing approaches to urban design, cities naturally impact on the prevalence of health-related behaviours. In this section we focus on the interface between the city and two aspects of health-related behaviour: the food desert and the walkable city.

Food deserts can be defined as areas where there is limited opportunity to purchase nutritious good quality raw food materials at affordable prices. It might seem unlikely that such areas would exist, certainly in western cities. However, food deserts develop both as a consequence of the outcomes of sequential planning decisions that have concentrated particular types of food retailing in particular locations and also as a result of the intra-urban ecology of food purchasing habits and the availability of income for food shopping. Much of what contributes to food deserts also stems from food retailer practices (Hawkes, 2008). Where they are located, what they stock, the price at which they sell, their discounting activities and their attitude to nutritional excellence are all important. Put simply these pressures can mean that raw food materials in poorer parts of cities are often of poorer quality. There may also be less choice and problems may be supplemented by difficulties in physical access to better food retail opportunities. Moreover deserts of raw food materials can occupy precisely the same locations as high carbohydrate, high fat, fast-food outlets. This results in a health damaging absence being accompanied by a health damaging presence, an 'obesogenic' environment (Lake and Townshend, 2006). Shaw (2006) has attempted a classification of food deserts based on spatial manifestations of financial and physical barriers to consumption of a healthy diet and the attitudes and knowledge of consumers. He notes that food deserts can manifest themselves in different ways, and perceptions of the existence of urban food deserts may not match the realities of raw food retail provision.

An attempt to review systematically the evidence for food deserts has cast some doubt on the methodological quality of the available studies (Beaulac et al., 2009). Clearest evidence appears to come from the USA where food deserts relate to racial and income inequality and individual poverty is compounded by area disadvantage (Black et al., 2010; Bovell-Benjamin et al., 2009; Morland and Evenson, 2009). In the UK case, a key study involved the Universities of Southampton, Leeds and Cardiff (Whelan et al., 2002; Wrigley, 2002; Wrigley et al., 2003; Wrigley et al., 2002) and used a range of approaches to investigate the Seacroft 'food desert' in Leeds as well as the impact of a new retail development on the nature of the food desert. Different population groups had varying success in adapting to living in the food desert. Economic constraints were important as were limitations on physical accessibility, but prior health and social responsibilities were also significant factors in determining individual behaviour. The idea that town planning and retail development policy could impact on health-related behaviour had not been subject to much research in the UK prior to the project. The research provided a sound evidence base confirming that such 'non-health' interventions could have a modest positive effect on behaviour. A second major study identified underlying complexity in this relationship (Cummins and Macintyre, 2002; Cummins et al., 2005; Cummins et al., 2008). A before-and-after study of dietary and food shopping behaviours in two equally deprived areas, one of which saw the opening of a new store, found that people tended to switch their shopping allegiance to the new store. Travel times to food retail outlets were also reduced. However, there was little impact on dietary behaviour. In Canada researchers have suggested that, while high-need neighbourhoods may have good raw food retail accessibility, they often lack access to the choice offered by supermarkets (Larsen and Gilliland, 2008; Smoyer-Tomic et al., 2006). This situation reflects the suburbanisation of large-scale food retail provision, a process evident in many western cities. Local cooperative initiatives can offer some respite (Larsen and Gilliland, 2009). Australian studies have reached similar conclusions indentifying food deserts in Adelaide, Melbourne and Brisbane among other cities (Ball et al., 2009; Burns and Inglis, 2007; O'Dwyer and Coveney, 2006; Winkler et al., 2006).

Many cities, and certainly many European cities, could be seen as walkable, particularly in terms of their historic cores and major tourist areas. Walkability, the concordance of urban design and the maximisation of pedestrian mobility, has emerged in recent years as a key research theme in urban health. In large part the focus has been on the absence of walkability, with the argument being that urban design in many cities has systematically reduced walkability. Consequently certain urban forms have become associated with reduced opportunities for everyday physical activity and labelled as health damaging.

Like the urban food desert, the walkable city can be seen as part of the potentially obesogenic nature of the urban environment (Herrick, 2009; Sui, 2003). The excess calorific intake in food deserts is matched by limited calorific output in urban areas with limited walkability (Moon, 2009). Limited walkability is fostered by land-use planning and urban design. Much research has focused on the low-density, suburban neighbourhoods that developed around the fringes of many cities in the twentieth century. Often characterised as urban sprawl (see above), such developments were and remain centred on a dependence on the private car, block land-use zoning and limited local services. Daily activities require sitting in a car rather than walking (Johnson and Marko, 2008). Increasingly urban planning is aiming to increase walkability, reduce traffic and lower environmental impacts in order to foster better health (Southworth, 2005). The 'new urbanism', promoting high-density developments with good public transport and high levels of walkability, forms part of this movement (Cozens and Hillier, 2008)

GIS technologies have featured extensively in research on walkable (and non-walkable) cities. Not only do these technologies provide a means of identifying and mapping land-use and its link to walkability, population density and the privatisation of transport, but they also allow the exploration of road connectivity and linkages. Communities with short street blocks and multiple connectivities within their boundaries tend to be more walkable (Cerin et al., 2007a). Other work has sought to develop survey instruments to capture local perceptions of walkability (Cerin et al., 2007b; Millington et al., 2009). For Ewing and Handy (2009) the walkable city is characterised by imageability, enclosure, human scale, transparency and complexity. Much evidence has inevitably been focused on the sprawling cities of the USA (Sallis et al., 2009). It is clear from this work that walkability affects levels of physical activity and low walkability is associated with higher levels of obesity. However, safety concerns can override positive effects, particularly for children (Holt et al., 2009; Holt et al., 2008). One intervention that has sought to counter safety concerns in an urban setting is the walking school bus which involves parent volunteers guiding groups of children to and from school along a set route and at a set time (Collins and Kearns, 2010).

Over recent years, the US focus of research on urban walkability and health has been supplemented and enhanced by a significant body of work on Australian cities from Billie Giles-Corti and colleagues (e.g. Crawford et al., 2008; Falconer et al., 2010; Giles-Corti and Donovan, 2002a, 2002b; Giles-Corti et al., 2009; Giles-Corti et al., 2008; Hume et al., 2009, McCormack et al., 2007; McCormack et al., 2004, Sugiyama et al., 2008, 2009; Wood et al., 2008). This work has shown that urban design contributes to mental and physical health outcomes as well as more generally to subjective well-being. While there has been a tendency to focus on non-walkability, policies to promote walkability can function as a positive instrument for enhancing urban health. Moreover, when considered alongside the enhanced presence of parks and other recreational opportunities in urban areas, it is possible to reconstruct the city as potentially health promoting, not least by recognising the social interaction that takes place in such settings.

Case Study: Consumption Landscapes and Problem Drinking in the City

There is little doubt that alcohol consumption can be a health-damaging behaviour when practised to excess and/or over a long period of time. Equally it is associated with conviviality, stress relief and relaxation. It is among more youthful populations that problem drinking tends to concentrate, and cities tend to be more youthful.

Problem drinking is particularly associated with city marketing and the growth of what has been termed the 'night-time economy'. Many cities have a thriving night-time economy. In some cases the development of this economy has been a deliberate strategy contributing to economic renewal and revival. Club destination areas and a 24-hour entertainment culture may make for a potent part of city marketing, drawing in young and not-so-young from a wide area. Drinking, aided in the UK by relaxed licensing laws, forms a major part of this urban phenomenon and has both positive and negative sides. Against the positive receipt of revenue to the city economy and the creation of jobs, we can stack the less happy consequences of violence, inappropriate behaviour and littering.

Urban drinking and night-time economy has become a significant area of research for health, social and cultural geographers as well as others concerned with the changing nature of cities. In Britain, research has shown how the topic links to wider issues concerning images of corporatisation and gentrification (Jayne et al., 2006; Jayne et al., 2008a, 2008b, 2008c); inclusivity, comfort and the experience of a night out in British city centres (Eldridge and Roberts, 2008); and images of women and femininity (Holloway et al., 2009; Ormerod and Wiltshire, 2009). As Kneale and French (2008) note, zones of problem drinking in British cities are by no means a new phenomenon. Nor is problem drinking by younger people exclusively an urban problem (Valentine et al., 2008). Indeed such concerns arguably intersect with long-standing moral panics regarding youth and youth culture (Collins and Kearns, 2001). The city planners' vision of an urbane European café culture has been challenged by its encounter with British drinking cultures (Roberts and Gornostaeva, 2007).

GOVERNING URBAN HEALTH

How is health governed in cities? Here we think not simply of the organisational and jurisdictional aspects of governance evident in, for example, the state or private agencies with responsibilities for delivering health care; rather our focus is on a more Foucauldian form of governance or governmentality. In this sense, the health of urban citizens is controlled, framed and regulated through a complex web of national and international programmes, laws, exhortations and projects. This web of influences results in an expression of governmentality – the governing of citizens' behaviour at-a-distance through persuasive as well as coercive attempts to get them to reshape their conduct, attitudes and behaviours. To continue the example of problem drinking and moral panics, health can arguably be (at least partially) governed through the state using the media to push people to 'conduct their conduct' in particular ways.

Ultimately ideology and collective behaviour have a role to play. For example, in some cities a high degree of social control over health behaviour is evident though legislation banning public smoking, drinking or even, in Singapore, spitting. Elsewhere the freedoms inherent within less-controlled polities see the development of 'skid row' zones within the downtown cores just as corrosive to health as the Victorian slum. This control and surveillance can be time- as well as space-specific. It is central to urban life, notably during times of health scares. Responses, both public and private, to avian influenza in a range of urban settings provide well-documented examples (Scoones, 2010). More recently epidemic cholera in the aftermath of the 2009 Haiti earthquake offers an instance of the intersection between health and the breakdown of urban governance.

Case Study: Governance in Action – SARS in Toronto

Within a few weeks in early 2003, SARS (Severe Acute Respiratory Syndrome) spread from the Chinese province of Guangdong to ultimately infect people in up to 37 countries. SARS had a particular impact within the health care system and ultimately the tourist industry in Toronto, Canada. Hospitals and health care workers became facilitators of disease diffusion with SARS occurring most frequently in hospitals where close contact with sick patients, particularly in emergency departments, and critical care units spread the disease.

In terms of governance, the federal agency Health Canada offered guidelines for clinicians as well as the general public. In April 2003, the World Health Organization (WHO) advised against all but essential travel to Toronto, advising that some travellers departing from Toronto appeared to have 'exported' SARS elsewhere. By the end of April, the WHO announced that the advisory would be withdrawn but already Toronto tourism had suffered as a result, thus illustrating the 'knock-on' effects of interventions to govern health behaviour and disease transmission (Affonso et al., 2004).

Beyond these facts and effects of the outbreak, we can observe deeper processes of globalisation: the transmission and response to SARS can be located within a broader global context that recognises the way cities are embedded in international networks of economy, information, and regulatory practices. Drawing on a bodily metaphor, Ali and Keil (2006) alert us to the 'intricate capillary structures of the globalised network' through which pathogens such as SARS can interact with economic, political and social factors. They maintain that these interactions can exist both in the connective networks and in global cities themselves. This embeddedness suggests new issues of governance for public health and epidemiological efforts which seek to contain disease and track its movement through the people and places.

As a further example of governmental technology focused on health, the Healthy Cities programme of the World Health Organization (WHO) illustrates many of our

contentions. It attempts to facilitate international collaboration on health development goals with local governments establishing political commitments, initiating
institutional change and engaging in capacity building, partnership-based planning
and innovative projects. Early articulations of the Healthy Cities' perspectives highlighted the potential for collective action for health. In the words of one commenta-
tor, because the city 'is a place with which its citizens identify, there are good
prospects for participation harnessed to neighbourhood or civic pride' (Ashton et al.,
1986: 319). The movement aimed (and continues to aim) to promote sustainable
urban change that addresses health inequalities and urban poverty, with attention
directed at the needs of vulnerable groups and the social, economic and environmental determinants of health. Healthy Cities takes an intersectoral approach in the
quest to include health considerations in economic, regeneration and urban development efforts (Davies and Kelly, 1993). In Europe over 1,200 cities and towns are
now designated as healthy cities (http://www.euro.who.int/healthy-cities). Their
association with the WHO has given municipalities a legitimacy to build bridges
between urban planning and health services, with intersectoral cooperation endorsed
by mayors and equity identified as a critical (if largely aspirational) value (Tsouros,
2009). Recent developments within the Healthy Cities programme include a widening, under the 2009 Zagreb Declaration to champion action on not only health, but
also – mirroring the *Closing the Gap in a Generation* report (Commission on Social
Determinants of Health, 2008) – sustainable development and social justice. Critics
have claimed, however, that too easily the essential social movement that underlies
Healthy Cities' thinking can be diluted and substituted with actions and approaches
that reduce it to a 'bureaucratic tool' (Baum, 1993).

   A quarter-century on from the inception of the Healthy Cities movement there
has arguably been a recognition of the limits to which its participative ideals can be
harnessed, especially when the conditions of everyday life place many households
under too much stress and preoccupation to permit engagement in broader goals
and projects. Against this backdrop, and in parallel with ongoing efforts, a range of
non-governmental organisations (NGOs) are persistent in their critique of the status quo, challenging not only policies that do not deliver on improving health but
also the very models of health care that inform them. Arguably, it is more likely to
be at the local neighbourhood level, where residents have stake in their community,
that citizens are most likely to agree to, and participate in, being 'governed' in the
interests of health. Moving from the global and regional to the national and local
scale, we can observe such ideas shaping the configuration and flavour of some
primary health services in urban New Zealand. In Wellington, the Newtown Union
Health Service opened in 1987 in a low-income neigbourhood as a joint venture
between the Service Workers' Union, health professionals and community activists
(Neuwelt and Crampton, 2005). As a community-owned-and-governed primary
care provider it has consistently been committed to community development with
a governance group including representatives from Samoan, Indian, Somali,
Cambodian and Cook Island communities, various community centres, labour unions
and mental health consumer groups. The structure and style of governance has resulted
in responsiveness to local need rarely seen in government or privately run services:

opening hours have been longer than usual, a drop-in clinic offered and outreach clinics established in various constituent communities. To an extent, the level of attention to the social and environmental determinants of health at community-owned centres such as Newtown mirrors earlier initiatives such as the Peckham Centre in England which focused on preventative rather than curative approaches to urban health.

The Wellington-based Newtown centre and the English Peckham initiative have been local, but nationally influential, expressions of alternative governance over bodies and services. At a broader scale they have their parallels in the commitments evident in programmes such as the Millennium Development Goals. They seek inclusion, participation and involvement. They challenge inequalities and hold out the possibility of a communal reshaping of urban health. Yet, at the same time, to return to the ideas at the start of this section, they are also expressions of govern-mentality. At root they represent metanarratives in which population health is controlled and framed in desirable directions by national and international coalitions of the powerful.

RESHAPING URBAN HEALTH CARE

From a demographic perspective cities are, in essence, spatial concentrations of population. As an outcome of population concentration, they become 'significant nodes' in terms of Christaller's classic 'Central Place Theory', and focal points of not just economic enterprise but also service activity. The apex of any health care hierarchy is to be found in cities: tertiary hospitals and associated clusters of medical expertise. Cities are also sites of innovation and the 'knowledge economy'. Ideas of what works within health care both quickly develop and can be quickly superseded. Hence, the health care landscape in cities often tends to be in a state of flux with openings and closing and reorganising of the landscape of care to accommodate new technology or staff. However, although in essence they are social constructions, cities at their most tangible comprise the 'bricks and mortar' of the built environment. So it is also the case with health care. Once built, hospitals and clinics can both constrain opportunities when the type and volume of patient demand outgrows them, and offer opportunities to capitalise on 'place-loyalty' and the heritage of local health care when under threat of closure.

Place-loyalty is invariably generated over years, if not generations. In cases where a clientele and sympathetic public is sought for a new development, a combination of branding and emphasis on novelty is evident. This approach was evident in the example of the Starship Hospital in Auckland where an innovative children's hospital was given this unlikely name in a quest to both appeal to a young clientele and to elicit financial support through its charitable foundation (Kearns and Barnett, 1999). The opposite of loyalty is disregard. In the reshaping of urban health care, we can see psychiatric hospitals rapidly accruing a public disregard through the period of deinstitutionalisation leading to widespread relief rather than protest at their closure (Kearns and Moon, 2012). With any closure of a building comes closure of opportunities and an inevitable movement of people and services elsewhere. In the case of mental health care, the closures of hospitals on urban fringes led to the ostensible relocation of patients in community settings and the frequent drift of many into destitution in inner cities.

Case Study: St Bartholomew's Hospital, London

In 1998, after a five-year struggle to remain open, St Bartholomew's Hospital was granted a reprieve when the Secretary of State for Health overturned a decision of the previous administration and saved the country's oldest hospital from closure. Inner London, it was contended, was served by too many hospitals, which provided too many hospital beds and whose services were costly and inefficient to run. As a result, a number of prominent inner London hospitals faced a severe rationalisation of their services, if not outright closure. In the process of resistance, Moon and Brown (2001) note the construction of communities dedicated to the retention of 'Barts' as well as four distinct representations of the hospital: as community resource; as a site of expertise; as a heritage symbol; and as a site pertinent to the identities of Londoners. One conclusion is that a health care facility can be more than a site of medical encounters; rather it can be a multi-faceted and potent symbol – of the city itself (in this case, London) and of a particular medical tradition. For St Bartholomew's, which had served Londoners since the twelfth century, those seeking to save the hospital used language which represented Barts as holding some form of symbolic or material link to its locality.

Significant inequalities in access to, and the quality of, primary health care in cities have been noted persistently (Moon and North, 2000). Too often, it seems, patients have a limited 'stake' in influencing the character of services available. This situation has implications for access inasmuch as valuable opportunities to mould a service around the needs of a community are lost when people are seen as consumers rather than participants. While there may be a concentration of GP practices in cities, access to after-hours care can be variable and patients are frequently diverted to hospital emergency departments, in turn sometimes hindering efficient treatment of genuine cases of emergency. Commercial enterprise has, in some cities, been responsive. In Auckland in the 1990s, for instance, new accident and medical clinics, often sited near or within shopping malls, were established featuring flashy interiors and comforting surrounds including televisions and free coffee. These branded clinics offered after-hours medical care for routine general practitioner (GP) consultation and minor accidents, employing shift-working doctors. This situation minimised the likelihood that one would encounter any continuity of care (Barnett and Kearns 1996). In the global south, the scale of urbanisation is such that primary health care is frequently fragmentary or aided by project-based NGO assistance. Poorer residents invariably rely on a range of treatment opportunities and, as Ergler et al.'s (2011) work in Chennai shows, this reliance can circulate between private and public sectors according to a household's financial means at the time. This work reveals ways in which slum-dwellers often overcome access barriers (e.g. through relying on their networks for loans to enable consultation with a private practitioner, or 'queue-jumping' to see a doctor if they know the staff). When they cannot afford further private treatment, poorer people often end up in the public system as a last resort or they partake of informal therapies that may result in unanticipated risks to their health.

In recent decades, attention on urban health and well-being has increasingly moved beyond a focus on medicalised health care and into the settings of everyday life. This is consistent with the influential urgings of the World Health Organization's 1978 International Conference on Primary Health Care. Held in Kazakhstan, this meeting generated what is known as the Alma Ata Declaration. It expressed the need for urgent action by all governments, health workers and the global community to protect and promote the 'health of all' largely through establishing primary health care that put people before professions and clinical practices. Housing was seen as central to this approach. People with low incomes are the most likely to live in sub-standard housing, yet they are the least likely to have the political power or financial capital to purchase better health. In lieu of working to enhance the health-promoting capacities of entire cities, an alternative is to return to the roots of the public health movement and focus on housing and its health implications. Since the birth of the public health movement, housing improvement has been regarded as a key intervention in the quest to reduce health problems (Lowry, 1989).

Often poorer households share household space with others in an effort to save money or because of family or cultural pressures. Aside from the stresses of overcrowding, there is the risk of transmission of infectious diseases, particularly those spread by respiratory means and direct contact. Maintaining a healthy thermal environment is also problematic. Howden-Chapman (2004) has noted that it is generally poorer people who have to pay more for heating in relation to income, while they are least able to improve the energy efficiency of their homes. Inadequate ventilation as well as overcrowding can also increase moisture in the home. High humidity makes it harder to heat a house and also encourages the proliferation of house dust mites which can play a role in the development and maintenance of asthma and other chronic respiratory diseases. Poor housing is also associated with mental health complications. Occupants of sub-standard housing may be reluctant to invite guests into their homes, leading to social isolation, a condition associated with mortality (Krieger and Higgins, 2002). On a larger scale, housing type influences the quality and quantity of interactions within neighbourhoods, affecting social cohesion, trust and a collective sense of belonging.

GEOGRAPHIES OF SOCIAL STIGMATISATION

While the scale of cities can offer a measure of anonymity for people with mental health problems, 'difference' in behaviour and appearance commonly results in stigmatisation. In many more developed countries the closure of large suburban or rural psychiatric asylums over the last 30 years has frequently led to a populating of the central city with former patients, either in boarding houses or homeless on the streets in part due to stigmatisation within urban housing and employment markets.

Evidence from a range of urban settings indicates that people with mental health problems have above average residential mobility (Curtis et al., 2009; Lix et al., 2007). Indeed, some suggest that stresses associated with mobility can compound mental health problems (Bhugra, 2004; DeVerteuil, 2003). High levels of mobility, particularly when accompanied by housing difficulties, may create discontinuities in the receipt of health care, disrupt employment, education and support networks, and precipitate relapse (Bachrach, 1987). Other work suggests that moving may benefit mental health if it brings a service user closer to sources of support. This apparent 'drift' into a 'service-dependent ghetto' has been emphasised by Dear and Wolch (1987). Others cite a 'breeder' hypothesis, first noted by Faris and Dunham (1939), who saw a higher than expected rate of people with first admissions for schizophrenia in the inner (and poorer) areas of Chicago. This view posited the urban environment as fundamentally implicated as a risk factor for this illness. Subsequently, crowded and noisy housing environments have also been placed under the spotlight for their corrosive effects on mental health. Yet social ties play a powerful role in maintaining psychological well-being. For it is not only sociality that is at stake, but the resources (informational, emotional, etc.) and the trust generated though 'the strength of weak ties' (Granovetter, 1973) that contribute to social capital and leave people feeling connected and compassionate towards a community of others.

The contemporary story of mental health care policy has seen an over-presumption of the capacity of communities to care for former patients. News travels fast in cities and the cumulative impact of otherwise isolated violent incidents has been a return to confinement as a response. Too easily 'community' in cities has been constructed in policy discourse as a container of possibilities 'out there' and beyond institutional walls, rather than the set of relationships at the heart of its meaning. In the absence of secure psychiatric settings, prisons have, at times, been a destination for individuals seen to pose a risk to others (Moon, 2000). The contemporary 'drift' hypothesis in this case is that, in the absence of an adequate fabric of community care, vulnerable people will end up in secure (and invariably carceral) institutions that may or may not be fully equipped to deal with their pathologies. Within this contemporary 'post-asylum' context, urban behaviour is increasingly etched with what we might call an 'anxiety about otherness'. Groups whose greatest need is compassion and support in the face of spiralling ill-health (e.g. drug addicts, people living with AIDS) are shunned as contours of perceived risk delineate 'secure' zones around 'middle class' residential areas. Elsewhere particular central city locations can become 'no-go zones' for children as parents acquiesce to geographies of fear. The net effect is that re-establishing the public spaces and centres of cities as safe spaces for all is a major planning challenge. Another challenge is the inclusion of diverse populations in civic life, given the impetus towards moral and visual cleansing (Shantz et al., 2007). Examples include removing the itinerant mentally ill from heritage, monument and 'project' areas of the city, especially in the lead-up to 'hallmark events' such as the Olympic Games.

An outgrowth of early studies of urban mental health and care services that focused on the analysis of the geographic distributions of mental disorders was a consideration of a particular generic place; the service dependent ghetto (see DeVerteuil – Chapter 4 in this volume). This mutually reinforcing concentration of services and clients invariably occurred in a similar urban area to that described by the Chicago urban ecologists as the 'zone of transition'. Here at its worst there was a 'landscape of despair' – a self-perpetuating cycle of poverty and social pathologies (Dear and Wolch, 1987) – still graphically seen in Vancouver's Downtown Eastside where some of Canada's highest rates of IV drug use, HIV/AIDS and homelessness all converge in the nation's most impoverished census tract (Bell et al., 2007). In the quest to ease the stress of poverty and addiction, services have increasingly acknowledged the needs of those experiencing entrapment. Safe injecting sites have been established as well as Aboriginal 'healing places', which seek to address health concerns in an integrated manner (Benoit et al., 2003).

Outside of specific 'pockets of misery', and notwithstanding the aforementioned return to confinement as a response to perceived risk, cities increasingly reveal small signs of hope for greater inclusion of those marked as different. Since the 1990s there has been an increasing focus on people's journeys towards independent living, assisted by support from 'third sector' organisations. The consumer rights movement, as well as a deepening of the 'qualitative turn', has facilitated research granting more agency to those experiencing mental illness and a more nuanced reading of sites of significance within the city. Coffee shops and 'donut stores', for instance, have been identified as critical sites of respite and de facto community care for those whose daily lives are 'restless journeys' around the city (Knowles, 2000). With the maturing of both the third sector and activism among psychiatric survivors, there has been strategic acquisition and transformation of sites such as gardens and art studios as sites of personal development rather than places of last resort (Parr, 2008).

CONCLUSION

In this chapter we began by discussing the 'penalty' of urban living and proceeded to examine a range of ways in which the city is generally less than health-enhancing. Arguably, we have over-emphasised the negative and granted less attention than we might to the positive and health-promoting aspects of urban life such as the density of possible support networks and the abundance of mentally uplifting parks and cultural opportunities. We have, however, endeavoured to be wide-ranging in surveying ways in which cities shape and affect human health. We have inevitably been selective, drawing on areas where we work ourselves and on topics recommended by colleagues. There are undoubtedly omissions, but in looking forward to a future research agenda it is clear that the subject matter of the chapter as a whole points to a relatively under-researched area. Although there is a journal devoted to urban health and much work implicitly considers health in urban areas (or indeed the provision of health care – a topic which we have barely touched) there is a sense in which much of this extensive body of work considers the urban only incidentally – as a space in which a study has been undertaken rather than an operational place or a living construct. Of course there are exceptions to this generalisation.

There is clearly a need for more work on the contemporary urban penalty in different urban settings. Its relevance in the global south is clear but how, for example, does it manifest in global cities, more affluent urban environments and the transition cities of China and the former Soviet Union? Walkability and food deserts have been well-researched but again they are very much concepts that are location-specific. Drinking spaces in cities have received significant attention but there has been less focus on places of smoking in the aftermath of bans on smoking in enclosed spaces. In terms of governance and urban health, there is a need for more work on how governance arrangements change under more neoliberal perspectives that stress responsibility, privatisation and self-reliance. There is also scope for better understandings of how new technologies are altering the experience and outcomes of health care provision in urban areas. How, for instance, are modes of telecare heralding change?

Urban areas are home to millions and give people a sense of place; their economic and educational potential drives in-migration, and their social and cultural potential is what makes them liveable and enjoyable places. Cities and towns provide children with resources to enable them to grow into healthy adults, and they enable older people to access necessary services, remain socially connected, and live in their homes longer. Yet some health trends are undermining the potential that cities have to offer. There is mounting evidence that the way urban areas have been designed is contributing to poor health outcomes, in addition to draining scarce resources and impacting on the global climate. New dialogues between a range of experts such as planners, public health specialists and environmental scientists will be needed to ensure cities of the twenty-first century are healthy places for residents and the generations to come.

Pedagogic guide

The International Society for Urban Health

http://www.isuh.org/
This is a membership organisation dedicated to the study of the health effects of urbanisation and the health of urban areas. The resources tab on its website is well worth a visit for its reviews of key issues.

UK Royal Town Planning Institute

http://www.rtpi.org.uk/item/1795/23/5/3
From here you can link to and learn about the UK Royal Town Planning Institute's policies regarding health.

USAID

http://urbanhealthupdates.wordpress.com/
This blog has some useful material on health issues in the cities of the global south but it tends to focus on biomedical research.

The World Health Organization

http://www.euro.who.int/en/what-we-do/health-topics/environmental-health/urban-health
This organisation has a strong commitment to urban health. This weblink provides a portal to related initiatives, notably the Healthy Cities programme.

10

Cities, Nature and Sustainability

Ian R. Cook and Erik Swyngedouw

INTRODUCTION

This chapter considers the nexus between cities, nature and sustainability. At first glance, the relationship between cities and the natural environment may sound like a peculiar nexus to focus on. Cities have long been viewed as places where nature ends and where urbanism begins, a perspective still prevalent today in many urban policy practices. Yet, cities are inhabited by a magnificent variety of flora and fauna, are built out of natural resources, produce vast quantities of pollution and effluents, contain mesmerising conduits for all manner of resource and other environmental flows, and have become central nodes in the commodification of nature (Heynen et al., 2006b; Hinchcliffe and Whatmore, 2006). What is more, under the banner of 'urban sustainability' cities have been pinpointed as primary places and producers of unsustainable practices, as well as being places where emerging policies and practices under the banner of urban sustainability are being constructed, targeted and at times fiercely contested.

Since the 1980s, the notions of urban sustainability have become omnipresent in academic and policy debates. The previous New Labour government in the UK, for instance, have positioned 'sustainability' as a key rhetorical cornerstone of how towns and cities will be planned, designed, managed, run and measured against in the future (Communities and Local Government, 2009; Office of the Deputy Prime Minister, 2003). In a variety of places across the global north and in many parts of the global south, many politicians, business people, non-governmental organisation representatives, activists and others have either demanded, or claimed to be rolling out, urban sustainability. From Malmö to Vancouver, Manchester to Curitiba, discourses of sustainability are being drawn up, discussed, circulated, disputed and considered. Whilst these discourses often vary with regard to what they mean by sustainability and how this looks in practice, they often assert a similar message: that in order to safeguard the social and ecological order of things, we need to change the ways in which we, as humans, interact with nature, and the relations between cities and nature. In other words, we need to make really important changes to make sure nothing really changes (Swyngedouw, 2009)!

In order to understand the relations between cities and nature, this chapter will begin by critically analysing the rise of urban sustainability as a political discourse and academic terrain of enquiry together with its conceptualisation of nature–cities relations. It will show that urban sustainability is wrapped up in the wider process of neoliberalisation, in which market-led economic development is prioritised over ecological or social justice (Heynen et al., 2006b). As a result, we shall argue, sustainability fails to understand or resolve the ways in which injustice and exploitation run through contemporary relations between cities and nature. The chapter will then critically explore the contributions of the environmental justice and urban political economy literatures, which foreground issues of (in)justice and (in)equality and their relationship with city-natures. In doing so, we shall show that the strength of the former approaches lies in its focus on the patterns of environmental injustice while the latter's strength is in its understanding of the way inequality is wrapped up in the process of urbanising and metabolising nature. The chapter considers how urban sustainability and environmental injustice can only be understood by examining the complex and interweaving 'extra-local' relations that constitute urban life, an issue that frequently gets overlooked in the literature. This will be done in two stages: firstly by demonstrating that socio-environmental inequality is not produced solely within the boundaries of a town or city, but is produced through wider and more complex processes of uneven geographical development and, secondly, by showing how social struggles over environmental (in)justice are often negotiated beyond the urban, operating at multiple scales and increasingly engaging in trans-local networks of support and solidarity.

THE PROBLEMATIC RISE OF URBAN SUSTAINABILITY

It is a commonly held belief today that cities in their present form and functioning are unsustainable. They use and abuse natural resources, they emit endless streams of pollution from car fumes to excessive food packaging, they are dependent on non-renewable fossil fuels such as oil and gas, and they are key contributors to the warming of the global climate (Blowers and Pain, 1999). Although cities in the global north, following deindustrialisation, seldom look like the smog-infested, chimney-stacked industrial cities of previous decades – as so famously depicted in the paintings of L.S. Lowry (see Figure 10.1) – it is widely understood that their relationship with nature continues to be reckless and short-sighted, in turn damaging the livelihoods of humans and the ecological conditions on this planet. In the cities of the global south – including many parts of Asia where smog-infested chimney-stacked industrial cities are now a common feature – poorly regulated industrialisation, grinding poverty, and expanding and barely inhabitable slums suggest that the cities of the global south are also completely unsustainable (Davis, 2006). A consensus has emerged that cities need to sever their ties with their unsustainable habits and become 'sustainable'.

Figure 10.1   LS Lowry *The Lake* 1937 © The Lowry Collection, Salford

Of course, the issues of sustainability and unsustainability are not new, even if the vocabulary is relatively so. Cities have long been troubled by environmental, social and economic problems and injustices. In 1844, for instance, Friedrich Engels already lamented the deplorable sanitary and ecological conditions of the working classes in industrialising English cities (Engels, 1844 [1969]). Furthermore, since the mid-1800s the urban elite in the West have selectively challenged particular urban socio-ecological problems, such as the rise of cholera and typhoid through the construction of sewer systems; the lack of green space through the construction of urban parks; and poor air quality through the introduction of air pollution regulations (Gandy, 2004; Kaika, 2005).

Nevertheless, urban sustainability and the problem of 'unsustainability' have both risen to the fore in political and public consciousness in recent years. A core element of urban sustainability is its emphasis on the repercussions of urbanising nature *beyond* the city, marking a contrast to previous insular city-nature understandings. It also views nature as being inherently benign and harmonious, desirable and in need of recovery from our ill-advised practices. Multiple visions, blueprints and models of sustainable urbanism reflecting these beliefs have been drawn up and circulated (see, for instance, Whitehead, 2007).

Redevelopment projects such as the Bo01 or the Hammarby Sjöstad waterfront developments in Malmö and Stockholm respectively have been framed as 'best practice' (see Figures 10.2 and 10.3). They are seen as examples for politicians and developers elsewhere to imitate, praised by some for their use of renewable energy sources, low energy use and green space, among other things. They are presented, not unproblematically, as technological advanced and ecological sensitive developments but also as catalysts for economic growth (cf. Hall, 2013; Jamison, 2008).

Figure 10.2   The Bo01 waterfront development in Malmö (photo: Ian Cook)

Figure 10.3   The Hammarby Sjöstad development in Stockholm (photo: Ian Cook)

Curitiba in Southern Brazil, meanwhile, has been widely cited as the destination of many policy holidays looking how to implement *low-costing* sustainable planning, examining its extensive and cheap to use overground public transportation and its recycling and litter picking reward schemes in particular (Moore, 2007).

Most blueprints of sustainable urban futures, including those of Malmö and Stockholm, actually envision small alterations to the current status quo. New Urbanism is a further example of such status quo sustainable urbanism. Popularised in North America and in parts of Western Europe since the 1980s, its advocates bemoan post-war urban sprawl, car-orientated and heavily zoned cities and the damage these have inflicted on surrounding green fields outside the city and on community spirit within the city. Their prescriptions tend to focus on design principles of compact and 'walkable' cities and mixed-use development (McCann, 2009; www.cnu.org). Some blueprints demand more fundamental changes in socio-environmental relations such as the increasingly popular Transition Towns movement. Its doyen, Rob Hopkins, argues in *The Transition Handbook* (2008) that communities must realign themselves now before peak oil and climate change forces a transition. A 'petropolis' is no longer viable. For Hopkins and his supporters, a transition to 'energy descent' where communities are more 'self-reliant, and prioritis[e] the local over the imported' is urgently required (Hopkins, 2008: 55; see also www.transition-towns.org; Mason and Whitehead, 2008).

Perhaps the most cited sustainability manifesto is the United Nations report, *Our Common Future* (World Commission for Environment and Development, 1987) – widely known as the Brundtland Report. Three core messages from the report have received much lip-service from urban policy-makers and practitioners throughout the world: firstly, its plea to make the three pillars of sustainability – economic development, social justice and the environment – work together rather than in opposition; secondly, its belief that we should 'adopt life-styles within the planet's ecological means' (ibid.: 9); and thirdly, its definition of sustainable development as 'development that meets the needs of the present without compromising the ability of future generations to meet their own needs' (ibid.: 5). Nonetheless, as we shall see, the issue of social justice, prevalent in the Brundtland formulation, is often a peripheral issue for those drawing up or implementing urban sustainability.

The rise of urban sustainability and 'unsustainability' has simultaneously created, and been shaped by, an emerging sustainability industry. This industry has myriad bodies who, according to their rhetoric at least, 'think', 'speak' and 'operationalise' sustainability. Companies now selectively manufacture and market 'sustainable', 'green' or 'organic' products from buildings to cars and food; provide supposedly more 'sustainable' energy sources; and fix and replace selected 'unsustainable' technologies. In addition vast numbers of 'sustainability experts' are involved in measuring sustainability on the one hand, and dreaming-up and promoting sustainable alternatives on the other. As Rydin (2007) has noted, numerous government agencies, academics and consultants devise and update catalogues of (often-competing) sustainability indicators, benchmarks and sustainability league tables that measure the sustainability of people, places and organisations (see, for instance, Forum for the Future, 2009). Comparing cities such as Malmö and Curitiba with other places, and extracting 'mobile' policy prescription, has become big business. Likewise, the numbers of 'how-to' sustainability guides, such as Rob Hopkins' (2008) *The Transition Handbook* or Douglas Farr's (2008) *Sustainable*

Urbanism are growing rapidly, as are online 'good practice' sustainability portals (e.g. www.sustainablecities.org.uk; www.sustainablecities.dk). Of course, it is right to be somewhat sceptical over the claims of many of these new 'sustainable' products, bodies, metrics and guides. Much sustainable labelling is somewhat superficial, vague and vacuous – a form of 'green-washing' which seeks to appeal to, and shape the mentalities of, more environmentally minded consumers (Jermier et al., 2006; Smith 2008).

More disconcerting, perhaps, is the neoliberalisation of sustainability and its associated inattention to social justice. Sustainability increasingly resembles the concept of ecological modernisation, a body of work which seeks to '"green" capitalism' through the reduction of corporate pollution and the mobilising of more 'ecological' production techniques (Harvey, 1996). In sustainability and ecological modernisation alike, economic development is unquestionably prioritised with the issues of social justice either not mentioned or receiving only limited consideration (Baker, 2007; Keil, 2007). Concurrently, a hegemonic consensus has emerged that (neoliberal) sustainability is a 'good thing' that can be achieved and managed through technological fixes and organisational change, while maintaining economic growth, rather than being viewed as an intensely political issue over possible or desirable future socio-ecological urban trajectories. Despite the varieties of urban sustainabilities, debates are confined to how to reduce carbon emissions, what technologies to use, the mix of organisational fixes, and the urgency of the timing and the implementation (Swyngedouw, 2007). With carbon being promoted as the external planetary villain, capitalism and neoliberalisation have been 'let off the hook' allowing the status quo to remain more or less intact. Following Žižek (1999), the opportunities for dissensus and real debate about possible and more radical futures are severely curtailed (Swyngedouw, 2007; 2009). Within the post-politisisation and neoliberalisation of sustainability, questions of socio-ecological justice and equality are downplayed and ignored. As Portney (2003: 158) argues, 'many cities that purport to be working toward becoming more sustainable do not address the issue of inequality at all'. As we shall discuss below, issues of socio-ecological injustice and inequality remain rife in towns and cities throughout the world, even in the self-styled sustainable cities (Agyeman, 2005). Access to environmental 'goods' remains starkly unequal as is the exposure to environmental 'bads' (Kaika and Swyngedouw, 2011). We cannot sideline these injustices when considering the relations between cities and nature. We shall now turn to consider two approaches that take injustice and inequality seriously: environmental justice and urban political ecology. We begin with urban environmental justice.

ENVIRONMENTAL JUSTICE AND INJUSTICE IN THE CITY

In towns and cities throughout North America and increasingly those in Europe and the global south, calls for 'environmental justice' are being made. Self-styled environmental justice movements are being formed, protests are being organised in the name of environmental justice, disadvantaged people are taking to the streets, and governments and businesses are being lobbied. While their messages and targets vary, these groups frequently share a similar belief that environmental 'goods' and 'bads' are unequally and unfairly distributed in society, and that environmental decision-making circles are unjustly insular and difficult to influence for those who suffer the most from the uneven distribution of environmental 'goods' or 'bads'. Furthermore, as encapsulated in the motto of a London-based environmental justice NGO, Capacity Global, these groups believe that 'living in a clean and healthy environment is everybody's right' (www.capacity.org.uk). In the field of social movements and, more recently, the social sciences, the question of environmental (in)justice has become increasingly prominent (see Holifield et al., 2009).

Concerns with environmental justice (hereafter EJ) emerged in the United States in the 1970s and 1980s. The community protests against the opening of a PCB-infested landfill site in Warren County, North Carolina, a predominately black and poor area, during 1982 marked a pivotal moment in the fledgling EJ movement. As McGurty (2007) notes, although the protests were unsuccessful in stopping the opening and running of the landfill, the injustice of the Warren County landfill, and the community struggle against it, galvanised other communities and citizens in the USA and beyond suffering from what they saw as environmental injustice or environmental racism to actively struggle against existing and proposed injustices. The burgeoning EJ movement would also go on to spur large volumes of academic research into environmental (in)justice in the USA, spearheaded by the academic-activist Robert Bullard (1983, 1990). This early work, with an emphasis on quantitatively mapping the spatial patterns of environmental injustice, demonstrated that hazardous waste facilities were disproportionately located and deliberately sited in disadvantaged and predominately black neighbourhoods. In doing so, these studies 'connected what had previously been largely isolated stories of risk into a racially identifiable pattern of injustice' (Byrne et al., 2002: 5).

EJ studies have become more empirically diverse and theoretically advanced in recent years. Recent work has focused more on environmental (in)justice beyond the USA and has revealed the social inequalities wrapped up in a variety of urban environmental issues, such as waste management, green space, water and transportation (e.g. Buckingham and Kulcur, 2009; Lucas, 2004; Sze, 2006; Walker, 2012). Research has also used the EJ framework to reveal the social inequalities that shape so-called 'natural disasters' such as hurricanes, floods and earthquakes across the world (Bullard and Wright, 2009; Cutter, 2006). In the words of Neil Smith (2006), the research has shown that 'there is no such thing as a natural disaster. In every phase and aspect of a disaster – causes, vulnerability, preparedness, results and response, and reconstruction – the contours of disaster and the difference between who lives and who dies is to a greater or lesser extent a social calculus'. The example of Hurricane Katrina in the box below demonstrates this thesis.

New Orleans and the Environmental Injustice of Hurricane Katrina

On 28 August 2005, Ray Nagin, the mayor of New Orleans, ordered a mandatory evacuation of the city, upgrading his previous orders for a voluntary evacuation the previous day. On the 29 August, as predicted, Hurricane Katrina hit New Orleans and the wider Gulf Coast of the USA. Although New Orleans did not receive the full brunt of the hurricane, the accompanying storm surge breeched the city's insufficient flood defences. As a result, 80 per cent of the city was severely flooded, hundreds died in the city, and billions of dollars of damage was caused.

Although the hurricane and the flood were in large part biophysical processes, it was socially mitigated with the lives of the black working class – who were already disadvantaged prior to Katrina – disproportionately victimised by the events. International news reports so famously showed a largely black working-class population, left behind in New Orleans on their attics and rooftops, in the Convention Center and the Superdome, to face the storm and flood with little or no food or water (see Spike Lee's (2007) documentary *When the Levees Broke*). Not only were the black and poor more vulnerable to the immediate threat of Katrina – through lack of private transportation and often low-lying and substandard housing – but they have continued to suffer disproportionately during the 'recovery' as it was, more often than not, they who were relocated haphazardly across the USA away from family and friends, and had little or no access to personal savings or flood, household and health insurance (Bullard and Wright, 2009). What is clear from Katrina, therefore, is that the environmental injustices do not simply erupt from the onset of 'natural' disasters but are conditioned in large part by pre-existing socio-ecological inequalities (see Bates and Swan, 2007).

Although early work on EJ was mostly preoccupied with the somewhat counter-productive question of which social group – ethnic minorities or the poor – suffers most from environmental justice (for critical reviews, see Downey, 1998 and Kurtz, 2009), more recent studies have demonstrated the *multiple and intersecting axes of inequalities* that are wrapped up in EJ (Bickerstaff and Agyeman, 2009; Sze et al., 2009). Studies, for instance, have shown that gender relations are shaping, and shaped by, environmental injustice. They have demonstrated how the positioning of women as unpaid labourers in the household division of labour and the biological workings of the female body (in particular their reproductive systems) mean that they are more exposed and vulnerable to particular toxicities than men (see Buckingham and Kulcur, 2009; Knopf-Newman, 2004). Moreover, women and gender-informed issues are often curtailed or ignored within patriarchal governing institutions and EJ movements (Buckingham and Kulcur, 2009; Kurtz, 2007). Gender inequalities, as studies have shown, intersect with a number of axes of inequality based around class, race, sexuality, age and disability (to name but a few) in contingent ways to produce particular urban socio-ecological landscapes of environmental justice and injustice (Buckingham and Kulcur, 2009; Sze, 2006). Another important insight is that environmental injustice is not simply the result of *deliberately* discriminatory acts and decision-making – for instance, a decision to put a toxic plant in a working-class black community (Morello-Frosch, 2002; Pulido, 2000). This, as Morello-Frosch (2002: 491) reasons, has implications for how we think about environmental justice:

> Given the insidious nature of discrimination in contemporary society, intent-based theories of environmental inequality are over-simplified by limiting inquiry to the most proximate causes while overlooking the institutional mechanisms and historical and structural processes that determine distributions of environmental hazards.

For Morello-Frosch the more subtle and structural inequalities in the housing markets, the racial division of labour and processes of economic restructuring as shaping patterns of environmental injustice, are pivotal to the workings of environmental injustice, and therefore cannot be overlooked. Pulido (2000), on a similar note, argues that institutional racism, or 'white privilege', is a key structural process creating these inequalities. In the words of Walker (2009), a complex and contingent mixture of factors – including those mentioned above as well as others such as access to insurance and health care – help structure the landscapes of vulnerability that toxicities and biophysical processes interact with.

At this point it is important to consider what is actually meant by 'environment' and 'justice' (with such definitional issues having received mixed attention from EJ scholars and activists). In terms of the environment, EJ activists and scholars have tended to emphasise its social relations and social production. As Dana Alston, a prominent EJ activist once said, 'the issues of the environment do not stand alone by themselves. They are not narrowly defined ... *The environment, for us, is where we live, where we work, and where we play*' (Alston, quoted in Whitehead, 2009: 664–5, emphasis added). In contrast to mainstream conservationist groups who seek to preserve and despoil the 'wilderness', EJ activists and scholars perceive the environment as deeply and unavoidably intertwined in social life.

Although environmental justice movements seem to bond around the need for justice, what justice actually means is not always so obvious. More often than not, EJ activists and scholars focus on the issue of *distributional justice*, arguing that environmental bads should not be concentrated in, or nearby, disadvantaged communities but (re)distributed more equally. However, as David Schlosberg (2003, 2007) has argued, drawing on the work of Iris Marion Young (1990), although distributional justice is key to environmental justice, other conceptions of justice are equally as important. For him, these are *procedural justice* (the desire for fairer and more democratic decision-making processes and the involvement of disadvantaged groups within this); *recognitional justice* (the desire for recognition and respect for the disadvantaged communities who suffer from environmental injustice and those who participate in the EJ movement); and the *justice of capabilities* (the desire for the production of healthy, functioning communities). Schlosberg insists that EJ scholars and activists must pay attention to all of these aspects of justice as they are inter-linked. For instance, the justice of capabilities necessitates a political focus on distributional justice: healthy communities require some form of redistribution of 'environmental bads'. And in order to achieve distributional justice and the justice of capabilities, procedural justice and recognitional justice (i.e. inclusive policy-making, respect and recognition) are necessary.

Success, in truth, has been mixed for EJ activists and scholars. Activists have often struggled to achieve their immediate goals, more often than not, of preventing particular toxicities from opening or worsening in disadvantaged communities (Cole and Foster, 2001). What is more, their victories are frequently isolated victories against a strong prevailing, discriminatory wind. Scholarly work, meanwhile, has suffered criticism that it is too often uncritical of the environmental justice movements themselves (Brulle and Pellow, 2005); that it tends to privilege distributional justice over other conceptions of justice (Lake, 1996); and that selected quantitative accounts are methodologically questionable (Bowen, 2002). Perhaps the most substantial criticism is that EJ accounts often focus on the patterns of environmental injustice (for instance, by mapping the geographies of injustice), while paying only limited attention to the often hidden processes that produce socio-environmental inequalities (Cook and Swyngedouw, 2012). We shall now turn to an approach – urban political ecology – which places emphases on structural processes in the production of city-natures.

METABOLISING THE CITY: URBAN POLITICAL ECOLOGY

Whereas the EJ literature tends to focus on the *patterns* of socio-spatial environment inequality, urban political ecology (hereafter UPE) is primarily concerned with the political-economic and ecological processes involved in the reworking of urban human-non-human assemblages and the *production* of socio-environmental inequalities. UPE is a school of critical urban political-environmental research (Heynen et al., 2006b) and takes many of its bearings from the wider and more voluminous academic school of political ecology (for reviews, see Castree and Braun, 2001; Keil, 2003). Led by the seminal work of Piers Blaikie (1985; Blaikie and Brookfield, 1987), Neil Smith (1984) and, of course, David Harvey (1996) – whose notorious statement that 'there is nothing unnatural about New York City' has been taken as a leitmotiv – urban political ecologists have sought to understand the social basis of urban environmental problems and conditions.

Two common misunderstandings about the relationship between society and nature have been exposed by UPE scholars. The first issue is the presumed ontological divide between nature and society that exists in popular and many academic understandings of nature/society. Political ecologists argue that nature and society do not exist independently of each other, but are intricately tangled, often to the point of blurring. To illustrate this point, there are few, if any, spaces of nature which are pristine or unaffected by human processes (think, for instance, of the global environmental effects of increasing carbon emissions). Furthermore, as Castree (2001) has demonstrated, capitalism has sought to reinvent and commodify (and, thus, socialise) more and more of what we traditionally see as 'natural' (e.g. water, CO_2, seeds, organs, genes). Similarly, UPE scholars have countered the myth that towns and cities are 'places where nature stops' (Hinchcliffe, 1999: 138), positing instead that nature has become urbanised and mobilised in the process of making and remaking cities. Drawing upon the work of Bruno Latour (1993) and Donna Haraway (1991), among others, several UPE scholars have claimed that capitalism and urbanisation are fundamentally hybrid processes through which social and bio-physical elements are assembled, entangled and transformed, and socio-natural cyborgs are produced (see Gandy, 2005b; Kaika, 2005; Swyngedouw, 1996, 2006). Such a lens permits grappling with the social and the physical in non-dualistic and deeply political ways. Natures and cities are always heterogeneously constituted, the product of a dynamic assemblage of human and non-human actants in metabolic circulatory processes. Rethinking nature and society relations in this way has important implications for how we think about the *politics* of socio-environmental relations. As Castree and Braun (1998: 34) state:

> The crucial issue therefore, is not that of policing boundaries between 'nature' and 'culture' but rather, of taking responsibility for how our inevitable interventions in nature proceed – along what lines, with what consequences and to whose benefit.

A second bone of contention for political ecologists is the Malthusian-influenced explanations of environmental degradation and resource depletion, which implicate over-population and poor people as the primary cause and culprits. Instead, it is argued that capitalism is responsible for these ongoing environmental atrocities. Drawing influence from Marx, scholars such as O'Connor (1996) and Henderson (2009) have shown that the ceaseless quest for surplus value compels capitalists to extract, commodify and urbanise more and more bio-physical resources. In doing so, capitalism degrades the very resources that are necessary for capitalism's reproduction and builds extraordinary landscapes of socio-ecological inequalities.

For many UPE scholars, both 'circulation' and 'metabolism' – first proposed by Karl Marx (1970 [1867]) in *Capital* – have become increasingly popular and theoretically advanced concepts through which to understand a series of interconnected, heterogeneous (human and non-human), dynamic and contested processes of continuous quantitative and qualitative transformations that re-arrange humans and non-humans in new, and often unexpected, assemblages like cities (Gandy, 2004; Swyngedouw, 2004). Metabolism is the process whereby bio-physical matters such as water, oil, pigs or whatever are transformed through the mobilisation of capital and labour in a circulatory process organised under distinct capitalist relations of production and exploitation (Swyngedouw, 2006). Metabolic circulation is the socially mediated process of environmental-technological transformation and trans-configuration, through which all manner of actants are mobilised, attached, collectivised and networked.

Urbanisation, in fact, is such a process of socio-environmental metabolisms. Such socially driven material processes produce extended and continuously reconfigured, intended and non-intended spatial (networked and scalar) arrangements (Heynen et al., 2006b). The urban political ecological approaches illustrate how the city and urbanisation more generally can be viewed as a process of de-territorialisation and re-territorialisation of metabolic circulatory flows, organised through social and physical conduits or networks of 'metabolic vehicles' (Virilio, 1986). These processes are infused by relations of power in which social actors strive to defend and create their own environments in a context of class, ethnic, racial and gender conflicts and struggles. As will be explored later in the chapter, circulatory metabolism is not confined to the boundaries of a city but involves a complex process of linking places, and the humans and non-humans within these places, in uneven and contingent ways. These perspectives reveal how city, nature and social power are fused together in constantly shifting and deeply uneven power relations and injustices wrapped up in its production (Swyngedouw, 2004). They also help us think critically about the types of cities we want to inhabit in the future, the type of political struggles to engage in, and what metabolisms and circulations make up these urban utopias.

In summary, then, UPE scholars focus less on the instances of environmental (in)justice than their EJ counterparts. Rather it is the socio-ecological production of urban inequality where emphasis is placed. These approaches are by no means incompatible. Indeed, UPE can draw upon the insights provided by EJ studies of the experiences and patterns of environmental injustice to highlight empirically the inequality produced through urban metabolism.

NETWORKS, SCALES AND THE POLITICAL ECOLOGY OF THE CITY

This section will move the debates further on by considering the *geographies* of the cities–nature nexus. In particular, it will critically examine the contention that environmental (in)justice and urban (un)sustainability can be understood through sole reference to the processes operating within the city. Echoing the work of urban political ecologists (see Heynen, et al., 2006a) and the work of Doreen Massey (1993, 2004, 2007), we reason that such a view is untenable. As Massey has argued, cities should be thought of as being porous, open and constituted in large part through their positions in wider power geometries. Cities cannot be understood by their internal characteristics alone but by their social and ecological relations which stretch beyond the city. Although at particular times, people, materials, energy, information and so on are territorialised or 'moored' in one or a small number of places, many such 'actants' move beyond, and operate across, the boundaries of a particular city (McCann and Ward, 2010; Swyngedouw and Kaika, 2000). Indeed, the processes that bring about urban (un)sustainability and environmental (in)justice are rarely, if ever, produced, circulated, mediated and consumed in one place. To take one example, when EJ activists campaigned against a maquiladora lead smelting plant in Tijuana (Northern Mexico), which was dumping lead slag and heavy metals on-site, poisoning workers and the water supplies for nearby residents, and subsequently abandoned the site in 1994 without remediation (Carruthers, 2008), they could not simply attribute blame to those working in the factory or the local authorities – for it was a San Diego-based company that owned and abandoned the plant; it was the Mexican government that drafted minimal environmental and safety regulations and failed to enforce these; it was pre-NAFTA agreements between the governments of Mexico and the United States that helped establish the maquiladoras; and so on. What is more, such an instance of environmental injustice cannot be understood independently of the geographies of capitalist uneven socio-ecological development – a global process that: thrives on global inequalities; ensures an endless quest for surplus value by capitalists; and necessitates others to compete to earn a wage. The example of the Tijuana plant shows that we should not be thinking about the political ecology *in* the city, but a political ecology *of* the city.

In the metabolism of the city, it is not always easy to see the somewhat hidden exploitative social relations that are wrapped up in this, not least because of the widespread fetishisation of commodities under capitalism (Swyngedouw, 2006). This remains the case in self-styled 'sustainable' cities, whose production, we argue, frequently involves the shadowy exploitation of people and ecologies inside and outside of the city as well as the conscious or unconscious mobilisation of resources and the production of environmental 'problems' elsewhere. Think, for instance, of recycling. Many urban governance institutions cite the recycling of household goods from bottles to newspapers (and, to a lesser extent, business waste) to be a linchpin of their environmental sustainability agenda. However, their rhetoric rarely tell us about who is doing the recycling, where this recycling is taking place, or the working practices, conditions and uneven power relations involved in it. Looking at the recycling of computers, for example, David Pellow (2007) has demonstrated that this business often involves hidden, trans-national exploitation. Computers are shipped illegally to China, India, Nigeria and other global south nations where they are either dumped or, more likely, disassembled by labourers by hand in unsafe working conditions for scant wages. Indeed, he estimates that approximately 80 per cent of the computers collected for recycling in the United States are exported to Asia. Although jobs can be created, profits can be made and re-usable resources can be salvaged in computer recycling plants, the health of the workers and the environmental conditions are always at risk from toxic substances in the computers such as mercury, lead, beryllium and cadmium. Another example of the transportation of socio-ecological problems elsewhere is the international ship-breaking industry in which vessels, largely from global north ports, are transferred to ports in poor nations, noticeably Bangladesh, India and Pakistan, to be dismantled in hazardous conditions and their parts recycled and sold onto other businesses. The boxed text below details the socio-ecological injustices and global networks involved in these through a case study of the ship-breaking yards in Chittagong, Bangladesh. The examples of e-waste and ship-breaking demonstrate that the people and environments of the global south frequently suffer at the expense of the profit-orientated 'sustainability here, exploitation elsewhere' strategies by capitalist firms and governments in the global north. Furthermore, these case studies show that due to the processes of capitalist uneven development, racism and patriarchy, labourers and communities in the global south are, in the words of one EJ activist, Jim Puckett, left 'with an untenable choice between poverty and poison' (quoted in Pellow, 2007: 191).

Ship-Breaking in and beyond Chittagong

On the beaches north of Chittagong (the second largest city in Bangladesh), ships are dying. They are being stripped down by the labour force of local businesses using simple tools such as blow-torches and winches. The ships' materials such as fire extinguishers, refrigerators, cables, lifeboats, foam, water hoses and (most important of all) steel are being removed and sold on to businesses in and beyond Chittagong (Buerk, 2006). Although ship-breaking can bring jobs, capital and resources to the area, it does so through the exploitation of labour. The labourers – most of whom are recruited from the poverty-stricken rural villages in North Bangladesh – work long hours outdoors, for very little money, with little or no protective clothing, footwear or safety training. The workers are potentially exposed to poisonous substances (e.g. asbestos, mercury), falling objects, sheets of steel cutting into their skin, and explosions and fires when blow-torches react with oil residues. Since the emergence of the ship-breaking yards in the 1970s, reports have estimated hundreds of deaths in the yards and thousands of workers sustaining severe injuries (e.g. limb-loss, burns) and illnesses (e.g. tuberculosis, skin diseases) as a result of working in the yards (see, for instance, International Federation for Human Rights, 2002). Compounding this, workers often continue to work with such illnesses and injuries as there is no sick pay and they fear being dismissed (Buerk, 2006).

Ship-breaking in Chittagong is part of a global process whereby ships owned by companies in the global north and often transporting commodities for urban consumption are broken up in poor countries, notably Bangladesh, India and Pakistan. Blaming 'excessive' regulations and high costs, merchants seldom use the dry docks in Western Europe for ship-breaking, preferring instead to sell 'end-of-life' ships onto businesses that use the 'regulation-light' yards and their cheap labour force in places such as Chittagong. Although the transfer of ships from countries with 'environmentally sound' disposal facilities to countries such as Bangladesh who lack such facilities contravenes the 1989 Basel Convention, many merchants continue to circumvent such laws and allegations of bribery are frequently voiced (Sonak et al., 2008). The growth of the industry has been perversely backed up by the Bangladeshi government's unwillingness to regulate strongly these yards or improve labour standards for fear of losing inward investment and cheap steel imports. The widespread poverty in Bangladesh, especially in its rural Northern villages – itself the result of capitalist uneven development, British imperialism and a retreat from a malign form of socialism – has left the villagers with few options other than to work in such yards.

With good reason, studies of environmental justice movements (EJMs) and, to a lesser extent, urban sustainability movements (USMs) have emphasised the contingent extra-local spatial relations of such movements. They have shown that these movements' abilities to act and the contexts in which they act are conditioned in part by actors, institutions and processes operating at scales and places elsewhere

Figure 10.4   Workers and ships on a ship-breaking beach in Alang, India (photo: Federico Demaria)

(Heynen and Swyngedouw, 2003; Sze et al., 2009). In addition, the organisational operations and 'repertoires of actions' of USMs and EJMs frequently go beyond the boundaries of particular communities and cities. In many instances, such extra-local engagement reflects a desire to influence the public and private institutions directly and indirectly responsible for 'unsustainability' or environmental injustice that are frequently located or headquartered elsewhere. As Kurtz (2002) argues, EJM and USMs often attempt to 'jump scale' in order to influence institutions such as national government departments and international organisations situated at other scales in order to further their campaigns. More horizontally, Bulkeley (2005) has shown that since the early 1980s, in the global north in particular, Transnational Municipal Networks (TMNs) such as the Cities for Climate Change Project have emerged, forming 'new political spaces' for engaging localities in resource-sharing activities and joint policy initiatives. Concurrently, incidents of joint campaigns and the sharing of resources between EJMs have grown substantially in the last decade or so. Carruthers (2008), for instance, shows how the struggle against the aforementioned lead-smelting plant in Tijuana involved a variety of Mexican and American EJ, human rights and labour movements and coalitions working alongside and in cooperation with each other. These movements and alliances have been underpinned by a number of beliefs, notably that environmental injustice rarely operates in one locality alone and therefore needs trans-local struggles, resource-sharing and networks of solidarity. Such alliances, it is also believed, help reduce the risk that 'environmental bads' that have been successfully 'fought off' by EJMs in one place will be displaced into a partner EJM's locality. Together with the growing numbers of formal and informal trans-boundary cooperations, trans-national EJMs such as the Basel Action Network (www.ban.org), Climate Justice Now! (www.climate-justice-now.org) and the Global Alliance for Incinerator Alternatives (www.no-burn.org) have formed, not least in the hope of operating at a similar scale to where the mechanisms that organised and sustain these injustices themselves are (re-)produced. For Faber (2005: 44), these new trans-national EJMs mark a significant departure from the 1980s in the United States where 'largely separate movements were organization-ally isolated or loosely connected to one another and engaged in primarily locally based battles for environmental justice'. Nonetheless, it must be remembered that comparatively isolated EJMs continue to exist and while the trans-national move-ments appear to be about cooperation and solidarity, we cannot overlook the real-ity that uneven power relations are inevitable and, as with other political movements, there is always the likelihood of disputes, splits and unproductive cooperation (Routledge, 2007). On a final note, the practices of 'creative destruc-tion' involved in forms of trans-boundary movements are also important, despite receiving little scholarly attention. It is necessary for further work to consider whether such trans-border EJMs transcends a parochial politics of place by devel-oping more universal and transcendent concepts of, and strategies towards, justice and equality (echoing David Harvey's (1996) conception of 'militant particular-ism'), or whether these movements sacrifice *necessary* localised requirements and beliefs of communities in particular places. It is vitally important, therefore, for academics and activists alike to continually (re)consider the socio-spatial and political strategies through which socio-environmental justice can be achieved.

CONCLUSION

Issues of injustice, inequality, exclusion and exploitation are central to the nexus of cities and nature. As this chapter has sought to demonstrate, we cannot under-stand city–nature relations without considering the uneven power relations that are wrapped up in the making and re-making of the urban environment. The lens of urban sustainability, although popular and arguably hegemonic, is unable to fully grasp the social aspects of city–nature relations. Its ecologically modernised, narrow focus on economic development through environmental sustainability fun-damentally downplays politics, social struggles and the plurality of natures in the city. An urban political ecology-inspired focus on the metabolised reworking of human-non-human assemblages and the inequalities infused within this is neces-sary, alongside the careful consideration of the spatial-temporal class-based, racial-ised and gendered patterns of environmental injustice. Such a synergy of the environmental justice and urban political ecology perspectives would provide a fruitful platform for exciting and nuanced understandings of the processes and patterns we have begun to explore in this chapter. Of course, these city–nature relations cannot be seen to operate solely within the boundaries of the city. We must not fetishise the urban, but look to the stretching and mooring of socio-nature assemblages and relations beyond the city boundaries to other places and scales. Not only does this alert us to the new cross-boundary networks of sustainability bodies and environmental justice movements, it also opens us up to the notion that the production of sustainable communities (for some) is potentially predicated on the exploitation of others in and beyond the city.

A critical eye when examining existing and proposed socio-environmental practices and policies is necessary if we are to understand and remove such injustices. As we have shown, such a view is particularly necessary when policy-makers, business-people and others herald their communities, cities or organisations to be leading the pathway to sustainability. Visions and practices of (un)sustainability and environmental (in)justice are constantly being re-imagined, revised and invented, often with a new-and-improved 'green' veneer, and we cannot simply assume that they are more sustainable just because they are new(er) or because their rhetoric claims them to be. Furthermore, researchers and students must use their critical evaluations to inform utopian ideas about what types of urban environments we want to be part of, and how we relate to other peoples and ecologies not just in our town or city but in places elsewhere – for instance, the places that our towns or cities are competing against for investment, places we see on the news, places the resources we use are extracted from, assembled in or disposed of, or the places we eerily hear little about.

Web resources

Basel Action Network

www.ban.org
This is the website of the NGO Basel Action Network who seek to monitor the international trade in international toxic waste (notably e-waste and ship-breaking).

Environmental Justice Foundation

www.ejfoundation.org
This is the website of perhaps the best known environmental justice charity in the UK that works to protect the environment and human rights.

Environmental justice research and resources

www.geography.lancs.ac.uk/envjustice
This is an educational resource portal on environmental justice maintained by Gordon Walker at Lancaster University.

Imagining Urban Futures

http://research.northumbria.ac.uk/urbanfutures

This is an educational resource from a collection of academics looking at urban policy mobilities and includes research on the circulation of 'best practice' sustainable urbanism.

Social Polis

www.socialpolis.eu

This is the website of a European Commission funded research project examining social cohesion in European cities. The Urban Ecology and Environment section hosts numerous documents on the nexus of cities, social cohesion and the environment.

11

Just Cities

James DeFilippis and Juan Rivero

TWO STORIES …

El Faro de Colón

In October 1992, as part of the celebration of the 500th anniversary of Columbus's arrival in the Americas, the Faro de Colón (Columbus's Lighthouse) opened in the eastern part of the city of Santo Domingo, in the Dominican Republic. It is a severe structure that, observed from the ground, does not look like a lighthouse, but like a set of 150ft-tall walls. From above – presumably the perspective of God and Columbus in the heavens – it is an 800ft-long cross capable of projecting enough light into the sky to make it visible throughout the Caribbean.

The building of the lighthouse can be told as a story of: the mass evictions from the neighbourhood of Maquiteria of mostly poor shanty-dwellers, only a lucky few of whom received relocation assistance; the physical separation of Maquiteria's remaining residents from the lighthouse, its square and their tourists by a massive wall behind which they have continued to live in poor quality housing with few services and intermittent electricity; the exacerbation of poverty in Santo Domingo – both in Maquiteria and elsewere in the city – due to the use of resources by the lighthouse project; the increased incidence of blackouts (which the wealthy handle by way of personal generators); and the priority given, by the small and wealthy elite, who have long governed this city, to tourism dollars over the concerns of the urban poor.

This way of telling this story would be fair and sound familiar to most observers of urban politics and urban economic development in contemporary cities. And this alone would make the story of the lighthouse and its construction an example (albeit an unremarkable one) of urban injustice. While such a reading would be mostly correct, it would overlook a whole set of issues of Dominican identity and its production via urban space that add a new layer to the expression of urban injustice in the contemporary city.

Santo Domingo is a rather remarkable city. As the first European settlement in the Americas, it boasts a whole set of historic firsts: the first European hospital, the first cathedral, the first university, and so on. These historic structures, which were renovated as part of the 1992 quincentennial in order to draw tourists from the beach to its capital city, play a part in Dominicans' self-identification with their Spanish heritage – often referred to on the island simply as *hispanidad*. This identification has entailed a denial of Dominican's African heritage. Dominicans are rarely 'black' in their self-identification (see Howard, 2001; Sagás, 2000). They have typically reserved the category of blackness for Haitians, with whom they share their island, collectively known as Hispaniola, and with whom they have historically had strained relations, often on account of race. It was Haitians who, during the Haitian revolution, when they controlled the whole island, first abolished slavery in the Dominican Republic, only to see Spanish colonists bring it back after a bloody struggle. Most violently, there was the 1937 'parsley massacre' when, over the course of five nights in October, the Dominican dictator Trujillo ordered the army to kill blacks in Dominican border towns who could not properly pronounce *perejil*. It is estimated that between 20 and 30 thousand people were murdered, many of whom were black Dominicans of Haitian descent (see Turits, 2002). While the dictator was certainly the one making the decisions during the 1937 massacre, the justification came from his resident scholar/intellectual, Joaquin Balaguer, who would govern the country for much of the post-Trujillo period (post-1961). It was Balaguer who, as president, drove the construction of the lighthouse.

The erasure of blackness in the dominant Dominican historical imagination has contributed to a reclamation of the Taíno (the indigenous people in Hispaniola and other parts of the Caribbean) heritage on the island. Dominicans, who will rarely self-identify as black, will often refer to themselves as *Indio*, which requires a suspension of disbelief regarding the island's history. When the Europeans arrived in late 1492 there were about 400,000 Taínos on the island. In less than three decades, that population was all but annihilated. By February 1519, there were fewer than 3,000 Taínos remaining on the island (Moya Pons, 1995). And so we return to Columbus. The physical imposition of a celebration of *Hispanidad* into the urban fabric of the national capital has required the forced displacement of poor, non-white residents and perpetuated the erasure of non-white identity in the Dominican Republic. As such, the lighthouse stands as an expression of the multiplicity of injustice in urban space.

Albee Square and Fulton Mall

Fulton Mall, an eight-block strip in downtown Brooklyn, New York, is a popular gathering place for African-Americans and recent immigrants from Brooklyn and beyond who visit this outdoor mall to shop, dine and take part in its vibrant street life. Despite its success – Fulton Mall is one of the most profitable retail strips in New York City (see FUREE, 2008) – the mall has been a target of recent revitalisation plans aimed at inducing investment in downtown Brooklyn and changing the composition and nature of the mall's commercial uses. At issue is the question of whose vision of the city drives redevelopment plans and how the benefits and costs of those plans are distributed across the population.

Fulton Street, where Fulton Mall is located, first emerged as a commercial corridor around the end of the nineteenth century in response to the increase in traffic generated by the new Brooklyn Bridge and the expansion of train service (the Elevated Line or El). From the outset, the development of the area set the interests of some against the interests of others. The expansion of train service made downtown Brooklyn accessible to a wider population, which benefited business-owners. Landowners, on the other hand, felt that the shadows, dirt and noise generated by the El service undermined the value of their property, and advocated for the dismantling of elevated rails. After several decades, in 1940, the rails came down; but this gave rise to a new round of conflict. The removal of the El revealed a hodge-podge of undistinguished buildings and numerous open store-fronts that sold cheap foods to passers-by. In response, larger business and property-owners organised a campaign to improve the character of the street by banning open store-fronts. Within a few years, they obtained an amendment to the city's zoning laws restricting the types of retail that could occupy the strip.

The subsequent decade is remembered by the post-war generation as the golden age of Fulton Street. From the late 1940s through the 1950s, major department stores catering to middle-class shoppers dominated the corridor. These stores came to symbolise bourgeois class advancement and serve as places for recreation and socialising. The ascendancy of Fulton Street's large department stores, however, proved short-lived. Sweeping demographic and economic changes in New York City throughout the 1950s, 1960s, and 1970s drastically changed the face of Brooklyn and of Fulton Street. De-industrialisation, suburbanisation, Puerto Rican immigration and African-American migration, and the economic crisis of the 1970s made the population of Brooklyn poorer and less white. This transformed the composition of the businesses and the Fulton Street shoppers. Gradually, discount retailers came to supplant the elegant department stores of the corridor's 'golden age'.

Despite Fulton Street's enduring profitability, its major business-owners viewed the transformation of their clientele and of the area's retail mix as a sign of decline and a harbinger of worse things to come. They successfully lobbied the City to formulate a plan for the 'revitalisation' of downtown Brooklyn. The core of the resulting plan consisted of class A office space and market-rate residential units, the development of which would presumably have a spill-over effect on Fulton Street and foster the environment sought by some of its businesses. Most aspects of the plan failed because of a lack of private investment. One of the few elements that survived was the construction of an arcade meant to enhance the pedestrian experience in a vain effort to draw suburban shoppers to the area – now renamed Fulton Street Mall.

The City's plans did not divert the ongoing transformation of Fulton Street. By the 1980s, all but one of the major shopping malls had been replaced by large discount stores and independent specialty stores tailored to tastes of the mall's new visitors – African-Americans from throughout Brooklyn. The retail composition, however, only tells part of the story. While the new pedestrian amenities failed to attract suburban shoppers, they did enable a lively, urban environment that allowed the mall to become a centre of hip-hop culture. Beyond the Afro-centric retailers and the purveyors of hip-hop fashion and music, the mall itself became a scene – a place for hanging out and socialising. In its new incarnation, Fulton Mall remained as profitable as ever.

During the 1990s, young professionals moved in droves into the gentrifying 'brownstone' neighbourhoods that abut downtown Brooklyn. They did not, however, frequent Fulton Mall, which they tended to view as vaguely threatening. The City, for its part, renewed its efforts to 'revitalise' downtown Brooklyn through the construction of office space. In 1992, it built a technology centre, MetroTech – a high-rise complex whose occupancy came to depend on public subsidies and public tenants. Contrary to expectations, MetroTech failed to stimulate the further development of office space. Moreover, since its campus was semi-enclosed, what activity it did generate had little impact beyond its immediate surroundings. Nonetheless, in the early 2000s, the dot-com boom led to a renewed call for office space, in response to which the City formulated an extensive re-zoning plan to dramatically increase the density of downtown Brooklyn.

The City passed the downtown Brooklyn re-zoning in 2004 and shortly thereafter created the Downtown Brooklyn Partnership (DBP). Charged with promoting and coordinating development, DBP subsumed the many BIDs and public–private partnerships that had previously operated in the area. The re-zoning had a tremendous, but largely unanticipated impact. No office development took place. Developers, instead, rode the housing bubble and produced thousands of units of luxury housing. The re-zoning fanned the flames of an already over-heated real estate market. Ground commercial rents sky-rocketed throughout downtown Brooklyn. Many commercial tenants lost their leases when landlords sold to developers. Entire city-blocks were vacated by landlords hoping to cash in on the development frenzy. Older buildings were demolished and parcels were assembled in order to make way for higher-density development. The most prominent example of this, and a representative one, was that of Albee Square, an indoor mall that had replaced Albee Square Theater in the late 1970s. For many Brooklyn African-Americans, Albee Square Mall was a landmark – a pre-eminent hang-out spot since the 1980s, frequented by hip hop artists such as Biz Markie, who immortalised the mall in one of his songs ('You wouldn't think it's a store, you would think it's my home').

Albee mall stood on city-owned land. A developer acquired its ground lease in 2001 for $25 million, paid little attention to its upkeep and became an outspoken supporter of the proposed re-zoning. In 2004, shortly after the re-zoning, he flipped the ground lease for $125 million to a development team that planned to build 1.6 million square feet of residential space and 125,000 square feet of office space with the assistance of public subsidies from the city. The mall was demolished in 2008.

In 2008, the real estate market collapsed. Some half-built luxury high-rises remained in mid-construction. Fully built condominiums struggled to find buyers. In Fulton Mall, store-fronts that had been vacated in anticipation of new development remained vacant. The development of the site where Albee Square once stood is proceeding; but only because developers secured yet another round of subsidies, this time federal, that required the construction of a portion of the project.

The question of who bore the costs and risks and who enjoyed the benefits of the downtown Brooklyn re-zoning merits consideration. But another fundamental question concerns what was left out from the discussions that surrounded the City's redevelopment plan. One of the most glaring omissions was Fulton Mall. The most active retail strip in all of Brooklyn never came up during the debates about the re-zoning and about the future of the downtown Brooklyn. Had it, the discussions might have considered the social and cultural function that the mall played for the African-American community; they might have considered improvements to enhance the experience of visitors; or they might have considered ways of protecting the mall's businesses from the speculative activity that would likely ensue. But the functions served by the mall and the preferences of its users had no place in a conversation about development premised almost exclusively on the question of demand for office space.

ON JUSTICE AND INJUSTICE

We started this chapter on social justice and cities with these two brief stories because they demonstrate the multiple ways in which processes of justice and injustice are produced and reproduced through urbanisation. Justice and injustice are not necessarily spatial processes. Many theorists of justice, such as Rawls and Nussbaum, have written elegantly elaborate theories of justice that are relatively devoid of space and place.[1] But justice and injustice do find expression in the production of material, built spaces – production that benefits some at the expense of others. And beyond the narrow distributive question of who benefits and who doesn't lay the processes and power relations that shape that production, inscribing the cultural narratives and memories of some groups in the built environment and suppressing those of others. This form of cultural affirmation and denigration reflects and reinforces the injustices of the cultural politics of societies writ large.

The stories we have chosen illustrate how much easier it is to identify injustice than justice. Injustice is evident in cities everywhere. We start with an understanding of injustice that leans heavily on Iris Marion Young's well-known 'five faces of oppression' (Young, 1990: Chapter 2). Central to Young's work is the recognition that oppression – that is, injustice – is a group-level process. It is groups that are oppressed, rather than simply individuals, and they are oppressed through one or more of the following five processes:

1 *exploitation*, which Young defines as 'the transfer of the results of the labor of one social group to benefit another' (1990: 49);

2 *marginalisation*, which is the exclusion of groups of people from the organisation of society;

3 *powerlessness*, which is the inability of groups to exert control over their working lives;

4 *cultural imperialism*, which entails stereotyping culturally subordinate groups and simultaneously rendering their members invisible as individuals; and

5 *violence*, which becomes a form of oppression when its infliction on certain groups is viewed as acceptable.

---

1 See Katznelson (1997) for an attempt to reconcile Rawls with more spatial theorists.

Young's categorisation of forms of injustice is not meant to be a laundry list or a crude yardstick against which we can measure 'injustice'. Instead, it is a way of thinking through the different ways in which injustice happens in society. Accordingly, it has the great virtue of being rooted not just in analytical reason, but also in an understanding of the operations and relations of actually existing social practices. It has the further virtue of moving us away from contemplating justice via sectarian lenses, which pit groups against each other in some perverse game of who is more oppressed.[2] We could therefore easily use Young's framing to discuss how the cases discussed earlier were unjust. Both cases are clear examples of the processes of marginalisation, cultural imperialism and powerlessness. And while the content and context of these cases vary, the larger injustices are not fundamentally different.

Young's work helps us understand injustice, but – and this is not to diminish the significance of her work – it does not help us in the harder task of identifying justice. The concept of justice has been thoroughly discussed and analysed by scholars and political activists; and, perhaps more importantly, it has been a banner behind which many urban social movements have marched. Despite this attention, however, the meaning of the concept remains elusive. From Plato's *Republic* onward, countless volumes have been written on social justice. We do not intend to summarise the many debates that have centred on this concept. Instead, we will highlight formulations of justice that have informed urban theorists' understanding of social justice and the city.

Liberal political philosophers have grappled at length with the question of justice, giving rise to a fundamental set of debates. The first is the issue of whether a universal understanding of justice is possible and, if so, desirable. The difficulty here is that the universal formulation of justice requires the erasure of difference – not difference in interests, but difference in values. Rawls posits a universal conception of justice in his seminal work *A Theory of Justice* (1971). In doing so, Rawls assumes a well-ordered, homogeneous society in which people use reason to determine the distribution of goods and services. People, however, value different things, and notions of justice vary and change. As Engels put it in *The Housing Question*, 'The conception of eternal justice, therefore, varies not only with time and place, but also with the persons concerned' (Engels, 1970: 86). Similar critiques have been advanced from different political perspectives by postmodern and poststructuralist theorists, who have argued that liberal conceptions of justice are rooted in a western Enlightenment tradition that generalises from the particular position of white, male property-owners.

But if justice cannot be understood universally, then by what criteria can we measure the desirability of particular policies, programmes or plans? An understanding of justice that lacks some kind of context-independent criteria threatens to leave us in the world of infinite regress, where everything can theoretically be just – if the

---

2 Such a destructive 'game' was enjoined by far too many leaders of the GLBT movement in their criticisms of African-Americans in California following the passage of Proposition 8, which outlawed same-sex marriage in that state.

context says that it is. Some have argued for an understanding of justice that tries to bridge the universal and the particular by recognising a place for the particular in the universal and vice-versa. That is, we can retain a basic set of universal principles of justice, as long as those universals are understood in ways that allow the content to vary from time to time, place to place, group to group, and person to person. Benhabib refers to this understanding as 'historically enlightened [i.e. particularistic] universalism' (Benhabib, 2002: 39). The work of Martha Nussbaum on this subject can be read as an elaboration of Benhabib's concept, although neither of them would probably see it quite that way.

Nussbaum, coming out of the liberal tradition has downplayed the significance of the universalism/relativism debate. She states bluntly, 'relativists tend ... to understate the amount of attunement, recognition, and overlap that actually obtains across cultures' (Nussbaum, 1993: 261, quoted in Fainstein, 2010). She posits that justice is really a function of human capabilities (a perspective she has worked out in conjunction with Amartya Sen). These capabilities are life, health, bodily integrity, access to education and control over one's environment (see Nussbaum, 2000). She views justice as requiring that all people have the opportunity to act on their capabilities. Her list constitutes a fair attempt at the kind of particularistic universal principles to which Benhabib refers. While capabilities are universal, their content – that is, what they actually mean in practice – can vary significantly by context and among different individuals and groups within the same larger context. Thus, Nussbaum defines justice as a minimum set of thresholds below which injustice occurs because individuals are not free to act on their capabilities.

The second big debate in theories of justice concerns the question of procedural vs. substantive justice. Most conceptions of justice, particularly those that emerge in liberal thought, focus primarily on substantive justice – the question of who gets, what and why? The dominant criterion for evaluating substantive justice for most of the last 200 years has been utilitarianism – a framework articulated by James and John Stuart Mill and by Jeremy Bentham, in *Principles of Morals and Legislation*. From a utilitarian perspective, actions are just if they create or enable a greater aggregate amount of pleasure than pain. This leads to Bentham's famous maxim of 'the greatest good for the greatest number'. This framework for justice, however, says very little about distribution. An action that causes great pleasure to one person and slight pain to many cannot necessarily be condemned on utilitarian grounds of justice.[3] Thus, depending on how one quantifies the pain caused to blacks in Brooklyn by the loss of Albee Square, the process that destroyed it might be justifiable on utilitarian grounds because of the massive amounts of pleasure realised by the developer who made money on the property.

Rawls famously rejected utilitarian thinking and argued that a just distribution must conform to the 'difference principle', which allows unequal distribution only when it benefits those who were worse off at the outset. In contrast to utilitarianism, then, Rawls offers a theory of substantive justice in which distribution plays a central role.

---

3 It is exactly this logic that is codified in every cost–benefit analysis – a methodology that Bentham himself spells out in *Principles*.

Critiques of substantive justice have emerged from those who argue that justice, properly understood, is about the decision-making processes, rather than the outcomes of those processes. Some of these critiques, particularly Marxist ones, argue that the prevailing (that is, liberal) notions of substantive justice take for granted the basic means and relations of production. In doing so, they empty the term of any intellectual or political utility. That is, if a conception of justice accepts all governing processes as given, whatever their tendencies may be, then what exactly is that conception of justice offering? Poststructuralists, postmodernists and feminists have also directed similar objections at distributive notions of justice, arguing that they fail to account for structural asymmetries of power.

For our purposes, the most important challenge to substantive notions of justice comes from advocates of procedural justice, specifically from proponents of communicative planning or deliberative democracy, who have become a significant force in political and urban planning theory. These writers and practitioners have relied heavily on the work of Jürgen Habermas. In his work on the deliberative process, Habermas posits an ideal speech situation in which all participants are able to speak and are given the chance to assert and defend any empirical, theoretical or normative claims. Such ideal speech leads to rational agreement, provided by the willingness and openness of the participants to come to a consensus. Practitioners working in what can be called a Habermasian tradition are less rigid in their speech requirements (although this might be a function of the move from theory to practice). But they also hew to the basic argument that open, transparent and free communication and discourse – that is, just decision-making processes – leads to just outcomes.

While we recognise the theoretical and political importance of critiques levied against all formulations of substantive justice, the alternatives, which focus on procedural justice, have problematic implications – particularly those with consensus-oriented understandings. The most thoughtful of those working in this framework, such as Fraser (1989, 1997), have long argued that just processes require a situation in which power relations within society enable something resembling Habermas's ideal speech, and have long understood that such a society does not yet exist. The most common form of procedural critique promotes consensus and participation as a way of arriving at a common deliberative ground. Consensus, however, often requires excluding from deliberation 'the big questions', those concerning institutional and structural inequality, and the value judgements involved in remedying them (or not) – the very questions that procedural critiques accuse others of eliding. Their inclusion would preclude consensus and cripple the entire process of deliberation.[4]

While the critiques of substantive justice are fair and important, we also believe them to be overstated. In the end, justice requires that both processes and outcomes be just. Any understanding of justice must include both clear guidelines for what constitutes a just process and a just outcome.

---

4 See Purcell (2008) for a partially sympathetic but highly trenchant critique of deliberative democracy as being inherently conservative.

URBANISING JUSTICE AND INJUSTICE

Thus far we have discussed theories of justice; but they have been largely a spatial and have not dealt with the relation of justice to cities. Those interested in making and understanding 'the just city' must grapple with political and theoretical questions of what justice means in cities and what role the 'city' part of the equation brings to these understandings. That is to say, what makes urban justice politically and conceptually different from rural justice or social justice writ large? There are a number of reasons why it might not make sense to frame or pursue justice at an urban scale. Firstly, cities are situated in a subordinate position to higher levels of government. This not only constraints their autonomy legally, but also limits the capacity of actions taken in one place to have larger social significance. One need not accept Dahl's (1967) famous 'Chinese box' understanding of scale and political participation (and we do not) to recognise that there are inherent limits to what can be done locally. The politically subordinate situation of cities in federalised government structures, such as exist in the United States, can place local governments in competition with other local jurisdictions for tax revenues and private investment (Peterson, 1981). A city that undertakes redistributive initiatives risks undermining its tax base if its efforts drive businesses and wealthy residents to move to more regressive pastures. Secondly, cities are products of larger-scale flows of capital that determine the economic context of local work. These flows also shape the political opportunity structure of local political projects – and they do so in ways that limit the capacity to challenge capitalist interests.

Given the above conceptual and practical limitations, why talk about 'urban' justice? For a variety of reasons, cities provide fertile ground for political projects concerned with social justice. Since antiquity, cities have been the focal point of human imaginings of utopias and emancipation (see Lees, 2004). As they grew, they concentrated great numbers of people and amassed vast amounts of capital and power. By the turn of the twentieth century, capitalism was exerting an incredible centripetal force. The resulting agglomeration brought with it massive exploitation; but it also brought social progress. Even Marx and Engels, the most eloquent of critics of capitalist urbanisation, observed that cities had 'rescued a considerable part of the population from the idiocy of rural life' (Marx and Engels, 1967: 84). Urban concentration also created the means for further social progress by allowing the working class to recognise itself as such and collectively pursue social change.

The focus on 'the urban', however, is not a mere matter of historic path dependency. City life typically unfolds within the relatively tight confines of highly populated urban space. It is characterised by a density and diversity of uses, activities and people. This has long been a central understanding of urban studies (Simmel, 1971; Wirth, 1938). Cities' ability to bring together people from different backgrounds – people who subscribe to different values and ways of life – plays a crucial role in the realisation of urban justice. It is this diversity that, in theory, makes possible Young's 'together in difference' ideal. It is also the presence of diversity that provides a cover of urban anonymity for those who seek transgression and emancipation. For sure, the coincidence of difference and proximity can be oppressive. But a greater understanding among different social groups is still less likely to emerge from remoteness and lack of exposure than from proximity and interaction.

At a political level, the claims about the futility of reform at an urban scale are overstated. While there may be considerable limits to cities' ability to effect social change without the cooperation of higher levels of government, there are policy areas that fall within the control of municipalities. Fainstein lists, among these, urban redevelopment, race relations, service provision and open space planning (Fainstein, 2010). More to the point, anyone who has visited Portland, OR and Dallas, TX – two cities within the same nation state and with the same legal constraints on them – could not fail to appreciate the capacity of local actors to have great impacts on the quality of life in their city. Local governance structures can and do vary in terms of how they make decisions and of the distributional outcomes of those decisions. Progressive city regimes have emerged (see Clavel, 1986, 2010; Gendron and Dumhoff, 2008) and act very differently from growth machine regimes (Logan and Molotch, 1987).

Moreover, urban concentration and diversity can function as catalysts for social transformation, providing the basis for cultural exchange and innovation, and facilitating mobilisation against injustice. For this reason, successful struggles for social justice almost always originate in cities, even when their outcome must be secured elsewhere. Cities, then, provide us with the tools and the freedom to transform them in the image of the city we wish to inhabit – just or unjust. That ideal city, in turn, is a reflection of the kind of people we wish to become.

We are not alone in recognising that cities play a central role in the production, reproduction, and contestations of justice and injustices. Urban scholars have long looked at urban issues and processes through the lens of justice. The recent turn in urban justice debates was provoked by David Harvey's landmark book *Social Justice and the City* (Harvey, 1973).[5] A couple of points about its impact in urban studies bear mention. Most important is that the book, following Marx, makes sense of social justice, 'as a matter of eternal justice and morality to regard it as something contingent upon the social processes operating in society as a whole' (Harvey, 1973: 15). This renders philosophical work on social justice suspect whenever it is abstracted from real socio-spatial relations (most centrally class relations) in urban areas.[6]

Harvey's critique corresponds well with the large body of urban studies work that has documented manifest injustices in cities, relying either on theory of justice per se or on implicit understandings of right and wrong. These injustices include racial segregation (Massey and Denton, 1993; S. Smith, 1989), racial oppression (Keith, 2005), class-based exploitation (Applebaum et al., 2006; Herod and Wright, 2001), the abuses that often surround trans-national migration (Samers, 2010), gentrification (Smith, 1996) and exclusionary urban space (Davis, 1990; Sorkin, 1992). This is not

---

5 See Merrifield and Swyngedouw (1995) for a useful set of discussions emanating from the book.

6 Young (1990) and Fraser (1989) also lodge this critique, but from different political perspectives than Harvey's.

meant to be a complete inventory of urban justice research, but a demonstration that
justice, or, more accurately, injustices have been well studied and documented by
urbanists in the last few decades. The common thread among these studies is the
recognition that socio-spatial relations in cities produce injustices. If justice is not to
be found in the abstract, then neither is injustice.

Empirical urban injustice research has been paralleled by efforts to understand the
spatialisation of justice. Most of this research has also focused on urban contexts. To
some extent, this has been because of the importance of the world-wide urban social
movements of the 1960s, which culminated in the uprisings of 1968. David Smith,
who has written at length about geography and social justice, bluntly states, 'The
explicit engagement of geography with morality and social justice dates from the
latter part of the 1960s' (D. Smith, 1994: 4). On some level, this is correct. However,
there is a related but distinct reason why urban researchers, and geographers in
particular, developed spatial theories of justice in the 1970s; and it is because of a
transformation in the understanding of space in social relations. When space was
treated as a mere container in which things happened, there was no need to explicitly
place social justice in space. Following the influence of Lefebvre, Soja and Harvey,
much of the field of human geography and parts of the social sciences more broadly
have come to a different understanding of space – one in which space is active in
producing and reproducing social relations. If this conception of space is correct
(and we believe it is) then the centrality of space in social justice work becomes clear.
Dikeç neatly summarises this point, stating that, 'the very production of space, which
is inherently a conflictual process, not only manifests various forms of injustice, but
actually produces *and* reproduces them' (Dikeç, 2001: 1787–8, emphasis in original). That is why the injustices in Brooklyn and Santo Domingo are about more than
just 'who gets what and why'. They are examples of the ways in which the production of the urban built environment constitutes in-and-of-itself a set of processes and
relationships that is central to the question of urban justice. This line of argument
has been recently taken to its logical conclusion by Soja's argument for an explicitly
geographic understanding of justice and injustice (Soja, 2010). This work is devoted
to asserting the importance of spatial explanations of injustice over sociological or
historical ones (although he is presumably compensating for the omission of space
in much social and political theory).

Finally, the influence of Lefebvre has recently been further enhanced by the
embrace of many urban theorists of his conception of 'the right to the city'.
Numerous urban scholars who in the past might have discussed urban issues
through the lens of justice and injustice have instead adopted Lefebvre's framing of
emancipatory urban politics (see, for instance, Harvey, 2008; Marcuse, 2009; Mayer,
2009; Mitchell, 2003; Purcell, 2008). The language of justice and the language of
rights are not unrelated; but they are distinct. The concept of the right to the city has
come to mean two related rights. The first is the right to claim entry to appropriate
urban spaces. This claim, which can appear relatively modest, is, in fact, a radical
call to jettison the centrality of private property and property ownership in controlling access to urban space, and opens up and democratises space – regardless of
issues of tenure and ownership. The second component is the right to participate in

the production of cities. The right is therefore not just, or even at all, about the right to the city as it currently exists. It is the right to remake the city, and thereby remake who we are as people. As Harvey put it:

> the question of what kind of city we want cannot be divorced from that of what kind of social ties, relationship to nature, lifestyles, technologies and aesthetic values we desire. The right to the city is far more than the individual liberty to access urban resources: it is a right to change ourselves by changing the city. (2008: 23)

While there are political organisations that have embraced the language of the right to the city, our reading of contemporary urban politics is that the academic theory is a bit ahead of the grounded urban politics, whose achievements, at least in American cities, are more modest than the flourishing of radical urban theory on the right to the city would suggest.

CONCLUDING THOUGHTS

We began this chapter with a pair of short discussions of different cases of urban injustice. We want to return to these by way of a conclusion. In some ways, the dislocations and erasures of the two cases are self-evident and widely recognised injustices, leaving us to wonder why academic analyses of them are needed. The stories, however, are more complicated than that; and those complications demonstrate the limits of 'justice' as a category of intellectual endeavour. Perhaps justice is a concept that has variable amounts of utility according to the level of abstraction and analysis involved. At the level of grounded urban politics, notions of justice and injustice have real power. They are the literal and figurative banners for those who demand a different distribution of goods and services or a different process for deciding what goods and services will be distributed. As Harvey put it simply, 'Right and wrong are words that power revolutionary changes and no amount of negative deconstruction of such terms can deny that' (Harvey, 2002: 398). And at the level of abstract philosophical inquiry, questions of justice and rights are important frames for analysis. Young's categorisation of oppression remains central to our thinking about injustice and, therefore, justice. Sen and Nussbaum's capabilities framework, for its part, is logical and compelling. Even Rawls, for all the criticism his work inspired, has been vitally important in forcing distribution back into liberal thought (from where it had been excluded for almost two centuries by the dominance of utilitarian thinking). And finally, Harvey has helped reframe questions of justice away from universalist ideals detached from social relations and processes (albeit in ways that were themselves often abstracted from any particular locality or struggle). But what is the analytic utility of questions of justice and rights at the meso-level of applied academic analysis?

In easy cases – those of self-evident oppression and deprivation – injustice is so easy to comprehend and analyse, that the contours of justice become irrelevant.

Discussion centres instead on the empirical questions about the processes that cause the injustice, the actors involved, and their impact on the circumstances. In difficult cases, on the other hand, the application of abstract notions of justice can often contradict our intuition or may not provide an adequate basis by which to decide among alternative scenarios. And in some cases, justice may have relatively little to do with the issue at hand. Outcomes and processes may not be more or less just; they may simply be different.

We are left with the question of what kind of city do we wish to inhabit? Whose voices will we count? Which activities will we value? We do not, and cannot, answer those questions in the abstract. Instead, our answers must come from rooting our analyses in localised contexts, without losing sight of the centrality of questions of justice and injustice in cities. We have discussed a set of important and useful ways of framing the issues involved in social justice and injustice in cities. There remains, however, more clarity in our understandings of injustices than in justice. Readers could thus legitimately ask, 'But what is social justice in cities?' To that, we are afraid, we find no convincing answer.

But maybe that is not the right question. Justice has to be understood in the context of actually existing social relations. It is those contexts that inspire questions about what justice is or might be. Can we have urban monuments devoted to national memory, and hence nation-building, which are not exclusionary in their meanings or brutal in their physical development processes? Can we value the uses and cultural significance of a space as much as we value its exchange value to property-owners? As these questions imply, making cities less unjust will require a different set of social relations then the ones that currently produce, and are produced by, cities. And the answer to such questions lies in the often frustrating dialectic of social change – a process that requires both a vision of what one is fighting for and a recognition that that vision will result from the fighting itself.

SECTION 4

REFLECTIONS ON CITIES AND SOCIAL CHANGE

12

The Good City?

Ananya Roy

The project of the good city has long been the utopian dream of urban planners, philosophers of space and urban social movements. Indeed, the very idea of the city carries within it a set of normative meanings – for example, that of *civitas* – and thereby far exceeds any simple description of human settlement. It is in this way that the search for the good city has come to be inextricably linked with the sheer fact of urban life, such that to talk about cities is to also inevitably talk about the good city, about arrangements of space and time that restore hope and dignity to the human condition. This utopian dream has persisted across centuries and has proliferated in a variety of urban ideologies and philosophies. It has done so despite the stark disjuncture between urban utopia and urban reality. It has done so in the face of urban segregation and alienation, amidst splintered and fragmented formations, as a stubborn refusal of the poverty, vulnerability and degradation so often apparent in cities around the world. The utopian dream of the good city therefore cannot be suppressed or denied; it deserves critical attention.

In this essay, I outline and discuss (re)emergent conceptualisations of the good city, from those that search for the just city to those that identify strategies of hope to those that seek to formulate an urban utopianism. I am interested in how such formulations of the good city face an impasse, how they stall around a few recurring themes: justice, collective good, difference, democracy. These themes represent desires and aspirations but they are also fictions, their power to inspire lost as soon as their precise meanings are pinned down and implemented (Hillier, 2009). New fictions often replace old ones but they too contain a 'fundamental fantasy for harmony' (Gunder, 2005: 192). Thus, in an essay on the 'just city', Susan Fainstein (2009: 29) asserts a 'collective enterprise' to create and defend 'collective goods'. Such an endeavour seems to be cast in opposition to the profession of city planning, which as Fainstein (2009: 19) notes was 'born of a vision of the good city … to achieve efficiency, order, and beauty through the imposition of reason'. But of course 'common-good politics', as Michael Gunder (2005: 153) calls it, is as subject to critique and contestation as are the ideas of 'efficiency, order, and beauty'. Indeed, common-good politics can be brutal and exclusionary, a staking of claims to the urban commons by the powerful. It is thus that in contemporary India, the good city with its mandates of public space and green urbanism, is claimed by the elite and the middle class, and actively excludes the urban poor. Such 'bourgeois environmentalism' – to borrow a phrase from Amita Baviskar (2003) – is also common-good politics. Not surprisingly, in an essay on the American neoliberal city, Neil Smith (1997: 133) expresses doubt about the productivity of the term 'justice', noting that it is steeped in desires and aspirations but unable to put forward a precise diagnosis of particular structural conditions of inequality.

It is not enough then to say that the good city is haunted by dark shadows, that there are worlds of urban living that remain excluded from the domain of such a city. Nor is it enough to say that the idea of the good city is often appropriated by powerful interests, those that impose a hegemony of will upon urban life. Instead it is important to pinpoint how conceptualisations of the good city are necessarily incomplete and indeterminate, that they are unable to bring normative closure to the project of urban utopianism. Jean Hillier (2009: 657) thus notes that 'doing justice will entail experimentation, an always-unfinished connecting and coming-together of trajectories'. Her reminder is worth applying to the broader project of the good city. In this essay, I argue that such indeterminacy is a matter of hope rather than lament, for it provides an opening to think about the city in political terms, to contemplate how agonism, uncertainty and even dystopia may provide the basis for a renewed commitment to urban life.

CIVIL CITY

In a bold statement on urban utopianism, John Friedmann (2000: 464) seeks to 'delineate some elements for a positive vision of the "good city"'. These elements run a familiar gamut of 'good' things: 'housing, affordable health care, adequately remu-nerated work, and adequate social provision', all delivered through a 'system of good governance' (Friedmann, 2000: 471). Who would disagree with such a list? But the logic of the good city does not rest in a list of elements. With this in mind, Friedmann (2000: 466) asserts 'human flourishing' – the right to the full development of human potential – as the key goal of the good city. Bearing uncanny resemblance to Amartya Sen's idea of human well-being, such a vision foregrounds humanist values. But Friedmann goes further. He situates this primary good – what he also calls 'multipli/city' – in civil society:

> By multipli/city, I mean an autonomous civil life relatively free from direct supervision and control by the state. So considered, a vibrant civil life is the necessary social context for human flourishing. Multipli/city acknowledges the priority of civil society, which is the sphere of freedom and social repro-duction – and it is for its sake that the city can be said to exist. (Friedmann, 2000: 467)

Friedmann's vision of the good city as a humanist space anchored by civil society is not an anomaly. John Dryzek (2005: 220) similarly calls for a 'deliberative democ-racy' that is located in a public sphere and that can 'handle deep differences'. Dryzek

(2005: 232) goes to considerable length to insist that such deliberative institutions must be 'at a distance from sovereign authority'. Such also is the work of Arjun Appadurai. His analysis of 'deep democracy' celebrates 'visions of emancipation and equity' put forward by 'grassroots political movements' and that are often 'at odds with the nationalist imagination' (Appadurai, 2002: 22). Most significant, according to Appadurai (2002: 24–5), are 'efforts to reconstitute citizenship in cities' that deploy 'new horizontal modes for articulating the deep democratic politics of the locality'. In more recent work, Appadurai (2007) reformulates such formations as the 'politics of hope'. In turn, he aligns the politics of hope with the 'politics of participation' (Appadurai, 2007: 30). With a focus on mass politics and the empowerment of the poor – what Partha Chatterjee (2006) has labeled 'popular politics of most of the world' – Appadurai (2007: 32) signals a 'great ethical shift' that is concerned with 'global poverty', i.e. 'human suffering and misery'. But it is 'participation' that remains central to Appadurai's politics of hope:

> Put in the sharpest terms, the new currency of democratic politics, stimulated by the emergence of poverty as a primary and measurable social ill and by the worldwide growth in mass agitational politics, makes participation the path to capacity rather than the reverse ... This reversal places a new value on the politics of hope, since it promises that mass participation in democratic politics can provide a more direct route to economic equality than the path of gradually improved qualifications for citizenship. (Appadurai, 2007: 30–1)

Appadurai (2007: 33) once again locates participation in the 'galactic explosion of civil society movements' that have 'brought into being a whole new range of practices that allow poor people to exercise their imaginations for participation'. It is thus that the sphere of civil society, with its practices of communication, deliberation, and participation, becomes central to the conceptualisation of the good city. Such a sphere is seen to be an alternative to the market, which Appadurai (2007: 32) argues substitutes 'enterprise' and 'calculation' for 'hope'. It is also seen to be, as Dryzek (2005) claims, 'at a distance from sovereign authority'.

Yet, in my work on the politics of inclusion, I have argued that civil society cannot be thus positioned: as an alternative to the market and at a distance from sovereign authority. The practices of economic solidarity of the urban poor that Appadurai describes – slum-dwelling, microcredit – are saturated with the movement of capital. They are the emergent frontiers of 'bottom billion capitalism', where transactions are thoroughly commodified and where practices of exploitation and accumulation are prominent. Such economies are instances of 'neoliberal populism', an authorisation of the people's economy that facilitates new circuits of market rule (Roy, 2010).

Similarly, formations of deep democracy can also be 'infrastructures of populist mediation' (Roy, 2008). Here, the 'horizontal modes' of political organising celebrated by Appadurai consolidate new forms of sovereign power with control over territory and inaugurate new forms of governmentality that shape how political subjects imagine themselves. Even if we are to concede that this is in fact 'autonomous civil life relatively free from direct supervision and control by the state' – Friedmann's vision of the good city – then it must also be asserted that this civil life is shot through with capital and power. Indeed, it is often distance from the sovereign authority of the state that opens up opportunity for other forms of sovereignty and territoriality. This multiplicity of sovereignty, the proliferation of federations, does not necessarily signify democratic practice or political empowerment. Instead, as AlSayyad and I (2006) have noted in an essay on 'medieval modernity', it may indicate a fractal feudalism that reduces citizenship to the sheer politics of patronage and protection. Most important, the call for distance from the state bears an uncanny resemblance to the logic of neoliberalism and its emphasis on the deregulation of space.

HABITS OF HABITATION

The vision of the good city put forward by Appadurai and others is anchored by civil society. Although this may loosely involve 'civil life', as in Friedmann's use of the term, it more commonly implies formal and informal associations that together constitute a public sphere. Appadurai quite explicitly directs his attention to non-governmental actors, grassroots political movements and federations of the poor. These, for him, constitute the infrastructure of the politics of hope and thus of the good city. A related, yet distinct, vision is that put forward by Ash Amin who calls for an 'urban ethic' organised as an 'ever-widening habit of solidarity' (2006: 1009). In place of the more formal language of civil society or deliberative democracy, Amin (2006: 1021) calls for a 'civic politics', one that can get the 'urban habit of living with diversity right'. This, he argues, can 'regain some mechanism for the distribution of hopefulness'. Strikingly similar to Appadurai in tone, Amin nevertheless strikes a different note. While Appadurai is seeking horizontal modes of organising and governing that defy the verticality of the nation-state, Amin (2006: 1021) rejects partnerships, stakeholder participation, decentralisation and devolution: 'The idea of good urban governance is an illusion not only for all that it cannot capture, but also for its panoptic authoritarianism veiled as stakeholder democracy.' In the place of these formations of governance he calls for 'an active and distributed democracy based around different registers of solidarity': 'repair, relatedness, rights, and re-enchantment' (Amin, 2006: 1021, 1012).

Amin's vision of the good city is ethereal – even though he himself designates it as a 'practical' utopianism. It is a city held together by webs of practices and meanings, not always embedded in associations and institutions. It is a city that lacks centre and hierarchy. It far exceeds Dryzek's call for 'distance from sovereign authority'. By relying on different registers of solidarity, Amin crafts a utopian dream where authority itself is inconsequential and where habits of habitation instead dominate. Neil Smith (2005: 894) presents a sharp critique of this urban vision: 'Insofar as neo-critical geographers see no hierarchy, then, they can show us no location of power that needs to be talked back to, challenged, or transformed.' Smith (2005: 898) goes further, arguing that this utopianism reinforces rather than challenges the ideas and practices of 'ethical Blairite capitalism'. As was the case with the 'civil city' could it be that these 'habits of habitation' unwittingly echo neoliberal populism and its dream of an 'active' and 'distributed' city, albeit one that functions through a distinctive register of solidarity: the market? Here it is worth remembering that neoliberalism itself is a set of both economic and ethical claims (Ong, 2006). These ethical claims – such as those of freedom, empowerment, efficiency – are also visions of the good city. At times, their echoes can also be found in the utopian dreams of those seeking to forge progressive visions of the good city.

In Amin's vision of the good city, formal systems of urban governance are replaced by habits of habitation, or registers of solidarity. But such is also the case in cities of crisis – those where economic crisis is an everyday lived experience. It is thus that Abdoumaliq Simone draws attention to urban colonial and neo-colonial contexts where hollowed-out states are unable to hold together infrastructures of governance and rule. Here, as Simone (2010: 72) notes, 'the "public" dimension is spread across as a variety of actors and modes of authority'. Urban residents survive and cope by experimenting with different registers of solidarity. The intersections of these practices do not make for a stable or formal apparatus of governance but they do create what Simone (2010: 2–3) calls 'cityness' – 'the city as a thing in the making', the capacity of urban residents to 'use the city in many different ways'. Simone's cityness seems to resemble the ethics of habitation favored by Amin. Yet, as Simone (2010: 114) argues, intersection cannot be interpreted as social harmony. Nor can platforms of repair and resilience, what Simone (2004b) has elsewhere designated as 'people as infrastructure', be read as civic politics. What then is the vision of the good city when the utopia of solidarity cannot be distinguished from the lived experience of crisis and its experiments of coping?

COSMOPOLITAN RESPONSIBILITY

The theme of difference is an important component of many visions of the good city. From Dryzek to Amin, there is a consistent concern with how associational forms and habits of solidarity may make possible a handling of 'deep difference' or a 'getting diversity right'. Many philosophers of the good city are also interested in how urban life overflows and transcends national borders. It is thus that Dryzek (2005) places hope in the 'transnationalization of the public sphere' and Appadurai (2002) sees urban deep democracy as a 'globalization from below'. Popke (2007) designates such formations as 'subaltern cosmopolitanisms'. He interprets Kant's call for cosmopolitanism as involving a 'wider, spatially extensive sense of responsibility toward others' (Popke, 2007: 509). Such an idea of extended responsibility can also be found in the work of Doreen Massey. She conceptualises the 'world city' not only as a command and control node of the world system but also as a site of 'local internationalism' (Massey, 2007: 184). Responsibility, Massey argues, cannot be restricted to the immediate or the local. Her transnational ethics of place imagines a cosmopolitanism where the imperial centre extends responsibility and recognition to its hinterland of resources, where the global poverty that Appadurai is concerned with is seen to be intimately connected to the financial centre of London:

> Such a reimagination poses to 'London', as a site of power within the networked relations of globalization, questions of its own responsibility. It is one of the ways in which is raised that question: what does this place stand for? (Massey, 2007: 85)

Such geographies of responsibility, of what Massey (2007: 177) calls 'extended responsibility', radically refashion dominant imaginations of global and world cities as economic centres of wealth and prosperity. They reposition cities like London as 'postcolonial' cities – those that must negotiate the distance and intimacy of colonialism and its present (see also Jacobs, 1996). But so too must the very enterprise of cosmopolitan responsibility. Can it transcend the epistemologies of colonialism in order to forge a new ethics of recognition and responsibility? Can the good city be fashioned thus? Popke makes note of an important contradiction in Kant's concept of cosmopolitanism – that its ethics of world citizenship can only be extended to citizens of sovereign states. It is against this limited idea of hospitality that Jacques Derrida (2000: 55, in Popke, 2007: 512) formulates an unconditional or absolute hospitality: 'that I open up my home and that I give not only to the foreigner ... but to the absolute, unknown, anonymous other, and that I *give place* to them, that I let them come, that I let them arrive, and take place in the place I offer them, without asking of them either reciprocity (entering into a pact) or even their names.'

Derrida's absolute hospitality is a radical conceptualisation of geographies of responsibility. It pivots on a distinctive reading of difference: the figure of the 'Other'. This is not a case of handling deep difference or getting diversity right. It is also not the politics of recognition. As Yiftachel et al. (2009: 123) note, 'liberal multicultural recognition' often reifies categories of difference and often assumes, in naïve fashion, that all groups marked as Other can be heard, counted and represented in the space of difference. Derrida's brilliant deconstruction points to how identity is constituted through practices of Othering. The good city, if we are to cast his vision as such, is one that seeks to transform Othering into the ethics of absolute hospitality. Here the Other remains 'absolute, unknown, anonymous'. The distance inscribed in this relationship – a colonial relationship of sovereign subject and constituted object – cannot be mediated by the type of extended responsibility that Massey has in mind. But an arrival, albeit marked by enigma and foreignness – to borrow a turn of phrase from Naipaul (1988) – is possible.

THE FREE CITIZEN

Visions of the good city often make reference to the Hellenic city-state. It is here that urban democracy and citizenship were seen to have been perfected and urbanism organised around a golden mean of public life. As Lewis Mumford (1961: 158–60) notes, the form of the Hellenic city was 'rustic' and 'crude', but the

> life it contained was more significant than the container … The highest product of that experience was not a new type of city, but a new kind of man … the free citizen.

The polis was thus a theatre for active public life, one that far exceeded military service and extended to the assembly, the law courts, the theatre, the spring festivals (Mumford, 1961: 166).

> Thus the public life of the Athenian citizen demanded his constant attention and participation, and these activities, so far from confining him to an office or limited quarter, took him from the temple to the Pnyx, from the agora to the theatre, from the gymnasium to the harbor of the Pireaus … For a while, city and citizen were one … In that brief period, Athens was rich in citizens as no city has ever been rich before (Mumford 1961: 168).

Mumford (1961: 171) laments that in the decades and centuries that followed, 'buildings began to displace men', that an obsession with ideal city form came to overshadow the golden mean of active public life. This urban utopia sought to suppress the 'dynamics of human development' (Mumford, 1961: 188) and to transform urban disorder into a controlled and segmented society. Urban citizenship gave way to immutable hierarchy, governed by immutable laws. It is thus that Mumford (1961: 176) levels a sharply worded critique of the Platonic ideal: 'Plato's polis might be described as a walled prison without room for the true activities of the city within its prison-yard.'

But the lament for the loss of the 'free citizen' and the sphere of active public life requires closer scrutiny. After all, the Hellenic city, with its realm of active and full citizenship, excluded a large number of city dwellers from citizenship. Mumford (1961: 189) rightly notes that 'the Greeks never repaired the error of slavery'. It is slavery that in rather obvious fashion marks the limits of the concept of the 'free citizen'. Yet, Mumford (1961: 16) argues that 'it is by its capacity to formulate that ideal – not by its failure to achieve it – that we still properly measure the Greek polis'.

The writings of Giorgio Agamben provide a radically different interpretation of the ideal of the 'free citizen'. At the limits of political community lies the figure of 'homo sacer' or 'sacred man', 'who may be killed and yet not sacrificed' (Agamben, 1995: 8). It is a figure that Agamben plucks from the legal philosophy of ancient Rome but traces in Aristotelian political thought and sees present in contemporary political formations. Contrary to Mumford's analysis, homo sacer does not signify the failure to achieve the ideal of the free citizen. Instead, the specter of homo sacer lies at the very heart of this ideal; it is the act of exclusion through which the good city is constituted. It is thus that Agamben (1995: 8) argues that 'human life is included in the juridical order … solely in the form of its exclusion (that is, of its capacity to be killed)'. This ban, and its relations of abandonment, exception and violence, are the key elements of political and ethical order.

He who has been banned is not, in fact, simply set outside the law and made indifferent to it but rather *abandoned* by it, that is, exposed and threatened on the threshold in which life and law, outside and inside, become indistinguishable. (Agamben, 1995: 28, emphasis in original)

Accordingly, Agamben shifts our attention from the city to the camp, this threshold of indistinction and exception. In an extension of Agamben's work, Achille Mbembe (2003: 24) discusses the various racialised materialisations of this threshold: death camps, refugee camps, slave plantations, the colony: 'the colonies are the location par excellence where the controls and guarantees of judicial order can be suspended – the zone where the violence of the state of exception is deemed to operate in the service of "civilization"'. In other words, it is at this threshold – in the camp and the colony rather than in the city – through practices of violence, abandonment and exception, that the norms of 'civilization' are upheld and enforced. Here the city can no longer be the locus of *civitas*. It is thus that Agamben's work marks the impossibility of the concept of the 'good' city.

AGONISM: BRIDGES AND REPLICANTS

The struggle to envision the good city is curiously averse to the idea of struggle. Various forms of urban utopianism coalesce around the hope of a civil city or celebrate habits of solidarity or assert cosmopolitan responsibility or make reference to the ideal of active and full urban citizenship. In doing so, they valorise a singular rather than fractured urban ethic; they propose common-good politics; and they map geographical relations, whether proximate or distant, of reciprocity, responsibility, and recognition. They thereby ignore what David Harvey and Cuz Potter (2009: 45) assert is the 'necessity of outright conflict and struggle'. How can visions of the good city incorporate practices of conflict and struggle? Can agonism form the heart of the good city? Harvey (2000b) himself wrestles with this notion. His call for 'dialectical utopianism' is inspiring and yet its materialisation in an urban utopia is nightmarish, befitting of the label of 'living hell' that Mumford (1961) reserves for Plato's ideal city.

It is against such visions of the good city that urban theorists have sought to put forward a critical interpretation of justice and utopia. David Pinder (2002: 238) thus adopts Leonie Sandercock's call for a 'utopia in the becoming ... a social project concerned with "living together in difference" that is open to dialogue, change and contestation'. He views utopian urbanism as an interruption in 'dominant conceptions about linear temporal progression or good spatial form in the effort to open up unrealized possibilities in the present'. Or, Jean Hillier (2009: 640) gives us a Deleuzoguattarian analysis of 'assemblages of justice', those that contain 'an oscillation between relations of presence and absence'. Such interventions are keenly attuned to the various forms of agonism that constitute urban life. Inspired by the philosophy of Chantal Mouffe, they replace 'the fundamental fantasy for harmony' with an 'agonistic pluralism':

> There is a requirement for a mode of planning that does not seek one dominant 'consensus', but rather actively promotes a planning related politics beyond that of liberal civil society. This is a proposed planning ethos predicated on affable but agonistic dis-sensus. (Gunder, 2005: 177)

In such analysis, it is the agonistic city or political city that is much more hopeful than the ideal city or the good city (see also Ploger, 2004; Purcell, 2009). Hope, in this case, derives not from common-good politics or achieved consensus but rather from the critical deconstruction of norms and ideals – that which reveals the founding acts of exclusion, absence, abandonment and violence:

> 'Acting in concert' requires the construction of a 'we', a political unity, but that a fully inclusive political unity can never be realized since wherever there is a 'we', there must also be an excluded 'them', a constitutive outside. Any agreement reached will thus be partial, based on acts of social regulation and exclusion. The 'surplus of meaning' … that remains uncontrolled is liable to challenge from the excluded other. (Hillier, 2003: 42)

In place of the vision of the good city, I am thus drawn to two inherently unstable critical formations: the bridge and the replicant. Each, I believe, can serve as an 'assemblage of justice' in the agonistic city, displacing ideals of the free citizen and maps of multicultural recognition and responsibility.

The concept-metaphor of the 'bridge' is central to the work of Chicana feminist theorist Gloria Anzaldua. Anzaldua's poetic writing makes visible structures of racialised and gendered oppression. The borderlands of which she writes, for example the US–Mexico border, bear resemblance to Agamben's threshold of life and death. They are, for Anzaldua (1999: 25), 'an open wound – where the Third World grates against the first and bleeds'. Yet, Anzaldua also asserts that these borderlands are more than spaces of violence and abandonment; they can also be occupied, they can also become home. In *this bridge we call home*, she repositions the back-breaking oppression of race, gender and class as a space of transformation:

> Bridges are thresholds to other realities, archetypal, primal symbols of shifting consciousness. They are passageways, conduits, and connectors that connote transitioning, crossing borders, and changing perspectives … Transformations occur in this in-between space lacking clear boundaries. (Anzaldua, 2002: 1)

Here the threshold of life and death becomes a threshold to transformation; here abandonment becomes recognition; here the open wound becomes home.

Is it a naïve fantasy, or an irresponsible political fiction, to imagine the racialised colony as a liberatory space? It is worth noting that for Anzaldua (2002: 1) the bridge remains irretrievably a 'liminal zone', a 'constant state of displacement', and home itself is thus an 'uncomfortable, even alarming feeling'. In other words, the bridge is a provisional space that calls into question the very idea of habitation and cosmopolitan belonging. But as a concept-metaphor the bridge also makes necessary what Sandoval (2002) has called 'technologies of crossing'. These threshold practices are not those of the free citizen; often they are acts of solidarity forged in the crucible of grave crisis, marking the limits of the agora and indeed the city. They are a making of space, provisionally habitable space, through the relations of agonism and strangeness.

Yet another useful concept-metaphor is that of the replicant. I derive this term from the famous dystopian cinematic text *Bladerunner*. A Hollywood rendering of Phillip K. Dick's novel *Do Androids Dream of Electric Sheep?*, *Bladerunner* is a montage of urban dystopian images set in Los Angeles 2019. At the heart of its dystopia is a theme of uncontrollability – of an imploded urban space made up of dizzying verticality and distant off-world colonies. Above all, this is a city of replicants, human replicas produced on the assembly line of a post-Fordist economy with a short shelf-life that signifies the disposability of the labouring body. The replicants are the *homo sacer* of this Brave New World; bodies that can be killed but not sacrificed. *Bladerunner* is a dystopia that not only erodes the idea of the city but also calls into question the very integrity of human identity. They are, as AlSayyad (2006: 140) notes, 'authentic reproductions, indistinguishable in almost all respects from human beings; they are simulacra, not robots'. How then do we know if we are human? Harvey (1989b) thus argues that this is a depressing film, one that erases the difference between human and replicant. Yet, the replicant can be seen to be a threshold figure, one whose indistinction is the basis of hope. Žižek (1993: 410) thus argues that the undecidability of replicant status – that liminal, intermediate, displaced state – makes us aware of the replicant quality of all human identity. Following Žižek, I argue that the replicant calls into question essentialist ideas of identity, such as that of free citizen. Instead, it makes us aware of the cyborg quality of all human identity, the fabrications and hybrid compositions through which we are put together (Haraway, 1991). This too is a bridge. What does it mean to forge solidarity and civility when the essence of human identity itself is under (de)construction? When the Other exists within the very self? In this way, the replicant forces a rewriting of imaginary communities:

> Policed by an unconstitutional, illegal order, it exterminates or indefinitely imprisons its others: 'terrorists', refugees, illegal immigrants, replicants. The workers and subjects of these offworld colonies have no place in the imperial, or even provincial, centers. But the center itself is laid waste, as is its law. (Hutchings, 2007: 397)

The good city that I am eager to embrace is this urbanism of bridges and replicants. It is a city of agonism and struggle, of fragmented and fractured identities, of precarious and provisional spaces of habitation. It is one where the centre itself – of geography and identity – is laid waste.

13

Conclusion: Engaging the Urban World

Eugene McCann and Ronan Paddison

The central aim of this book is to provide a relatively advanced, theoretically informed, yet empirically grounded discussion of the social experience of urban life; one that critically addresses the excitement, contradictions, conflicts and tensions of living in cities and that, through the range of authorial voices, highlights the rich diversity of urban social geography. The chapters are written by leading scholars – people well positioned to survey the field, critically comment on its contours, and point out intellectually and politically important pathways for future research. It is not a recipe book, however. One cannot (and should not!) expect to be provided with clearly defined research questions upon which to build one's own research. Rather, the chapters are suggestive of numerous possibilities for future research and, in combination, they highlight the breadth of work that is possible and the variety of likely approaches that can be deployed in urban social research.

In this chapter we do what we hope readers of this book will do: reflect back on the arguments and case studies the authors have presented for the purpose of combining and interconnecting them in ways that generate questions about, and perspectives on, a particular urban social geography. Then, based on our reading of the chapters, we take a stance – an intellectual and normative position – on how urban social geography and urban studies more generally should develop in the future. We argue for an analytical approach that pays close attention to the intersections of difference and connection and of localisations and globalisation. We outline an approach that 'unpacks' the specificities and apparent 'here-and-now-ness' of one place to better understand it through its position within wider socio-spatial processes and historical legacies. In doing so, we argue, following many of the chapter authors, that such an approach allows an engagement with the world that emphasises social justice in its many forms. Before elaborating on these arguments, however, we will address the concerns, themes and approaches highlighted by the chapter authors. We'll start from one of the most-tapped wells of urban social research.

CHICAGO SCHOOL

A recurring reference in the preceding chapters is to the work of the Chicago School of urban sociology that flourished in the 1910s, 1920s and 1930s. This is not surprising, of course. As scholars of cities, we have all been taught, at one time or another, the ins-and-outs of Burgess's Concentric Zone model. In fact, we are willing to bet that the vast majority of you – even if you are not from the Midwest, or from anywhere else in the US – have a vision of the model in your mind's eye right now. It has been a remarkably resilient and well-travelled representation of the city. Indeed, one of us (Eugene) went to high school in a relatively small west of Scotland steel town called Motherwell. He distinctly remembers being taught the concentric zone model and its later variants (sectors, nuclei, etc.) in a geography classroom and being encouraged by his teacher to go out and explore the town to see if there could be something like a 'zone in transition' there. This was a clever pedagogical technique, rather than a misguided attempt to discover some ontologically real similarity between early industrial Chicago and (very soon to be) post-industrial Motherwell. It was a strategy to get a group of budding geographers out into the built environment and to see it not only as bricks, mortar, concrete and steel works, but to understand its connections to social life. Yet, reflecting back, the high school exercise also speaks to the geographical scope and dominance of the Chicago School, for better or worse. (And as a recent debate on the particularity of Chicago highlights, its concentric patterning has become critiqued for having less bearing on other major North American cities, such as New York, than might be imagined (Judd and Simpson, 2011)).

These qualifications aside, some among you will, as a result of your own disciplinary initiation into urban geography, be able to conjure up more than the mere image of Burgess's concentric zones but also other dominant names associated with the School – Park and Wirth as well as Hoyt, Harris and Ullman – and key terms they lent to the study of cities – the Central Business District, among others. Most likely, other elements of the School's approach, perhaps including its appeal to ecological metaphors or its pioneering use of social survey and ethnographic techniques, will also ring some bells. The School, like planners and academics before and after, dealt in what Koch and Latham define as powerful, generative representations of cities. Speaking of Daniel Burnham's plan for Chicago, but in a way that resonates also with the Chicago sociologists, Koch and Latham (this volume, page 18) argue that, '[r]epresentations can facilitate [certain forms of rational governance] by both creating information (giving a problem a certain definition or shape) and neutralising it (through making this information technical)'. Through its abstract representations, the Chicago School has long been an influence and a reference for those studying cities, particularly the social geographies of cities.

And yet it is clear, from the discussions of the School's work in the preceding chapters, that contemporary geographers, like their peers in cognate disciplines, tend to view the work of the Chicago School with ambivalence or outright scepticism. The authors who invoke it in this book tend, however, to use it as a foil. They show how the conditions, conceptualisations, methods and politics of contemporary critical urban scholarship have become – and must necessarily continue to be – quite distinct from an approach that, while still prominent in introductory high school and undergraduate texts and classrooms, is increasingly difficult to square with the experience of, and intellectual and political challenges presented by, contemporary urbanism. As Deborah Martin (2009: 79), in her essential entry in the *Dictionary of Human Geography*, puts it, '[t]he Chicago School is clearly situated in and thus limited by its time and place – because of its reliance on human ecology and Darwinian metaphors, and upon the city of Chicago as the main case study'.

But are things really so clear-cut? The answer is probably yes and no. Martin is certainly cautious about throwing the baby out with the bath water:

> Yet Park's (1967 [1925]) original description of an agenda for research included population and demography, land use, patterns of home ownership and migration, community development and character, neighbourhood history, occupational and class mobility, social unrest and social control (including policing and urban policies). Many of these topics remain of vital interest to urban geographers, and draw upon ideas from the Chicago School about pattern, process and community, although our contemporary approaches to and theories of these topics are necessarily different. (Martin, 2009: 79–80)

So, perhaps we can acknowledge that today some of the key concerns associated with cities and urban life that drew the attention of the Chicago School researchers are still relevant in broad terms, if somewhat different in their particulars. It is in this way that the Chicago School may still serve as some sort of resource or reference. But why is their work so clearly a foil or point of marked contrast for contemporary critical urban scholars? A key reason relates to the how the key members of the School conceptualised, categorised and generalised its objects of study and, in turn, what their own and subsequent analyses elided.

Gill Valentine, for example, points out that the Chicago School's

> theory of how 'natural communities' emerge in cities … led to the development of techniques to map segregation within cities on the basis of ethnicity and class … [that were] heavily criticised by radical geographers and black political activists (see P. Jackson, 1987) for [their] narrow empiricism and the assumptions made about 'race' (that it was an essential category). (page 75, this volume)

These assumptions are 'now out of kilter with contemporary understandings of identity and "difference"' (page 75, this volume), she notes. Clearly, there is a telling and productive distinction between 'traditional' work on cities (work that has tended to seek out or create categorical similarities and stabilities, like the sharply defined zones, sectors, belts and identities of the Chicago School) and contemporary critical work that seeks, among other things, to acknowledge and work *with*, rather than against, difference, complexity, multiplicity and even confusion.

Diversity and multiplexity are certainly key characteristics of this volume. The chapters represent the provocative range of topics, approaches and narrative styles that characterise contemporary critical urban social geography. Cities shape, and are shaped by, a multitude of social practices, identities or processes, and the varied critical approaches found in the preceding chapters help unpack cities' complex diversity (without aspiring to necessarily clear and simple 'answers' nor to agree entirely with each other in the details of their perspectives). Yet, one strategy that is common among many of the authors is the use of one site or one social phenomenon – e.g., a ship-breaking yard (Cook and Swyngedouw – Chapter 10), a lighthouse or a mall (DeFilippis and Rivero – Chapter 11), gentrification (Lees – Chapter 3), the stigmatisation of poor people (DeVerteuil – Chapter 4), exclusionary walling (MacLeod – Chapter 8), obesogenic environments (Moon and Kearns – Chapter 9), etc. – as a microcosm of wider social processes that constitute cities and urban life. The specific, concrete and 'graspable' site or phenomenon then allows researchers to demonstrate the workings of processes that are more abstract and more extensive – stretching spatially across wider geographical fields than one specific site or city and stretching historically back into the past and forward to multiple potential futures, beyond the specific temporal bounds of the case at hand.

This technique can also be used to unpack the implications of the arguments about the state of cities and the state of urban studies that are embedded in the chapters. So, let's use Chicago as such a site. But let's return to the city about 80 years after the publication of Burgess's Concentric Zone model and, in the spirit of the method, let's not focus primarily on the whole city but on one small place within it. Our aim, then, is to use one place in the city as an example that emphasises the strategy found in many of the preceding chapters – to draw out the connections between present and past, local and global, 'the social' and other elements of urban life that are often artificially separated from it, such as 'the economic' or 'the environmental'.

CHICAGO COOL

On the night of 4 November 2008, as the results of the US presidential election rolled in, people across the country and the world realised that Barack Obama was about to be elected the first African-American president. Obama himself was in Chicago, where he had lived for a number of years and from where he had been elected to Congress. It was from there that he would accept victory. Politicians and their campaign managers are sensitive to place. They choose the sites of their 'set-piece' speeches carefully and with full knowledge of the symbolic weight that the right place at the right time can lend their message and their identity. For example, in February 2007, Obama announced his intention to run for the presidency in a speech from the steps of the Old State Capitol building in Springfield, Illinois – a building closely associated with Abraham Lincoln's early political career, including his 'House Divided' speech that set the terms for debate about slavery in the subsequent years. As the realisation of Obama's victory spread, most interested people gathered around televisions, but Chicagoans had the opportunity to congregate in

Grant Park, a large lakefront public space in the city's downtown that had been chosen as the site of Obama's post-election victory address.

We were not in Chicago that night but we were struck by the television coverage of growing crowds in the park and the air of excited expectation. Echoing in some ways the arguments of Koch and Latham, the early-evening television shots of the park were from high above, highlighting the purposeful movement of large groups of people along its pathways. In these shots the park was illuminated by streetlights that, due to the camera lenses, seemed to shine like stars in the night, while the converging crowds beneath them gave a sense of a culminating mass movement. As the evening progressed and Obama's victory became increasingly likely, coverage turned to ground-level cameras shooting the emotional, racially diverse crowd crammed around the speaker's podium. By the time the president-elect's address ended, Grant Park had entered the national and international consciousness as a profoundly meaningful public space: a meeting ground for a reported 240,000 people, the setting for expressions of joy, pride and relief (the cheers of t-shirt-clad supporters, Jesse Jackson's streaming tears, the excited skipping of the Obamas' daughter, Malia, on stage), and a symbolic building ground for what Obama identified as his and his allies' hard work ahead.

These images contrasted sharply with the gathering of John McCain's supporters in the grounds of the Biltmore Hotel in Phoenix, Arizona. The city's 'swankiest hotel' according to *The Economist* (2008), the Biltmore's thoroughly private space held a much smaller, 'affluent crowd, done up to the nines' with their 'stiletto heels sinking into the lawn' who took every opportunity to boo Obama's name even as McCain praised his achievement. Grant Park, unlike the Biltmore, seemed to be a social, inclusive, celebratory, meaningful space – a 'space of hope' – that symbolised a landmark in American history and offered an opportunity for connections to be made among those who had come to recognise their equivalent interests, concerns and desires across the lines of segregation. And, of course, it was that notion of hope that had propelled Obama's media-savvy campaign. If the previous Democratic US president, Bill Clinton, had campaigned as 'the man *from* Hope', street artist Shepard Fairey's iconic campaign poster allowed Obama to represent himself as the man *of* hope; embodying a brighter possible future. It also helped him embody *cool*, both in the sense of calm assuredness (Obama's composure is often commented upon in the media and it seems to radiate from the portrait Fairey chose for his poster design) and in the sense of hipness (*Shepard Fairey* made a poster of him). Certainly, it seemed that being an Obama supporter in Chicago on that November night, perhaps with an image of the Hope poster on your t-shirt, made you cooler, more forward-thinking, than those well-heeled Republicans down in Phoenix.

And yet, no one person, place, or gathering can be seen as offering a new future untethered to the past or to currently hegemonic ideas. Nor can it offer a new political consensus untrammelled by conflicting interests. The celebration of a pivotal moment in US presidential election history was grounded in a public space that had been witness to a diversity of political events, most often less convivial than was that November night. Indeed, Grant Park, like most urban public spaces, is a palimpsest with a complex history, frequently marked by political struggle, injustice and violence of one form or another. While Obama's campaign team justified its choice of location for the post-election gathering by noting that 'Grant Park is regularly used as an open-air venue for concerts, charity events and sporting activities such as the Chicago Marathon and Taste of Chicago' (quoted in Sweet, 2008), and while it afforded the television cameras spectacular background views of the city skyline, the park's connection to political history could have been no more lost on them than the significance of those steps in Springfield. In August 1968 the park was the site of a police riot against those gathered legally to protest the Democratic National Convention, another unpopular war, and to demand civil rights. Television pictures then featured billowing tear gas and baton-wielding police officers beating unarmed civilians. There were tears in Grant Park that night too, but certainly not tears of joy.

Clearly, then, an analysis of the social geographies of a particular place, as the chapter authors have shown, must involve a sensitivity to the multiple and complex construction and associations of that place, including, in the case of Grant Park, its history. A method of social, spatial and historical 'unpacking' then allows a deeper, if never complete, account of the place in the world. Thus, we might also extend our analysis of the social geography of Grant Park back further in time, back before the era of the Chicago School, to unpack how this place highlights some of the pivotal trends in urban planning, architecture, design, public health and political ecology. The park itself is a product of big plans and literal terraforming. It was extended increasingly far out into Lake Michigan from the late nineteenth century until the 1920s – out to where Burgess's imaginary concentric circles disappear beneath the water. This landfilled park can be understood in terms of the complex and power-laden relationships between nature and cities that Cook and Swyngedouw outline in Chapter 10, even if they are on a lesser scale than the towering skyscrapers that rise over it, the sprawling urban region that extends out from it, or the city's mutually constitutive relationship with its vast agricultural hinterland that made it what Cronon (1991) called 'nature's metropolis'. Grant Park (or Lake Park to use its original name) is, in its most basic sense, a product of labour. But this labour did not end as the last piece of land was filled. Rather, each of its eastward extensions set in train visions, debates, struggles and negotiations on its proper uses. From Chicago's earliest days, the park was to remain free of buildings. In the early twentieth century, Daniel Burnham argued that it should be built on to some extent, and eventually a compromise landscape – largely open, but with a few public buildings and monuments, not far from Burnham's vision – emerged.

In the tradition of the influential American Parks Movement, most associated with Central Park in New York, Grant Park was to act as a pocket of 'nature' and a space for outdoor recreation and exercise in a cramped and polluted industrial city. It was to be a place to promote physical, but also societal, health and well-being. The goal of promoting physical health through the reshaping and management of urban built environments is, as Moon and Kearns show in Chapter 9, a central theme in the emergence of the twin institutions of urban planning and public health. The goal of promoting and reproducing particular social structures, behaviours and mores was also central to the Parks Movement (see also Koch and Latham – Chapter 2). Parks were to be spaces where classes would mingle – or at least be co-present – not because nineteenth-century urban elites subscribed to ideals of equality but because these were spaces in which problematic difference could be dealt with through the socialisation of the working class. Hegemonic norms of moral behaviour, civility and taste were to be taught and, thereby, difference – and class conflict – was to be polished away; airbrushed out of popular consciousness. Immigrants and the poor would, it was hoped, learn to be American – in all the classed and ethnicised ways in which we might imagine that ideal was defined – through watching and engaging with their 'betters' in the park. Parks, then, are social creations imbued, from their very founding, with power but also with resistance as, for example, in the increased class conflict that emerged in nineteenth-century cities, through the very mingling that was intended to stop it (see Taylor, 1999).

Of course, the relationship between the control and management of parks and always incomplete and contested attempts by elites to 'order' 'disorderly' society is not something restricted to a previous era (see Herbert and Grobelski – Chapter 7). If we move back to present-day Grant Park, we can identify similar, if not identical, themes of power, social distinction and the continual production of urban space in its north-western reaches, now rebranded as 'Millennium Park'. Built from the late 1990s through the 2000s, Millennium Park is a hugely expensive collection of gardens, pavilions and public art pieces, most commonly associated with Anish Kapoor's sculpture *Cloud Gate*, colloquially known as 'The Bean'. Like an enormous blob of mercury, the highly polished sculpture reflects and distorts the surrounding skyline and the many visitors who come to have their picture taken with it. It has now become a feature of tourist merchandise and is considered by some to be an unofficial symbol of the city. Yet, the cost of the park – $475m, $270m of which was borne by city tax-payers (Cohen and Ford, 2004) – has been an object of contention, as has its corporatisation through naming rights. The Bean stands on AT&T Plaza, which is surrounded by the McDonald's Cycle Centre, BP Bridge, the Exelon Pavilions, the Chase Promenades and the Boeing Galleries, among other features.

Figure 13.1   'The Bean' in Millennium Park, Chicago, 2006 (photo: Geoff DeVerteuil)

The corporatisation of public space through public–private partnerships and the use of carefully designed urban landscapes as opportunities for 'imagineering' and branding purposes has long been documented as an element of the rise of the entrepreneurial, neoliberal city. Corporate public art and the creations of global 'starchitects' feature prominently in this story and it is no surprise that some of Millennium Park's features are designed not only by Kapoor, but also by Frank Gehry and Renzo Piano – brands in themselves. Their creations involve the sorts of powerful re-presentations of cities referenced by Koch and Latham in Chapter 2, and also the 're-sensing' of the city that Degen discusses in Chapter 6, particularly as redesigned public spaces like Millennium Park often involve the erasure of older landscapes – with all their distinctive sounds, smells, sights and feelings – in favour of new ones that are often critiqued for their 'sanitised' character. While none of this is entirely new, as we have seen, it suggests a context-specific recalibration of the intensity and prominence of certain long-running strands that link present-day cities and power relations with those of the past.

This latest calibration involves branding cities as cool, attractive places to live. But it is clearly the latest gloss on a standard neoliberal strategy that invokes narrowly-defined notions of 'creativity', a fealty to the needs of certain groups of young middle-class workers, and a related acceptance of gentrification and middle-class consumption as a necessary, welcome and inevitable economic development strategy. In many cities, these orientations have raised questions about the right to the city, social justice, and debates about what constitutes a 'good' city (see DeFilippis and Rivero – Chapter 11, and also Roy – Chapter 12). Who, in other words, is welcome in the new city, especially the new, 'vibrant', 'creative' and increasingly gentrified, 'packaged', surveilled and controlled city centre?

Millennium Park, since it was carved from Grant Park, has exhibited some of the tensions and struggles around security and appropriate use of public spaces that Herbert and Grobelski and also MacLeod highlight in their chapters (7 and 8 respectively) and, more generally, it speaks to many of the class-based concerns raised by both Lees (Chapter 3) and DeVerteuil (Chapter 4). Accusations have been made of undemocratic restrictions on access to and use of its spaces and criticism has focused in part on the argument that the public resources used to create and manage it might have been better spent on poverty alleviation and improving the city's schools. Chicago's entrepreneurial, neoliberal business and political elites argue, on the other hand, that the park helps improve the city's image and attracts tourist dollars. In words that echo the goal of a previous era's elites to improve the livability of the city through park design but that also highlight the shift to entrepreneurial concerns with urban brands, one local business leader argued that '[w]hether you are a tourist or a resident, Millennium Park is one of the most extraordinary public spaces in the world' and went on to 'salute' the corporate sponsors, people [and] cultures and arts organisations that make Chicago such a special place to live' (Chapman, quoted in City of Chicago Mayor's Press Office, 2004).

The multiple faces, uses and connotations of Grant Park persist, however. Its neoliberal incarnation has not prevented it being a place of oppositional political action. In October 2011 it was twice the site of confrontations between members of the Occupy movement, looking to set up a permanent camp, and police, enforcing the city's bylaws on overnight presence in parks. In May 2012, the park was a staging ground for protestors opposing the Chicago NATO Summit. Obama, exhibiting his tempered demeanour, argued that the anti-NATO protestors had every right to express their disagreement and then, at the end of the summit, speaking as a local booster, he invoked the new 'official' symbol of Chicago's world-class cool: '[At the end of the summit,] I encouraged [the world leaders] to shop. Want to boost the hometown economy. We gave each leader a bean, a small model [of the sculpture] for them to remember ... Obviously Chicago residents who had difficulties getting home or getting to work [because of security during the meeting] ... What can I tell you? That's part of the price of being a world city. But this was a great showcase' (quoted in Sweet, 2012). The bean and the park in which it is set are now powerful fetishes and the city is now a carefully manicured brand in the service of neoliberal place-boosterism. The reifying elements of this public discourse must be, and can be, countered by urban studies research that digs beneath their polished exteriors.

BEYOND CHICAGO

Neither of us would claim to be experts on Chicago. Our point in the narrative is simply that it is possible, indeed necessary, to carefully and creatively unpack a specific site and the contexts against which it is positioned – temporally, spatially, socially, politically – for the purposes of insightful analysis. As we have indicated, the analytical 'tools' provided by the authors of the preceding chapters generate questions and conceptual orientations that guide that unpacking. They do not provide answers, but they facilitate research into the power relations that constitute particular places. Importantly, the authors also show how we must balance a necessary 'inward' and 'downward' gaze with a 'heads up' orientation to the world outside. We must, as Doreen Massey (1991) advised us almost a quarter of a century ago, have a 'global sense of place', recognising the flows from and to elsewhere and the wider social, political, economic and environmental contexts that shape and interconnect specific places.

Massey's work is only one example of the ways in which geographers have sought to develop analyses of the mutually constitutive relationships between cities and wider geographical fields, or scales, ranging 'upwards' or 'outwards' to the regional, the national, the international and the global (e.g. Brenner and Keil, 2006; Brenner and Theodore, 2002; Harvey, 1985; McCann and Ward, 2011; Roy and Ong, 2011; Smith, 2001). For her, it is both a necessary analytical point and also a crucial political point to assert that places like urban neighbourhoods are best understood not as bounded entities that are clearly defined by specific histories and identities. Rather, urban places, like all places, are constituted by their 'external' relations. We put 'external' in quotes here because, of course, the use of that term reaffirms the very inside/outside binary that Massey and others have deconstructed. Rather than falling into this binary trap, we can think critically and creatively about the co-constitutive and inter-referential relationships between a neighbourhood in

Vancouver, for example, and the *apparently* very different and distant social and physical fabrics of Hong Kong and Dubai. In doing so, we can trace the flows of people, knowledge and capital that are, in fact, simultaneously internal to and stretched externally among these sites, tying them into a network that has, since the 1980s, involved processes of borrowing, emulation and inter-referencing that shape their urban built environments into distinct but resonant forms. In these cities, where certain aspects of their landscapes look similar not because of coincidence or any sort of natural isomorphism, but because of the deliberate actions of developers and planners, we can see how the 'internal' elements of places are always already 'externally' relational in ways that make the binary largely unsustainable as an analytical tool (Lowry and McCann, 2011; Olds, 2001).

The idea that cities are defined by their connections to other places as much as by their locally manifest characteristics is not to suggest that these inter-local connections are unproblematic or smooth. In fact, geography is defined by its attention to unevenness and clustering. Very few, if any, geographical phenomena are spread uniformly across space and a similarly limited number of spatial relations are characterised by easy and straightforward connection. Rather, critical human geography is about the study of power relations as they are manifest in and produced by various types of spatial connections/disconnections, clustering, unevenness, tensions and contradictions. For example, David Harvey's (1982) conceptualisation of the contradictory relationship between the fixity and mobility of capital is a classic case of a relational understanding of a socio-spatial process. For him, capital is defined by its contradictory need to move around in order to exploit the best situations for the generation of profits and its simultaneously and equally necessary imperative to be fixed or embedded in specific places – invested in particular landscapes of production, for example – where the work needed to add value to a commodity is actually done. Thus, work-*places* are not delimited by the walls of the factory, office cubical, or design studio. Instead, they are moments within wider, globally extensive processes of circulation. This conceptualisation therefore entails a particular methodological orientation: one that addresses both the specific site of production but also its wider context and the tensions and contradictions that define them both.

The city, then, is a 'multiplex' assemblage of here and there, near and far, difference and connection, the social, the cultural, the political, the natural and the economic (Allen and Cochrane, 2007; Amin and Graham, 1997; Robinson, 2006). Conceptual discussions and empirical research designs are developed in reference to how best to study this multi-scalar, socio-spatial complexity. Debates and decisions revolve around questions of categorisation, for example, in which typologies, such as those of certain brands of the 'global cities' approach are criticised for the narrowness of their definition of what counts as 'globalness' in cities and in the world system of cities (McCann, 2002, 2004; Robinson, 2006). Other discussions focus on the experiences and strategies of migrants and forced refugees as they produce a 'transnational', 'multicultural', or 'cosmopolitan' urbanism, framed by connections across diasporic networks that are made manifest in and shaped by neighbourhoods like Koreatowns, Chinatowns, Little Indias and Little Italys in cities across the world. Still other discussions emphasise the role of the internet, the web and social media in 'extending' and accelerating relations between specific places across the globe but also the tendency for these types of communications to differentiate the world into technological haves and have-nots through the profoundly physical, infrastructural geographies of what Graham (1999) calls the 'global grids of glass', or fibre-optic cable networks, etc., through which 'virtual' connections are channelled.

These sorts of socio-spatial connections and differences, movements and immobilities are fundamentally about power. As anthropologist Donna Haraway (1991) once provocatively put it: 'Some differences are playful; some are poles of world historical systems of domination. "Epistemology" is about knowing the difference.' In more prosaic terms, we might think, as those interested in mobilities have done in recent years, about the differences that pertain to people's ability to move through space, from place to place. This literature, which involves sociologists and geographers among others, addresses questions of difference at scales ranging from the city to the globe. In the former sense, the sorts of mobilities discussed involve modes of transportation – from automobiles, to various forms of mass transit – while in the latter, researchers have focused on such movements as migration and tourism. This literature has been conceptualised with attention to the contributuions made by Massey, Harvey and various geographers who have theorised scale in recent decades. The mobilities researchers take seriously the notion that a social process, like the movement of people from place to place, can only be understood if both transit through space and also the fixed infrastructures of various types that allow movement to occur are held in dual focus. In other words, one can't understand air travel only by standing in the departure lounge waiting for one's family to emerge from the baggage claim area. Yet, similarly, one can't understand it without investigating the emotional (re)connections that are manifest on the ground in those very airport waiting areas. The point, as Haraway suggests, is to make careful decisions about one's research questions, methods and conceptualisations since the framing of one's approach – how one knows what one knows about a specific topic – is both enhanced but also delimited by those frames.

Certainly, these crucial questions of focus, emphasis and method of analysis are evident in debates around the relative balance of local and global orientation and around the relative balance of the social and the economic in the study of cities. Massey's argument about the 'global sense of place', for example, was in part a critique of the (unrecognised or unstated) positionality and focus of what she characterised as a group of largely white, male, privileged, economistic, western scholars. Yet, in turn, her narrative of the globalness of her neighbourhood in London was subsequently criticised for not fully unpacking the identity politics in her own account (McGuinness, 2000). Those who study globalisation and mobility are often critiqued for an over-attention to and even a glamourisation of those who can move freely and who have command over space. Yet, many have recognised the problematic differences between 'kinetic elites', on the one hand, and those who cannot move when they might want to or who move because they have no choice. On the other hand, urban scholars have noted, as Herbert and Grobelski and also Lees show (in Chapters 7 and 3 respectively), that there is an important right to stay put in cities that is often disrupted by gentrification pressures and other government policies (see also Blomley, 2011). Geographies at all scales, then, are often characterised by differences in social groups' relationships to processes of emancipation and dispossession. In turn, communications technologies have helped social justice struggles in particular places to be almost instantaneously (although always partially) global, as the 'Arab Spring' and subsequent Occupy protests have indicated. Even then, however, identity, difference, connection and disconnection are complex intersecting processes that order and stratify access to and control over space.

All of these phenomena – and many more, of course – can be studied by unpacking the sites and situations in which they intersect and become manifest in cities. This is what we have suggested in the previous section and it is the model for the preceding chapters. What the chapters show, however, is that there are many ways in which to unpack the 'local' and to understand it in a 'global' way, just as there are many ways to understand the 'social' in the context of the complex urbanism. The diversity and difference in the approaches is fundamental to the strength and continued potential of contemporary research into the socio-spatial character of contemporary cities.

FROM CHICAGO TO ORDINARY CITIES

Diversity and difference are not only characteristic of analysis in contemporary urban studies. They are also concepts that are crucial to the local practice of urban life, as many of the chapter authors have indicated. Difference is celebrated, 'tolerated' and experienced in every city every day. Yet difference is also constantly policed, constrained and suppressed through the actions of individuals, communities and institutions. Difference is lived each day in cities through the tension between these two impulses. Thus the study of difference, however defined, is crucial to the study of urban social geography. Yet, the field of critical urban studies has, in recent years, also been characterised by debates over difference in another register. These discussions revolve around the question of how we might better conceptualise and research differences among cities. Many involved in thinking through this issue engage in a politics of knowledge that moves beyond a hierarchical and exclusionary vision of the world towards a cosmopolitan and post-colonial vision which focuses on embracing rather than trying to 'wall out' difference from our conceptualisations.

One of the most important figures in this approach is Jennifer Robinson who has, since the 2000s, been developing conceptual arguments and empirical research that take seriously the opportunities and worthwhile challenges of conducting global research on cities from what she terms a post-colonial and cosmopolitan perspective. Her argument for an urban studies that embraces difference, specificity and diversity is set out in her book *Ordinary Cities* (2006). Interestingly, but perhaps no longer surprisingly for us, Robinson contrasts her vision of how to understand cities with the work of the Chicago School. Rather than Burgess, Robinson's focus is largely on Louis Wirth. Wirth is renowned for his essay 'Urbanism as a way of life' (1938) in which he argued, following Georg Simmel and his Chicago School colleague Robert Park, that a defining feature of modern urban life is a detached, indifferent and 'blasé' attitude toward others. Maintaining a certain social distance, even in the cheek-by-jowl living situations and face-to-face encounters of urban life was, Wirth suggested, necessary for survival in modern cities. This, then, is a sociological analysis of late-nineteenth- and twentieth-century urbanism that naturalises and valorises individualism and guardedness over any impulse towards connection and community. It is built, Robinson argues, on a very small data set: the analyses of a handful of scholars in a few cities, like Chicago and Paris. Yet, she notes that it is an understanding that, like Wirth's colleague Burgess's concentric zones, has travelled widely and become a dominant part of the urban studies canon, one that is generally understood to be applicable to any city in any part of the world; any city that can be considered 'modern,' at least.

Robinson's argument is about the production and valorisation of knowledge. On the remarkably wide influence and resilience of Wirth's 'indifferent modern city-dweller', she notes that '[a] large number of scholars, both within and outside the West, contested this rather simplistic claim. Yet it remains a constant component of contemporary urban theory and is often reproduced in urban readers, while the critiques of comparative urbanists have largely been ignored' (Robinson, 2006: 8). Through the representational strategies of powerful, well-connected and well-published urban scholars and their editors, she argues,

> Parochial descriptions of urban ways of life have sedimented into universalizing theories of cities, with disturbing consequences. The diverse urbanisms of different cities have not been allowed to transform the theoretical categories ... through which cities are understood. (Robinson, 2006: 39)

The simplicity of Wirth's argument and its wide influence, despite its parochialism, is, she continues, in great part fostered by an uncritical acceptance of its core category: modernity. What and where is 'modern' have been very narrowly defined and associated with only certain sets of social practices and certain cities. Different practices – attempts to make connections rather than refusing them – and different cities – those in so-called 'primitive', 'traditional,', or 'developing' societies – have been assigned to places that are supposedly 'static and closed, the antithesis of urban modernity'. By following the example of comparative anthropologists in the mid-twentieth century, Robinson shows how urban life in the Zambian Copperbelt was modern, in a fuller definition of the concept, but was by no means characterised by cold indifference to others. Rather, through the lens of Zambian urban modernity, she argues that 'we learn that urbanites have generated fictive kin, eagerly sought to make connections where none really existed, carefully nurtured neighbours and family, built communities and defended difference' (Robinson, 2006: 9).

Thus 'modernity' itself is a category to be critically unpacked, differentiated and put in its place, rather than being accepted as a received, well-defined, universal and hermetically sealed wisdom. The fact that it *has been* a received wisdom is an indication of particular power relations in cities and in writing about cities that are, in themselves, something to critically consider. Robinson also does this through examples of the ways

in which cities on both sides of the modern/traditional divide were all active in processes of borrowing and 'inter-referencing' (Roy and Ong, 2011) architectural styles
that are usually considered 'modern' and 'western'. In this way she breaks down the
'diffusionist' notion that all innovations emerge from a few centres of innovation and
then spread to imitators (see also Blaut, 1987, 1993). This damaging vision of how
social change works can only be sustained through a vision of the world as discretely
categorised around the modern/traditional binary.

The fact that Wirth perceived widespread indifference around him on the streets
of Chicago does not mean that such coolness towards others (another sense of
'Chicago cool', perhaps) is necessarily a defining feature of all modern cities. Even
more importantly, from Robinson's perspective, is the argument that it does not even
necessarily define life in cities like Chicago. Rather, as we have seen, she questions
the categories and assumptions that underpin this Chicago School analysis, just as
some of our chapter authors question the categories and assumptions underpinning
other aspects of the School's work. Robinson, like the other authors, is at best indifferent about Chicago as a point of reference in urban studies. It certainly should not
be a privileged referent, she argues. Instead, she suggests that by being open to forms
of analysis undertaken in very different places and being willing to learn from their
findings and apply their approaches, it is possible to develop more cosmopolitan
urban studies in which the innovativeness and mutually constitutive interconnected-
ness of all places are acknowledged, valorised, researched and used to inform a more
worldly urban studies.

So what to make of all this? How is Robinson's perspective related to, and how can
it inform, ongoing and newly forming research on the urban social geographies of
cities? An important point to make, first of all, is that this is *not* a call for everyone
to go off studying 'exotic' places. 'In fact, the opposite is closer to my personal ambi-
tion', she argues:

> I would be horrified if the consequence of this book was that well-resourced
> scholars went globe-trotting, in the wake of their late colonial predecessors,
> to study cities around the world ... [Rather,] any research on cities needs to
> be undertaken in a spirit of attentiveness to the possibilities that cities else-
> where might perhaps be different and shed stronger light on the processes
> being studied. The potential to learn from other contexts, other cities, would
> need always to be kept open and hopefully acted upon ... The primary tac-
> tic that I propose for postcolonializing urban studies, then, is one of decen-
> tring the reference points of international scholarship. Thinking about cities
> ought to be willing to travel widely, tracking the diverse circulations that
> shape cities and thinking across both similarities and difference amongst
> cities, in search of understandings of the many different ways of urban life.
> (Robinson, 2006: 168–9)

The point then is develop a critical openness to what is already around us: a world of
interconnection and difference where agency, influence and innovation are not naturally or necessarily centred in specific places. This is an analytical and methodological

point. It is about being open to the various practices and conceptualisation of 'world-ing' (Roy and Ong, 2011) that can inform our work, even if we conceive of that work as primarily local. It is also a political point. If power and agency are not naturally and necessarily centred in one place or institution, then there is, by definition, an opportunity to change the configurations of power and agency. This is the point DeFilippis and Rivero (Chapter 11) and Roy (Chapter 12) make most explicitly in their chapters on justice and the good city, but it is one highlighted by all the essays in this volume.

A FINAL WORD

Understandably, it is the conceit of the contemporary age, its scholarship and the frameworks within which it attempts to understand the world – here, the social geographies of the city – that its own epistomologies are considered to offer a robust and coherent account of how the world works. Their privileged position is justifiable by their imputed strengths. To read the canonical texts of the Chicago School is to appreciate how its understanding of the city and its framing within the ideas of social Darwinism was embraced as both a powerful lens through which to explore and understand the then rapidly growing city of Chicago and one which could be exported. In the historiography of urban social geography, the fragilities of both were to be exposed through subsequent analysis, though in the case of the Chicago School its influence was to be more pervasive than was the case for many other theoretical ideas apparent elsewhere in human geography.

The chapters in this volume are suggestive of ways in which future research into how urban societies work might be conceived and conducted. We do not want to conclude by reifying these suggestive accounts into a list of the 'most important' issues or 'most' insightful approaches for future urban social research. Readers will make their own judgements. Certainly, our approach in this volume will be super-seded by analyses of the social geography of the city to come. Yet, the bypassing of the pitfalls of meta-theoretical reasoning (such as the uncritical lionising of paradig-matic cities or paradigm-defining thinkers) and the harnessing of the diversity and multiplexity of urban social processes should be robust building blocks for the urban social geographer. The strengths of contemporary analysis lie in the appreciation of difference and diversity not only within the city but also between cities and in the unpacking of the interconnections – the complex interweavings of global and local, the impress of path dependency and the ruptures to it – that contribute to the mak-ing of social spaces, the meanings given to them and of the experiences of urban life.

References

Abrams, J. & Hall, P. (2006) *Else/where: Mapping New Cartographies of Networks and Territories*. Minneapolis: University of Minnesota Design Institute.

Adams, M. & Guy, S. (2007) 'Editorial: Senses and the city', *Senses and Society*, 2(2): 133–6.

Affonso, D., Andrews, G. & Jeffs, L. (2004) 'The urban geography of SARS: Paradoxes and dilemmas in Toronto's health care', *Journal of Advanced Nursing*, 45: 568–78.

Agamben, G. (1995) *Homo Sacer: Sovereign Power and Bare Life* (trans. D. Heller-Roazen, 1998). Stanford, CA: Stanford University Press.

Agamben, G. (2006) 'Metropolis *Light in the Fridge*', from lightinthefridge.blogspot.com. Available at http://www.generation-online.org/p/fpagamben4.htm.

Agyeman, J. (2005) *Sustainable Communities and the Challenge of Environmental Justice*. London: New York University Press.

Ahmed, S. (2000) *Strange Encounters: Embodied Others in Post-Coloniality*. London: Routledge.

Albertsen, N. (1988) 'Postmodernism, postfordism, and critical social theory', *Environment and Planning D: Society and Space*, 6: 339–65.

Ali, H. & Keil, R. (2006) 'Global cities and the spread of infectious disease: The case of Severe Acute Respiratory Syndrome (SARS) in Toronto, Canada', *Urban Studies*, 43: 491–509.

Allen, C. (2008) *Housing Market Renewal and Social Class*. London: Routledge.

Allen, I.L. (1995) *The City in Slang: New York Life and Popular Speech*. Oxford: University of Mississippi Press.

Allen, J. & Cochrane, A. (2007) 'Beyond the territorial fix: Regional assemblages, politics, and power', *Regional Studies*, 41: 1161–75.

Allport G.W. (1954) *The Nature of Prejudice*. Reading, MA: Addison-Wesley.

AlSayyad, N. (2006) *Cinematic Urbanism: A History of the Modern from Reel to Real*. London: Routledge.

AlSayyad, N. & Roy, A. (2006) 'Medieval modernity: On citizenship and urbanism in a global era', *Space and Polity*, 10(1): 1–20.

Ames, H. (1897 [1972]) *The City Below the Hill*. Toronto: University of Toronto Press.

Amin, A. (2002) 'Ethnicity and the multicultural city: Living with diversity', *Environment and Planning A*, 34: 959–80.

Amin, A. (2004) 'Regions unbound: Towards a new politics of place', *Geografiska Annaler*, 86B: 33–44.

Amin, A. (2006) 'The good city', *Urban Studies*, 43: 1009–23.

Amin, A. & Graham, S. (1997) 'The ordinary city', *Transactions of the Institute of British Geographers* NS, 22: 411–29.

Amin, A. & Thrift, N. (2002) *Cities: Reimagining the Urban*. Cambridge: Polity Press.

Anderson, K. (1991) *Vancouver's Chinatown: Racial Discourse in Canada, 1875–1980*. Montreal: McGill-Queen's University Press.

Anderson, E. (1992) *Streetwise: Race, Class and Change in an Urban Community*. Chicago: University of Chicago Press.

Anvik, C. (2009) 'Embodied spaces in the making: Visually impaired people, bodies and surroundings', *Scandinavian Journal of Disability Research*, 11(2): 145–57.

Anzaldua, G. (1999) *Borderlands: The New Mestiza/La Frontera*. San Francisco: Aunt Lute Books.

Anzaldua, G. (2002) '(Un)natural Bridges, (Un)safe Spaces', in G. Anzaldua and A. Keating (eds) *This Bridge We Call Home: Radical Visions for Transformation*. New York: Routledge, pp. 1–6.

Appadurai, A. (2002) 'Deep democracy: Urban governmentality and the horizon of politics', *Public Culture*, 21(1): 21–47.

Appadurai, A. (2007) 'Hope and democracy', *Public Culture*, 19(1): 29.

Applebaum, E., Bernhardt, A. & Murnane, R. (eds) (2006) *Low-Wage America: How Employers Are Reshaping Opportunity in the Workplace*. New York: Russell Sage Foundation Press.

Ashton, J., Grey, P. & Barnard, K. (1986) 'Healthy cities, WHO's New Public Health initiative', *Health Promotion International*, 1: 319–24.

Ashworth, G. & Kavaratzis, M. (2007) 'Beyond the logo: Brand management for cities', *Journal of Brand Management*, 16(8): 520–31.

Atkins, P. (1993) 'How the West End was won: The struggle to remove street barriers in Victorian London', *Journal of Historical Geography*, 19(3): 265–77.

Atkins, P., Simmons, I. & Roberts, B. (1998) *People, Land and Time*. London: Arnold.

Atkinson, R. (2008) 'The great cut: The support for private modes of social evasion by public policy', *Social Policy and Administration*, 42: 593–610.

Atkinson, R. & Blandy, S. (2005) 'Introduction: International perspectives on the new enclavism and the rise of gated communities', *Housing Studies*, 20: 177–86.

Aw, Tash (2013) *Five Star Billionaire*. London: Fourth Estate.

Bachrach, L. (1987) 'Geographic mobility and the homeless mentally ill', *Hospital and City Psychiatry*, 38: 27–8.

Badcock, B. (1984) *Unfairly Structured Cities*. London: Blackwell.

Badyina, A. and Golubchikov, O. (2005) 'Gentrification in central Moscow – a market process or a deliberate policy? Money, power and people in housing regeneration in Ostozhenka', *Geografiska Annaler B*, 87: 113–29.

Baker, S. (1994) 'Gender, ethnicity, and homelessness', *American Behavioral Scientist*, 37: 476–504.

Baker, S. (2007) 'Sustainable development as symbolic commitment: Declaratory politics and the seductive appeal of ecological modernisation in the European Union', *Environmental Politics*, 16: 297–317.

Ball, K., Timperio, A. & Crawford, D. (2009) 'Neighbourhood socioeconomic inequalities in food access and affordability', *Health & Place*, 15: 578–85.

Banerjee, T. (2001) 'The future of public space: Beyond invented streets and reinvented places', *Journal of the American Planning Association*, 67: 9–24.

Banfield, E. (1970) *The Unheavenly City*. Boston: Little Brown Company.

Bannister, J., Fyfe, N. & Kearns, A. (2006) 'Respectable or respectful? (In) civility and the city', *Urban Studies*, 43: 919–37.

Barnes, T. (1996) *Logics of Dislocation: Models, Metaphors, and Meanings of Economic Space*. New York: Guilford Press.

Barnes, T (1998) 'A history of regression: Actors, networks, machines, and numbers', *Environment and Planning A*, 30: 203–24.

Barnett, C. (2005) 'Ways of relating: Hospitality and the acknowledgement of otherness', *Progress in Human Geography*, 29: 5–21.

Barnett, J.R. & Kearns, R.A. (1996) 'Shopping around? Consumerism and the use of private accident and medical clinics in Auckland, New Zealand', *Environment and Planning A*, 28: 1053–75.

Bassi, C. (2003) 'Asian gay counter hegemonic negotiations of Birmingham's pink pound territory'. PhD thesis, University of Sheffield.

Bates, K. & Swan, R.S. (2007) *Through the Eye of Katrina*. Durham, NC: Carolina Academic Press.

Baum, F. (1993) 'Healthy cities and change: Social movement or bureaucratic tool?', *Health Promotion International*, 8: 31–40.

Bauman, Z. (1998) *Work, Consumerism and the New Poor.* Buckingham: Open University Press.

Baumgartner, M. (1991) *The Moral Order of a Suburb.* New York and Oxford: Oxford University Press.

Baviskar, A. (2003) 'Between violence and desire: Space, power, and identity in the making of metropolitan Delhi', *International Social Science Journal*, 55(175): 89–98.

Beaulac, J., Kristjansson, E. & Cummins, S. (2009) 'A systematic review of food deserts, 1966–2007', *Preventing Chronic Disease,* 6. Available at: http://www.cdc.gov/pcd/issues/2009/jul/08_0163.htm (accessed December 2010).

Beauregard, R.A. (1993) *Voices of Decline: The Postwar Fate of U.S. Cities.* Oxford: Blackwell.

Beck, U. (1997) *The Reinvention of Politics: Rethinking Modernity in the Global Social Order.* Cambridge: Polity Press.

Beck, U. (2002) 'The cosmopolitan society and its enemies', *Theory, Culture and Society*, 19: 17–44.

Beck, U. (2006) *The Cosmopolitan Vision.* Cambridge: Polity Press.

Beck, U. & Sznaider, N. (2006) 'Unpacking cosmopolitanism for the social sciences: A research agenda', *The British Journal of Sociology*, 57: 1–23.

Beckett, A. (1994) 'Take a walk on the safe side', *Independent on Sunday*, 27 February.

Beckett, K. & Herbert, S. (2009) *Banished: Social Control in the Contemporary American City.* New York and Oxford: Oxford University Press.

Belina, B. (2007) 'From disciplining to dislocation: Area bans in recent urban policing in Germany', *European Urban and Regional Studies*, 14: 321–36.

Bell, D., Binnie, J., Cream, J. & Valentine, G. (1994) 'All hyped up and no place to go', *Gender, Places and Culture*, 1: 31–47.

Bell, N., Schuurman, N., Oliver, L. & Hayes, M.V. (2007) 'Towards the construction of place-specific measures of deprivation: A case study from the Vancouver metropolitan area', *The Canadian Geographer*, 51: 444–61.

Benhabib, S. (2002) *The Claims of Culture.* Princeton, NJ: Princeton University Press.

Benjamin, W. (1968) 'Paris – capital of the 19th century', *New Left Review*, 48.

Benjamin, W. (1997) 'On some motifs in baudelaire', in N. Leach (ed.) *Rethinking Architecture*, London: Routledge, pp. 125–32.

Benoit, C., Carroll, D. & Chaudry, M. (1993) 'In search of a healing place: Aboriginal women in Vancouver's Downtown Eastside', *Social Science & Medicine*, 56: 821–33.

Berman, M. (1983) *All That is Solid Melts into Air: The Experience of Modernity.* London: Verso.

Berman, M. (2006) *On the Town: One Hundred Years of Spectacle in Times Square.* New York: Random House.

Berry B J. L. & Garrison W. L. (1958) 'A note on central place theory and the range of a good', *Economic Geography* 34: 304–311.

Besancenot, J.P. (2002) 'Vagues de chaleur et mortalité dans les grandes agglomérations urbaines', *Environnement, Risques & Santé*, 1: 229–40.

Beveridge, A.A. (2011) 'Commonalities and contrasts in the development of major United States urban areas: A spatial and temporal analysis from 1910 to 2000', in M.P. Guttman, G.D. Deane, E.R. Merchant & K.M. Sylvester (eds) *Navigating Time and Space in Population Studies,* Springer for the International Union for the Scientific Study of Population, pp. 185–216.

Bhugra, D. (2004) 'Migration and mental health', *Acta Psychiatratrica Scandinavica*, 109: 243–58.

Bickerstaff, K. & Agyeman, J. (2009) 'Assembling justice spaces: The scalar politics of environmental justice in North-east England', *Antipode*, 41: 781–806.

Binnie, J., Holloway, J., Millington, S. & Young, C. (eds) (2006) *Cosmopolitan Urbanism*. London: Routledge.

Bittner, E. (1967) 'The police on skid row: A study in peacekeeping', *American Sociological Review*, 32: 699–715.

Black, J.L., Macinko, J., Dixon, L.B. & Fryer, J.G.E. (2010) 'Neighborhoods and obesity in New York City', *Health & Place*, 16: 489–99.

Blaikie, P. (1985) *Political Ecology of Social Erosion in Developing Countries*. Oxford: Longman.

Blaikie, P. & Brookfield, H. (1987) *Land Degradation and Society*. London: Routledge.

Blakely, E. & Snyder, M. (1999) *Fortress America: Gated Communities in the United States*. Washington: Brookings Institute Press.

Blaut, J.M. (1987) 'Diffusionism: A uniformitarian critique', *Annals of the Association of American Geographers*, 77(1): 30–47.

Blaut, J.M. (1993) *The Colonizer's Model of the World: Geographical Diffusionism and Eurocentric History*. New York: Guilford.

Blomley, N. (2011) *Rights of Passage: Sidewalks and the Regulation of Public Flow*. New York: Routledge.

Blowers, A. & Pain, K. (1999) 'The unsustainable city?', in S. Pile, C. Brook & G. Mooney (eds) *Unruly Cities? Order/Disorder*. London: Routledge, pp. 247–98.

Boddy, T. (1992) 'Underground and overhead: Building the analogous city', in M. Sorkin (ed.) *Variations on a Theme Park: The New American City and the End of Public Space*. New York: Hill & Wang, pp. 123–53.

Booth, C. (1902) *Life and Labour of the People in London: First Series Poverty*. London: MacMillan and Co Ltd. (see also http://lse.booth.ac.uk/static/a/4.html).

Borsdorf, A. & Hidalgo, R. (2009) 'The fragmented city: Changing patterns in Latin American cities', *The Urban Reinventors Paper Series*, 3/09.

Bounds, M. (2004) *Urban Social Theory: City, Self and Society*. Oxford: Oxford University Press.

Bourdieu, P. and Wacquant, L. (2001) 'Neoliberal newspeak: Notes on the new planetary vulgate', *Radical Philosophy*, 108: 1–6.

Bourgois, P. (1995) *In Search of Respect: Selling Crack in El Barrio* (first edition). Cambridge: Cambridge University Press.

Bourgois, P. (2003) *In Search of Respect: Selling Crack in El Barrio* (second edition). Cambridge: Cambridge University Press.

Bovell-Benjamin, A.C., Hathorn, C.S., Ibrahim, S., Gichuhi, P.N. & Bromfield, E.M. (2009) 'Healthy food choices and physical activity opportunities in two contrasting Alabama cities', *Health & Place*, 15: 429–38.

Bowen, W. (2002) 'An analytical review of environmental justice research: What do we really know?', *Environmental Management*, 29(1): 3–15.

Bowling, B. (1999) 'The rise and fall of New York murder: Zero tolerance or crack's decline?', *British Journal of Criminology*, 39: 531–54.

Bowser, E. (1990) *The Transformation of Cinema, 1907–1915*. Berkeley and Los Angeles: University of California.

Boyd, R. (2006) 'The value of civility?', *Urban Studies*, 43: 863–78.

Boyer, C. (1993) 'The city of illusion: New York's public spaces', in P. Knox (ed.) *The Restless Urban Landscape*. Englewood Cliffs, NJ: Prentice Hall, pp. 111–26.

Boyer, M.C. (1988) 'The return of aesthetics to city planning', *Society*, 25(4): 49–56.

Brandes, S. (2002) *Staying Sober in Mexico City*. Austin, TX: University of Texas Press.

Bratton, W. (1998) *Turnaround: How America's Top Cop Reversed the Crime Epidemic*. New York: Random House.

Brenner, N. (2009) 'What is critical urban theory?', *City*, 13(2): 198–207.

Brenner, N. & Keil, R. (2006) *The Global Cities Reader.* New York: Routledge.

Brenner, N., Peck, J. and Theodore, N. (2010) 'After neoliberalization?', *Globalizations*, 7(3): 327–45.

Brenner, N. & Theodore, N. (eds) (2002) *Spaces of Neoliberalism.* Malden, MA: Blackwell.

Bridge, G. & Watson, S. (2002) 'Lest power be forgotten: Networks, division and difference in the city', *The Sociological Review*, 50: 507–24.

Brody, H., Rip, M.R., Vinten-Johansen, P., Paneth, N. & Rachman, S. (2000) 'Map-making and myth-making in Broad Street: The London cholera epidemic, 1854', *The Lancet*, 356: 64–8.

Brulle, R.J. & Pellow, D.N. (2005) 'The future of environmental justice movements', in D.N. Pellow & R.J. Brulle (eds) *Power, Justice, and the Environment: A Critical Appraisal of the Environmental Justice Movement.* London: New York University Press, pp. 293–300.

Buckingham, S. & Degen, M. (2012) 'Sensing our way: Using yoga as a research method', *Senses and Society*, 7 (3): 329–344.

Buckingham, S. & Kulcur, R. (2009) 'Gendered geographies of environmental injustice', *Antipode*, 41: 659–83.

Budds, J. & Teixeira, P. (2005) 'Ensuring the right to the city: Pro-poor housing, urban development and tenure legalization in Sao Paulo, Brazil', *Environment and Urbanization*, 17: 89–113.

Buerk, R. (2006) *Breaking Ships: How Supertankers and Cargo Ships are Dismantled on the Beaches of Bangladesh.* New York: Chamberlain Books.

Bulkeley, H. (2005) 'Reconfiguring environmental governance: Towards a politics of scales and networks', *Political Geography*, 24: 875–902.

Bullard, R.D. (1983) 'Solid waste sites and the black Houston community', *Sociological Inquiry*, 53: 273–88.

Bullard, R.D. (1990) *Dumping in Dixie: Race, Class, and Environmental Quality.* Boulder, CO: Westview Press.

Bullard, R.D. & Wright, B. (2009) (eds) *Race, Place, and Environment Justice after Hurricane Katrina.* Boulder, CO: Westview Press.

Burgess, E. (1925) 'The growth of the city', in R. Park, E. Burgess & R. McKenzie (eds) *The City.* Chicago: University of Chicago Press.

Burnham, D. & Bennett, E. ([1909] 1993) *Plan of Chicago.* New York: Princeton Architectural Press.

Burns, C.M. & Inglis, A.D. (2007) 'Measuring food access in Melbourne: Access to healthy and fast foods by car, bus and foot in an urban municipality in Melbourne', *Health & Place*, 13: 877–85.

Burt, M. (1992) *Over the Edge: The Growth of Homelessness in the 1980s.* New York: Russell Sage. Foundation.

Butterfield, F. (1998) 'Prisons replace hospitals for the nation's mentally ill', *The New York Times*, 5 March, p. A1.

Butler, R. & Parr, H. (1999) *Mind and Body Spaces: Geographies of Illness, Impairment and Disability.* London: Routledge.

Butler, T. (1997) *Gentrification and the Middle Classes.* Aldershot: Ashgate.

Butler, T. & Lees, L. (2006) 'Super-gentrification in Barnsbury, London: Globalisation and gentrifying global elites at the neighbourhood level', *Transactions of the Institute of British Geographers*, 31: 467–87.

Butler, T. with Robson, G. (2003) *London Calling: The Middle Classes and the Remaking of Inner London.* London: Berg.

Butler, T. & Watt, P. (2007) *Understanding Social Inequality.* London: Sage.

Buttimer, A. & Seamon, D. (1980) *The Human Experience of Space and Place.* New York: St. Martin's Press.

Byrne, J., Martinez, C. & Glover, L. (2002) 'A brief on environmental justice', in J. Byrne, L. Glover & C. Martinez (eds) *Environmental Justice: Discourses in International Political Economy.* London: Transaction Publishers, pp. 3–17.

Caldeira, T.P.R. (1996) 'Fortified enclaves: The new urban segregation', *Public Culture*, 8: 303–28.

Caldeira, T. (2000) *City of Walls: Crime, Segregation and Citizenship in São Paulo.* Los Angeles and Berkeley: University of California Press.

Cameron, D. 2000: *Good to Talk? Living and Working in a Communication Culture.* London: Sage.

Carruthers, D.V. (2008) 'The globalization of environmental justice: Lessons from the U.S.–Mexico border', *Society and Natural Resources*, 21: 556–68.

Castells, M. ([1972] 1979) *The Urban Question: A Marxist Approach.* Cambridge, MA: MIT Press.

Castells, M. (1977) *The Urban Question.* London: Edward Arnold.

Castells, M. (2000) *The Rise of the Network Society.* Malden, MA: Blackwell.

Castree, N. (2001) 'Socializing nature', in N. Castree & B. Braun (eds) *Social Nature.* Oxford: Blackwell, pp. 1–21.

Castree, N. (2006) 'The detour of critical theory', in N. Castree & D. Gregory (eds) *David Harvey: A Critical Reader.* Oxford: Blackwell, pp. 247–69.

Castree, N. & Braun, B. (1998) 'The construction of nature and the nature of construction: Analytical and political tools for building survivable futures', in N. Castree & B. Braun (eds) *Remaking Reality: Nature at the Millennium.* London: Routledge, pp. 2–41

Castree, N. & Braun, B. (2001) (eds) *Social Nature: Theory, Practice, and Politics.* Oxford: Blackwell.

Caulfield, J. (1989) 'Gentrification and desire', *Canadian Review of Sociology and Anthropology,* 26: 617–32.

Caulfield, J. (1994) *City Form and Everyday Life: Toronto's Gentrification and Critical Social Practice.* Toronto: University of Toronto Press.

Cerin, E., Leslie, E., Toit, L.D., Owen, N. & Frank, L.D. (2007a) 'Destinations that matter: Associations with walking for transport', *Health and Place*, 13: 713–24.

Cerin, E., Macfarlane, D.J., Ko, H.H. & Chan, K.C.A. (2007b) 'Measuring perceived neighbourhood walkability in Hong Kong', *Cities*, 24: 209–17.

Chakravorty, S. (2006) *Fragments of Inequality: Social, Spatial and Evolutionary Analyses of Income Distribution.* New York: Routledge.

Chambliss, W. (1964) 'A sociological analysis of laws of vagrancy', *Social Problems,* 12: 67–77.

Chan, C.K. & Yao, X. (2008) 'Review: Air pollution in mega cities in China', *Atmospheric Environment,* 42(1): 1–42.

Charney, L. & Schwartz, V.R. (1995) *Cinema and the Invention of Modern Life.* Berkeley: University of California.

Chatterjee, P. (2006) *The Politics of the Governed: Reflections on Popular Politics in Most of the World.* New York: Columbia University Press.

Christopherson, S. (1994) 'The fortress city: Privatized spaces, consumer citizenship', in A. Amin (ed.) *Post-Fordism: A Reader.* Oxford: Blackwell, pp. 409–27.

Citizenship 21 (2003) *Profiles of Prejudice.* London: Citizenship 21.

City of Chicago Mayor's Press Office (2004) 'Press release: Millennium Park grand opening July 16–18; weekend long celebration features free events and performances'. Available at: http://www.pbcchicago.com/content/about/press_detail.asp?pID=151 (accessed 29 May 2012).

Clark, E. (2005) 'The order and simplicity of gentrification – a political challenge', in R. Atkinson & G. Bridge (eds) *Gentrification in a Global Context: The New Urban Colonialism.* London: Routledge, pp. 256–64.

Clarke, D.B. (2003) *The Consumer Society and the Postmodern City*. London: Routledge.

Classen, C. (1993) *Worlds of Sense: Exploring the Senses in History and across Cultures*. London: Routledge.

Classen, C., Howes, D. & Synnott, A. (1994) *Aroma: The Cultural History of Smell*. New York: Routledge.

Clavel, P. (1986) *The Progressive City*. New Brunswick, NJ: Rutgers University Press.

Clavel, P. (2010) *Activists in City Hall*. Ithaca, NY: Cornell University Press.

Coaffee, J. (2009) 'Protecting the urban: The dangers of planning for terrorism', *Theory, Culture and Society*, 26(7–8): 343–55.

Coaffee, J. & Murakami Wood, D. (2009) 'Terror and Surveillance', in T. Hall, P. Hubbard & J.R. Short (eds) *The Sage Companion to the City*. London: Sage, pp. 352–72.

Coates, B., Johnston, R.J. & Knox, P. (1977) *Geography and Inequality*. London: Oxford University Press.

Cohen, L. & Ford, L. (2004) '$16 million in lawsuits ensnare pavilion at Millennium Park', *Chicago Tribune*, 18 July. Available at: http://articles.chicagotribune.com/2004-07-18/news/0407180277_1_gehry-millennium-park-lawsuits (accessed 29 May 2012).

Cole, L.W. & Foster, S.R. (2001) *From the Ground Up: Environmental Racism and the Rise of the Environmental Justice Movement*. London: New York University Press.

Coleman, R. (2004) 'Images from a neoliberal city: The state, surveillance and social control', *Criminology*, 12: 21–42.

Coleman, R. & Sim, J. (2000) '"You'll never walk alone": CCTV surveillance, order, and neoliberal rule in Liverpool city', *British Journal of Sociology*, 51: 623–39.

Coleman, R., Tombs, S. & Whyte, D. (2005) 'Capital, crime control and statecraft in the entrepreneurial city', *Urban Studies*, 42: 2511–30.

Collins, D.C.A. & Kearns, R.A. (2001) 'Under curfew and under siege? Legal geographies of young people', *Geoforum*, 32: 389–403.

Collins, D.C.A. & Kearns, R.A. (2010) 'Walking school buses in the Auckland region: A longitudinal assessment', *Transport Policy*, 17: 1–8.

Commission on Social Determinants of Health (2008) *Closing the Gap in a Generation* report. Geneva: WHO.

Communities and Local Government (2009) *Planning Policy Statement: Eco-Towns: A supplement to Planning Policy Statement 1*. London: CLG.

Connell, J. (1999) 'Beyond Manila: Walls, malls, and private spaces', *Environment and Planning A*, 31(3): 417–39.

Conradson, D. (2003) 'Spaces of care in the city: The place of a community drop in centre', *Social and Cultural Geography*, 4: 507–28.

Cook, I. R. and Swyngedouw, E. (2012) Cities, social cohesion and the environment: Towards a future research agenda, *Urban Studies*, 49(9): 1959–79.

Cooper, D. (2007) 'Being in public: The threat and promise of stranger contact', *Law & Social Inquiry*, 43: 203–32.

Corbin, A. (1986) *The Foul and the Fragrant: Odor and the French Social Imagination*. Cambridge, MA: Harvard University Press.

Corburn, J. (2009) *Toward the Healthy City: People, Places, and the Politics of Urban Planning*. Boston: MIT Press.

Cosgrove, D. (1999) *Mappings*. London: Reaktion Books.

Cozens, P. & Hillier, D. (2008) 'The shape of things to come: New urbanism, the grid and the cul-de-sac. *International Planning Studies*, 13: 51–73.

Crawford, D., Timperio, A., Giles-Corti, B., Ball, K., Hume, C., Roberts, R., Andrianopoulos, N. & Salmon, J. (2008) 'Do features of public open spaces vary according to neighbourhood socio-economic status?', *Health and Place*, 14: 887–91.

Cresswell, T. (1996) *In Place/Out of Place: Geography, Ideology and Transgression*. Minneapolis, MN: University of Minnesota Press.

Crocker, J., Majo, B. & Steele, C.M. (1998) 'Social Stigma', in D. Gilbert, S.T. Fiske & G. Lindzey (eds) *Handbook of Social Psychology*. Boston: McGraw-Hill, pp. 504–53.

Cronin, A.M. (2006) 'Advertising and the metabolism of the city: Urban spaces, commodity rhythms', *Environment and Planning D: Society and Space*, 24(4): 615–32.

Cronin, A. & Hetherington, K. (2008) 'Introduction', in A. Croning & K. Hetherington (eds) *Consuming the Entrepreneurial City*. London: Routledge, pp. 1–17.

Cronin, A.M. & Hetherington, K. (2008) *Consuming the Entrepreneurial City: Image, Memory, Spectacle*. London: Routledge.

Cronon, W. (1991) *Nature's Metropolis: Chicago and the Great West*. New York: W.W. Norton.

Crump, J.R. (2002) 'Public housing, poverty and urban space', *Environment and Planning D: Society and Space*, 20: 581–96.

Cummins, S. & Macintyre, S. (2002) '"Food deserts" – evidence and assumption in health policy making', *British Medical Journal*, 325: 436–8.

Cummins, S., Findlay, A., Petticrew, M. & Sparks, L. (2005) 'Healthy cities: The impact of food retail-led regeneration on food access, choice and retail structure', *Built Environment*, 31: 288–301.

Cummins, S., Findlay, A., Petticrew, M. & Sparks, L. (2008) 'Retail-led regeneration and store-switching behaviour', *Journal of Retailing and Consumer Services*, 15: 288–95.

Curtis, S., Setia, M.S. & Quesnel-Vallee, A. (2009) 'Socio-geographic mobility and health status: A longitudinal analysis using the National Population Health Survey of Canada', *Social Science & Medicine*, 69: 1845–53.

Cutter, S.L. (2006) (ed.) *Hazards, Vulnerability and Environmental Justice*. London: Earthscan.

Dahl, R. (1967) 'The city in the future of democracy', *American Political Science Review*, 61: 953–70.

Datta, K., McIlwaine, C., Evans, T., Herbert, J. & Wills, J. (2007) 'From coping strategies to tactics: London's low-pay economy and migrant labour', *British Journal of Industrial Relations*, 45(2): 404–32.

Davies, J.K. & Kelly, M.P. (1993) *Healthy Cities: Research and Practice*. London: Psychology Press.

Davies, K. (2001) 'Responsibility and daily life: Reflections over timespace', in N. Thrift & J. May (eds) *TimeSpace*. London: Routledge, pp. 133–48.

Davis, M. (1990) *City of Quartz: Excavating the Future in Los Angeles*. New York: Verso.

Davis, M. (2006) *Planet of Slums*. London and New York: Verso.

Davis, M. & Monk, D. (eds) (2007) *Evil Paradise: Dreamworlds of Neoliberalism*. New York: The New Press.

Dawkins, A. & Loftus, A. (2013) 'The senses as direct theoreticians in practice.' *Transactions of the Institute of British Geographers*, 38 (4): 665–77.

de Certeau, M. (1984) *The Practice of Everyday Life*. Berkeley, CA: University of California.

de Certeau, M. (2000) 'Walking in the City', in G. Ward (ed.) *The Certeau Reader*. London: Blackwell, pp. 101–18.

Dear, M. (1980) 'The Public City', in W. Clark and G. Moore (eds) *Residential Mobility and Public Policy*. Beverly Hills, CA: Sage, pp. 219–41.

Dear, M. (2000) *The Postmodern Urban Condition*. Oxford: Blackwell.

Dear, M. & Dahmann, N. (2008) 'Urban politics and the Los Angeles school of urbanism', *Urban Affairs Review*, 44: 266–79.

Dear, M. & Flusty, S. (2002) 'Los Angeles as postmodern urbanism', in M. Dear (ed.) *From Chicago to LA: Making Sense of Urban Theory*. London: Sage, pp. 61–93.

Dear, M. & Wolch, J. (1987) *Landscapes of Despair*. London: Polity Press.

Dear, M., Wolch, J. & Wilton, R. (1994) 'The service hub concept in human services planning', *Progress in Planning*, 42: 179–267.

Debord, G. ([1967] 1983) *Society of the Spectacle*. London: Rebel Press.

Degen, M. (2008) *Sensing Cities: Regenerating Public Life in Barcelona and Manchester*. London: Routledge.

Degen, M. (2010) 'Consuming urban rhythms: Let's ravalejar', in T. Edensor (ed.) *Geographies of Rhythm: Nature, Place, Mobilities and Bodies*. Aldershot: Ashgate, pp. 21–31.

Degen, M., Rose, G. & Basdas, B. (2010) 'Bodies and everyday practices in designed urban environments', *Science Studies*, 23 (2): 60–76.

Degen, M. & Rose, G. (2012) 'Experiencing designed urban environments: the senses, walking and perceptual memory', *Urban Studies*, 49 (15): 3271–3287.

Degen, M., Melhuish, C., Rose, G. (2014) 'Producing digital place atmospheres: architecture, digital visualisation practices and the experience economy', *Journal of Consumer Culture*.

DeLanda, M. (2006a) *A New Philosophy of Society: Assemblage Theory and Social Complexity*. London: Continuum.

DeLanda, M. (2006b) 'Deleuzian social ontology and assemblage theory', in M. Fuglsang & B. Sorensen (eds) *Deleuze and the Social*. Edinburgh: University Press, pp. 250–66.

Dennis, K. & Urry, J. (2009) *After the Car*. Cambridge: Polity Press.

DETR (Department of the Environment, Transport and Regions) (1999) *Towards an Urban Renaissance. Final Report of the Urban Taskforce*, chaired by Lord Rogers of Riverside, London: Spon/The Stationery Office.

DeVerteuil, G. (2000) 'Reconsidering the legacy of urban public facility location theory in human geography', *Progress in Human Geography*, 24(1): 47–69.

DeVerteuil, G. (2001) *Welfare Reform and Welfare Neighborhoods: Institutional and Individual Perspectives*. Dissertation University of Southern California, Los Angeles.

DeVerteuil, G. (2003) 'Homeless mobility, institutional settings, and the new poverty management', *Environment and Planning A*, 35(2): 361–79.

DeVerteuil, G. (2005) 'Welfare neighborhoods: Anatomy of a concept', *Journal of Poverty*, 9(2): 23–41.

DeVerteuil, G. (2006). 'The local state and homeless shelters: Beyond revanchism?', *Cities*, 23: 109–20.

DeVerteuil, G. (2009) 'Inequality', in R. Kitchin & N. Thrift (eds) *International Encyclopedia of Human Geography*. London: Elsevier Press, pp. 433–45.

DeVerteuil, G. (2011) 'Survive but not thrive? Geographical strategies for avoiding absolute homelessness among immigrant communities', *Social and Cultural Geography*, 12(8): 929–45.

DeVerteuil, G., Marr, M. & Snow, D. (2009) 'Any space left? Homeless resistance by place-type in Los Angeles County', *Urban Geography*, 30(6): 633–51.

DeVerteuil, G., May, J. & von Mahs, J. (2009) 'Complexity not collapse: Recasting the geographies of homelessness in a "punitive" age', *Progress in Human Geography*, 33(5): 646–66.

Dick, H. & Rimmer, P. (1998) 'Beyond the third world city: The new urban geography of South-East Asia', *Urban Studies*, 35: 2303–21.

Dikeç M. (2001) 'Justice and the spatial imagination', *Environment and Planning A*, 33(10): 1785–805.

Dikeç, M. (2002) 'Police, politics, and the right to the city', *GeoJournal*, 58: 91–8.

Dikeç, M. (2007) *Badlands of the Republic: Space, Politics and Urban Policy*. Oxford: Blackwell.

Dines, N. & Cattell, V. (2006) *Public Spaces, Social Relations and Well-Being in East London*. York: Joseph Rowntree Foundation Report.

Dixon, J., Levine, M. & McAuley, R. (2006) 'Locating impropriety: Street drinking, moral order, and the ideological dilemma of public space', *Political Psychology*, 27: 187–206.

Dorling, D., Rigby, J., Wheeler, B., Ballas, D., Thomas, B., Fahmy, E., Gordon, D. & Lupton, R. (2007) *Poverty, Wealth and Place in Britain, 1968 to 2005*. Bristol: Policy Press.

dos Santos, M.C. (2009) 'How can design education contribute to illuminating issues of homelessness representation?', presented at Lumpen-City Conference, York University, Toronto.

Douglas, M. (1966) *Purity and Danger, An Analysis of the Concepts of Pollution and Taboo*. London: Routledge, Kegan & Paul.

Douglass, M. (2000) 'Mega-urban regions and world city formation: Globalisation, the economic crisis and urban policy issues in Pacific Asia', *Urban Studies,* 3: 2315–35.

Douglass, M. & Huang, L. (2007) 'Globalizing the city in Southeast Asia: Utopia on the urban edge – the case of Phu My Hung, Saigon', *International Journal of Asia-Pacific Studies,* 3: 1–42.

Dovey, K. (1999) *Framing Places: Mediating Power in the Built Form.* London: Routledge.

Downey, L. (1998) 'Environmental injustice: Is race or income a better predictor?', *Social Science Quarterly,* 79: 766–78.

Dreier, P., Mollenkopf, J. & Swanstrom, T. (2001) *Place Matters: Metropolitics for the Twenty-First Century.* Lawrence, KS: University Press of Kansas.

Dreier, P., Mollenkopf, J. & Swanstrom, T. (2005) *Place Matters: Metropolitics for the 21st Century.* Lawrence, KS: University Press of Kansas.

Dryzek, J. (2005) 'Deliberative democracy in divided societies: Alternatives to agonism and analgesia', *Political Theory,* 33(2): 218–42.

Dubber, M. (2005) *The Police Power: Patriarchy and the Foundations of American Government.* New York: Columbia University Press.

Duneier, M. (1999) *Sidewalk.* New York: Farrar, Straus & Giroux.

Durkheim, E. (1893) *The Division of Labour in Society.* New York: Free Press

Eaton, R. (2001) *Ideal Cities: Utopianism and the (Un)Built Environment.* London: Thames & Hudson.

Edensor, T. (2000) 'Moving through the city', in D. Bell & A. Haddour (eds) *City Visions.* Harlow: Pearson Education, pp. 121–40.

Edensor, T. (2005) *Industrial Ruins: Space, Aesthetics and Materiality.* Oxford: Berg.

Edgerton, R. (1979) *Alone Together: Social Order on an Urban Beach.* Berkeley and Los Angeles: University of California Press.

Ehrenreich, B. & Eherenreich, J. (1979) 'The professional-managerial class', in P. Walker (ed.) *Between Labor and Capital.* South End Press: Boston, pp. 5–45.

Elden, S. (2004) *Understanding Henri Lefebvre: Theory and the Possible.* London: Continuum.

Eldridge, A., & Roberts, M. (2008) 'A comfortable night out? Alcohol, drunkenness and inclusive town centres', *Area,* 40(3): 365–74.

Elias, N. (1978 [1939]) *The Civilising Process Vol 1: The History of Manners.* Oxford: Basil Blackwell.

Ellickson, R. (1994) *Order Without Law: How Neighbors Settle Disputes.* Cambridge, MA: Harvard University Press.

Ellickson, R. (1996) 'Controlling chronic misconduct in city spaces', *Yale Law Journal,* 105: 1167–228.

Engels, F. (1844 [1971]) *The Condition of the Working Class in England.* Oxford: Blackwell.

Engels, F. (1872) *The Housing Question.* Moscow: Progress Publishers.

Engels, F. (1970 [1887]) *The Housing Question.* Moscow: Progress Publishers.

Engels, F. & Kiernan, V. (1987) *The Condition of the Working Class in England in 1844.* London: Penguin Classics.

Ergler, C., Sakdapolrak, P., Bohle, H. & Kearns, R.A. (2011) 'Entitlements to health care: Why is there a preference for private facilities among poorer residents of Chennai, India?', *Social Science & Medicine,* 72(3): 327–37.

Ewing, R. & Handy, S. (2009)' Measuring the unmeasurable: Urban design qualities related to walkability', *Journal of Urban Design,* 14: 65–84.

Faber, D. (2005) 'Building a transnational environmental justice movement: Obstacles and opportunities in the age of globalization', in J. Bandy & J. Smith (eds) *Coalitions Across Borders: Transnational Protest and the Neoliberal Order.* Oxford: Rowman & Littlefield, pp. 43–70.

Fainstein, S. (2009) 'Planning and the just city', in P. Marcuse et al. (eds) *Searching for the Just City*. New York: Routledge, pp. 19–39.

Fainstein, S. (2010) *The Just City*. Ithaca, NY: Cornell University Press.

Fairbanks, R. (2009) *How it Works: Recovering Citizens in Post-Welfare Philadelphia*. Chicago: University of Chicago Press.

Falconer, R., Newman, P. & Giles-Corti, B. (2010) 'Is practice aligned with the principles? Implementing New Urbanism in Perth, Western Australia', *Transport Policy*, 17(5): 287–94.

Faris, R.E.L. & Dunham, H.W. (1939) *Mental Disorders in Urban Areas*. Chicago: University of Chicago Press.

Farr, D. (2008) *Sustainable Urbanism: Urban Design with Nature*. Hoboken, NJ: John Wiley & Sons.

Ferguson, G (1994) *Building the New Zealand Dream*. Palmerston North: Dunmore Press.

Fernandes, L. (2004) 'The politics of forgetting: Class politics, state power and the restructuring of urban space in India', *Urban Studies*, 12: 2415–30.

Fernandes,L. (2006) *India's New Middle Class: Democratic Politics in an Era of Economic Reform*. Minneapolis: University of Minnesota Press.

Few, R., Harpham, T. & Atkinson, S. (2003) 'Urban primary health care in Africa: A comparative analysis of city-wide public sector projects in Lusaka and Dar es Salaam', *Health and Place*, 9: 45–53.

Field, A. (1974) *Picture Palace: A Social History of the Cinema*. London: Gentry Books.

Fincher, R. (2003) *Planning for Cities of Diversity, Difference and Encounter*. Available at: www.planning.sa.gov.au/congress/pdf/Papers/Fincher.pdf (accessed 19 June 2007).

Fincher, R. & Iveson, K. (2008) *The Social Logics of Urban Planning: Towards a Just Diversity in Cities*. London: Palgrave.

Fincher, R. and Jacobs, J. (eds) (1998) *Cities of Difference*. New York and London: Guilford Press.

Fine, M., Weis, L., Addleston, J. & Mazuza, J. (1997) '(In)secure times: Constructing white working class masculinities in the late twentieth century', *Gender and Society*, 11: 52–68.

Fishman, R. (1982) *Urban Utopias in the Twentieth Century: Ebenezer Howard, Frank Lloyd Wright, Le Corbusier*. London: MIT Press.

Fix, M. (2007) *São Paulo Cidade Global: Fundamentos Financeiros de Uma Miragem*. São Paulo: Boitempo.

Fix, M., Arantes, P. & Tanaka, G. (2003) *The Case of São Paulo (Understanding Slums Series)*. New York: United Nations-HABITAT.

Flint, J. & Nixon, J. (2006) 'Governing neighbours: Anti-social behaviour orders and new forms of regulating conduct in the UK', *Urban Studies*, 43: 939 –55.

Florida, R. (2002) *The Rise of the Creative Class: and How it's Transforming Work, Leisure, Community and Everyday Life*. New York: Basic Books.

Florida, R. (2005) *Cities and the Creative Class*. New York and London: Routledge.

Florida, R. (2007) *The Flight of the Creative Class: The New Global Competition for Talent*. New York: HarperBusiness.

Florida, R. (2009) 'How the crash will reshape America', *The Atlantic*, March. Available at: http://www.theatlantic.com/magazine/archive/2009/03/how-the-crash-will-reshape-america/307293/?single_page=true (accessed 29 April 2014).

Flusty, S. (2001) 'The banality of interdiction: Surveillance, control and the displacement of diversity', *International Journal of Urban and Regional Research*, 25: 658–64.

Forum for the Future (2009) *The Sustainable Cities Index: Ranking the Largest 20 British Cities*. London: Forum for the Future.

Foscarinis, M (1996) 'Downward spiral: Homelessness and its criminalization', *Yale Law and Policy Review*, 14: 1–63.

Fotso, J.C. (2007) 'Urban–rural differentials in child malnutrition: Trends and socioeconomic correlates in sub-Saharan Africa', *Health and Place*, 13: 205–23.

Frankenberg, R. (1993) *The Social Construction of Whiteness: White Women, Race Matters*. London: Routledge.

Fraser, N. (1989) *Unruly Practices: Power, Discourse and Gender in Contemporary Social Theory*. Minneapolis: University of Minnesota Press.

Fraser, N. (1997) *Justice Interruptus: Critical Reflections on the 'Postsocialist' Condition*. New York: Routledge.

Frieden, B. & Sagalyn, L. (1989) 'Downtown malls and the city agenda', *Social Science and Modern Society*, 27: 43–7.

Friedmann, J. (2000) 'The good city: In defense of utopian thinking', *International Journal of Urban and Regional Research*, 24(2): 460–72.

Frisby, D. (1986) *Fragments of Modernity: Theories of Modernity in the Work of Simmel, Kracauer and Benjamin*. Cambridge, MA: MIT Press.

Fritzsche, P. (1996) *Reading Berlin, 1900*. Cambridge, MA: Harvard University.

FUREE and the Community Development Project of the Urban Justice Center (2008) *Out of Business*. New York: FUREE.

Fyfe, N. and Bannister, J. (1996) 'City watching: Closed circuit television surveillance in public spaces', *Area*, 28: 37–46.

Gandy, M. (2004) 'Rethinking urban metabolism: Water, space and the modern city', *City*, 8: 363–79.

Gandy, M. (2005a) 'Learning from Lagos', *New Left Review*, 33: 37–52.

Gandy, M. (2005b) 'Cyborg urbanization: Complexity and monstrosity in the contemporary city', *International Journal of Urban and Regional Research*, 29: 26–49.

Gans, H. (1963) *The Urban Villagers: Groups and Class in the Life of Italian-Americans*. New York: Free Press.

Garreau, J. (1991) *Edge City: Life on the New Frontier*. New York: Doubleday.

Gendron, R. & Dumhoff, W. (2008) *The Leftmost City: Power and Progressive Politics in Santa Cruz*. Boulder, CO: Westview Press

Gibson, T. (2003) *Securing the Spectacular City: The Politics of Homelessness and Revitalization in Downtown Seattle*. Lanham, MD: Lexington Books.

Gilbert, M. (1998) '"Race", space, and power: The survival strategies of working poor women', *Annals of the Association of American Geographers*, 88: 595–621.

Giles-Corti, B. & Donovan, R.J. (2002a) 'The relative influence of individual, social and physical environment determinants of physical activity', *Social Science and Medicine*, 54: 1793–812.

Giles-Corti, B. & Donovan, R.J. (2002b) 'Socioeconomic status differences in recreational physical activity levels and real and perceived access to a supportive physical environment', *Preventive Medicine*, 35: 601–11.

Giles-Corti, B., Kelty, S.F., Zubrick, S.R. & Villanueva, K.P. (2009) 'Encouraging walking for transport and physical activity in children and adolescents: How important is the built environment?', *Sports Medicine*, 39: 995–1009.

Giles-Corti, B., Knuiman, M., Timperio, A., Van Niel, K., Pikora, T.J., Bull, F.C.L., Shilton, T. & Bulsara, M. (2008) 'Evaluation of the implementation of a state government community design policy aimed at increasing local walking: Design issues and baseline results from RESIDE, Perth, Western Australia', *Preventive Medicine*, 46: 46–54.

Gill, K. (2009) *On Poverty and Plastic: Scavenging and Scrap Trading Entrepreneurs in India's Urban Informal Economy*. Oxford: Oxford University Press.

Glasze, G., Webster, C. & Frantz, K. (2006) 'Introduction: Global and local perspectives on the rise of private neighbourhoods', in G. Glasze, C. Webster and K. Frantz (eds) *Private Cities: Local and Global Perspectives*. London: Routledge, pp. 1–8.

Gleeson, B. (2002) 'Geographies of disability', in G. Bridge & S. Watson (eds) *The Blackwell City Reader*. Oxford: Blackwell, pp. 304–14.

Gleeson, B. & Kearns, R.A. (2001) 'Remoralising landscapes of care', *Environment and Planning D: Society and Space,* 19: 61–80.

Goffman, E. (1963) *Behavior in Public Places.* New York: Free Press.

Goonewardena, K., Kipfer, S., Milgrom, R. & Schmid, C. (2008) *Space, Difference, Everyday Life.* London: Routledge.

Goss, J. (1993) 'The "magic of the mall": An analysis of the form, function, and meaning in the contemporary retail built environment', *Annals of the Association of American Geographers,* 83: 18–47.

Goss, J. (1999) 'Once-upon-a-time in the commodity world: An unofficial guide to Mall of America', *Annals of the Association of American Geographers,* 89(1): 45–75.

Gould, W.T.S. (1998) 'African mortality and the new "urban penalty"', *Health and Place,* 4: 171–81.

Grabher, G. (2001) 'Locating economic action: Projects, networks, localities, institutions', *Environment and Planning A,* 33(8): 1329–31.

Grabher, G. (2002) 'Cool projects, boring institutions: Temporary collaboration in social context', *Regional Studies,* 36(3): 205–14.

Graham, S. (1999) 'Global grids of glass: On global cities, telecommunications and planetary urban networks', *Urban Studies,* 36(5–6): 929–49.

Graham, S. & Marvin, S. (2001) *Splintering Urbanism.* London: Routledge.

Graham, S. & Wood, D. (2003) 'Digitizing surveillance: Categorization, space, inequality', *Critical Social Policy,* 23: 227–48.

Granovetter, M. (1973) 'The strength of weak ties', *American Journal of Sociology,* 78: 1360–80.

Grant, R. & Nijman, J. (2002) 'Globalization and the corporate geography of cities in the less-developed world', *Annals of the Association of American Geographers,* 92: 320–40.

Greater London Authority (2007) *Health in London: Looking Back, Looking Forward.* London: London Health Commission.

Greenberg, M. (2008) *Branding New York: How a City in Crisis Was Sold to the World.* New York: Routledge.

Greene, J. (1999) 'Zero tolerance: A case study of police policies and practices in New York City', *Crime & Delinquency,* 45: 171–87.

Gregory, D. (1994) *Geographical Imaginations.* Oxford: Blackwell.

Gregory, I., Dorling, D. & Southall, H. (2001) 'A century of inequality in England and Wales using standardized geographical units', *Area,* 33: 297–311.

Guagliardo, M.F., Ronzio, C.R., Cheung, I., Chacko, E. & Joseph, J.G. (2004) 'Physician accessibility: An urban case study of pediatric providers', *Health and Place,* 10: 273–83.

Gunder, M. (2005) 'The production of desirous space: Mere fantasies of the utopian city?', *Planning Theory,* 4(2): 173–99.

Hackworth, J. & Smith, N. (2001) 'The changing state of gentrification', *Tijdschrift voor Economische en Sociale Geografie,* 22: 464–77.

Hajat, S., Armstrong, B., Gouveia, N. & Wilkinson, P. (2005) 'Mortality displacement of heat-related deaths: A comparison of Delhi, São Paulo, and London', *Epidemiology,* 16: 613–20.

Halfacree, K.H. (1995) 'Talking about rurality: Social representations of the rural as expressed by residents of six English parishes', *Journal of Rural Studies,* 11: 1–20.

Hall, P. (1988) *Cities of Tomorrow.* Oxford: Blackwell.

Hall, P. (2002) *Urban and Regional Planning.* London: Routledge.

Hall, P. (2013) *Good Cities, Better Lives: How Europe Discovered the Lost Art of Urbanism.* London: Routledge.

Hall, S. (2012) *City, Street and Citizen: The Measure of the Ordinary.* London: Routledge.

Hall, S. (1993) 'Culture, community, nation', *Cultural Studies,* 7: 349–63.

Hall, T. & Hubbard, P. (1998) *The Entrepreneurial City: Geographies of Politics, Regime and Representation.* Chichester: John Wiley & Sons.

Haraway, D. (1991) *Simians, Cyborgs and Women: The Reinvention of Nature*. London and New York: Routledge.

Harcourt, B. (2001) *The Illusion of Order: The False Promise of Broken Windows Policing*. Cambridge, MA: Harvard University Press.

Harley, J.B. (2001) *The New Nature of Maps: Essays in the History of Cartography* (edited by P. Laxton). Baltimore, MD: Johns Hopkins University Press.

Harpham, T. (2009) 'Urban health in developing countries: What do we know and where do we go?', *Health and Place*, 15: 107–16.

Harris, A. (2008) 'From London to Mumbai and back again: Gentrification and public policy in comparative perspective', *Urban Studies*, 45(12): 2407–28.

Harvey, D. (1973) *Social Justice and the City*. London: Edward Arnold.

Harvey, D.(1982) *The Limits to Capital*. Oxford: Oxford University Press.

Harvey, D. (1985) *The Urbanization of Capital*. Oxford: Blackwell.

Harvey, D. (1987) 'Flexible accumulation through urbanization: Reflections on "post-modernism" in the American city', *Antipode*, 19(3): 260–86.

Harvey, D. (1989a) 'From managerialism to entrepreneurialism: The transformation in urban governance in late capitalism', *Geografiska Annaler. Series B, Human Geography*, 71(1): 3–17.

Harvey, D. (1989b) *The Condition of Postmodernity*. Oxford: Blackwell.

Harvey, D. (1989c) *The Urban Experience*. Oxford: Blackwell.

Harvey, D. (1996) *Justice, Nature and the Geography of Difference*. Oxford: Blackwell.

Harvey, D. (2000a) *Cities of Hope*. Edinburgh: Edinburgh University Press.

Harvey, D. (2000b) *Spaces of Hope*. Berkeley, CA: University of California Press.

Harvey, D. (2002) 'Social Justice, Postmodernism, and the City', in S. Fainstein and S. Campbell (eds) *Readings in Urban Theory*. 2nd edn. Oxford: Blackwell pp. 386–402.

Harvey, D. (2003) *Paris: Capital of Modernity*. New York: Routledge.

Harvey, D. (2008) 'The right to the city', *New Left Review*, 53: 23–40.

Harvey, D. (2009a) *Social Justice and the City*. Athens, GA: University of Georgia Press.

Harvey, D. (2009b) 'The crisis today @ Marxism 2009'. Available at www.david-harvey-the-crisis-today-marxism-2009/.

Harvey, D. & Potter, C. (2009) 'The right to the just city', in P. Marcuse, J. Connolly, J. Nory, I. Olivo, C. Potter and J. Steil (eds) *Searching for the Just City*. New York: Routledge, pp. 40–51.

Hasan, A. (2007) 'Confronting the urban development paradigm'. Available at: http://www.india-seminar.com/2007/579/579_arif_hasan.htm.

Hawkes, C. (2008) 'Dietary implications of supermarket development: A global perspective', *Development Policy Review*, 26: 657–92.

Hayami, Y., Dikshit, A. & Mishra, S. (2006) 'Waste pickers and collectors in Delhi: Poverty and environment in an urban informal sector', *Journal of Development Studies*, 42: 41–69.

He, S. (2007) 'State-sponsored gentrification under market transition: The case of Shanghai', *Urban Affairs Review*, 43(2): 171–98.

He, S. (2010) 'New-build gentrification in central Shanghai: Demographic changes and socio-economic implications', *Population, Space and Place*, 16(5): 345–61.

Hebbert, M. (1999) 'A city in good shape: Town planning and public health', *The Town Planning Review*, 70(4): 433–53.

Henderson, G. (2009) 'Marxist Political Economy and the Environment', in N. Castree, D. Demeritt, D. Liverman & B. Rhoads (eds) *A Companion to Environmental Geography*. Oxford: Wiley-Blackwell, pp. 266–93.

Herbert, S. (1996) 'Morality in law enforcement: Chasing "bad guys" with the Los Angeles Police Department', *Law & Society Review*, 30: 799–818.

Herbert, S. (1997) *Policing Space: Territoriality and the Los Angeles Police Department*. Minneapolis, MN: University of Minnesota Press.

Herbert, S. (2006) *Citizens, Cops and Power: Recognizing the Limits to Community*. Chicago: University of Chicago Press.

Herbert, S. (2007) 'The "Battle of Seattle" revisited: Or, seven views of the protest-zoning state', *Political Geography*, 26: 601–17.

Herbert, S. & Brown, E. (2006) 'Conceptions of space and crime in the punitive neo-liberal city', *Antipode*, 38: 755–77.

Herod, A. & Wright, M.W. (eds) (2001) *Labor Geographies: Workers and the Landscapes of Capitalism*. New York: Guilford Press.

Herrick, C. (2009) 'Designing the fit city: Public health, active lives, and the (re) instrumentalization of urban space', *Environment and Planning A*, 41: 2437–54.

Heynen, N. (2010) 'Cooking up non-violent civil disobedient direct action for the hungry: Food not bombs and the resurgence of radical democracy'. *Urban Studies*, 47(6): 1225–40.

Heynen, N. & Swyngedouw, E. (2003) 'Urban political ecology, justice and the politics of scale', *Antipode*, 34: 898–918.

Heynen, N., Kaika, M., & Swyngedouw, E. (eds) (2006a) *In the Nature of Cities: Urban Political Ecology and the Politics of Urban Metabolism*. London: Routledge.

Heynen, N., Kaika, M. & Swyngedouw, E. (2006b) 'Urban political ecology: Politicizing the production of urban natures', in N. Heynen, M. Kaika & E. Swyngedouw (eds) *In the Nature of Cities: Urban Political Ecology and the Politics of Urban Metabolism*. London: Routledge, pp. 3–20.

Hillier, J. (2003) 'Agonizing over consensus: Why Habermasian ideals cannot be "real"', *Planning Theory*, 24(1): 37–59.

Hillier, J. (2009) 'Assemblages of justice: The "ghost ships" of Graythorp', *International Journal of Urban and Regional Research*, 33(3): 640–61.

Hinchcliffe, S. (1999) 'Cities and Nature – Intimate Strangers', in J. Allen & M. Pryke (eds) *Unsettling Cities*. London: Routledge, pp. 137–80.

Hinchliffe, S. & Whatmore, S. (2006) 'Living cities: Towards a politics of conviviality', *Science as Culture*, 15: 123–38.

Hirt, S. & Petrovic, M. (2011) 'The Belgrade wall: The proliferation of gated housing in the Serbian capital after socialism', *International Journal of Urban and Regional Research*, 35: 753–77.

Holifield, R., Porter, M. & Walker, G. (2009) 'Spaces of environmental justice: Frameworks for critical engagement', *Antipode*, 41: 591–612.

Holland, C., Clark, A., Katz, J. & Peace, S. (2007) *Social Interactions in Urban Public Places*. York: Joseph Rowntree Foundation.

Holloway, S.L., Valentine, G. & Jayne, M. (2009) 'Masculinities, femininities and the geographies of public and private drinking landscapes', *Geoforum*, 40: 821–31.

Holloway, S. & Wyly, E. (2001) 'The color of money expanded: Geographically contingent mortgage lending in Atlanta', *Journal of Housing Research*, 12: 55–90.

Holsten, J. (1989) *The Modernist City: Architecture, Politics and Society in Brasilia*. Chicago: University of Chicago.

Holt, N.L., Cunningham, C.T., Sehn, Z.L., Spence, J.C., Newton, A.S. & Ball, G.D.C. (2009) 'Neighborhood physical activity opportunities for inner-city children and youth', *Health and Place*, 15: 1022–8.

Holt, N.L., Spence, J.C., Sehn, Z.L. & Cutumisu, N. (2008) 'Neighborhood and developmental differences in children's perceptions of opportunities for play and physical activity', *Health and Place*, 14: 2–14.

Home Office (2001) *Community Cohesion: A Report of the Independent Review Team*. London: Home Office.

Hopkins, R. (2008) *The Transition Handbook: From Oil Dependency to Local Resilience*. Totnes: Green Books.

Howard, D. (2001) *Coloring the Nation: Race and Ethnicity in the Dominican Republic*. Oxford: Signal Books.

Howard, E. (1945) *Garden Cities of Tomorrow* (first published as *Tomorrow, a Peaceful Plan to Real Reform*. London: Swan, Sonnerschein, 1898), reissued (1902) and reprinted with a preface by Sir Frederic Osborn and introductory essay by Lewis Mumford. London: Faber and Faber.

Howden-Chapman, P. (2004) 'Housing standards: A glossary of housing and health', *Journal of Epidemiology & Community Health*, 58: 162–8.

Howes, D. (1991) *The Varieties of Sensory Experience: A Sourcebook in the Anthropology of the Senses*. Toronto: University of Toronto Press.

Howes, D. (2005) *Empire of the Senses*. Oxford: Berg.

Howes, D. (2006) 'Scent, sound and synaethesia: Intersensoriality and material culture theory', in C. Tilley, W. Keane, S. Kuechler, M. Rowlands and P. Spyer (eds) *Handbook of Material Culture*. London: Sage, pp. 161–72.

Howes, D. (2007)' Multi-sensory marketing in cross-cultural perspective (Part 1): From synergy to synaesthesia'. Available at www.perceptnet.com (accessed 26 February 2009).

Huang, M.T.S. (2004) *Walking Between Slums and Skyscrapers*. Hong Kong: Hong Kong University Press.

Hubbard, P (1996) 'Urban design and city regeneration: Social representation of entrepreneurial landscapes', *Urban Studies*, 33(8): 1441–62.

Hubbard, P. (2006) *City*. London and New York: Routledge.

Huey, L. (2010) 'False security or greater social inclusion? Exploring perceptions of CCTV use in public and private spaces accessed by the homeless', *British Journal of Sociology*, 61: 63–82.

Hughes, T.P. (1993) *Networks of Power: Electrification in Western Society, 1880–1930*. Baltimore, MD: Johns Hopkins University Press.

Hume, C., Timperio, A., Salmon, J., Carver, A., Giles-Corti, B. & Crawford, D. (2009) 'Walking and cycling to school: Predictors of increases among children and adolescents', *American Journal of Preventive Medicine*, 36: 195–200.

Hutchings, P.J. (2007) 'From offworld colonies to migration zones: Bladerunner and the fractured subject of jurisprudence', *Law, Culture and the Humanities*, 3: 381–97.

Hyndman, J.C.G. & Holman, C.D.A. (2001) 'Accessibility and spatial distribution of general practice services in an Australian city by levels of social disadvantage', *Social Science and Medicine*, 53: 1599–609.

Imrie, R. (1996) *Disability and the City: International Perspectives*. London: Paul Chapman Publishing.

International Federation for Human Rights (2002) *Where Do the 'Floating Dustbins' End Up?* Paris: IFHR.

Isenberg, A. (2004) *Downtown America: A History of the Place and the People Who Made it*. Chicago: University of Chicago Press.

Isin, E. (ed.) (2000) *Democracy, Citizenship and the Global City*. London: Routledge.

Isin, E. & Siemiatycki, M. (2002) 'Making space for mosques: Claiming urban citizenship', in S. Razack (ed.) *Race, Space and the Law: The Making of White Settler Society*. Toronto: Between the Lines, pp. 185–210.

Iveson, K. (2006) 'Strangers in the Cosmopolis', in J. Binnie, J. Holloway, S. Millington & C. Young (eds) *Cosmopolitan Urbanism*. London: Routledge, pp. 70–85.

Iveson, K. (2007) *Publics and the City*. Oxford: Blackwell.

Jackson, K. (1987) *Crabgrass Frontier: The Suburbanization of the United States*. New York and Oxford: Oxford University Press.

Jackson, P. (ed.) (1987) *Race and Racism: Essays in Social Geography*. London: Allen & Unwin.

Jacobs, J. (1961) *The Death and Life of the Great American Cities*. New York: Vintage.

Jacobs, J. (1996) *Edge of Empire: Postcolonialism and the City*. New York: Routledge.

Jameson, F. (1984) 'Postmodernism or the cultural logic of late capitalism', *New Left Review*, 146: 53–92.

Jamison, A. (2008) 'Urban environmentalism from Mumford to Malmö', in M. Hård & T.J. Misa (eds) *Urban Machinery: Inside Modern European Cities*. London: MIT Press, pp. 281–98.

Jankowski, M. (1991) *Islands in the Street: Gangs and American Urban Society*. Berkeley, CA: University of California Press.

Jargowsky, P. (2003) *Stunning Progress, Hidden Problems: The Dramatic Decline of Concentrated Poverty in the 1990s*. Washington, DC: Brookings Institution.

Jayne, M. (2006) *Cities and Consumption*. London: Routledge.

Jayne, M., Holloway, S.L. & Valentine, G. (2006) 'Drunk and disorderly: Alcohol, urban life and public space', *Progress in Human Geography*, 30: 451–68.

Jayne, M., Valentine, G. & Holloway, S.L. (2008a) 'Geographies of alcohol, drinking and drunkenness: A review of progress', *Progress in Human Geography*, 32: 247–63.

Jayne, M., Valentine, G. & Holloway, S.L. (2008b) 'The place of drink: Geographical contributions to alcohol studies', *Drugs: Education, Prevention and Policy*, 15: 219–32.

Jayne, M., Valentine, G. & Holloway, S.L. (2008c) 'Fluid boundaries – British binge drinking and European civility: Alcohol and the production and consumption of public space', *Space and Polity*, 12: 81–100.

Jeffrey, P. & Pounder, J. (2000) 'Physical and environmental aspects', in P. Roberts & H. Sykes (eds) *Urban Regeneration*. London: Sage, pp. 86–108.

Jermier, J.M., Forbes, L.C., Benn, S. & Orsato, B.J. (2006) The new corporate environmentalism and green politics', in S. Clegg, C. Hardy, T. Lawrence & W. Nord (eds) *The Sage Handbook of Organisational Studies*, London: Sage, pp. 618–50.

Johnsen, S. and Fitzpatrick, S. (2007) *The Impact of Enforcement on Street Users in England*. Plymouth: The Policy Press.

Johnsen, S., May, J. & Cloke, P. (2008) 'Imag(in)ing "homeless places": Using auto-photography to (re)examine the geographies of homelessness', *Area*, 40: 194–207.

Johnson, D.P. & Wilson, J.S. (2009) 'The socio-spatial dynamics of extreme urban heat events: The case of heat-related deaths in Philadelphia', *Applied Geography*, 29: 419–34.

Johnson, S. & Marko, J. (2008) 'Designing healthy places: Land use planning and public health', *Environments*, 35: 9–19.

Johnston, R.J., Gregory, D., Smith, D.M. (eds) (1994) *The Dictionary of Human Geography* (third edition). Oxford: Blackwell.

Joyce, P. (2005) *The Rule of Freedom: Liberalism and the Modern City*. London: Verso.

Judd, D. (1995) 'The Rise of the New Walled Cities', in H. Liggett & D. Perry (eds) *Spatial Practices: Critical Explorations in Social/Spatial Theory*. Thousand Oaks, CA: Sage, pp. 144–66.

Judd, D. (2005) 'Everything is always going to Hell: Urban scholars as end-times prophets', *Urban Affairs Review*, 41: 119–35.

Judd, D.R. & Simpson, D. (eds) (2011) *The City, Revisited: Urban Theory from Chicago, Los Angeles, and New York*. Minneapolis, MN: University of Minnesota Press.

Julier, G. (2007) 'Urban designscapes and the production of aesthetic consent', in R. Paddison & S. Miles (eds) *Culture-Led Urban Regeneration*. London: Routledge, pp. 29–47.

Kaika, M. (2005) *City of Flows – Modernity, Nature and the City*. London: Routledge.

Kaika, M. & Swyngedouw, E. (2011) 'The urbanization of nature: great promises, impasse, and new beginnings', in G. Bridge & S. Watson (eds) *The New Blackwell Companion to the City*. Oxford: Wiley-Blackwell.

Karmen, A. (2006) *New York Murder Mystery: The True Story of the Crime Crash of the 1990s*. New York: New York University Press.

Kasarda, J. & Lindsay, G. (2011) *Aerotropolis. The Way We'll Live Next*. London: Allen Lane.

Katz, C. (2006) 'Messing with "the Project"', in N. Castree & D. Gregory (eds) *David Harvey: A Critical Reader*. Oxford: Blackwell, pp. 234–46.

Katznelson, I. (1995) 'Social justice, liberalism, and the city: Considerations on David Harvey, John Rawls, and Karl Polanyi', in A. Merrifield & E. Swyngedouw (eds) *The Urbanization of Injustice*. New York: New York University Press, pp. 45–64.

Kavaratzis, M. (2009) 'Cities and their brands: Lessons from corporate branding', *Place Branding and Public Diplomacy*. 5(1): 26–37.

Kearns, G. & Philo, C. (1993) *Selling Places: The City as Cultural Capital, Past and Present*. Oxford: Pergamon.

Kearns, G. (1988) 'Private property and public health reform in England 1830–70', *Social Science and Medicine*, 26: 187–99.

Kearns, R.A. & Barnett, J.R. (1999) 'To boldly go? Place, metaphor and the marketing of Auckland's Starship Hospital', *Environment and Planning D: Society and Space*, 17: 201–26.

Kearns, R.A., Joseph, A.E. & Moon, G. (2012) 'Traces of the New Zealand psychiatric hospital: Unpacking the place of stigma', *New Zealand Geographer* 68: 175–86.

Keil, R. (2003) 'Urban political ecology', *Urban Geography*, 24: 723–38.

Keil, R. (2007) 'Sustaining modernity, modernizing nature: The environmental crisis and the survival of capitalism', in R. Krueger & D. Gibbs (eds) *The Sustainable Development Paradox: Urban Political Ecology in the United States and Europe*. London: Guildford Press, pp. 41–65.

Keith, M. (2005) *After the Cosmopolitan? Multicultural Cities and the Future of Racism*. New York: Routledge.

Kelling, G. & Coles, C. (1998) *Fixing Broken Windows: Restoring Order and Reducing Crime in Our Communities*. New York: Free Press.

Kitchin, R. & Dodge, M. (2007) 'Rethinking maps', *Progress in Human Geography*, 31(3): 331.

Kitchin, R. & Dodge, M. (2011) *Code/Space: Software and Everyday Life*. Cambridge, MA: MIT Press.

Klinenberg, E. (2002) *Heat Wave: A Social Autopsy of Disaster in Chicago*. Chicago: University of Chicago Press.

Klingmann, A. (2007) *Brandscapes: Architecture in the Experience Economy*. Cambridge, MA: MIT Press.

Kneale, J. & French, S. (2008) 'Mapping alcohol: Health, policy and the geographies of problem drinking in Britain', *Drugs: Education, Prevention and Policy*, 15: 233–49.

Knopf-Newman, M.J. (2004) 'Public eyes: Investigating the causes of breast cancer', in R. Stein (ed.) *New Perspectives on Environmental Justice: Gender, Sexuality, and Activism*. London: Rutgers University Press, pp. 161–76.

Knopp, L. (1998) 'Sexuality and urban space: Gay male identity politics in the United States, the United Kingdom and Australia', in R. Fincher & J. Jacobs (eds) *Cities of Difference*. London: Guilford Press, pp. 149–76.

Knowles, C. (2000) 'Burger King, Dunkin Donuts and community mental health care', *Health & Place*, 6: 213–24.

Knox, P. (2008) *Metroburbia, USA*. New Brunswick, NJ: Rutgers University Press.

Koch, R. & Latham, A. (2013) 'On the hard work of domesticating public space', *Urban Studies*, 55(12): 1–16.

Kodras, J. (1997) 'The changing map of American poverty in an era of economic restructuring and political realignment', *Economic Geography*, 73: 67–93.

Kohn, M. (2004) *Brave New Neighborhoods: The Privatization of Public Space*. New York: Routledge.

Kosinets, R.V. & Belk, R.W. (2007) 'Camcorder society: Quality videography in consumer and market research', in R.W. Belk (ed.) (2007) *Handbook of Qualitative Research Methods in Marketing*. Cheltenham: Edward Elgar Publishing, pp. 335–44.

Kovats, S. & Akhtar, R. (2008) 'Climate, climate change and human health in Asian cities', *Environment and Urbanization*, 20: 165–75.

Kowinski, W. (1985) *The Malling of America*. Bloomington, IN: Xlibris Corporation.

Kozol J. (1988) *Rachel and Her Children*. New York: Crown Press.

Kracauer, S. (1927) *The Mass Ornament*. Frankfurt: Surhkamp.

Krieger, J. & Higgins, D.L. (2002) 'Housing and health: Time again for public health action', *American Journal of Public Health*, 92(5): 758–68.

Kurtz, H.E. (2002) 'The politics of environmental justice as the politics of scale: St. James Parish, Louisiana, and the Stintech Siting Controversy', in A. Herod & M. Wright (eds) *Geographies of Power: Placing Scale*. Oxford: Blackwell, pp. 249–73.

Kurtz, H.E. (2007) 'Gender and environmental justice in Louisiana: Blurring the boundaries of public and private spheres', *Gender, Place and Culture*, 14: 409–26.

Kurtz, H.E. (2009) 'Acknowledging the racial state: An agenda for environmental justice research', *Antipode*, 41: 684–704.

Kusenbach, M. (2003) 'Street phenomenology: The go-along as ethnographic research tool', *Ethnography*, 4: 455–85.

Ladd, B. (1990) *Urban Planning and Civic Order in Germany, 1860–1914*. Boston: Harvard University Press.

Lake, A. & Townshend, T. (2006) 'Obesogenic environments: Exploring the built and food environments', *The Journal of the Royal Society for the Promotion of Health*, 126: 262–7.

Lake, R. (1996) 'Volunteers, NIMBYs, and environmental justice: Dilemmas of democratic practice', *Antipode*, 28: 160–74.

Lanchester, J. (2012) *Capital*. London: Faber and Faber.

Lang, R. & Nelson, A. (2007) 'Boomburb politics and the rise of private government', *Housing Policy Debate*, 18(3): 627–34.

Larsen, K. & Gilliland, J. (2008) 'Mapping the evolution of "food deserts" in a Canadian city: Supermarket accessibility in London, Ontario, 1961–2005', *International Journal of Health Geographics*, 7.

Larsen, K. & Gilliland, J. (2009) 'A farmers' market in a food desert: Evaluating impacts on the price and availability of healthy food', *Health and Place*, 15: 1158–62.

Larson, E. (2003) *The Devil in the White City: Murder, Magic, and Madness at the Fair that Changed America*. New York: Random House.

Lash, S. & Lury, C. (2007) *Global Culture Industry: The Mediation of Things*. Cambridge: Polity Press.

Lash, S. & Urry, J. (1994) *Economies of Signs and Space*. London: Sage.

Latham, A. & McCormack, D.P. (2004) 'Moving cities: Rethinking the materialities of urban geographies', *Progress in Human Geography*, 28(6): 701–24.

Latour, B. (1993) *We Have Never Been Modern*. Cambridge, MA: Harvard University Press.

Laurier, E. & Philo, C. (2006) 'Cold shoulders and napkins handed: Gestures of responsibility', *Transactions of the Institute of British Geographers*, 31: 193–207.

Laurier, E., Whyte, A. & Buckner, K. (2002) 'Neighbouring as an occasioned activity: "Finding a lost cat"', *Space & Culture*, 5: 346–67.

Law, L. (2001) 'Home cooking: Filipino women and geographies of the senses in Hong Kong', *Ecumene*, 8: 264–83.

Law, L. (2002) 'Defying disappearance: Cosmopolitan public spaces in Hong Kong', *Urban Studies*, 39: 1625–45.

Leach, W. (1994) *Land of Desire: Merchants, Power, and the Rise of a New American Culture*. New York: Vintage.

Lee, J. & Ingold, T. (2006) 'Fieldwork on foot: Perceiving, routing, socialising', in S. Coleman & P. Collins (eds) *Locating the Field: Space, Place and Context in Anthropology*. Oxford: Berg, pp. 67–85.

Lee, S. 2006: *When the Levees Broke: A Requiem in Four Parts*. HBO documentary.

Lees, L. (1998) 'Urban renaissance and the street: Spaces of control and contestation', in N. Fyfe (ed.) *Images of the Street: Planning, Identity and Control in Public Space*. London: Routledge, pp. 236–53.

Lees, L. (2000) 'A reappraisal of gentrification: Towards a "geography of gentrification"', *Progress in Human Geography*, 24(3): 389–408.

Lees, L. (2002) 'Rematerializing geography: The new urban geography', *Progress in Human Geography*, 26(1): 101–12.

Lees, L. (2003a) 'Visions of "urban renaissance": The urban taskforce report and the urban white paper', in R. Imrie & M. Raco (eds) *Urban Renaissance? New Labour, Community and Urban Policy*. Bristol: Policy Press, pp. 61–82.

Lees, L. (2003b) 'The ambivalence of diversity and the politics of urban renaissance: The case of youth in downtown Portland, Maine', *International Journal of Urban and Regional Research*, 27: 613–34.

Lees, L. (ed.) (2004) *The Emancipatory City: Paradoxes and Possibilities?* London: Sage.

Lees, L. (2008) 'Gentrification and social mixing: Towards an urban renaissance?', *Urban Studies*, 45(12): 2449–70.

Lees, L. (2009) 'Urban renaissance in an urban recession: The end of gentrification?', *Environment and Planning A*, 41(7): 1529–33.

Lees, L. (2012a) 'The geography of gentrification: Thinking through comparative urbanism, *Progress in Human Geography*, 36(2): 155–171.

Lees, L. (2012b) 'Gentrifying the world city', in B. Derudder,, M. Hoyler, P. Taylor and F. Witlox (eds) *International Handbook of Globalization and World Cities*. Cheltenham: Edward Elgar, pp. 628–642.

Lees, L. & Ley, D. (2008) 'Gentrification and public policy', *Urban Studies*, 45(12): 2379–2648.

Lees, L., Shin, H. and Lopez, E. (eds) (in press) *Gentrification, Globalization and the Postcolonial Challenge*. Bristol: Policy Press.

Lees, L., Slater, T. & Wyly, E. (2008) *Gentrification*. New York: Routledge.

Lees, L., Slater, T. & Wyly, E. (2010) *The Gentrification Reader*. London: Routledge.

Lefebvre, H. (1991 [1974]) *The Production of Space*. Oxford: Blackwell.

Lefebvre, H. (1996 [1968]) *Writings on Cities*. Translated and edited by E. Kofman & E. Lebas. Oxford: Blackwell.

Lemanski, C. (2006) 'Spaces of exclusivity or connection? Linkages between a gated community and its poorer neighbour in a Cape Town master plan development', *Urban Studies*, 43(2): 397–420.

Leon, D.A. (2008) 'Cities, urbanization and health', *International Journal of Epidemiology*, 37: 4–8.

Levin, K.A. & Leyland, A.H. (2006) 'A comparison of health inequalities in urban and rural Scotland', *Social Science & Medicine*, 62: 1457–64.

Lewis, O. (1966) *Vida: A Puerto Rican Family in the Culture of Poverty – San Juan and New York*. New York: Random House.

Ley, D. (1974) *The Black Inner City as Frontier Outpost: Images and Behavior of a Philadelphia Neighborhood*. Washington, DC: Association of American Geographers.

Ley, D. (1980) 'Liberal ideology and the post-industrial city', *Annals of the Association of American Geographers*, 70(2): 238–58.

Ley, D. (1994) 'Gentrification and the politics of the new middle class', *Environment and Planning D: Society and Space*, 12: 53–74.

Ley, D. (1996) *The New Middle Class and the Remaking of the Central City*. Oxford: Oxford University Press.

Ley, D. (2003) 'Artists, aestheticisation and the field of gentrification', *Urban Studies*, 40(12): 2527–44.

Leyshon, A. (1995) 'Missing worlds: Whatever happened to the geography of poverty?', *Environment and Planning A*, 27: 1021–8.

Liebow, E. (1967) *Tally's Corner: A Study of Negro Streetcorner Men*. Boston: Little, Brown.

Lindner, R. (1996) *The Reportage of Urban Culture: Robert Park and the Chicago School*. Cambridge: Cambridge University Press.

Lirish Dean, A. (2007) 'Albee Square: When the mall's no longer home', *Gotham Gazette*, July.

Lirish Dean, A. (2009) 'Confronting the condo glut', *Gotham Gazette*, February.

Livingstone, D. (1992) *The Geographical Tradition: Episodes in the History of a Contested Enterprise*. Oxford: Blackwell.

Lix, L., DeVerteuil, G., Hinds, A., Robinson, R., Walker, J. & Roos, L. (2007) 'Residential mobility of individuals with severe mental illness: A comparison of frequent and infrequent movers', *Social Psychology and Psychiatric Epidemiology*, 42: 221–8.

Lloyd, R.D. (2006) *Neo-bohemia: Art and Commerce in the Postindustrial City*. London: Routledge.

Lofland, L. (1998) *The Public Realm: Exploring the City's Quintessential Social Territory*. Hawthrone, NY: Aldine de Gruyter.

Logan, J. & Molotch, H. (1987) *Urban Fortunes: The Political Economy of Place*. Berkeley, CA: University of California Press.

Lonsway, B. (2009) *Making Leisure Work: Architecture in the Experience Economy*. Cambridge, MA: MIT Press.

Lopez-Morales, E.J. (2010) 'Real estate market, state-entrepreneurialism and urban policy in the "gentrification by ground rent dispossession" of Santiago de Chile', *Journal of Latin American Geography*, 9(1): 145–73.

Lorentzen, A. (2009) 'Cities in the Experience Economy'. *European Planning Studies*, 17(6): 829–45.

Low, K. (2005) 'Ruminations on smell as a sociocultural phenomenon', *Current Sociology*, 53(3): 397–417.

Low, S. (2000) *On the Plaza: The Politics of Public Space and Culture*. Austin, TX: University of Texas.

Low, S. (2002) 'Introduction: Theorizing the city', in S. Low (ed.) *Theorizing the City: The New Urban Anthropology Reader*. New Brunswick, NJ: Rutgers University Press, pp. 1–33.

Low, S. (2003) *Behind the Gates: Life, Security, and the Pursuit of Happiness in Fortress America*. New York: Routledge.

Lowry, G. & McCann, E. (2011) 'Asia in the mix: urban form and global mobilities – Hong Kong, Vancouver, Dubai', in A. Roy & A. Ong (eds) *Worlding Cities: Asian Experiments and the Art of Being Global*. Malden, MA: Wiley-Blackwell, pp. 182–204.

Lowry, S. (1989) 'Housing and health: Temperature and humidity', *British Medical Journal*, 299: 1326.

Lucas, K. (ed.) (2004) *Running on Empty: Transport, Social Exclusion and Environmental Justice*. Bristol: Policy Press.

Lynch, K. (1979) *The Image of the City*. Cambridge, MA: MIT Press.

Macgaffey, J. (1991) *The Real Economy of Zaire: The Contribution of Smuggling and Other Unofficial Activities to National Wealth*. London: James Currey.

MacLeod, G. (2002) 'From urban entrepreneurialism to a revanchist city? On the spatial injustices of Glasgow's renaissance', *Antipode*, 34: 602–24.

MacLeod, G. (2011) 'Urban politics reconsidered: growth machine to post-democratic city?', *Urban Studies*, 48(12): 2629–60.

MacLeod, G. (2012) '"Entrepreneurial city" revisited: governmentalizing landscapes, de-amplifying politics', *Urban Worlds*, Working Paper, University of Durham.

MacLeod, G. & Johnstone, C. (2012) 'Stretching urban renaissance: privatizing space, civilizing place, summoning "community"', *International Journal of Urban and Regional Research*, 36: 1–30.

MacLeod, G. & Ward, K. (2002) 'Spaces of utopia and dystopia: Landscaping the contemporary city', *Geografiska Annaler*, 84B: 153–69.

Manning, P. (1977) *Police Work*. Boston: MIT Press.

Marcuse, P. (1997) 'Walls of fear and walls of support', in N. Ellen (ed.) *Architecture of Fear*. New York: Princeton Architectural Press, pp. 101–14.

Marcuse, P. (2009) 'From critical urban theory to the right to the city', *City*, 13(2/3): 185–97.

Marcuse, P., Connolly, J., Novy, J., Oivio, I., Potter, C. & Steil, J. (2009) *Searching for the Just City: Debates in Urban Theory and Practice*. New York: Routledge.

Marcuse, P. (2009) 'Postscript: Beyond the just city to the right to the city', in P. Marcuse, J. Connolly, J. Novy, I. Oivio, C. Potter & J. Steil, *Searching for the Just City: Debates in Urban Theory and Practice*. New York: Routledge, pp. 240–54.

Martin, D.G. (2009) 'Chicago School', in *The Dictionary of Human Geography*. Oxford: Blackwell.

Marx, K. (1970 [1867]) *Capital*, Vol. 1. New York: Penguin.

Marx, K. & Engels, F. (1967 [1848]) *The Communist Manifesto*. New York: Penguin Books.

Mason, K. & Whitehead, M. (2008) 'Transition urbanism and the contested politics of spatial practice', paper presented at the Royal Geographical Society–Institute of British Geographers annual conference, London.

Massey, D. (1991) 'A global sense of place', *Marxism Today*, 24–29 June.

Massey, D. (1993) 'Power-geometry and a progressive sense of place', in J. Bird, B. Curtis, T. Putnam, G. Robertson & L. Tickner (eds) *Mapping the Futures: Local Cultures, Global Change*. London: Routledge, pp. 60–70.

Massey, D. (2004) 'Geographies of responsibility', *Geografiska Annaler: Series B, Human Geography*, 86: 5–18.

Massey, D. (2005) *For Space*. London: Sage.

Massey, D. (2007) *World City*. Cambridge: Polity Press.

Massey, D. & Denton, N. (1991) *American Apartheid: Segregation and the Making of the Underclass*. Cambridge, MA: Harvard University Press.

Massey, D. & Denton, N. (1993) *American Apartheid*. Cambridge, MA: Harvard University Press.

May, J. (2000) 'Of nomads and vagrants: Single homelessness and narratives of home as place', *Environment and Planning D: Society and Space*, 18: 737–59.

May, J. et al. (2007) 'Keeping London working: Global cities, the British state and London's new migrant division of labour', *Transactions of the Institute of British Geographers*, 32: 151–67.

Mayer, M. (2009) 'The "Right to the City" in the context of shifting mottos of urban social movements', *City*, 13(2–3): 362–74.

Mbembe, A. (2003) 'Necropolitics', *Public Culture*, 15(1): 11–40.

McCann, E. (2002) 'The urban as an object of study in global cities literatures: Representational practices and conceptions of place and scale', in A. Herod & M.W. Wright (eds) *Geographies of Power: Placing Scale*. Cambridge, MA: Blackwell, pp. 61–84.

McCann, E. (2004) 'Urban political economy beyond the "global" city', *Urban Studies*, 41: 2315–33.

McCann, E. (2009) 'New Urbanism', in R. Kitchin & N. Thrift (eds) *The International Encyclopedia of Human Geography*. Oxford: Elsevier, pp. 438–43.

McCann, E. & Ward, K. (eds) (2011) *Mobile Urbanism: Cities and Policymaking in the Global Age*. Minneapolis, MN: University of Minnesota Press.

McCann, E. and Ward, K. (2010) 'Relationality/territoriality: Towards a conceptualization of cities in the world', *Geoforum*, 41 (2): 175–84.

McCormack, G. R., Giles-Corti, B. & Bulsara, M. (2007) 'Correlates of using neighborhood recreational destinations in physically active respondents', *Journal of Physical Activity & Health*, 4: 39–53.

McCormack, G., Giles-Corti, B., Lange, A., Smith, T., Martin, K. & Pikora, T.J. (2004) 'An update of recent evidence of the relationship between objective and self-report measures of the physical environment and physical activity behaviours', *Journal of Science and Medicine in Sport/Sports Medicine Australia*, 7: 81–92.

McGuinness, M. (2000) 'Geography matters? Whiteness and contemporary geography', *Area*, 32(2): 225–30.

McGuirk, P. & Dowling, R. (2009) 'Neoliberal privatisation? Remapping the public and the private in Sydney's masterplanned residential estates', *Political Geography*, 28: 174–85.

McGurty, E. (2007) *Transforming Environmentalism: Warren County, PCBs, and the Origins of Environmental Justice*. London: Rutgers University Press.

McKenzie, E. (1994) *Privatopia: Homeowner Associations and the Rise of Residential Private Government*. New Haven, CT: Yale University Press.

McKenzie, E. (1996) *Privatopia: Homeowner Associations and the Rise of Residential Private Government*. New Haven, CT: Yale University Press.

McKenzie, E. (2005) 'Constructing the pomerium in Las Vegas: A case study of emerging trends in American gated communities', *Housing Studies*, 20: 187–203.

McKenzie, E. (2006) "The Dynamics of Privatopia: Private Residential Governance in the USA', in G. Glasze, C. Webster and K. Frantz (eds) *Private Cities: Local and Global Perspectives*. London: Routledge, pp. 9–30.

McKeown, T. (1979) *The Role of Medicine: Dream, Mirage or Nemesis*. London: Blackwell.

McKirr, L. (2002) *Suburban Warriors: The Origins of the New American Right*. Princeton, NJ: Princeton University Press.

McLaughlin, E. & Muncie, J. (1999) 'Walled cities, surveillance, regulation and segregation', in S. Pile, C. Brook & G. Mooney (eds) *Unruly Cities?* London: Routledge/Oxford University Press, pp. 96–136.

McLeod, K.S. (2000) 'Our sense of Snow: The myth of John Snow in medical geography', *Social Science & Medicine*, 50: 923–35.

Mehta, S. (2008) 'What they hate about Mumbai', *New York Times* Available at: http://www.nytimes.com/2008/11/29/opinion/29mehta.html?_r=0 (accessed 29 April 2014).

Mele, C. (2000a) *Selling the Lower East Side: Culture, Real Estate, and Resistance in New York City*. Minneapolis, MN: University of Minnesota Press.

Mele, C. (2000b) 'The materiality of urban discourse: rational planning in the restructuring of the early twentieth-century ghetto', *Urban Affairs Review*, 35(5): 628.

Melosi, M. (1999) *The Sanitary City: Urban Infrastructure in America from Colonial Times to the Present*. Baltimore, MD: Johns Hopkins University Press.

Merrifield, A. (2000) 'The dialectics of dystopia: Disorder and zero tolerance in the city', *International Journal of Urban and Regional Research*, 24: 473–89.

Merrifield, A. (2006) *Henri Lefebvre: A Critical Introduction*. New York: Routledge.

Merrifield, A. & Swyngedouw, E. (eds) (1995) *The Urbanization of Injustice*. London: Lawrence & Wishart.

Merry, S. (1981) *Urban Danger: Life in a Neighborhood of Strangers*. Philadelphia: Temple University Press.

Merry, S. (2001) 'Spatial governmentality and the new social order: Controlling gender violence through law', *American Anthropologist*, 103(1): 16–29.

Milbourne, P. (2004) 'The local geographies of poverty', *Geoforum*, 35: 559–75.

Miles, M. (2000) *The Uses of Decoration*. Chichester: Wiley.

Miles, M. (2007) *Cities and Cultures*. London: Routledge.

Miles, M. & Miles, S. (2004) *Consuming Cities*. London: Palgrave Macmillan.

Millington, C., Ward Thompson, C., Rowe, D., Aspinall, P., Fitzsimons, C., Nelson, N. & Mutrie, N. (2009) 'Development of the Scottish Walkability Assessment Tool (SWAT)', *Health and Place*, 15: 474–81.

Mingay, G.E. (1989) *The Rural Idyll*. London: Routledge.

Minton, A. (2009) *Ground Control: Fear and Happiness in the Twenty-First-Century City*. London: Penguin.

Mitchell, D. (1997) 'The annihilation of space by law: The roots and implications of anti-homeless laws in the United States', *Antipode*, 29: 303–35.

Mitchell, D. (2001) 'Postmodern geographical praxis? The postmodern impulse and the war against homeless people in the "post-justice" city', in C. Minca (ed.) *Postmodern Geography: Theory and Praxis*, Oxford: Blackwell, pp. 57–92.

Mitchell, D. (2003) *The Right to the City: Social Justice and the Fight for Public Space*. New York: Guilford Press.

Mitchell, T. (1991) *Colonising Egypt*. Berkeley, CA: University of California.

Mitchell, W.J. (1996) *City of Bits: Space, Place, and the Infobahn*. Cambridge, MA: MIT Press.

Molina, E. (2000) 'Informal non-kin networks among homeless Latino and African American men: Form and functions', *American Behavioral Scientist*, 43: 663–85.

Molotch, H. (1996) 'LA as design product in a regional economy', in A. Scott and E.W. Soja (eds) *The City: Los Angeles and Urban Theory at the End of the Twentieth Century*, Berkeley, CA: University of California Press pp. 225–75.

Moon, G. & Brown, T. (2001) 'Closing Barts: Community and resistance in contemporary UK hospital policy', *Environment and Planning D*, 19: 43–60.

Moon, G. & North, N. (2000) *Policy and Place: General Medical Practice in the UK*. London: Macmillan.

Moon, G. (2000) 'Risk and protection: The discourse of confinement in contemporary mental health policy', *Health & Place*, 6(3): 239–50.

Moon, G. (2009) 'Residential environments and obesity: estimating causal effects', in J. Pearce & K. Witten (eds) *Geographies of Obesity: Environmental Understandings of the Obesity Epidemic*. London: Ashgate, pp. 251–75.

Mooney, G. (2002) 'Shifting sex differentials in mortality during urban epidemiological transition: The case of Victorian London', *International Journal of Population Geography*, 8: 17–47.

Mooney, G. (2007) 'Infectious diseases and epidemiologic transition in Victorian Britain? Definitely', *Social History of Medicine*, 20: 595–606.

Moore, S. (2007) *Alternative Routes to the Sustainable City: Austin, Curitiba, and Frankfurt*. Plymouth: Lexington Books.

Morello-Frosch, R.A. (2002) 'Discrimination and the political economy of environmental inequality', *Environment and Planning C*, 20: 477–96.

Morland, K.B. & Evenson, K.R. (2009) 'Obesity prevalence and the local food environment', *Health & Place*, 15: 491–5.

Morrill, C., Snow, D. & White, C. (2005) *Together Alone: Personal Relationships in Public Spaces*. Berkeley and Los Angeles: University of California Press.

Mort, F. (1996) *Cultures of Consumption: Masculinities and Social Space in Late Twentieth-Century Britain*. London: Routledge.

Mountz, A. & Curran, W. (2009) 'Policing in drag: Giuliani goes global with the illusion of control', *Geoforum*, 40: 1033–40.

Moya Pons, F. (1995) *The Dominican Republic: A National History*. New Rochelle, NY: Hispaniola Books.

Mumford, L. (1961) *The City in History: Its Origins, Its Transformations, and Its Prospects*. New York: Harcourt, Brace & World, Inc.

Murray, M. (2004) 'The spatial dynamics of postmodern urbanism: Social polarization and fragmentation in São Paulo and Johannesburg', *Journal of Contemporary African Studies*, 22: 141–64.

Murray, M. (2008) *Taming the Disorderly City: The Spatial Landscape of Johannesburg After Apartheid*. Cape Town: CTP Cornell University Press.

Naipaul, V.S. (1988) *The Enigma of Arrival*. New York: Vintage.

Nava, M. (2006) 'Domestic Cosmopolitanism and structures of feeling: The specificity of London', in N. Yuval-Davis, K. Kannabiran & U.M. Vieten (eds) *The Situated Politics of Belonging*. London: Sage, pp. 42–53.

Neuwelt, P. & Crampton, P (2005) 'Community participation in primary health care', in K. Dew & P. Davis (eds) *Health and Society in Aotearoa/New Zealand* (second edition). Auckland: Oxford University Press, pp. 194–210.

Newburn, T. and Jones, T. (2007) 'Symbolizing crime control: Reflections on zero tolerance'. *Theoretical Criminology*, 11: 221–43.

Nijman, J. (2008) 'Against the odds: Slum rehabilitation in neoliberal Mumbai', *Cities*, 25: 73–85.

Norris, C. & Armstrong, G. (1999) *The Maximum Surveillance Society: The Rise of CCTV*. Oxford: Berg.

Norton, P.D. (2008) *Fighting Traffic: The Dawn of the Motor Age in the American City*. Cambridge, MA: The MIT Press.

November, V., Camacho-Hübner, E. & Latour, B. (2010) 'Entering a risky territory: Space in the age of digital navigation', *Environment and Planning D: Society and Space*, 28: 581–99.

Nussbaum, M. (2000) *Women and Development*. Cambridge: Cambridge University Press.

O'Connor, J. (1996) 'The second contradiction of capitalism', in T. Benton (ed.) *The Greening of Marxism*. London: Guilford Press, pp. 197–221.

O'Dwyer, L.A. & Coveney, J. (2006) 'Scoping supermarket availability and accessibility by socio-economic status in Adelaide', *Health Promotion Journal of Australia*, 17: 240–6.

Office of the Deputy Prime Minister (2003) *Sustainable Communities: Building for the Future*. London: ODPM.

Olds, K. (2001) *Globalization and Urban Change: Capital, Culture, and Pacific Rim Mega-Projects*. Oxford: Oxford University Press.

Oney, S. (1987) 'Portman's complaint', *Esquire* (June): 182–9.

Ong, A. (2006) *Neoliberalism as Exception: Mutations in Citizenship and Sovereignty*. Durham, NC: Duke University Press.

Ooi, C. (2008) 'Reimagining Singapore as a creative nation: The politics of place branding', *Place Branding and Public Diplomacy*, 4(4): 287–302.

Orfield, G. & Ashkinaze, C. (1991) *The Closing Door: Conservative Policy and Black Opportunity*. Chicago: University of Chicago Press.

Ormerod, P. & Wiltshire, G. (2009) '"Binge" drinking in the UK: A social network phenomenon', *Mind and Society*, 8: 135–52.

Pacione, M. (2005) 'City profile: Mumbai', *Cities*, 23: 229–38.

Paddison, R. (1993) 'City marketing, image reconstruction and urban regeneration', *Urban Studies*, 30(2): 339–50.

Paddison, R. (2009) 'Some reflections on the limitations to public participation in the post-political city', *L'Espace Politique*. Available at http://espacepolitique.revues.org/index1393.html.

Padilla, F. (1992) *The Gang as an American Enterprise*. New Brunswick, NJ: Rutgers University Press.

Pager, D. (2007) *Marked: Race, Crime and Finding Work in an Era of Mass Incarceration*. Chicago: University of Chicago Press.

Pallasmaa, J. (2005) *The Eyes of the Skin*. Chichester: Wiley.

Park, R.E. ([1925] 1967) 'The city: Suggestions for the investigation of human behavior in the urban environment.', in R. Park, E. Burgess & R. McKenzie (eds) *The City*. Chicago: The University of Chicago Press, pp. 1–46.

Park, R., Burgess, E. & R. McKenzie (1925 [1967]) *The City*. Chicago: University of Chicago Press (Midway Reprints).

Parr, H. (2001) 'Feeling, reading and making bodies in space', *The Geographical Review*, 91(1–2): 158–67.

Parr, H. (2008) *Mental Health and Social Space*. London: Blackwell Publishing.

Peach, C. (ed.) (1975) *Urban Social Segregation*. London: Longman.

Peck, J. (2001) *Workfare States*. New York: Guilford.

Peck, J. (2005) 'Struggling with the creative class', *International Journal of Urban and Regional Research*. 29(4): 740–70.

Peck, J. (2010) *Constructions of Neoliberal Reason*. Oxford: Oxford University Press.

Peck, J. & Theodore, N. (2008) 'Carceral Chicago: Making the ex-offender employability crisis', *International Journal of Urban and Regional Research*, 32: 251–81.

Peet, R. (1975) 'Inequality and poverty: A Marxist-geographic theory', *Annals of the Association of American Geographers*, 65: 564–71.

Pellow, D. (2007) *Resisting Global Toxics: Transnational Movements for Environmental Justice*. London: MIT Press.

Peterson, J.A. (1979) 'The impact of sanitary reform upon American urban planning, 1840–1890', *Journal of Social History*, 13: 83–103.

Peterson, P. (1981) *City Limits*. Chicago: University of Chicago Press

Phillimore, P. & Reading, R. (1992) 'A rural advantage? Urban–rural health differences in Northern England', *Journal of Public Health*, 14: 290–9.

Phillips, D. (2006) 'Parallel lives? Challenging discourses of British Muslim self-segregation', *Transactions of the Institute of British Geographers*, 24: 25–40.

Phillips, T. (2005) 'After 7/7: Sleep-walking into segregation', 22 September. Available at http://www.cre.gov.uk/Default.aspx.LocID-0hgnew07r.RefLocID-0hg00900c001001.Lang-EN.htm.

Phillips, T. & Smith, P. (2006) 'Rethinking urban incivility research: Strangers, bodies and circulations', *Urban Studies*, 43: 879–901.

Philo, C. (2000) 'More words, more worlds: Reflections on the "cultural turn" and human geography', in I. Cook, D. Crouch, S. Naylor & J.R. Ryan (eds) *Cultural Turns/Geographical Turns*. Harlow: Pearson, pp. 109–39.

Philo, C. et al. (eds) (1995) *Off the Map: The Social Geography of Poverty in the UK*. London: Child Poverty Action Group.

Philo, C., Parr, H. & Burns, N. (2003) 'Rural madness: A geographical reading and critique of the rural mental health literature', *Journal of Rural Studies*, 19: 259–81.

Pickles, J. (2004) *A History of Spaces: Cartographic Reason, Mapping, and the Geo-Coded World*. London: Routledge.

Pile, S. (2005) *Real Cities*. London: Sage.

Pinder, D. (2002) 'In defence of utopian urbanism: Imagining cities after the "end of utopia"', *Geografiska Annaler*, 84(3/4): 229–41.

Pinder, D. (2005) *Visions of the City: Utopianism, Power and Politics in Twentieth-Century Urbanism*. Edinburgh: Edinburgh University Press.

Pinder, D. (2007) 'Cartographies unbound', *Cultural Geographies*, 14(3): 453.

Pine, B.J. & Gilmore J.H. (1999) *The Experience Economy: Work is Theatre and Every Business a Stage*. Harvard, MA: Harvard Business School Press.

Pink, S. (2008) 'An urban tour: The sensory sociality of ethnographic place-making', *Ethnography*, 9(2): 175–96.

Ploger, J. (2004) 'Strife: Urban planning and agonism', *Planning Theory*, 3(1): 71 –92.

Popke, J. (2007) 'Geography and ethics: Spaces of cosmopolitan responsibility', *Progress in Human Geography*, 31(4): 509–18.

Popper, F. (1988) 'Understanding American land use regulation since 1970', *Journal of the American Planning Association*, 54: 291–301.

Porteous, J.D. (1985) 'Smellscapes', *Progress in Human Geography*, 9(3): 356–78.

Porteous, J.D. (1990) *Landscapes of the Mind*. Toronto: University of Toronto Press.

Porter, D. (1999) *Health, Civilization and the State*. London: Routledge.

Portney, K.E. (2003) *Taking Sustainable Cities Seriously: Economic Development, the Environment, and Quality of Life in American Cities*. London: MIT Press.

Power, D. & Scott, A.J. (2004) *Cultural Industries and the Production of Culture*. New York: Routledge.

Pulido, L. (2000) 'Rethinking environmental racism: White privilege and urban development in Southern California', *Annals of the Association of American Geographers*, 90: 12–40.

Purcell, M. (2008) *Recapturing Demcracy: Neoliberalization and the Struggle for Alternative Urban Futures*. New York: Routledge.

Purcell, M. (2009) 'Resisting neoliberalization: Communicative planning or counter-hegemonic movements?', *Planning Theory*, 8(2): 140–65.

Raban, J. (1974) *Soft City*. London and New York: Fontana.

Raco, M. (2003) 'Remaking place and securitising space: Urban regeneration and the strategies, tactics and practices of policing in the UK', *Urban Studies*, 40: 1869–87.

Rahimian, A. (1990) *Migration and Mobility of the Urban Homeless*. Unpublished PhD thesis, Department of Urban Planning, University of Southern California, Los Angeles.

Rappaport, E.D. (2001) *Shopping for Pleasure: Women in the Making of London's West End*. Princeton, NJ: Princeton University.

Rawls, J. (1971) *A Theory of Justice*. Cambridge, MA: Harvard University Press.

Reher, D.S. (2001) 'In search of the "urban penalty": Exploring urban and rural mortality patterns in Spain during the demographic transition', *International Journal of Population Geography*, 7: 105–27.

Reis, J. (2009) 'Urban premium or urban penalty? The case of Lisbon, 1840–1912', *Historia Agraria*, 47(5): 69–94.

Relph, E. (1976) *Place and Placelessness*. London: Pion.

Report of the Group of Eminent Persons of the Council of Europe (2011) *Living Together: Combining Diversity and Freedom in 21st Century Europe*. Available at www.coe.int.

Reps, J. (1965) *The Making of Urban America: A History of City Planning in the United States*. Princeton, NJ: Princeton University Press.

Rey, G., Fouillet, A., Jougla, Ã. & Hémon, D. (2007) 'Heat waves, ordinary temperature fluctuations and mortality in France since 1971', *Population*, 62: 457–86.

Rishbeth, C. (2001) 'Ethnic minority groups and the design on public open space: An inclusive landscape?', *Landscape Research*, 26: 4.

Roberts, B. (2005) 'Globalization and Latin American cities', *International Journal of Urban and Regional Research*, 29: 110–23.

Roberts, M. & Gornostaeva, G. (2007) 'The night-time economy and sustainable town centres: Dilemmas for local government', *International Journal of Sustainable Development and Planning*, 2: 134–52.

Robertson, K. (1995) 'Downtown redevelopment strategies in the United States: An end-of-the-century assessment', *Journal of the American Planning Association*, 61(4): 429–37.

Robins, S. (2002) 'At the limits of spatial governmentality: A message from the tip of Africa', *Third World Quarterly*, 23(4): 665–89.

Robinson, F. and Gregson, N. (1992) 'The "underclass": A class apart?', *Critical Social Policy*, 12: 38–51.

Robinson, J. (2002) 'Global and world cities: A view from off the map', *International Journal of Urban and Regional Research*, 26: 531–54.

Robinson, J. (2006) *Ordinary Cities: Between Modernity and Development*. New York: Routledge.

Rodaway, P. (1994) *Sensuous Geographies*. London: Routledge.

Rollinson, P. (1990) 'The everyday geography of poor elderly residents in Chicago', *Geografiska Annaler*, 72: 47–57.

Rose, D. (1984) 'Rethinking gentrification: Beyond the uneven development of Marxist urban theory', *Environment and Planning D: Society and Space*, 1: 47–74.

Rose, G. (1993) *Feminism and Geography: The Limits of Geographical Knowledge*. Minneapolis, MN: University of Minnesota.

Rose, G., Degen, M. & Basdas, B. (2009) 'Using the web to disseminate research on urban space', *Geography Compass*, published online, (available at http://onlinelibrary.wiley.com/doi/10/1111/j.1749-8198.2009.00285.x/pdf) 16 September.

Rose, G., Degen, M. & Basdas, B. (2010) 'More on "big things": building events and feelings', *Transactions of the Institute of British Geographers*, 35 (1): 334–349.

Rose, N. (1999) *Powers of Freedom: Reframing Political Thought*. Cambridge: Cambridge University Press.

Ross, A. (2000) *The Celebration Chronicles: Life, Liberty, and the Pursuit of Property Value in Disney's New Town*. London: Verso.

Ross, R. (2013) 'Picturing the profession', *Journal of Planning History*, 12(3): 269–81.

Rossi, U. & Vanolo, A. (2011) *Urban Political Geographies: A Global Perspective*. London: Sage.

Rothman, H. (2003) *Neon Metropolis: How Las Vegas Started the 21st Century*. New York: Routledge.

Routledge, P. (2007) 'Transnational Political Movements', in M. Low, K.R. Cox & J. Robinson (eds) *The Sage Handbook of Political Geography*. London: Sage, pp. 335–49.

Rowe, S. & Wolch, J. (1990) 'Social networks in time and space: Homeless women in Skid Row, Los Angeles', *Annals of the Association of American Geographers*, 80: 184–205.

Roy, A. (2008) 'Civic governmentality: The politics of inclusion in Mumbai and Beirut', *Antipode*, 41(1): 159–79.

Roy, A. (2010) *Poverty Capital: Microfinance and the Making of Development*. New York: Routledge.

Roy, A, & Ong, A. (eds) (2011) *Worlding Cities: Asian Experiments and the Art of Being Global*. Malden, MA: Wiley-Blackwell.

Ruddick, S. (1996a) *Young and Homeless in Hollywood*. London: Routledge.

Ruddick, S. (1996b) 'Constructing difference in public spaces: Race, class and gender as interlocking systems', *Urban Geography*, 17: 132–51.

Ruwanpura, K. (2006) 'Conflict and survival: Sinhala female-headship in eastern Sri Lanka', *Asian Population Studies*, 2: 187–200.

Rydin, Y. (2007) 'Indicators as a governmental technology? The lessons of community-based sustainability indicator projects', *Environment and Planning D*, 25: 610–24.

Sagás, E. (2000) *Race and Politics in the Dominican Republic*. Tallahassee, FL: University Press of Florida.

Sallis, J.F., Saelens, B.E., Frank, L.D., Conway, T.L., Slymen, D.J., Cain, K.L., Chapman, J.E. & Kerr, J. (2009) 'Neighborhood built environment and income: Examining multiple health outcomes', *Social Science and Medicine*, 68: 1285–93.

Samers, M. (2010) *Migration*. New York: Routledge.

Sampson, R. & Raudenbush, S. (1999) 'Systematic social observation of public spaces: A new look at disorder in urban neighborhoods', *American Journal of Sociology*, 105: 603 –51.

Sanchez, T. W., Lang, R. E., & Dhavale, D. (2005) 'Security versus status? A first look at the census's gated community data', *Journal of Planning Education and Research*, 24: 281–91.

Sandercock, L. (1998) *Towards Cosmopolis: Planning for Multi-Cultural Cities*. Chichester: John Wiley & Sons.

Sandercock, L. (2003) *Cosmopolis II: Mongrel Cities in the 21st century*. London: Continuum.

Sandoval, C. (2002) 'Technologies of Crossing', in G. Anzaldua & A. Keating (eds) *This Bridge we Call Home: Radical Visions for Transformation*. New York: Routledge, pp. 21–27.

Sassen, S. (1991) *The Global City: New York, London and Tokyo*. First Edition. Princeton, NJ: Princeton University Press.

Sassen, S. (2001) *The Global City: New York, London and Tokyo*. Second Edition. Princeton, NJ: Princeton University Press.

Savage, M., Warde, A.M. & Ward, K. (2003) *Urban Sociology, Capitalism and Modernity*. Basingstoke: Macmillan.

Schivelbusch, W. (1995) *Disenchanted Night: The Industrialization of Light in the Nineteenth Century*. Berkeley, CA: University of California.

Schlosberg, D. (2003) 'The justice of environmental justice: reconciling equity, recognition, and participation in a political movement', in A. Light & A. de-Shalit (eds) *Moral and Political Reasoning in Environmental Practice*, London: MIT Press, pp. 77–106.

Schlosberg, D. (2007) *Defining Environmental Justice: Theories, Movements, and Nature*. Oxford: Oxford University Press.

Schwartz, V.R. (1999) *Spectacular Realities: Early Mass Culture in Fin-de-Siècle Paris*. Berkeley, CA: University of California Press.

Schwieterman, J. & Caspall, D. (2006) *The Politics of Place: A History of Zoning in Chicago*. Chicago: Lake Claremont Press.

Scoones, I. (2010) *Avian Influenza: Science, Policy and Politics*. London: Earthscan Publications.

Scott, A.J. (2000) *The Cultural Economy of Cities*. London: Sage.

Sennett, R. (1990) *The Conscience of the Eye*. London: Norton.

Sennett, R. (1992) *The Uses of Disorder: Personal Identity and City Life*. New York: W.W. Norton.

Sennett, R. (1994) *Flesh and Stone: The Body and the City in Western Civilisation*. London: Faber and Faber.

Sennett, R. (1999) 'The Spaces of Democracy', in R. Beauregard. & S. Body-Gendrot (eds) *The Urban Moment: Cosmopolitan Essays on the Late 20th Century City*. Thousand Oaks, CA and London: Sage, pp. 273–85.

Sennett, R. (2000) 'Cities without care or connection', *New Statesman*, 5 June, pp. 25–7.

Sennett, R. (2001) 'New capitalism, new isolation: A flexible city of strangers', posted on CRIT-GEOG-FORUM, 16 February.

Sennett, R. (2003) *Respect: The Formation of Character in an Age of Inequality*. London: Penguin Books.

Shantz, B.-M., Kearns, R.A. & Collins, D. (2007) 'Intolerance for noise and disorder: Questioning the "publicness" of Auckland's lower Queen Street', *Urban Policy and Research*, 26: 39–55.

Shatkin, G. (2007) 'Global cities of the South: Perspectives on growth and inequality', *Cities*, 24: 1–24.

Shatkin, G. (2008) 'The city and the bottom line: Urban megaprojects and the privatization of planning in Southeast Asia', *Environment and Planning A*, 40(2): 383–401.

Shaw, C. & McKay, H. (1942) *Juvenile Delinquency in Urban Areas*. Chicago: University of Chicago Press

Shaw, H.J. (2006) 'Food deserts: Towards the development of a classification', *Geografiska Annaler, Series B: Human Geography*, 88: 231–47.

Shengjian, Z. (2004) 'The city-map and consumerist ideology', in Y. Xuanmeng & H. Xirong (eds) *Shanghai: its Urbanization and Culture*. The Council for Research in Values and Philosophy, pp. 125–40.

Sheridan, S.C. & Dolney, T.J. (2003) 'Heat, mortality, and level of urbanization: Measuring vulnerability across Ohio, USA', *Climate Research*, 24: 255–65.

Shields, R. (1996) 'A guide to urban representations and what to do about it: Alternative traditions of urban theory', in A. King (ed.) *Re-presenting the City: Ethnicity, Capital and Culture in the 21st-Century Metropolis*. New York: New York University.

Shields, R. (1998) *Lefebvre, Love, and Struggle: Spatial Dialectics*. London: Routledge.

Sibley, D. (1995) *Geographies of Exclusion: Society and Difference in the West*. London: Routledge.

Silverman, E. (1999) *NYPD Battles Crime: Innovative Strategies in Policing*. Boston: Northeastern University Press.

Simmel, G. (1903 [1997]) 'The metropolis and mental life', in D. Frisby & D. Featherstone (eds) *Simmel on Culture*. London: Sage, pp. 174–85.

Simmel, G. (1950 [1903]) 'The metropolis and mental life', in *The Sociology of Georg Simmel*. Trans. Kurt Wolff. New York: Free Press, pp. 409–24.

Simmel, G. (1971) 'The metropolis and mental life', in D.N. Levine (ed.) *On Individuality and Social Forms*. Chicago: University of Chicago Press, pp. 324–39.

Simmel, G. (1997) [1907] 'The Sociology of the Senses', in D. Frisby and M. Featherstone (eds) *Simmel on Culture*. London: Sage, pp. 109–19.

Simone, A. (2004a) *For the City Yet to Come: Changing African Life in Four Cities*. Durham, NC: Duke University Press.

Simone, A. (2004b) 'People as infrastructure: Intersecting fragments in Johannesburg', *Public Culture*, 16(3): 407–29.

Simone, A. (2010) *City Life from Jakarta to Dakar: Movements at the Crossroads*. New York: Routledge.

Sklar, R. (1994) *Movie-Made America: A Cultural History of American Movies*. New York: Vintage.

Slater, T. (2006) 'The eviction of critical perspectives from gentrification research', *International Journal of Urban and Regional Research*, 30(4): 737–57.

Slater, T. (2008) '"A literal necessity to be replaced": A rejoinder to the gentrification debate', *International Journal of Urban and Regional Research*, 32(1): 212–23.

Slater, T. (2009) 'Missing Marcuse: On gentrification and displacement', *CITY: Analysis of Urban Trends, Culture, Theory, Policy, Action*, 13(2): 292–311.

Slater, T., Curran, W. & Lees, L. (2004) 'Gentrification research: New directions and critical scholarship', *Environment and Planning A*, 36(7): 1141–50.

Sloane, D.C. (2006) 'Longer view: From congestion to sprawl: Planning and health in historical context', *Journal of the American Planning Association*, 72: 10–18.

Smith, C. (2006) *The Plan of Chicago: Daniel Burnham and the Remaking of the American City*. Chicago: University of Chicago Press.

Smith, D.M. (1987) *Geography, Inequality and Society*. Cambridge: Cambridge University Press.

Smith, D.M. (1994) *Geography and Social Justice*. London: Blackwell.

Smith, M.P. (2001) *Transnational Urbanism: Locating Globalization*. Cambridge, MA: Blackwell.

Smith, M. (2007) *How Race is Made: Slavery, Segregation and the Senses*. Chapel Hill, NC: University of North Carolina Press.

Smith, M. & Davidson, J. (2008) 'Civlity and etiquette', in P. Hubbard, T. Hall & J.R. Short (eds) *The SAGE Companion to the City*. London: Sage, pp. 231–49.

Smith, N. (1982) 'Gentrification and uneven development', *Economic Geography*, 58: 139–55.

Smith, N. (1984) *Uneven Development*. Oxford: Blackwell.

Smith, N. (1986) 'Gentrification, the frontier, and the restructuring of urban space' in N. Smith, and P. Williams (eds) *Gentrification of the City*. London: Allen & Unwin, pp. 15–34.

Smith, N. (1987) 'Of yuppies and housing: Gentrification, social restructuring and the urban dream', *Environment and Planning D: Society and Space*, 5: 151–72.

Smith, N. (1996a) *The New Urban Frontier: Gentrification and the Revanchist City*. London: Routledge.

Smith, N. (1996b) 'Social justice and the new American urbanism: The revanchist city', in A. Merrifield & E. Swyngedouw (eds) *The Urbanization of Injustice*. London: Lawrence & Wishart, pp. 117–36

Smith, N. (2002) 'New globalism, new urbanism: Gentrification as global urban strategy', *Antipode*, 34(3): 427–50.

Smith, N. (2005) 'Neo-critical geography, or, the flat pluralist world of business class', *Antipode*, 37: 887–99.

Smith, N. (2006) 'There's no such thing as a natural disaster'. Available at: http://understanding-katrina.ssrc.org/Smith/.

Smith, N. (2008) 'Afterword to the third edition', in N. Smith, *Uneven Development*. Athens, GA: Georgia University Press, pp. 239–66.

Smith, P.J. (1994) 'Slum clearance as an instrument of sanitary reform: The flawed vision of Edinburgh's first slum clearance scheme', *Planning Perspectives*, 9: 1–27.

Smith, S.J. (1987) 'Residential segregation: A geography of English racism', in P. Jackson (ed.) *Race and Racism: Essays in Social Geography*. London: Allen & Unwin pp. 25–49.

Smith, S. (1989) *The Politics of 'Race' and Residence*. Cambridge: Polity Press.

Smoyer, K.E. (1998) 'Putting risk in its place: Methodological considerations for investigating extreme event health risk', *Social Science and Medicine*, 47: 1809–24.

Smoyer-Tomic, K.E., Spence, J.C. & Amrhein, C. (2006) 'Food deserts in the prairies? Supermarket accessibility and neighborhood need in Edmonton, Canada', *Professional Geographer*, 58: 307–26.

Snow, D. & Anderson, L. (1993) *Down on Their Luck: A Study of Homeless Street People*. Los Angeles, CA: University of California Press.

Söderström, O. (2005) 'Representation', in D. Atkinson, P. Jackson, D. Sibley & N. Washbourne (eds) *Cultural Geography: A Critical Dictionary of Key Concepts*. London: I.B.Tauris.

Soja, E. (1989) *Postmodern Geographies: The Reassertion of Space in Critical Social Theory*. London: Verso.

Soja, E. (1996) *Thirdspace: Journeys to Los Angeles and Other Real-and-Imaginary Places*. Oxford: Blackwell.

Soja, E. (2000) *Postmetropolis: Critical Studies of Cities and Regions*. Oxford: Blackwell.

Soja, E. (2010) *Seeking Spatial Justice*. Minneapolis, MN: University of Minnesota Press.

Sonak, S., Sonak, M. & Giriyan, A. (2008) 'Shipping hazardous waste: Implications for economically developing countries', *International Environmental Agreements*, 8: 143–59.

Sorkin, M. (ed.) (1991) *Variations on a Theme Park: The New American City and the End of Public Space*. New York: Hill & Wang.

Sorkin, M. (ed.) (1992) *Variations on a Theme Park: The New American City and the End of Public Space*. New York: Hill & Wang.

Southworth, M. (2005) 'Designing the walkable city', *Journal of Urban Planning and Development*, 131: 246–57.

Speak, S. & Tipple, G. (2006) 'Perceptions, persecution and pity: The limitations of interventions for homelessness in developing countries', *International Journal of Urban and Regional Research*, 30: 172–88.

Spivak, G. (1988) 'Can the subaltern speak?', in C. Nelson & L. Grossberg (eds) *Marxism and the Interpretation of Culture*. Urbana, IL: University of Illinois Press, pp. 271–313.

Stack, C. (1987) *All Our Kin: Strategies for Survival in a Black Community*. New York: Basic Books.

Staeheli, L. (2003) 'Cities and citizenship', *Urban Geography*, 24: 97–102.

Staeheli, L. & Mitchell, D. (2008) *The People's Property: Power, Politics, the Public*. London: Routledge.

Statistics Canada (2007) *Income in Canada*. Ottawa: Statistics Canada.

Stedman Jones, G. (1971) *Outcast London: A Study in the Relationship Between Classes in Victorian Society*. Oxford: Oxford University Press.

Stewart, K. (2007) *Ordinary Affects*. Durham, NC and London: Duke University Press.

Stoller, P. (1989) *The Taste of Ethnographic Things: The Senses in Anthropology*. Philadelphia: Philadelphia University Press.

Stringer, M.D. (2013) *Discourses on Religious Diversity: Explorations in an Urban Ecology*. Farnham and Burlington, VT: Ashgate.

Sugiyama, T., Leslie, E., Giles-Corti, B. & Owen, N. (2008) 'Associations of neighbourhood greenness with physical and mental health: Do walking, social coherence and local social interaction explain the relationships?', *Journal of Epidemiology and Community Health*, 62(5): 1–6.

Sugiyama, T., Leslie, E., Giles-Corti, B. & Owen, N. (2009) 'Physical activity for recreation or exercise on neighbourhood streets: Associations with perceived environmental attributes', *Health and Place*, 15: 1058–63.

Sui, D.Z. (2003) 'Musings on the fat city: Are obesity and urban forms linked?', *Urban Geography*, 24: 75–84.

Sutherland, E. (1955) *Principles of Criminology*. Philadelphia: Lippincott.

Swanson, K. (2007) 'Revanchist urbanism heads south: The regulation of indigenous beggars and street vendors in Ecuador', *Antipode*, 39: 708–28.

Swanson, K. (2010) *Begging as a Path to Progress: Indigenous Women and Children and the Struggle for Ecuador's Urban Spaces*. Athens, GA: University of Georgia Press

Sweet, L. (2008) 'Obama makes it official: Chicago's Grant Park on election night', *Chicago Sun-Times* blog. Available at: http://blogs.suntimes.com/sweet/2008/10/obama_makes_it_official_chicag.html (accessed 29 May 2012).

Sweet, L. (2012) 'Obama on NATO Summit: Said global leaders "loved the city", were encouraged to shop', *Chicago Sun-Times* blog. Available at: http://blogs.suntimes.com/sweet/2012/05/obama_on_nato_summit_said_glob.html (accessed 29 May 2012).

Swyngedouw, E. (1996) 'The city as a hybrid – On nature, society and cyborg urbanisation', *Capitalism, Nature, Socialism*, 7: 65–80.

Swyngedouw, E. (2004) *Social Power and the Urbanization of Water: Flows of Power*. Oxford: Oxford University Press.

Swyngedouw, E. (2006) 'Circulations and metabolisms: (Hybrid) natures and (cyborg) cities', *Science as Culture*, 15: 105–21.

Swyngedouw, E. (2007) 'Impossible "Sustainability" and the Postpolitical Condition', in R. Krueger & D. Gibbs (eds) *The Sustainable Development Paradox: Urban Political Economy in the United States and Europe*. London: Guilford Press, pp. 13–40.

Swyngedouw, E. (2009) 'The antinomies of the post-political city: In search of a democratic politics of environmental production', *International Journal of Urban and Regional Research*, 33: 601–20.

Swyngedouw, E. (2011) 'Interrogating post-democratization: Reclaiming egalitarian political spaces', *Political Geography*, 30(7): 370–80.

Swyngedouw, E. & Cook, I.R. (2009) 'Cities, social cohesion and the environment', *Social Polis Survey Paper*, University of Manchester.

Swyngedouw, E. & Kaika, M. (2000) 'The Environment of the City ... or the Urbanization of Nature', in G. Bridge & S. Watson (eds) *A Companion to the City*. Oxford: Blackwell, pp. 567–80.

Sze, J. (2006) *Noxious New York: The Racial Politics of Urban Health and Environmental Justice*. Cambridge, MA: MIT Press.

Sze, J., London, J., Shilling, F., Gambirazzio, G., Filan, T. & Cadenasso, M. (2009) 'Defining and contesting environmental justice: Socio-natures and the politics of scale in the Delta', *Antipode*, 41: 807–53.

Takahashi, L. (1996) 'A decade of understanding homelessness in the USA: From characterization to representation', *Progress in Human Geography*, 20(3): 291–310.

Takahashi, L. (1997) 'The socio-spatial stigmatization of homelessness and HIV/AIDS: Toward an explanation of the NIMBY syndrome', *Social Science and Medicine*, 45: 903–14.

Taylor, D.E. (1999) 'Central Park as a model for social control: Urban parks, social class and leisure behavior in nineteenth-century America', *Journal of Leisure Research*, 31(4): 420–77.

Taylor, R. (2001) *Breaking Away from Broken Windows: Baltimore Neighborhoods and the Nationwide Fight Against Crime, Grime, Fear and Decline*. Boulder, CO: Westview Press.

Teaford, J. (1979) *City and Suburb: The Political Fragmentation of Metropolitan America, 1850–1970*. Baltimore, MD: Johns Hopkins University Press.

The Economist (2008) 'Scenes from a wake: The defeated candidate outclassed his supporters', 6 November. Available at: http://www.economist.com/world/unitedstates/displaystory.cfm?story_id=12573193 (accessed 29 May 2012).

Thrift, N. (1996) 'New urban eras and old technological fears: Reconfiguring the goodwill of electronic things', *Urban Studies*, 33(8): 1463–94.

Thrift, N. (2004) 'Summoning life', in P. Cloke, P. Crang & M. Goodwin (eds) *Envisioning Human Geographies*. London: Arnold, pp. 81–103.

Thrift, N. (2005) 'But malice aforethought: Cities and the natural history of hatred', *Transactions of the Institute of British Geographers*, 30: 133–50.

Thrift, N. & French, S. (2002) 'The automatic production of space', *Transactions of the Institute of British Geographers*, 27(3): 309–35.

Thrush, C. (2008) *Native Seattle: Stories from the Crossing-Over Place*. Seattle, WA: University of Washington Press.

Tickell, A. & Peck, J. (2003) 'Making global rules: Globalization or neoliberalization?', in J. Peck & H. Yeung (eds) *Remaking the Global Economy: Economic–Geographical Perspectives*. London: Sage, pp. 163–81.

Till, K. (2005) *The New Berlin: Memory, Politics, Place*. Minnesota, MN: University of Minnesota Press.

Toll, S. (1969) *Zoned American*. New York: Viking.

Tonkiss, F. (2005) *Space, the City and Social Theory: Social Relations and Urban Forms*. London: Polity Press.

Tonnies, F. (1887) *Community and Society*. New York: Harper & Row.

Toulemon, L. & Barbieri, M. (2008) 'The mortality impact of the August 2003 heat wave in France: Investigating the "harvesting" effect and other long-term consequences', *Population Studies*, 62: 39–53.

Towers, G. (2000) 'Applying the political geography of scale: Grassroots strategies and environmental justice', *The Professional Geographer*, 52: 23–36.

Tsouros, A. (2009) 'City leadership for health and sustainable development: The WHO European Healthy Cities Network', *Health Promotion International*, 24: 4–10.

Tuan, Y. (1977) *Space and Place*. London: Arnold.

Turits, R. (2002) 'A world destroyed, a nation imposed: The 1937 Haitian massacre in the Dominican Republic', *Hispanic American Historical Review*, 82(3): 589–635.

Turner, R. (2002) 'Politics of design and development in the postmodern downtown', *Journal of Urban Affairs*, 24(5): 533–48.

Uitermark, J., Rossi, U. & van Houtum, H. (2005) 'Reinventing multiculturalism: Urban citizenship and the negotiation of ethnic diversity in Amsterdam', *International Journal of Urban and Regional Research*, 29: 622–40.

UK Royal Commission on Environmental Pollution (2006) *The Urban Environment: Summary of the Royal Commission on Environmental Pollution's Report*. Available at: http://www.rcep.org.uk/reports/26-urban/documents/urb-env-summary.pdf (accessed December 2010).

Underwood-Bultmann, E. (2010) 'Zoning', in B. Warf (ed.) *Encyclopedia of Geography*. Thousand Oaks, CA: Sage Publications.

UNFPA (United Nations Population Fund) (2007) *State of World Population 2007*. New York: UNFPA.

UN-HABITAT (2003) *Understanding Slums: Case Studies for the Global Report 2003*. London: University College.

Urry, J. (2004) 'The "system" of automobility', *Theory, Culture & Society*, 21(4–5): 25–39.

Valentine, G. (1989) 'The geography of women's fear', *Area*, 21: 385–90.

Valentine, G. (2004) *Public Space and Culture of Childhood*. Aldershot: Ashgate Publishing.

Valentine, G. (2006) 'Good relations? Negotiating pan-equality strand politics'. Paper available from the author, School of Geography, University of Leeds, Leeds, LS2 9JT, UK.

Valentine, G. (2007) 'Theorising and researching intersectionality: A challenge for feminist geography', *The Professional Geographer*, 59: 10–21.

Valentine, G. (2010) 'Prejudice – rethinking geographies of oppression', *Social & Cultural Geography*, 11: 521–37.

Valentine, G. & Skelton, T. (2003) 'Living on the edge: The marginalisation and resistance of D/deaf youth', *Environment & Planning A*, 35: 301–21.

Valentine, G. & Skelton, T. (2007) 'The right to be heard: Citizenship and language', *Political Geography*, 26: 121–40.

Valentine, G., Holloway, S., Knell, C. & Jayne, M. (2008) 'Drinking places: Young people and cultures of alcohol consumption in rural environments', *Journal of Rural Studies*, 24: 28–40.

Valentine, G., Sporton, D. & Nielsen, K.B. (2009) 'Identities and belonging: A comparative study of Somali refugees and asylum seekers living in the UK and Denmark', *Environment & Planning D: Society & Space*, 27: 234–50.

van Deusen Jr., R. (2002) 'Public space design as class warfare: Urban design, the "right to the city" and the production of Clinton Square, Syracuse, NY', *GeoJournal*, 58(2): 149–58.

van Praag, B. and Ferrer-Carbonell, A. (2006) *Ask the Poor About Poverty: A Subjective Multidimensional Concept of Poverty*. Amsterdam: University of Amsterdam.

Vanderbeck, R.(2007) 'Intergenerational geographies: Age relations, segregation and re-engagements', *Geography Compass*, 1/2: 200–21.

Vanderbilt, T. (2008) *Traffic: Why We Drive The Way We Do (And What It Says About Us)*. New York: Knopf.

Vertovec, S. (2007) 'Super-diversity and its implications', *Ethnic and Racial Studies*, 29: 1024–54.

Vidler, A. (2000) 'Photourbanism: Planning the city from above and below', in G. Bridge & S. Watson (eds) *A Companion to the City*. Blackwell: Oxford, pp. 35–45.

Virilio, P. (1986) *Speed and Politics: An Essay on Dromology*. New York: Semiotext(e).

Visser, G. & Kotze, N. (2008) 'The state and new-build gentrification in central Cape Town, South Africa', *Urban Studies*, 45(12): 2565–93.

Vlahov, D. & Galea, S. (2003) 'Urban health: A new discipline', *Lancet*, 362: 1091–2.

Vögele, J. (2000) 'Urbanization and the urban mortality change in Imperial Germany', *Health & Place*, 6: 41–55.

Wacquant, L. (1999) 'Urban marginality in the coming millennium', *Urban Studies*, 36: 1639–47.

Wacquant, L. (2008) *Urban Outcasts: A Comparative Sociology of Advanced Marginality*. Cambridge: Polity Press.

Waley, P. (2007) 'Tokyo-as-world-city: Reassessing the role of capital and the state in urban restructuring', *Urban Studies*, 44: 1465–90.

Walker, G. (2009) 'Beyond distribution and proximity: Exploring the multiple spatialities of environmental justice', *Antipode*, 41: 614–36.

Walker, G. (2012) *Environmental Justice: Concepts, Evidence and Politics*. London: Routledge.

Waltzer, M. (1997) *On Toleration*. New Haven, CT and London: Yale University Press.

Wang, J. and Lau, S. (2009) 'Gentrification and Shanghai's new middle-class: Another reflection on the cultural consumption thesis', *Cities*, 26(2): 57–66.

Ward, K. (2007) '"Creating a personality for downtown": Business improvement districts in Milwaukee', *Urban Geography*, 28: 781–808.

Ward, K. (2010) 'Towards a relational comparative approach to the study of cities', *Progress in Human Geography*, 34(4): 471–87.

Warde, A. (2002) 'Production, consumption and the "cultural economy"', *Cultural Economy*, in P.D. Gay and M. Pryke (eds) *Cultural Analysis and Commercial Life*. London: Sage. pp. 185–200.

Watkins, F. & Jacoby, A. (2007) 'Is the rural idyll bad for your health? Stigma and exclusion in the English countryside', *Health and Place*, 13: 851–64.

Watt, P. (1998) 'Going out of town: Youth, "race" and place in the South East of England', *Environment & Planning D: Society & Space*, 16: 687–703.

Watt, P. & Stenson, K. (1998) '"It's a bit dodgy round here": Safety, danger, ethnicity and young people's use of public space', in T. Skelton & G. Valentine (eds) *Cool Places: Geographies of Youth Cultures*. London: Routledge, pp. 249–65.

Webster, C. (1996) 'Local heroes: Violent racism, localism, and spacism among Asian and white young people', *Youth and Policy*, 53: 15–27.

Webster, C., Glasze, G. & Frantz, K. (2002) 'Guest editorial: The global spread of gated communities', *Environment and Planning B: Planning and Design,* 29: 315–20.

Weymss, G. (2006) 'The power to tolerate: Contests over Britishness and belonging in East London', *Patterns of Prejudice,* 40: 215–36.

Whelan, A., Wrigley, N., Warm, D. & Cannings, E. (2002) 'Life in a "food desert"', *Urban Studies,* 39: 2083–100.

Whitehead, M. (2007) *Spaces of Sustainability: Geographical Perspectives on the Sustainable Society.* London: Routledge.

Whitehead, M. (2009) 'The wood for the trees: Ordinary environmental injustice and the everyday right to urban nature', *International Journal of Urban and Regional Research,* 33: 662–81.

Williams, K.S. & Johnstone, C. (2000) 'The politics of the selective gaze: Closed circuit television and the policing of public space', *Crime, Law and Social Change,* 34: 183–210.

Williams, N. & Mooney, G. (1994) 'Infant mortality in an "age of great cities": London and the English provincial cities compared, c. 1840–1910', *Continuity & Change,* 9: 18 –212.

Williams, R. (1973) *The Country and the City.* London: Chatto & Windus.

Williams, T. (1989) *The Cocaine Kids: The Inside Story of a Teenage Drug Ring.* Reading, MA: Addison-Wesley.

Wilson, D. (2007) *Cities and Race: America's New Black Ghetto.* New York: Taylor & Francis.

Wilson, D. (2004) 'Towards a contingent urban neoliberalism', *Urban Geography,* 25: 771–83.

Wilson, D. & Keil, R. (2008) 'The real creative class', *Journal of Social and Cultural Geography,* 9: 841–7.

Wilson, J. (1968) *Varieties of Police Behavior.* Cambridge, MA: Harvard University Press.

Wilson, J. (1987) *The Truly Disadvantaged: The Inner City, the Underclass, and Public Policy.* Chicago: University of Chicago Press.

Wilson, J. (1996) *When Work Disappears: The World of the New Urban Poor.* New York: Vintage Books.

Wilson, J. & Kelling, G. (1982) 'Broken windows: Police and neighborhood safety', *Atlantic Monthly* (March), pp. 29–38.

Wilson, W.H. (1989) *The City Beautiful Movement.* Baltimore, MD: Johns Hopkins University Press.

Wilson, W. (1987) *The Truly Disadvantaged: The Inner City, the Underclass, and Public Policy.* Chicago: University of Chicago Press.

Winkler, E., Turrell, G. & Patterson, C. (2006) 'Does living in a disadvantaged area mean fewer opportunities to purchase fresh fruit and vegetables in the area? Findings from the Brisbane food study', *Health & Place,* 12: 306–19.

Wirth, L. (1938) 'Urbanism as a way of life', *American Journal of Sociology,* 44(1): 1–24.

Wiseman, J. (1970) *Stations of the Lost: The Treatment of Skid Row Alcoholics.* Englewood Cliffs, NJ: New York: Prentice-Hall.

Wolch, J. & Dear, M. (1987) *Landscapes of Despair: From Deinstitutionalization to Homelessness.* Princeton, NJ: Princeton University Press.

Wolch, J. & Dear, M. (1993) *Malign Neglect: Homelessness in an American city.* San Francisco: Jossey-Bass Publishers.

Woo, R., TenHoor, M. & Rich, D. (2010) *Street Value: Shopping, Planning, and Politics at Fulton Mall.* New York: Princeton Architectural Press.

Wood, D. (2010) *Rethinking the Power of Maps.* New York: The Guilford Press.

Wood, L., Shannon, T., Bulsara, M., Pikora, T., Mccormack, G. & Giles-Corti, B. (2008) 'The anatomy of the safe and social suburb: An exploratory study of the built environment, social capital and residents' perceptions of safety', *Health and Place,* 14: 15 –31.

Woods, R. (2003) 'Urban-rural mortality differentials: An unresolved debate', *Population and Development Review,* 29: 29–46.

World Bank (2009) *Urban Health: Overview*. Available at: http://go.worldbank.org/ J8633XN9M0 (accessed December 2009).

World Commission for Environment and Development (1987) *Our Common Future*. Oxford: Oxford University Press.

World Health Organization (2003) *The Health Impacts of 2003 Summer Heat-waves*. Copenhagen: WHO.

Wrigley, N. (2002) '"Food deserts" in British cities: Policy context and research priorities', *Urban Studies*, 39: 2029–40.

Wrigley, N., Warm, D. & Margetts, B. (2003) 'Deprivation, diet, and food-retail access: Findings from the Leeds "food deserts" study', *Environment and Planning A*, 35: 151–88.

Wrigley, N., Warm, D., Margetts, B. & Whelan, A. (2002) 'Assessing the impact of improved retail access on diet in a "food desert": A preliminary report', *Urban Studies*, 39: 2061–82.

Yeoh, B. (2004) 'Cosmopolitanism and its exclusions in Singapore', *Urban Studies*, 41: 2431–45.

Yiftachel, O., Goldhaber, R. & Nuriel, R. (2009) 'Urban Justice and Recognition: Affirmation and Hostility in Beer Sheva', in P. Marcuse, J. Connolly, J. Nory, I. Olivo, C. Potter & J. Steil (eds) *Searching for the Just City*. New York: Routledge, pp. 120–43.

Young, I.M. (1990) *Justice and the Politics of Difference*. Princeton, NJ: Princeton University Press.

Young, I.M. (2002) *Inclusion and Democracy*. Oxford: Oxford University Press.

Young, L. (2003) 'The "place" of street children in Kampala, Uganda: Marginalisation, resistance, and acceptance in the urban environment', *Environment and Planning D: Society and Space*, 21: 607–27.

Young, M. & Willmott, P. (1962) *Family and Kinship in East London*. Harmondsworth: Penguin.

Zick, A., Kupper, B. & Hovermann, A. (2010) *Intolerance, Prejudice and Discrimination: A European Report*. Berlin: Friedrich Ebert Stiftung. Available at www.fes-gegen-rechtsextremismus.de.

Žižek, S. (1993) *Tarrying with the Negative*. Durham, NC: Duke University Press.

Žižek, S. (1999) *The Ticklish Subject: The Absent Centre of Political Ontology*. London: Verso.

Zorbaugh, H. (1929) *The Gold Coast and the Slum: A Sociological Study of Chicago's Near North Side*. Chicago: University of Chicago Press.

Zukin, S. (1991) *Landscapes of Power: From Detroit to Disneyland*. Berkeley, CA: University of California Press.

Zukin, S. (1995) *The Cultures of Cities*. Oxford: Blackwell.

Zukin, S. (2008) 'Consuming authenticity', *Cultural Studies*, 22(5): 724–48.

Zukin, S. (2009) *Naked City: The Death and Life of Authentic Urban Places*. Oxford: Oxford University Press.

Index

272 INDEX